Conflict *or* Co-operation?

The Growth of Industrial Democracy

John Elliott

Kogan Page

First published 1978 in Great Britain by
Kogan Page Limited, 120 Pentonville Road, London N1 9JN
Reprinted 1978
Second edition 1984

Copyright © John Elliott 1978, 1984

British Library Cataloguing in Publication Data

Elliott, John,
   Conflict or cooperation?: The growth of
   industrial democracy. — 2nd ed
   1. Employee's representation in management
   — Great Britain
   I. Title
   331'.01'120941   HD5660.G7
ISBN 0–85038–747–7 (Hb)
ISBN 0–85038–758–2 (Pb)

Printed in Great Britain by
Spottiswoode Ballantyne Ltd, Colchester, Essex

Contents

Preface   *ix*

List of Abbreviations   *xii*

Author's Note   *xv*

Part I Living with the Unions

1. *Introduction: Industrial Democracy*   3
    A definition 4; Transfer of power 4; The new responsibilities 5; Different perspectives 6; The issue of responsibility 6; Contradictory answers 7

2. *A Decade of Union Victories: Winning Responsibility*   9
    The rule of law 10; 'A giant's strength' 10; Pay laws of the 1960s 11; The Donovan Report 11; Barbara Castle's 'In Place of Strife' 13; The Conservatives' Industrial Relations Act 15; Tripartism on pay 17; Heath's initiatives 18; The miners' crisis 21; The Conservative failure 21; The role of the law 21; Employment Protection Act 22; A 1977 perspective 23

3. *The Social Contract: Programme for a Government*   25
    Jack Jones in the lead 26; Tea party politics 26; Union personalities 28; Unity at Brighton 29; Liaison in the movement 30; The social contract 33

4. *Social Contract Methods: Tripartism in Government*   34
    Wider industrial democracy 26; Planning agreements 37; Industrial strategy and the Bullock Report 38; The institutions 39; NEDC and the Little Neddies 39; Tripartite-style commissions 40; The Manpower Services Commission (MSC) 42; The Advisory Conciliation and Arbitration Service (ACAS) 45; Summary 48

5. *Social Contract Methods: The TUC and the Industrialists*   49
    How the TUC works 49; Methods of influencing events 51; Government agencies 52; The TUC in action – policies on wealth 52; The corporate state partners – unions and the TUC 54; Closed shops 55; The corporate state partners – industrialists and the CBI 56; Political lobbying 57; A capitalist movement? 60; Conclusion 61

Part II The Path to Industrial Power

6. *The Unions: Traditions, Roles and Policies*   65
    Reforms for the unions 67; A question of method 67; Shop

stewards 68; A change of role 69; A TUC lead 71; The conflict tradition 72; The TUC and its dissidents 74; Left and right 76

7. *The Unions: Ambitions, Expertise and Organisation*   78
Subjects for participation 78; Government policies 79; 'Socially useful' Lucas 80; Possible exemptions: newspapers and finance 82; Research, training and expertise 83; Shop steward education 84; Research facilities 86; Harland and Wolff 88; Sweden 90; Management initiatives 90; Union influence and organisation 91; Authority for shop stewards 91; Inter-union co-operation 93; The union official 93; Confidentiality 94; The balance of power 94; Commercial secrecy 96; Conclusion 97

8. *Employers: The Industrialist, his Company and the Manager*   98
Legitimacy of management 98; Management and conflict 99; Property and managerial rights 100; Hierarchies within management 103; The company 103; The industrialist 104; The manager 104; The manager as an employee 106; Managers in unions 107; Trade union expansion 108

9. *Employers: Company Views and Styles of Management*   111
Company accountability 112; Arnold Weinstock's journey 114; Realities at Ford Motor 116; CBI policy develops 117; Styles of management 118; A step at a time 119; Education and training 119; Leyland's troubles 120; A new 'legitimacy' 121

10. *Methods of Participation*   123
General terminology 123; Industrial traditions 126; The terminology in practice 126; Collective bargaining 127; Consultation 128; Participation 129; 'Single channel' 129; Extended collective bargaining 131; Worker directors 134; Foreign experience 135; Minorities in Sweden 135; One-third in Germany 136; Conclusions 137

11. *Participation Trends: The Private Sector*   139
Communication and consultation 139; Communicating the facts 140; Consultative developments – three surveys 142; Consultative developments – some company examples 145; ICI 145; Unilever 147; Ford Motor 149; GEC 150; Towards power sharing 151; Charters for workpeople in GKN 151; Chrysler 153; British Leyland 154; Worker directors 158; Conclusion 160

12. *Participation Trends: The Public Sector, from Whitley to Worker Directors*   161
Whitley traditions 162; Electricity supply 164; Gas supply 166; Coal 167; Worker directors 168; Fairfields 168; British Steel 169; Benn and the Bullock era 175; Harland and Wolff 176; Post Office 178; Summary 181

13. *Shopfloor Democracy*   182
Power to the individual 182; The collective alternatives 183; Experience abroad 183; Employee share ownership 184; 'Sharing wealth' at ICI 185; Industrialists become interested 186; Ownership and co-operation 187; Labour's collective fund alternative 188; Sit-ins and co-operatives 190; Labour disputes 190; Redundancy sit-ins and work-ins 191; Workers' co-operatives 192; New enterprises 193; Capital needs 194; Mondragon in Spain 196;

Management expertise 196; Summary 197; Satisfaction at work 197; 'Descending participation' 198; From Scandinavia to Britain 199; Volvo's scheme 199; Experience in Britain 200; Government interest 201; Conclusions 202

Part III Bullock and the Future

14. *Britain's Road to Bullock*   205
First steps in the 1960s 205; The Donovan Commission 206; The Jones working party 207; Government consultations 208; Morrison and the public sector 209; Impetus from Brussels 211; Britain joins the EEC 212; TUC goes 50-50 212; Conservative indecision 213; Summary to 1974 215; Battles in Whitehall 215; The Radice Bill 216; Cabinet rows 217; Terms of reference 218; Search for members 218; Conclusion 220

15. *The Bullock Committee and its Report*   221
Evidence to the Committee 222; Political parties 222; Evidence from Europe 224; The Committee at work 225; Months of debate 226; The Bullock-Bain 'core report' 227; Encouragement abroad 228; Methven resigns 230; Conflict at Sunningdale 231; The Report 233; The majority report 233; How *'2x + y'* would work 234; Mr Wilson's dissent 237; The industrialists' minority report 238

16. *Reactions to Bullock and Issues for Debate*   241
Rough deal for Bullock 242; Practical issues ignored 243; The CBI's campaign 244; The TUC stands back 245; Lack of government enthusiasm 247; 'Single channel' of union power 249; Points for debate 251; Employees' rights and interests 251; The parity issue 252; Role of the unions – a 'single channel'? 254; Tiers of power 257; Shareholders' rights 259; Shareholders and takeovers 261; Summary and the European significance 262; The 1978 White Paper 263

17. *Other Campaigns: The Public Sector and Control of Pension Funds*   264
Plans for the public sector 264; Nationalised industries 266; The Civil Service 169; Local government 271; Summary 273; Control of pension funds 273; Direction of investment 274; Mr Orme's White Paper 276

18. *Summary*   278
Compacts with governments 279; Tripartism in government agencies 281; Co-operation at work 282; Catalysts through the boardroom 284; Flexibility and safeguards 285; A boardroom scheme and individual rights 286; Could it work — could people cope? 288

Part IV Addendum 1983

19. *The start of the Thatcherite '80s*   293
Tripartism out of fashion 294; From democracy to involvement 294

20. *Systems*   297
Backwards and Forwards: Some Practical Examples 297; A short life at BL 297; Disagreement in the Post Office 300; Changes at BSC 302; Suvival at ICI 303; Steady growth in Unilever 304; Worker co-operatives flourish 306; Financial participation 308; Other examples 308

21. *Statutory Policies*   310
Statutory developments 310; Vredehng and the Fifth 311; Policies
in the UK develop from Bullock 312

22. *Conclusions*   314
A lack of progress 314
The management and trade union challenge 315

Bibliography   317
Index   323

Preface

by Lord Bullock, Chairman of the Committee
on Industrial Democracy

I have read John Elliott's book with the greatest interest and I am sure that anyone who shares my view that industrial relations is the most important problem confronting this country will do the same.

It is an unusual, and at times disconcerting, experience (especially for an historian) to read about an episode of history in which he has so recently been an actor. To avoid any misunderstanding, let me say that Mr Elliott has not consulted me at any stage about the account which he gives of the Committee of which I was chairman, any more than he has discussed with me his conclusions: in both cases they are his own views, not mine, which he expresses.

As his contributions to the *Financial Times* have shown, however, Mr Elliott is an acute and well-informed observer, and his account of British politics and industrial relations in the 1970s has the great merit of placing the Committee on Industrial Democracy and its report, for the first time, in its historical context. His account may be challenged on detail, but it provides easily the most comprehensive and intelligible explanation I have seen of what has been happening in this decade and how the inquiry on industrial democracy is related to other developments in the relations between Government, unions and management.

It was clear to me as chairman, and I think to most of the other members of the Committee on Industrial Democracy, that we had a double task to perform. The first was to advise the Government on the best way of carrying out their commitment 'to a radical extension of industrial democracy in the control of companies by means of representation on boards of directors'. The second – whatever use the Government might make of our advice – was to produce a report which would have sufficient impact to start a continuing debate on industrial democracy.

Although they were clearly different, I did not regard these two objectives as incompatible. Even if the Government were to implement our recommendations, this would only be the beginning of a new phase of development, further stages of which would require to be discussed in the light of experience. It also seemed likely that the only way to start a serious debate was to produce a coherent and detailed set of recommendations which, whatever the Government might decide to do with them, would attract and focus attention in a way which well-meaning generalities would never do.

Naturally enough it is on the first question–what action the Committee would recommend and the Government decide to take–that attention so far has largely been concentrated. By the time this book is published, the Government's answer may be known. But, whatever that may be, I am sure, as I said on the day the Report was published, that the issue of employees' representation has been placed on the agenda of British politics and will not easily be removed.

If this forecast proves to be correct, then the second object the Committee had in view, to start a continuing debate, becomes much more important. Mr Elliott's book carries this debate further by offering a careful and dispassionate examination of the arguments which the Committee's report has provoked. Having read most of what has been written and said about 'Bullock', I am impressed by the skilful way in which Mr Elliott has carried this out and cleared the way for the next stage of the discussion. In the process he has also corrected a number of mistakes and misrepresentations about what was actually said in the Report, for example about two-tier boards.

Most people, I believe, would agree that this country's situation would be very different if we could draw out more initiative, create a greater sense of commitment and tap more of the unused potential of those who are employed in our manufacturing and service industries. The majority report of the Committee on Industrial Democracy argued that the way to do this is by giving them a greater opportunity to take part in making decisions about the undertakings in which they are employed and a greater share of the responsibility for them, instead of leaving both the decisions and the responsibility to management alone. There is plenty of room for differences of opinion about the best way in which to secure this and there is, surely, more than one way. But these questions of ways and means should not be allowed to obscure the challenge of the main argument which I believe has not been met, let alone answered, in the debate so far.

My final reason for recommending Mr Elliott's book is his sense not only of historical context but of historical perspective.

The concluding paragraph of the majority report drew attention to the fears expressed in the 19th century that to give more people the right to vote would lead to the subversion of the constitution and the dissolution of society.

Once the franchise was extended, however, the fears were forgotten and the Reform Acts were seen as essential to the country's stability and prosperity. We believe that over 100 years later an extension of industrial democracy can produce comparable benefits and that our descendants will look back with as much surprise to the controversy which surrounded it as we do to that which surrounded the extension of the political suffrage in the 19th century.

I do not mean to suggest by this that there is a simple historical parallel between political and industrial democracy. The point I wish to make is that changes which appeared to many at the time to be alarming in their irresponsibility and destruction of the power of decision-making can be seen, in retrospect, to have had very different results from those which were feared. The conclusion I draw from this is that it is a mistake to view changes of the sort we discussed in the report on industrial democracy against too short a time-scale, thinking only of the next few months or even the next few years. Mr Elliott avoids that mistake and by standing back from the developments he discusses enables, and indeed obliges, the reader to consider them in relation not to the programme of a particular government but to the way our industrial society is going to develop between now and the end of the century.

Many people who see clearly enough that industry is dependent on, and productive of, technological change are unwilling to see that this will produce other changes as well, in the organisation of industry just as much as in society at large. One example of this – although much of the evidence given to the Bullock Committee showed unwillingness to recognise it – is the managerial revolution which has transferred the effective control of companies from their 'owners', the shareholders, to the professional managers. There is no reason to suppose that the process of change will stop at this point. It could be that the next stage of development will lead to the representatives of all sections of employees, and not just those employed in management, sharing in the responsibility for the undertaking they work in – and that by the end of the century it will seem as natural that this should be so as it does now that the management and no longer the owners of a business, its shareholders, should make the decisions. The Bullock Report started from the assumption of a mixed economy and it is my firm belief that nothing would do as much to guarantee the continuation and success of a mixed economy as change along these lines. This *could* be the way in which things go, with immense benefit to our future as an industrial nation. But such change will not take place without an effort of imagination and will on the part of those engaged both in industry and politics, and this will need to be greater in Britain than in the other countries which have already started on this road.

The alternative, as Mr Elliott concludes, is for companies and unions to carry on with the traditional tactics of conflict: 'That is the easy answer, the one that has done Britain little good over the past few decades.' Mr Elliott has written his book, as I agreed to serve as chairman of the Committee on Industrial Democracy, in the belief that it is possible to find a better way to conduct industrial relations, and that there is no more important task than to start the process of debate and experimentation now.

St. Catherine's College, Oxford,
6 November 1977   *Alan Bullock*

List of Abbreviations

ACAS	Advisory Conciliation and Arbitration Service
APEX	Association of Professional, Executive, Clerical and Computer Staff (the clerical workers union)
ASLEF	Associated Society of Locomotive Engineers and Firemen
ASTMS	Association of Scientific, Technical and Managerial Staffs
AUEW	Amalgamated Union of Engineering Workers (the engineers)
BIM	British Institute of Management
BSC	British Steel Corporation
CBI	Confederation of British Industry
CDA	Co-operative Development Agency
CSD	Civil Service Department
EEC	European Economic Community
EEF	Engineering Employers Federation
EPEA	Electrical Power Engineers Association
EPTU	Electrical and Plumbing Trades Union (the electricians)
GMWU	General and Municipal Workers' Union
ISTC	Iron and Steel Trades Confederation
JoTT	Journalists of The Times
JRC	Joint Representation Committee of shop stewards in a company recommended by the Bullock Report
JUC	Joint Union Committee
KME	Kirkby Manufacturing and Engineering workers' co-operative
MSC	Manpower Services Commission (Manpower Commission)
NAFF	National Association for Freedom
NALGO	National and Local Government Officers' Association (local government workers)
NCB	National Coal Board
NEDC	National Economic Development Council (Neddy)
NEDO	National Economic Development Office
NUB	National Union of Blastfurnacemen
NUBE	National Union of Bank Employees (bank employees)
NUM	National Union of Mineworkers (miners)
NUR	National Union of Railwaymen
POEU	Post Office Engineering Union
SDP	Social Democratic Party
SOGAT	Society of Graphical and Allied Trades
SSRC	Social Science Research Council
TASS	Technical and Supervisory Section of AUEW
TUC	Trades Union Congress
TGWU	Transport and General Workers Union
UCATT	Union of Construction, Allied Trades and Technicians

UCS	Upper Clyde Shipbuilders
UCW	Union of Communication Workers (formerly the UPW)
UNICE	Union des Industries de la Communauté Européenne
UNM	Union Nominated Members
UPW	Union of Post Office Workers
USDAW	Union of Shop, Distributive and Allied Workers (shopworkers)

Author's Note

This book started out in the late summer of 1976 as a response to an invitation to write a quick work on employee participation. The catalyst was the Bullock Committee of Inquiry which was then looking into the TUC's worker director plans. Gradually however the book has expanded into the whole area of trade union operations in national and economic as well as industrial affairs, which has meant that the 1974 Labour Government's 'social contract' with the unions has become a central feature.

Throughout the following year, until the book was completed in July 1977, a series of events occurred on the social contract and the Bullock exercise, all to do with how Britain lives with its unions and how it mixes its industrial conflict and co-operation. This book is about how governments and industrialists have tried to come to terms with unions and workers during the past decade. In this way the Bullock Report and the social contract are put into the broader context in which they belong.

But the book does not for example attempt to analyse the rights or wrongs in economic terms of incomes policies (which is a key issue for monetarist economists and Conservative politicians), nor does it examine whether companies might be more efficient without unions (which some industrialists and other protagonists would claim). Rather it starts from the premise that unions exist as part of British society and then goes on to examine how their role could become more constructive under the broad responsibilities of industrial democracy.

Inevitably, a journalist writing such a book will be criticised for being a theorist with no practical experience – and indeed my own direct industrial experience is limited to a relatively short period as a management trainee with a construction company. But over the years that I have reported labour and industrial affairs on the *Financial Times* I have seen (in Fleet Street itself as well as elsewhere) enough of the failure of many unions and management to run business effectively to believe that it would often be difficult to change things for the worse. More often than not, a labour reporter is a student of trouble and a purveyor of bad news and so will see companies at their worst; and I must apologise in advance if on occasion I seem to be forgetting the thousands of industrialists, managers, union officials, shop stewards, and the several million workers who daily go about their business in relatively co-operative and constructive relationships.

As a reporter, one builds up over the years a large number of kind, patient and helpful 'contacts' who are experts and activitsts in their own fields, without whose knowledge and wisdom one would have little chance of making sense of many of the events that have to be reported. Many of these people have helped me directly with this book, but there are many others to whom I must apologise for the fact that, with so little time available, I was not able to talk to them again during the past year. To both groups however I owe a great debt of gratitude because without their help I could not have produced this book. If some of them feel I have not done their ideas justice, or have sometimes ducked out of arguments they urged me to follow to conclusions, I hope they will not be too disappointed.

So to all of them, at the TUC and in individual unions, in the CBI and a large number of companies, and elsewhere in Whitehall and the academic world, I would like to say 'thank you'. Some of the people who have given me special help have asked not to be mentioned by name here, and some of them appear during the course of the book. I would especially mention two life peers of the labour academic world – Bill McCarthy, who has patiently taught and explained to me the mysteries of the business over several years, and Bill Wedderburn, who has given invaluable help with the legal aspects of the subject. In addition, Mike Bett has read many chapters for me and has tried to bring me down to earth with the crisp logic of a management practitioner.

My thanks also go to Andrew Best, who has guided me through the intricacies of the art of book writing, and to Anne Cooke and Ruth Lees-Jones, who at amazing speeds typed most of the drafts. I must also thank friends and colleagues at the *Financial Times* for their help and especially John Wyles, who has discussed and analysed many of my ideas and has read every word in this book at least once in successive drafts. Without his tactful, critical encouragement, the errors of fact and the gaps in the arguments would be far greater than they are.

Above all I would like to thank my wife Margie, but for whose cheeful and understanding patience and support there would have been no chance of this book being written. With our two young sons, Mark and Nick, she adapted our home and their lives to the distracting demands of the work, and this book is dedicated to them.

Addendum 1983

On June 9 1983, when Mrs Thatcher's Conservative Government won a second term of office by a landslide victory, it became clear that many of the assumptions of the 1970s would need to be reassessed on a long-term basis. During her first 1979-1983 period of Government, a combination of her policies and the recession had dramatically changed the balance of power in industry. 'Bullockry', as it has become known, had been swept aside as an irrelevancy along with the participative debates and experiments of the 1970s.

The addendum to this book, written while Mrs Thatcher was winning her votes and then forming her second administration, attempts to put some of these events in context, and to look ahead to the future relations between employers and employees at work.

I am extremely grateful to the contacts, friends, and colleagues who have helped me prepare the addendum. My thanks also to Geoffrey Owen, Editor of the *Financial Times*, for allowing me the necessary time off to do the work in between my departure from being industrial editor of the *Financial Times* and my arrival in New Dehli in August 1983 as the newspaper's first South Asia correspondent.

Part I
Living with the Unions

Chapter 1

Introduction: Industrial Democracy

The power and the responsibilities of trade unions have been subjects of continuous political controversy and debate since the unions first started developing more than a century ago. In the second half of the twentieth century this controversy has become more intense. Technological and social developments and natural economic problems have increased the powers of the unions, and politicians of all parties have tried various methods of curbing these powers, as well as, sometimes, encouraging the unions to shoulder greater responsibilities.

These attempts to come to terms with the unions have gradually and almost unobtrusively broadened into a concept of what can be called 'industrial democracy'. This involves far more workers' rights in the board room and on the shop floor because it takes the issue into the realms of national economic and other policies of governments. What has been learned in the postwar years is that the powers and influence of the unions – albeit often negatively operated – are such that governments cannot run the country, and most managements cannot run efficient companies, without the co-operation of their unions. Equally, the unions cannot achieve the advances they want for their members and for their own organisations without coming to terms with governments and industrialists. Under the broad heading of 'industrial democracy', this involves the community tacitly recognising the rights and aspirations of workers to be collectively represented – normally by unions – in a widening area of industrial and economic affairs that affect their working lives. On the other hand, the unions and their members are expected to recognise the corresponding responsibilities to the community that this involves and to exercise constructive and positive, rather than negative and defensive, powers, especially on wages.

During the past ten years in particular, the British Parliament and public have swung almost irrationally from one extreme to another in their views on how to live with the unions, as governments have searched for incomes and other labour and economic policies. On the one hand there have been laws to curb the unions and their members' freedom of action. On the other hand there have been laws (from the same political parties) to help them strengthen their hold on industry and to enforce through the law matters they used to have to bargain about with employers. However aggressively governments may sometimes start down a path of 'curbing the power of the unions', they generally switch back after a year or so to trying to do deals. This is because they have increasingly found themselves turning to incomes policies rather than facing the social and industrial unrest of 'monetarist' and other policies that would lead to widespread unemployment, and other unpopular policies such as cuts in public spending.

A definition

The 1974 Labour Government's 'social contract' with the unions, and the Bullock Committee of Inquiry on Industrial Democracy which was set up at the end of 1975, are both products of the more positive aspect of these developments, and the central purpose of this book is to put these two events into an overall context.

The term 'industrial democracy' means many things to different people and has been much abused during the debate over worker directors that followed publication of the Bullock Report early in 1977. The first thing to say about it therefore is that it is a far wider and older issue than just about worker directors, possessing both industrial and political dimensions. Broadly, industrial democracy involves workers (normally through their trade unions) claiming rights to have a greater say over matters affecting their working lives. This involves the running of the country's economic and industrial affairs which in turn involves those who are in positions of authority handing over some of their powers to representatives of the workers.

Transfer of power

This transfer of power fits in with the political ambitions of British trade unions to change society. (In any discussion of British politics and industrial relations it should always be remembered that British unions are both political and industrial bodies, being part of the Labour movement and the founders of the Labour Party. The leaders of the unions therefore operate both at an industrial level in companies and on the shop floor and at a political level both within the Labour Party and in dealings with the government in power. And while looking after their members' day-to-day interests with governments and employers, they have longer-term, albeit often vague, socialist ambitions to change society.)

So the concept of industrial democracy in its broadest terms—that is, harnessing the influence of workers to change the balance of power in the nation and at work—is what the unions have been about since their inception. And it is a concept that has been boosted on the shop floor, where workers are now better educated, more affluent and more demanding than they were a couple of decades ago. They are consequently less willing to accept without question or challenge the legitimacy of managerial authority (or trade union or many other forms of authority, for that matter), especially at times of economic and industrial failure.

But in the context of Britain in the 1970s there is a further dimension to the subject of legitimate authority. This is the extent of new responsibilities for the co-operative running of the country's economy and industry that the unions are prepared and able to shoulder in return for their increased powers. This is not merely a question, for example, of how Jack Jones or Hugh Scanlon or their successors or some labour theoretician might view the role of the unions. It is a question of how the union members themselves would react permanently to such a development, or whether they might not turn away from the established unions to find new standard-bearers if they felt that their old unions had become too permanent a part of the Establishment. There is also the practical problem of whether the shoestring approach of British unions to their own organisations makes them capable of bearing the burden themselves and of how the unions' shop stewards would cope with the duality of roles.

The problem of the role of the unions emerges in all forms of industrial democracy but it is seen at its most potent in the debate about worker directors (or board employee representatives, as the TUC prefers them to be called) which could be a far more drastic step than all the other forms of industrial democracy that will be examined. This is because it means changing permanently the whole basis of British company law, the rights of the shareholders as the providers of industrial capital, and the relative status and powers of people who work together every day.

The new responsibilities

Industrial democracy thus puts the unions and their members into positions where they shoulder new responsibilities in dealings with governments and employers. The implications of this emerged during the mid-1970s, when the emphasis of public policy (under both Conservative and Labour Governments) swung away from trying to restrict unions by law and towards harnessing their positive support by involving them constructively in the formulation and execution of policy.

Indications of this trend were first the Heath Government's attempts at tripartism and understanding with the unions on pay and economic affairs, in 1972 and then, in a slightly different form, in 1973. This led on to the 1974 Labour Government's much more radical partnership with the unions called the 'social contract', which involved the unions and their members (for a time at least) donning a new responsibility in their wage negotiations in return for the Government's introducing union-favoured social and industrial reforms.

Second, the unions moved into new policy-making and executive roles, helping to run quasi-governmental agencies such as the Manpower Services Commission and the Advisory Conciliation and Arbitration Service with civil servants and employers. They have also demanded wider economic and financial influence over the way pension funds and other industrial investment are managed.

Third, there have been demands for a greater say in industrial and company affairs—which brings in the employee participation dimension—through extended consultative and participative systems ranging from employees being given more company information by their employer to the worker director issue. The union leaders' aim here is to extend their influence beyond the day-to-day immediate shopfloor interests into the power centres of major companies where decisions are made that will affect the livelihoods of their members in the future. This target lies at the heart of the ambitions both of those union leaders who want to see worker directors appointed and of those who want to extend their collective bargaining systems up from the shop floor to the level of long-term corporate decisions outside the board room. The trade union logic here is that, in the highly developed international industrial world of the 1970s and 1980s, union negotiators should no longer only rely on shop-floor negotiations, where they can only react to top-level decisions which may have been taken by boards of directors and top management long before.

Different perspectives

Despite its central semi-political theme of increasing the role and status of workers in an industrial society, industrial democracy means different things to different people. To some on the far left it is perceived as a path to full workers' control, while for many employers and Conservative politicians, who dislike its political connotations, it should be called simply 'employee participation' and only involve a partnership between employer and employee in making the company and the present social and economic system work more efficiently and productively without any changes in power-relationships. To union leaders, as part of their long-term aim of changing society, it is a method of shifting the balance of power in industry so that they and their members increasingly share in that power, with the trade union organisation being the vehicle for linking national economic, industrial, and shopfloor aspects.

Industrial democracy as a concept is not new, however. As long ago as 1898 Sidney and Beatrice Webb, the socialist philosophers who have had a lasting impact on the thinking of the Labour movement, discussed it. But they saw a democracy for workers built on trade unions through collective bargaining in which unions negotiated on behalf of the workers with managements, who in turn reflected the wishes and demands of the consumer. 'Thus it is for the consumers,' wrote the Webbs,

acting either through capitalist entrepreneurs or their own salaried agents, to decide what shall be produced. It is for directors of industry, whether profit-makers or officials, to decide how it shall be produced, though in this decision they must take into account the objections of the workers' representatives as to the effect on the conditions of employment. And, in settlement of these conditions, it is for the expert negotiators of the Trade Unions, controlled by the desires of their members, to state the terms under which each grade will sell its labour. *(Webb and Webb, 1897.)*

The Webbs saw this as a continuing role for the trade unions in any form of society, however collectivist or otherwise it might become, and their views helped to underline the main adversary base of British industrial relations into the second half of the twentieth century.

The issue of responsibility

Now however the spread of industrial democracy poses for the unions the problem of whether they can and should shoulder a new role of joint responsibility, in which they can no longer operate fully according to their old traditions because to do so would ultimately endanger society's acceptance of their new powers. So partnership with governments on economic policies, with the agents of governments in the running of organisations like the Manpower Services Commission, and even with managers on the boards of companies, inevitably depends for its success on more co-operation and less conflict.

The question of whether the unions envisage Britain being run on its traditional undercurrents of conflict or by new-style co-operation was put succinctly by one of the best and toughest managed companies in Britain, Ford Motor, which in its written evidence to the Bullock Committee said rhetorically that there was one fundamental issue to be faced:

Do the trade unions perceive their long term role as becoming one of constructive opposition, increasingly involved in and thereby able to influence the various aspects of the company's business – a perfectly valid role which would, however, exclude Board participation but lead to further development of the collective bargaining and consultative machinery? Or do they see their long term role as one of full coalition partner in the management job, sharing alike all the obligations, and all the responsibility, which go with the authority? This latter role would involve a fundamental change in what the trade unions perceive as their current role, and it is only if and when such a fundamental change takes place that we see even the question of Board participation arising.

Ford was in effect asking (from its vantage point as a multinational operating in one of the world's toughest industries) whether the British unions were preparing to abandon their political interests and behave more like the business-oriented unions of America (which have been interested primarily not in changing society but in maximising the profits of the capitalist system and then fighting for their members to have as big a share of the proceeds as possible) or like the German unions (which have some UK-style society-reforming ideals but put these aside on a day-to-day basis in a spirit of co-determination). In Britain however even the unions' rule books stress their politically oriented purpose of changing society through means such as nationalisation and workers' control. So the blunt answer to Ford is 'No'.

The *best* answer that one could give however is more pragmatic, and is that giving workers greater responsibilities through their unions might well lessen industrial conflict. To pose the issue as starkly as Ford did is rather a case of the relative position of the cart and the horse – whether a change can come without some catalyst, like the statutory right to the responsibilities of board representation, to encourage it.

It is true of course that politicians and industrialists can point to experiences over the years where they have tried to give unions extra responsibilities and where either the unions themselves or their members have shown, sooner or later, a preference to fall back on their old-style tactics. The history of the social contract's wages policy illustrates this, with union leaders eventually having to recognise their members' waning interest in an industrial democracy-style social contract relationship which held down wages but, while providing union members with various gains through employment legislation, seemed to do little for unemployment or prices, which was what most concerned the workers.

Contradictory answers

The purpose of this book therefore is to set the trends of the past decade

7

or so in some sort of perspective and to see how far trade unions and workers and industrialists and managers want to, and can, change the way that Britain manages its affairs. It is not a study that can lead anyone but the most ideologically committed to a single solution. There is no way for example that the blanket enforcement of worker directors or of corporate state wage levels would solve Britain's problems. Indeed, as the book progresses, different possible conclusions are thrown up.

Hence in Part II, Chapters 6 and 7 on, trade unions basically sympathise with the TUC aspirations but raise doubts about whether the role of the unions and their activists can change sufficiently to sustain an efficient industry run in the near future on a widespread worker director basis: a conclusion that leads one towards the alternative of collective bargaining being extended into a widening range of corporate decisions if union aspirations are to be satisfied. The conclusions that could be drawn from Chapters 8 and 9 on companies, industrialists and managers are partially inspired by the author's personal belief that management (as well as unions) in Britain needs a major reforming catalyst. They therefore tend towards the idea of giving an option for worker directors in the boardroom to provide some necessary shock treatment when unions meet certain preconditions. Then Chapter 11 on the methods of participation criticises the notion of extended collective bargaining, first because it could restrict managerial functions, second because it would perpetuate conflict-based tactics, and third because its statutory enforceability is open to doubt. So one is back to worker directors. And at that point one is also back to the starting point of whether the trade unions can, or whether their activists want them to, change their role into one of semi or total partnership.

Lord Bullock has seen the development of worker directors in a historical context of extending individual rights through the unions and providing a new legitimacy for the existence of the mixed economy system. His Committee's report also talked of managerial functions being seen in a new light of legitimacy of consent on the shop floor. This book suggests that industrial democracy and a changing union role could also increase the legitimacy of the unions and especially their shop stewards as positive as opposed to negative forces in the eyes of industrialists, the country at large, and the politicians, at a time when respect for authority of all sorts is on the wane.

Chapter 2

A Decade of Union Victories: Winning Responsibility

The sharp increase in the power and influence of the unions in the management of Britain's affairs that developed in the early 1970s marks a significant chapter in the history of the country's political and industrial life. Under the overall umbrella of what can be seen as industrial democracy, new rights were given to unions and their members and they were expected to shoulder new responsibilities in return.

The most important political catalyst for this change was the move away from the efforts of the previous decade to tame the unions by legislating them into respectable behaviour patterns of responsibility. At the same time the confrontation politics, with which the Heath Government was launched in 1970 and removed from office in 1974, were also abandoned. Politicians and industrialists, tired and frustrated by the battles they had lost over the preceding years, realised the attractions of trying an alternative co-operative policy that was presented to them by the Labour Party and the TUC. This new approach involved harnessing the unions' co-operation by giving them opportunities to shoulder positive responsibilities.

At a national political and economic level this took the form from 1974 of Labour's social contract, where the unions were brought in on national planning and policy formulation in a more substantial way than ever before. In the machinery of government the unions' voice was increasingly heard – though not always followed – and their responsible co-operation was sometimes harnessed. In industry the TUC prepared policies to enable the unions, partly through various employment and industrial safety legislation, to share in the role of management by some means of industrial democracy, even though, in its ultimate manifestation of proposed Bullock-style worker directors and the plan for joint control of pension schemes, it did not always inspire the enthusiasm even of individual workers and union officials.

There was one other important factor, and it followed the defeat of the Conservative Government in February 1974: the repeal by the new Labour Government of the Conservatives' Industrial Relations Act. Even though the Act had not restrained them much, many union leaders had seen during its three-year life how they *might* be restricted by law. Consequently they adopted a new positive attitude and went out with the 1974 Labour Government to gain all the legislative advantages and insurances that they could find. Their objective was to underpin with statutory force many of their freely negotiated collective bargaining

9

gains. At the same time the unions were also sensitive about the strength of their own organisations and became specially aggressive about potential infiltration of employer attitudes into their organisations through staff associations and other non-TUC bodies. This partly emerged in their approach to the training of shop stewards. Such training, the TUC said with increasing insistence and success, was a matter of education in trade unionism; it was not industrial training, and so should be under the sole control of the unions (Chapter 7). In short, the unions showed some signs of having emerged from the Industrial Relations Act period more aggressive and more wary of being caught short.

The rule of law

To appreciate the changes in attitudes towards the unions, as well as the unions' own outlook, one needs to trace the history of earlier developments. Up to the late 1950s, governments did little to try to curb the trade unions, and in the later postwar years Conservative ministers of labour increasingly seemed to regard it as their role to establish close and almost paternal relations with the top trade union leaders of their day, who themselves were generally powerful right-wing rather than radical figures. Only the emergence of incomes policies towards the end of the 1950s started to change this and led, in 1959, to a Conservative minister of labour—Iain Macleod—initiating his Party's first anti-union-power move when he cancelled a long-established arbitration system which employers considered to be inflationary.

'A Giant's Strength'

But there had already been concern about what was seen by some people as the growing power and lack of responsibility of the trade unions as Britain's economy improved in the postwar years. This was illustrated by an historic pamphlet called *A Giant's Strength* which was published in 1958 by the Inns of Court Conservative and Unionist Society. It took its title from Shakespeare's *Measure for Measure:* 'It is excellent to have a giant's strength but it is tyrannous to use it as a giant.' Associated with the Conservative lawyers who prepared this booklet was a one-time Conservative parliamentary candidate who later became famous as the first and last president of the Conservatives' National Industrial Relations Court–Sir John Donaldson.

The pamphlet quoted Sir Winston Churchill as having said that 'the great power that the trade unions now hold entitles them to be considered a new estate of the realm in company with other ancient estates', and went on to say:

By each upsurging thrust a different group in the community in its turn has sought and in time achieved, power. Each group on reaching the pinnacle, being human, used that power in a way that did not meet with the full approval of the group arising behind it. It tended to do this simply because it was composed of men drawn from a particular section of the people. But in the course of time it was, like a wild horse, tamed and schooled so that it could be used for a useful and worthy purpose without harm to any man. From a group liable to exert its strength in any direction, regardless of the country's good, it was converted into a constitutional force directing its energies into those channels the common weal demanded. In every case there was first a struggle between the old and the new followed by a settlement accepted by both sides, the settlement itself becoming part of the constitutional law of the land. . . . The trade unions as the most recently developed of these upsurging groups have not, as we have seen, in their genesis and growth followed the happy pattern of the earlier estates. . . From being rigidly circumscribed they were put by the Acts of 1871, 1875 and 1906 in a position that in many ways placed them beyond the rule of law. *(Inns of Court Conservative and Unionist Society, 1958.)*

Therefore, the Conservative lawyers concluded, a settlement was needed that 'would regulate the relationship of trade unions with the State by bringing them under the rule of law'. Provided such a settlement was 'just', they believed that the unions would be 'disposed to direct their vast power into a course beneficial to their own members and to their fellow Englishmen'. They would then become 'the new estate of the realm'.

Pay laws of the 1960s

But it was not till ten years later that Barbara Castle, by then secretary of state for employment and productivity, took up a not too dissimilar cry. First, however, the 1964 Labour Government tried to win the trade unions' voluntary co-operation with a declaration of intent on pay and productivity jointly signed by the Government, CBI and TUC. Second, in 1965 it introduced voluntary pay norms around the 3 to 3½ per cent mark. But neither the declaration nor the norms worked well, and a series of economic problems led the Wilson Government to introduce a statutory pay freeze. The basic unity of the Government and TUC withstood this test, despite opposition from such figures as Frank Cousins of the TGWU who resigned from the Government, and the TUC accepted with some reluctance the legal restraint involved.

The significance here is that by this time the unions had still not developed the hypersensitivity over legal restraint of their affairs that was to develop by 1975, when they refused to accept formal legal restraint on pay from a Labour Government. Traditionally they have not mounted major confrontations with governments on the principle of pay restraint for short periods, even though individual unions have been involved in confrontations on the detailed application of such policies. So the pay laws remained in force, and even though the pay policy became less and less effective towards the end of the 1960s, there were no serious challenges to the role of the law. At the same time the way that the pay policy developed in meetings between the Government and the TUC, as well as the CBI, showed the way that the Government was trying to harness the responsibility of the unions for unpalatable policies.

The Donovan Report

While all this was happening, there were parallel developments on the industrial relations front. In 1965 the Labour Government passed a Trades Disputes Act that was intended to restore some legal immunities for strikes and other forms of industrial action that had been limited by case law during the life of previous Conservative governments. Later that year the Wilson Government set up the Royal Commission on Trade Unions and Employers' Associations under the chairmanship of Lord Donovan to look into the question of labour law and to examine relationships between unions and employers 'in promoting the interests of their members and in accelerating the social and economic advance of the nation'.

Unions do not like being controlled or examined by outsiders; but the Donovan Commission suited the purpose of George Woodcock, the TUC's general secretary, who had rhetorically asked the TUC Congress in 1963 'What are we here for?' and was not meeting with much success in getting an answer. For him the Donovan Commission, provided it was not too legalistic in its approach (which it was not) and provided he was appointed to it (which he was), could be a useful catalyst in encouraging the trade unions to modernise themselves. For the Government, the Commission showed that it was doing something to appease public concern about the power of trade unions and was not just re-instituting the unions' old freedoms with the 1965 Act.

The Donovan Commission, after many splits between its employer and union-orientated members, produced in June 1968 a main report broadly favouring voluntary reforms in industrial relations. But it did include one victory for the legalistic hawks, who forced through a qualified idea connected with commercial contracts that unconstitutional strikers should not receive full legal immunities in tort. This illustrated the preoccupation of the period with unconstitutional strikers (that is, those who strike without going through all the constitutional stages of their disputes procedure agreements) and with unofficial strikers (those who strike without the official blessing of their unions). The report however did not back another option – legally binding labour agreements – which was favoured by some 'hawks' and eventually emerged in the Conservatives' 1970 Industrial Relations Bill.

The strong and growing undercurrent in the country that favoured some sort of legal restraint on unions was illustrated by minority reports appended to the main Donovan findings. These called for legal teeth with power to enforce labour reforms to be given to a new Commission on Industrial Relations, which the main Donovan Report was proposing as a voluntary institution. They wanted a new national statutory register of unions to be created which would have some disciplinary power over unions, and there were also calls for a more general legal framework.

The general drift of the report, heavily influenced by one of the country's leading labour academics, Professor Hugh Clegg of Warwick University, diagnosed as the problem that the country's industrial relations were fragmented on two levels and needed voluntary reform. The two levels were the formal national arena, where official agreements were negotiated, and the informal world, where individual managements and union representatives developed their own ways of negotiating the sort of loose agreements needed to keep their factories functioning. It stressed the primary role of management to instigate reforms and was widely interpreted as advocating the development of more formal company and plant negotiations and settlements in order to rationalise the increasing number of *ad hoc* shopfloor arrangements which could not be regulated by industry-wide agreements.

Expert and well argued though it was, the Donovan Report left a lot under-studied. This was particularly true of the national, political and economic role of unions and their potential for establishing new industrial democracy rights. As Dr Bill (now Lord) McCarthy of Oxford University, who was the Commission's research director, wrote five years later 'Donovan contains no general statement concerning the nature of trade unionism and its role in contemporary society' (McCarthy and Ellis, 1973). McCarthy went on to add three further criticisms:

First it oversimplified what was involved in introducing bargaining change. Second it underestimated the legitimate conflict that could arise on the way. Third it advanced an alternative structural model that was itself too simple to be applied universally.

So while the Donovan Report fulfilled an important function in providing a bible for advocates of voluntariness as opposed to legalism, and while it also induced some managements and unions to modernise their practices, it did not tackle some increasingly important immediate issues: in particular it did not examine the role of the unions in the management of the economy. Nor, although a minority of its members wanted some worker director initiatives, did it look ahead to the unions' growing interest in expanding their industrial role beyond pay rises and allied matters which were explored in a Labour Party discussion document published in 1967 calling for positive advances for unions and their members—see Chapter 14. Donovan did not in fact satisfy many people, and with the Government doing little to implement its voluntary reforms, it was soon overtaken by events.

Barbara Castle's 'In Place of Strife'

British industry was hit by some serious strikes in the following months with a seemingly never-ending stream of trouble in the motor industry and the docks. The pressure on the Government to act to curb the unions and their members increased and found a willing minister in Barbara Castle when she moved to be secretary of state at a new Department of Employment and Productivity—formerly the Ministry of Labour—in 1968.

In characteristic style she set about developing a policy that would carve out a new role for a modernised union movement able and willing to share in the planning of the country's economy. While the Conservative lawyers ten years earlier in *A Giant's Strength* had talked about legislating union power into a course beneficial to Englishmen, Barbara Castle wanted to legislate it into responsibility within a new socialist order. Peter Jenkins of *The Guardian* explained Barbara Castle's thoughts in *The Battle of Downing Street*, a book that reported on these events:

The problem was not merely to repair and strengthen the higgledy-piggledy system which had grown out of economic and social conditions which no longer applied but to strike a new balance of rights and obligations. The union movement must be made stronger in order to become a fit partner for a Labour Government engaged in the task of constructing Social Democracy. . . . That also meant a stronger trade union movement. Basic trade union rights—the right to join a trade union, the right to bargain, the right of redress against arbitrary dismissal—these had to be secured. But there were also some basic obligations, one of which was to honour bargains freely entered into. . . . And surely the trade union movement existed for something more than the aggregation of the sectional interests of the individual unions. Was not that why they had created the Labour Party? And if so was there not some obligation to assist it in the planning of the economy as a whole and in serving the interests of all? *(Jenkins, 1970.)*

But, like so many politicians, civil servants and commentators, she was frustrated by their inadequacies, and felt the unions should be helped by the law to help themselves–not apparently appreciating the unions' century-long tradition of resisting laws affecting their organisations. Her White Paper, *In Place of Strife,* was published in January 1969 with the backing of her Department's senior civil servants who had been toying with strike law ideas for some years. Her initiative led to a massive bust-up between the Labour Government and the unions. The victors were the unions, but, partly as a result of being shown incapable of managing the unions, the Labour Government was removed from office in June 1970.

At first the trade union opposition to the White Paper was fairly muted, partly because George Woodcock at the TUC saw the policy as a complete package with advantages for the uniòns that outweighed the attempts to restrict them by law. Also Mr Woodcock secured for himself the post of chairman of a new Commission on Industrial Relations (CIR) which he thought would enable him to stop any laws being misused. One or two union leaders on the left of the TUC wanted to fight the policy but no real opposition built up for some weeks. Other events then intervened and, for a variety of political and economic reasons, the Government swung round within a few months to the idea of having a short piece of legislation, culled from *In Place of Strife,* enacted quickly to restrict unions in two ways: the Government would be able to order twenty-eight-day cooling off periods (called 'conciliation pauses') in unconstitutional strikes, with workers who continued to strike facing financial penalties; also, it could enforce settlements in inter-union disputes when voluntary conciliation methods had failed. Balancing this, the unions were intended to gain from provisions that included employers being required to recognise a union and the establishment of a basic legal right to belong to a union.

It was, in the spirit of the times, a balanced package–and there were more advantages, such as protection against unfair dismissal, left behind for a later piece of legislation. But gradually opposition grew, fuelled in particular by a row in which Ford Motor took its unions (unsuccessfully) to court over the negotiation of a wage agreement that included financial bonuses for workers who did not go on strike. This bonus idea was quickly re-interpreted by left-wingers as a 'penal clause' against those who did strike. It therefore helped to illustrate how penalties could weaken the essential basic organisation and rights of a trade union and thus provided a catalyst for those who wanted to stop the Castle measure. This movement of opposition was aided by Vic (later Lord) Feather, who had taken over at the TUC when Woodcock left for the CIR, and by Jim Callaghan, who opposed Barbara Castle's ideas inside and outside the Cabinet (so incidentally starting to cement a relationship with union leaders that helped him to become prime minister seven years later).

Eventually the combined strength of the TUC and the Labour MPs at Westminster defeated Castle and the TUC signed a 'solemn and binding' agreement under which the legislation was dropped and the TUC itself shouldered the responsibility of trying to stop unconstitutional and inter-union strikes. In 1970 a new industrial relations bill, containing the Donovan-style advances for unions, was launched, but this fell with the June 1970 general election.

The pendulum had therefore begun to swing. The Labour Government had learned the dangers of trying to legislate the unions into respectability and instead, trying to salvage something in its defeat, decided to give them some responsibility. The event also gave a boost to the TUC's limited central authority and influence over its affiliated unions, a trend that has since increased. This is significant, because, traditionally, individual unions jealously guard their right to autonomy in the way they write and operate their rule books and prepare and execute their policies. The idea of a central bureaucratic style of body—the TUC or anyone else—trying to influence them is usually therefore strongly resisted. But some authority was given to the TUC in the strikes deal (enlarging existing powers on inter-union disputes), and this increased in later years when the TUC was fighting the Conservatives' Industrial Relations Act and drawing up social contract pay policies with the 1974 Labour Government.

The TUC's victory was shortlived, however. The TUC, and Mr. Feather in particular, did their best to deal with strikes but they soon proved to be an Aunt Sally for critics of the deal because they obviously could not stop every outbreak of industrial action.

The Conservatives' Industrial Relations Act

In some people's eyes, therefore, the TUC had failed in a crucial test of its responsibility and authority. So it was politically quite logical that the Conservative Government, elected in June 1970, should go ahead with its own laws aimed at achieving responsibility through legal restraint, which it had set out in April 1968 (two months before Donovan reported) in a document *'Fair Deal at Work'*. Indeed, so determined were the Conservatives to demonstrate that there was a new order that they did not even want to consult the unions on basic policies.

Two ministers were primarily responsible for preparing the new legislation. One was Robert (now Lord) Carr, who was appointed secretary for employment in the new Conservative Government, and the other was Sir Geoffrey Howe, appointed solicitor-general with an extra office in the Department of Employment.

The package Carr produced was what he regarded as a fair balance between restrictions and bonuses for the unions. It was intended to control the ways unions ran their own affairs, kept agreements and staged strikes. But it also gave help for unions to gain recognition with employers, though at the price of parallel legal constraints. And it provided advantages for individual workers, including protection against unfair dismissal and the right *not* to belong to a union (so outlawing the enforcement of a closed shop). It thus had some of the elements of the Castle White Paper and attempted to strike a similar though broader balance. But its supreme advantage over the Castle proposals seemed to be that, instead of tinkering with limited ideas around the edges of labour strike problems as she had done, it attempted to introduce an overall, balanced and complete framework of law in one package.

The hope was that the framework would settle down gradually over a number of years and would generally provide a basis on which the years of indecision about 'what to do with the unions' could come to an end. If there was a battle with the unions, supporters of the Act argued, the

Government would win and peace would prevail. And provided the Act was not used too much in its early controversial years, the legislation would become part of the background against which industry operated. Its penal aspects would be used only in dire emergencies, while its other provisions would constantly encourage reforms of trade union methods and labour relations practices.

But this was not to be, because the Act was too potent an issue. On the one hand, with some people arguing that the TUC's defeat of the Castle measures had paved the way for the Conservatives to win the election, Vic Feather could not go down in history as the TUC general secretary who had defeated his own people and had consequently shackled the trade union movement with Tory laws. On the other hand, there were too many lawyers, employers and eager Conservative back-benchers who did not understand the niceties of labour relations and the ways of unions. They were keen to have the Act used at every opportunity, which meant it never had a chance to settle in quietly.

The TUC chose union registration–which Feather described as the replacement of 'existing social rights by a state licence to operate'–as the central plank on which to fight the legislation. Eventually it persuaded almost all its unions not to be registered, although unions such as the Shopworkers wanted to remain registered in order to cash in on some of the Act's advantages, and even Clive Jenkins at the Association of Scientific, Technical and Managerial Staffs saw how he could use the Act to rout employers reluctant to recognise him for their white-collar staff. Others were also worried about the problems that refusing to join the new register might bring, including among them Jack Jones of the TGWU, who was concerned because non-registration meant a union losing its traditional tax advantages on its provident funds and other facilities.

Gradually however, fuelled by a growing emotional reaction among union members, opposition to the legislation built up and its lack of effectiveness became evident. At the centre of events was Sir John Donaldson, president of the National Industrial Relations Court (NIRC) which was the main institution policing the Act. This court had a number of successes, notably its handling of unfair dismissals, the way it coaxed some TUC leaders to co-operate with it, and the way its ban on the railwaymen's industrial action in 1972 was obeyed (even though the Government mishandled the dispute subsequently and called for a strike ballot). But these successes were overwhelmed by the Court's calamities, the most notable being the jailing and rapid release of five dockers in 1972.

The problem stemmed from the view held by the Conservatives, and by Sir John from his *Giant's Strength* background, of the way a trade union operated. They wrongly regarded unions as autocratic organisations which could and should be structured and disciplined. This meant that union officials from the general secretary downwards could and should issue orders to their members who would obediently obey them–in much the same way as companies are structurally run from the top.

Thus, according to the theory on which the whole Act was built, the courts would need to deal only with the union leaders and there would be no risk of having to jail masses of workers. The leaders would be held accountable for their members' actions, the Act would be obeyed, and unions would become 'responsible'. This however was a basic misconception of how the unions operate and it meant that in their search for 'responsibility' the Conservatives had not understood the representative nature of unions. Union officials are primarily accountable *to* their members, not *for* them; they are primarily responsible for doing to others what their members want, not for imposing the wishes of others on their members. That is the principle of the way the unions operate, and it makes it very difficult to find ways of enforcing labour laws against them. Obviously these lines become blurred in practice because a union general secretary or other official can have a lot of influence over the views of his members and should feel responsible for making his members keep to an agreement he has signed; but that is different from holding him accountable in law if they do not.

(Ironically, the more recent moves in the mid-1970s towards trade union-based worker directors not only have made the unions' view of accountability absolutely clear but are also part of a general union attempt to stop companies being run in the autocratic corporate style that the Conservatives had wanted to wish on the unions. Under a worker director or other participation system, the workers' representatives would be accountable to their members whose views they would echo on the board. But this would not mean that the worker representatives would be responsible on the board or accountable for what their members did.)

So the NIRC found itself trying to enforce the Act on a trade union movement that did not accept their preconceived ideas or rules. The Court stumbled on from one confrontation to another, with its statute-based, flexibly oriented judgements often being overturned by the more common law-minded appeal court, until Conservative ministers became embarrassed by what they had created, although they were too tied to their general election mandate to do much about it. In any case, any attempt to persuade the TUC to talk about amendments to the Act at this stage would have been fruitless unless the Government was prepared to agree to the virtual wholesale repeal of the legislation, because the unions were by then agreeing on such a repeal with the Labour Opposition Leaders as a policy for a future Labour Government.

Far from reforming and improving labour relations, then, the Act had created an unco-operative atmosphere throughout industry. Employers sometimes found their union officials and shop stewards more difficult to deal with on routine matters, especially where the unions feared that signed agreements might carry the force of law. The TUC-led battle-lines were not only drawn in London but affected practical dealings in individual companies, even though the Act was generally ineffectual.

Tripartism on pay

Meanwhile the Conservatives were also having trouble on the pay front and as a result the Government launched an historically significant initiative with the TUC and CBI, and the Industrial Relations Act faded into the background. Having shunned all forms of formal pay restraint when elected, the Government had relied on squeezing public sector pay rises so as to start a downward trend from the 15 per cent levels that one or two settlements were reaching within months of their taking office in 1970. But they conducted these policies at arm's length from union leaders, whom they did not consult, and soon lost major disputes to groups such as local council dustmen, electricity supply workers and miners. The only group that took the Government on and lost was the postmen, who alone discovered they did not have the solid economic muscle to beat a Government determined to show who was in charge.

Heath's initiatives
And so, facing problems on economic policies, the Conservatives allowed the pendulum to swing a little and Edward Heath tried to woo the unions. Vic Feather was at long last back in the power bargaining game he wanted, doing business as the TUC traditionally does with a government of any political colour, and talks started. Although they ended in deadlock and were followed by a statutory pay freeze, these talks are significant because they involved a Conservative prime minister dipping his toe into a social contract style of running the country and inviting leaders of both sides of industry to Downing Street (and Chequers) to thrash out an economic policy. The stumbling block was that Mr Heath was not prepared to trade major policies, which he regarded as the sole prerogative of the Government, such as housing, pensions, food subsidies and what the TUC called 'non-operation' of the Industrial Relations Act, in order to obtain a deal with the unions.

The initiative started after the miners' strike of 1971-2 which left the Prime Minister fuming in Downing Street because his pay strategy had been roundly defeated by the Wilberforce Report that ended the strike. Mr Heath then told the nation tersely on television: 'We have to find a more sensible way of settling our differences.' The way he chose was to start talks on a wide range of economic and employment subjects with both sides of industry in the spring of 1972, long before a new pay policy would need to be finalised for the following winter's wage round. Then, at the end of September 1972, he lodged the Goverment's pay offer based on £2 a week rises. A little more than a month later–2 November–the talks broke down. They did so because the Prime Minister and his party were not really prepared to budge on his first offer, an attitude that was illustrated by two remarks Heath made. One, widely reported, was when he launched the offer and, clearly choosing his words carefully, said: 'I don't mind how much argument there is about it. We are quite prepared to correct figures if figures need to be corrected.' But 'correct' was not the verb that the TUC would have preferred to hear, and its precise meaning became clear when in an explosive private aside during the subsequent talks Mr Heath said, 'I am not negotiating. This is Her Majesty's Government'. After the talks broke down, Mr Heath said, 'We've always emphasised that these talks were not carried on as a bargaining session. They were carried on . . . in an endeavour to find a rational way of handling these economic problems and to try to get people to agree upon the figures.' The TUC however said it had thought that the Government had wanted a real partnership with both sides of industry in the management of the economy and those involved understood Mr Heath wanted to move on to the creation of some form of economic council. Unfortunately Mr

Heath and his closest advisor, Sir William (now Lord) Armstrong, who was then head of the Civil Service and who played a major role in the talks, failed to understand the nature of trade unions and the type of relationships that they expected to have with other centres of power and influence.

According to some of the participants, Heath and Armstrong both gave every impression after the early introductory phases that they were conducting a consultation exercise of the sort that takes place between government departments when a common policy has to be agreed. In such a forum, while the battles may be fierce, everyone knows, understands and accepts common objectives and proceeds according to common assumptions about relationships and targets. It is an intellectual argument that will reach a conclusion, rather than an across-the-table haggle that might – as this did – fail to reach agreement.

That was not the world the TUC is used to, and even though the CBI, which is more accustomed to such informal arrangements, was present it was the unions' instinctive need for negotiation that eventually prevailed. 'The human relations were good but the industrial relations were bad', is how one participant puts it.

There were also problems with the CBI team. Unlike the TUC leaders, who had had years of experience of negotiating with all sorts of people including ministers, they were all individualists used to consulting with governments but not at all used to closing ranks and negotiating: if there is one thing that union leaders are good at, on the other hand, it is knowing when and how to put their internal squabbles and differences aside and unite in a solid negotiating flank.

Because of the CBI's lack of experience, its representatives were not well prepared and did not have the same sort of detailed background papers that were provided for the TUC's team. (This was something the CBI was painfully aware of by the end of the exercise, and it also knew that the Prime Minister had developed a very low opinion of its capability. Subsequently the CBI improved both its back-up work and the negotiating abilities of its representatives for the following year when there were bipartite talks between the Government separately with the CBI and TUC.)

The seating arrangements, at least in Downing Street, where the final and toughest sessions in the autumn of 1972 took place, also made it difficult to develop a tripartite negotiating type of forum. Ranged along one side of the long oval Cabinet table were all the government ministers and senior civil servants with the Prime Minister sitting at the centre. Opposite him was Sir Frank Figgures, director-general of the National Economic Development Office, with the CBI stretching away from him on one side and the TUC on the other. Consequently the three teams did not coalesce into identifiable, evenly balanced, groups able to see each other – because for a start the seating meant that there could not be a consistent interchange between the CBI and TUC along their side of the table.

The inexperience of the parties in what they were about also emerged sometimes through a lack of contact during long adjournments when there was no 'honest broker' type of labour dispute chief conciliator moving between them to try to find common ground. Armstrong, who might have played this role, was seen by both the CBI and TUC teams as Heath's chief aide, while Sir Frank Figgures was not given the leeway to conciliate although at the National Economic Development Office (NEDO) he was responsible for running some effective working party sub-groups and also tried to patch up the widening differences when the talks were near their final breakdown point, during the evening of 2 November.

In effect, the parties were not ready for the roles they were assuming. The CBI was ill-prepared and relatively unskilled, while the Prime Minister thought he would eventually be able to deal on common ground with men who would put aside their ideological and sectional interests for the good of the nation. But Heath was also aware both of a need for the Government to show that it was itself acting as the guardian of those interests outside the tripartite discussions, and that his Party and backbenchers had reservations about the exercise because of the union power and 'corporate state' aspects.

There is also room for considerable doubt as to whether the TUC really wanted a deal at all with a Conservative Government. Vic Feather was co-architect of the talks with Heath and undoubtedly was striving for a deal; some of his fellow elder TUC statesmen probably wanted one too, but there were recurring doubts about the real interests of Jack Jones and Hugh Scanlon, who made it clear that they had problems with their members about doing deals with Tories. Such qualifications show the doubts any Conservative administration would have about the real motives of the TUC. What is most significant historically however is that Heath started what was then called 'tripartism' (in the present context, the political dimension of industrial democracy) despite his opponents and critics who included some senior civil servants at the Department of Employment. These civil servants did not believe that the TUC was interested in or capable of striking and keeping voluntary deals with any government, especially with a Conservative one, and especially against the background of the Industrial Relations Act.

Heath's offer of partnership, however limited, had nevertheless been a genuine one, as ministers continued to stress. Indeed the following May, Maurice Macmillan, secretary for employment, in a speech on employee participation (see Chapter 14), said:

At the highest level in our national life we are seeking to complement power with responsibility by offering the TUC and CBI, as representative bodies, a say in the management of the economy, no less. Participation par excellence. It is true that we did not achieve this at the first attempt in the Chequers series of talks last autumn. But I am convinced that the Prime Minister's offer of such an opportunity had–and continues to have–a profound effect on the thinking of these major industrial institutions.

The talks also served a purpose for Labour leaders, then in opposition, because they showed the sorts of things on which the unions would want to influence government policies within what was to become the social contract. 'There should be no arbitrary restriction on the range of matters for discussion between the trade union movement and the Government', declared the TUC after the talks had broken down.

The miners' crisis

A year later–after the successful and peaceful introduction of statutory pay restraint–Edward Heath held more talks separately with both sides of industry, but in a less formalised form than the tripartite gatherings of the year before. Again, these talks did not lead to a formal agreement and the statutory policy continued. But Heath did something else that demonstrated industrial democracy overtones of a prime minister recognising the power of, and trying to come to terms with, the unions. He tried to make sure that the pay limits were so designed that they would satisfy the miners. Unfortunately for him, he was dealing with Joe Gormley, the right-wing president of the National Union of Mine-workers, who underestimated the mood of even his traditionally less militant areas. He told Heath what would be needed for a peaceful deal and, with characteristic supreme self-confidence, let it be known that there would be no trouble in the pits. Heath, believing that at long last he had found a national leader who was prepared to speak for his members and who could deliver their loyalty, had the statutory pay policy designed accordingly. But Gormley found he could not deliver his members on a plate, partly because the Government failed to take account (again) of the union's impulsive need to negotiate, and so gave everything away immediately and left nothing for the miners to win at the negotiating table. So to sum up one of Britain's most harrowing postwar winters in just one short sentence, the miners eventually struck and the TUC backed them. Heath, with his battle-thirsty back-benchers wanting a show down with the unions, ultimately refused to operate his pay laws as flexibly as he could have and called a general election, with the back-benchers in full cry on the issue of 'Who rules Britain?' In the event, Labour was returned to power.

The Conservative failure

Elected in 1970 to tame the unions and legislate them into respectability, the Heath Government was swept from office by union power less than four years later. It was a lesson in how not to share power and encourage responsibility–the opposite in fact of an industrial democracy approach, despite the attempt at tripartite talks. Not only had the Government failed to introduce effective labour laws and to establish a concordat with the unions; it had in effect allowed the unions to build up their own morale by giving them opportunities to discover and demonstrate their strength. At the same time the respect for restrictive laws passed by Parliament and the authority of the country's legal system in enforcing them suffered. In addition the Left in British politics was strengthened for a time by such demonstrations of the relative strengths of industrial and legal power.

The role of the law

But contrary to the views of arch critics of the Industrial Relations Act, the period did not show that a framework of labour laws, including some restrictions on the unions, cannot work. Nor did it show that statutory pay policies are unworkable. On the other hand, the unions were able to give the latest and most effective demonstration of their historic determination to fight laws that could endanger the freedom of their organisations. This determination dates back to the last century and was specially evident with the 1901 Taff Vale case in which the House of Lords ruled that a union could be sued in tort for the actions of its servants or agents. This judgement was set aside by the 1906 Trades Disputes Act, but ever since, unions have been on their guard against legal attacks on their basic freedoms and were reminded of the importance of this in 1964 with the Rookes *v.* Barnard case which extended the civil liability of unions in strikes and was in turn corrected by Labour's 1965 Act. The long-term preservation of these organisational freedoms is more important to the unions than short-term issues, and this means that most union leaders do not mount major fights against the principle of pay laws, which only have a short-term effectiveness. Indeed, the 1974 social contract eventually showed how the unions are prepared to trade short-term (and even semi-statutory) pay restraint in return for wider industrial democracy advances.

In addition, there are two wider lessons from the 1970-4 period. The first is that laws have less chance of being introduced and operated effectively if they are not accepted both by an overwhelming proportion of the population (especially when they aim to change the basic social structure) and by the people liable to be restrained by them. Second, the style and methods by which a government introduces unpopular policies is crucial for their success, as is the flexibility with which they are administered. The Heath Government lost out partly because it imposed laws on an unwilling work force and also because it introduced and administered both its strike and pay laws with a catastrophic degree of rigidity.

Employment Protection Act

The period also served to remind union leaders about the potential usefulness of laws, so that, when designing new legislation to kill off the Industrial Relations Act, they also designed new rights and protections for themselves and their members (which had in fact first emerged in a Labour Party report called *Industrial Democracy* in 1967 – see Chapter 14). This has sometimes been construed as being a contradiction for a union movement which is opposed to a legal framework for labour relations. But one needs to distinguish here between the relationship of law to collective labour relations and to individual employment matters. While opposing collective restrictions, the unions have frequently sought legal protection for their individual members so as to provide a 'floor of rights' (Wedderburn, 1971) from which to begin their bargaining with employers. The unions' latest achievements in this area were included in the 1975 Employment Protection Act which, among other benefits, contained legal minimum terms of employment and dismissal for workers – and built a comprehensive framework of employment law. It also went further by moving into the collective bargaining area and laying down statutory procedures for unions to follow in order to gain recognition from employers. The risk here is that such laws, designed to benefit the unions as organisations, can be turned by the courts through judgements into case law that restricts union operations. This is a problem that the unions may have to face up to in the future with the Employment

Protection Act (1975) and for that matter as a result of any legislation on industrial democracy.

A 1977 perspective

While the unions' attitudes towards the law were hardening, however, it should not be thought that all their opponents had given up the idea of curbing union power in the courts. Ironically, this issue was to arise again in 1977 just at the time when the TUC was trying to persuade the Government to enshrine industrial democracy in the law, after publication of the Bullock Report, by introducing legislation on worker directors. It arose then because there were the beginnings of a swing in public and political opinion on union power, a shift of view that was to pose problems for the TUC over the Bullock issue (Chapter 16).

The first glimmerings of the change came in January 1977 with a row over an attempt to use the law to stop the Union of Post Office Workers (UPW) taking industrial action as part of an international trade union protest over South African apartheid. The union called off its proposed action in response to a court order (and the issue later finished up on appeal in the Lords). The special significance of the event was that it resulted from legal proceedings initiated by a prominent member of a relatively new right-wing pressure group, the National Association for Freedom (NAFF), after the Government's Attorney-General had failed to try to stop the industrial action.

NAFF insisted it was not being anti-union though it was against closed shops. It said it was interested in ensuring that the unions upheld the law and did not usurp either the legal or the Parliamentary system. Put crudely, the Association represented, from a fringe but powerful political position, a feeling among some people that the Government had swung too far in placating the unions in the wake of earlier experience. The issue came to a head in a clash with the Attorney-General, Sam Silkin, who, coincidentally on the day after the Bullock Report was published, said that he had himself not initiated action agaist the UPW because (according to reports in *The Times* on 28 January, 1977) 'there was a great risk that wider industrial action would be taken' if he had intervened. For what were nicely described as 'historical reasons', Mr Silkin thought it unwise for the Government to intervene in the industrial field – a clear indication that ministers were scared of the problems that might arise for their social contract with the unions and for their pay and economic policies if they were to initiate legal action.

Next, in May 1977 there was a political row involving remarks made by Michael Foot alleging that judges were biased against unions; and then in June 1977 a dispute involving NAFF and the issue of union power arose at a north London film processing factory called Grunwick. The actual dispute at Grunwick concerned union recognition and employee dismissal problems, but it rapidly became one of the most important anti-union *causes célèbres* for many years as it was enlarged into issues about the role of unions and the law. This concentrated on the wrongs of mass picketing (which erupted in violent scenes at the factory's gates) and the closed shop (which was not really an issue in the dispute at all). Conservative back-bench MPs and others, who still really hankered after an Industrial Relations Act, used the dispute to relaunch their views, and Margaret

Thatcher, the Conservative leader, became increasingly interested in introducing laws and procedures that would curb picketing, change recognition procedures and protect individuals in closed shops.

Then, later in 1977, the CBI produced a new policy document calling for a change in the balance of law on unions and strikes and its first national conference became a focal point for frustrated employers anxious for legal changes.

So, just five years after the Conservatives had started to move towards deals with the unions through Heath's tripartite talks, the issue of union power and the law seemed to be swinging back again towards statutory controls. Early in 1974, however, when the Conservatives were swept from office by the miners' strike, the reverse was the case: laws were out and co-operation was in.

Chapter 3

The Social Contract: Programme for a Government

While the Conservatives' resolute determination to rule the country according to their interpretation of their 1970 general election manifesto was foundering, a new style of industrial and economic government was being thrashed out in the Labour movement. The 'social contract' (or 'social compact' in its early days), which took over where tripartism stopped, rapidly became one of the most misunderstood, most unfairly attacked, and at the same time most powerful innovations on Britain's political scene for many decades.

The basic concept was that the trade unions should have a bigger role in formulating and helping with the success of government policies, in return for which they would regard the wage bargaining and other aspects of their operations in a new and responsible way. This was a direct extension of the Heath tripartite approach, indeed the Heath meetings with both sides of industry in the spring of 1972 gave a new urgency to talks that had started only a month or two earlier between Labour leaders and the unions. The form in which the Heath talks developed helped to concentrate the minds of Labour and TUC leaders about what they should be producing.

In practice this would mean not legislating against the unions on pay or strikes without the consent – or at least acquiescence – of those involved, and not featherbedding the higher earners in society. Instead, the future Labour Government should make radical moves towards changing the social balance of Britain, partly by squeezing the rich and cutting incomes differentials at all levels through taxation policies. It should give workers a new deal with legislation protecting their livelihoods at work and increasing their power over the companies in which they were employed, thereby reducing the shareholders' power and (primarily) the power of big, often unrepresentative, financial institutions. At the same time, essentially voluntary systems for dealing with industrial relations problems should be created with the co-operation of the unions. In return for this a Labour Government would receive, if necessary, the major prize from the unions – co-operation in pay and other industrial and economic policies.

But it should not be thought that the Labour Party as a whole – that is all its MPs, constituency parties and members – had suddenly come round to this way of thinking about union power. Indeed, there have always been strong reservations about such power among many Labour MPs – as was to emerge in 1977 in the post-Bullock Report debate. They had all

25

shuddered with horror however at what had happened towards the end of Labour's 1964-70 administration, and they realised that they had to learn to get on with the union wing of their movement if they were to persuade the electorate to return them to office.

So it was the unions that emerged in the early 1970s to dominate new Labour policies, with the support of Labour Party leaders and MPs in the Parliamentary Labour Party. Together these three groups—the TUC, the party leaders through Labour's National Executive Committee, and the Parliamentary Labour Party—formed a new body in 1971-2 called the Liaison Committee, which was to provide a powerful uniting force through the period of opposition, and then in government after Labour was returned to power in 1974, giving the unions a direct voice in the running of the country's affairs.

Jack Jones in the lead

The moves towards this new union-oriented approach to running the country started to develop towards the end of 1971, a little more than a year after Labour's general election defeat. The main forum was the Labour Party's annual conference at Brighton in the October of 1971, when Jack Jones began to change his public posture. From being the leader of left-wing opponents of governments, he changed into the instigator of policies that would help Labour to regain and to hold on to power. In doing this he was beginning to fulfil the traditional role of the general secretary of the country's largest union, the TGWU, in relation to the Labour Party—a role fulfilled earlier in a different way by his predecessors, Ernie Bevin and Frank Cousins. This is a unique relationship quite unlike any other union leader's and stems partly from the sheer size of the union, with its membership of nearly two million and by far the biggest bloc vote at TUC and Labour Party conferences, but also from the union's powerful role representing general workers in Britain's key industries such as docks, road haulage, buses and motor factories. Other unions—notably the National Union of Mineworkers—also have both a long history of actively helping to support the Labour Party and of proven industrial power; but their general secretaries do not often play anything like the same role in the running of the Labour Party either in government or in opposition.

Jones comes from Merseyside, where he was a docker, and spent many of his early years as a trade union official in the Midlands. A confident negotiator before all else, he has a sharp sense of how to exploit situations. He likes to give the impression that he has little time for intellectuals, even less time for managers, and that he has scant regard for anyone who has not at some time or other worked on the shop floor. He also instinctively dislikes and distrusts the right wing of the Labour Party. These views and attitudes underline the significance of an event that happened at the 1971 Labour Party annual conference, which was to open the way for the development of the social contract.

Tea party politics
On the fringe of a Labour Party conference, during the lunch breaks, immediately after the conference finishes for the day, and during the

evening, various political and other interest groups hold meetings that are addressed by the famous, the experts, as well as by the fanatics who could never get near the main conference rostrum. One group that always has a meeting is the Fabians, one of the founding groups of the Labour Party, which is regarded as an intellectual wing of the Party playing a significant role from right-of-centre in formulating Labour policies through the pamphlets it publishes and the meetings it organises. At the Labour conference it holds what it calls a tea meeting, a genteel affair where the more sedate and comfortable members of Labour's fraternity sip cups of tea and nibble at small sandwiches while listening to a speaker who normally says the sorts of things they want to hear. Few trade union leaders are to be found among the tea-cups. The exception was on Monday, 4 October 1971, when a serious looking middle-aged man, soberly suited and without a glimmer of pleasure in his taut face, entered their stuffy tea party room. His hosts looked little more at ease with the new arrival. Invited by them a couple of months earlier to be the main speaker, Jack Jones was about to make a historic speech burying the hatchet of *In Place of Strife,* calling for a new unity, and even foreseeing the possibility of a wages policy. There should be an end to the 'stress and strain between the trade union and intellectual wings of the Party', he said, and new policies should be worked out together.

Jack Jones was speaking at a time when the Party leaders and the unions were preparing for talks later in the winter and he left his audience in no doubt about what he wanted to emerge from them: higher pensions, a completely free health service, a reduction in poverty levels, industrial democracy based on the unions, and more besides. This, he explained, was why the unions had to be active in politics–they had wide interests which all people should share in.

Reported in *The Guardian* by Keith Harper the next day under the headline, 'Jones sees "marriage" of Labour minds', the event thus provided a key to what was to emerge later as the trade-off that the unions would want for co-operating with incomes policy. As Harper wrote:

Drawn into a discussion on an incomes policy, Mr Jones said: 'If we have to make some sort of sacrifice involving incomes, then we have to decide how it can be done equably. It cannot be done as it was tried under the last Labour Government. It is impossible to put a ceiling on wages while one man works for another man's profit.' Pressed further, he said it was impossible to talk about incomes without thinking in terms of prices. 'If you can find a way of keeping down retail prices and rents, you will get a reaction from the unions, but it needs thinking out'.

He also talked about what was to emerge later as the TUC–Labour Party Liaison Committee and said that the three groups–the Parliamentary Labour Party, the Labour Party's National Executive and the TUC–should meet often to discuss common policies.

This was the first public event to provide evidence that the unions were soon to emerge in a new guise, adopting responsibilities for national policies and demanding positive power in return. This was personified in the change in Jones himself, who was soon to become a national statesman and leader, proposing unpopular but constructive left-wing policies. Jones believed such policies would be for the good of a Labour Government and therefore for the country–and especially (though he rarely emphasised this for fear of the possible backlash) for his general worker members, who would be among those to gain most from a redistribution of the nation's wealth and power.

There can be no doubt that Jack Jones started what was to become the social contract moving in 1971 at the Fabian meeting because he, and other Labour leaders, were horrified at how the Labour Government's failure in its 1964-70 period to come to terms with, and understand the ambitions and limitations of, the unions had been largely instrumental in their losing to the Conservatives in 1970. Jones in particular at this time saw the potential for forwarding his own beliefs in the need for increasing both socialism and trade union power at both a political and a grass-roots level, while keeping bureaucrats at bay and giving workers a better deal. If such an alternative were not put forward, Labour could not be a credible alternative government when the almost inevitable showdown between the Conservatives and the unions came about. As time went on and the social contract came into force with the 1974 Labour Government, Jones was also undoubtedly increasingly motivated by a conviction that the trade unions should be seen to emerge with credit from the country's economic crises.

Union personalities

Such an initiative had to be taken by an individual trade union leader, not by the TUC general secretary, because the TUC is (or was at that time) supposed to stay one stage removed from party politics. This is a distinction that is still maintained, although the social contract inevitably has drawn the TUC into a close formal liaison with the Labour Party both in opposition and in government. In addition union leaders, who cherish their individual autonomy, often especially resent being led by the TUC general secretary. Apart from Vic Feather, who was therefore disqualified, there was no trade union leader of stature and ability to match Jones. Heading the country's second largest union, the Engineers, there was Hugh Scanlon, who seemed perpetually confined at the time to the left-wing style of negative opposition which Jones was about to abandon in an attempt to deal constructively with economic problems. At the General and Municipal Workers there was the ageing Lord Cooper, firmly ensconced on the unimaginative and ineffectual right wing of the union movement and of no great political consequence. At the end of 1972 he was succeeded by David Basnett, an enigmatic figure who sometimes encouraged his union to take a more radical line and saw the emerging social contract as a major development. In the subsequent years he joined Jones on many economic issues, but opposed him sometimes on worker directors. Other notable union figures included Sir Sidney (later Lord) Greene of the Railwaymen, Alf (later Lord) Allen of the Shopworkers, Joe Gormley and Lawrence Daly of the Mineworkers, and others. But none of them had the stature and intellect, or the instinctive political feel, ability and power, to operate in the world of national politics that Jones demonstrated.

Until this time Jones had often been 'twinned' with Scanlon. The two had operated together in their opposition to the Labour Government's policies and had also stood together at the beginning of the Conservative Government's period. Together they were an important force, with their unions' membership dominating the nation's most important industries, especially engineering. Above all they held a powerful combined bloc of well over three million votes out of the TUC's total ten or eleven million membership, and a similarly high proportion in the Labour Party. They did not always win – but they were also a powerful negative force in defeat.

Gradually however the leaders grew apart in the early 1970s. Jones, worried about the impact of the Conservatives' Industrial Relations Act on the wellbeing of what he regarded as the TGWU's essential trade union organisation, was prepared to soften his principled opposition to the Act and so allowed his union to appear in the NIRC to ward off fines. But Scanlon, from the more doctrinaire background of a proud craft union built on an intransigent rule book and racked by constant internal political infighting, was more interested in maintaining the principle of opposition, whatever that might do to his union's finances and organisation. The singlemindedness with which he opposed the Industrial Relations Act undoubtedly made it easier for the TUC to insist that the Act should be repealed by the 1974 Labour Government. Such a wholesale repeal of the laws the unions opposed would have been less likely if the Engineers had been prepared, like the TGWU, to compromise the opposition and, for example, deal with the National Industrial Relations Court.

Unity at Brighton
The coincidence of unions like Scanlon's being determined to destroy the Act and of men like Jones being determined to avoid another Labour Government battle over pay restraint made the development of the social contract during Labour's opposition period possible because it meant they could all group around the development of the new relationship for their own interests. But it was only Jones who could launch the initiative, and after his Fabian tea party appearance he told the main Labour Party conference later in the week: 'The unions and the Party leadership are closer now than for many years and will remain firm and united.' An immediate response came from the Right of the Party. Roy Jenkins called for talks to begin between the politicians and unions 'on the basis that none of us want a return to the past'. No one was confident at the time about where all this would lead but a possible shape of the future emerged in a speech by Bill Simpson, a leading trade union figure (from the engineering industry) in Labour Party affairs, who subsequently became chairman of the Health and Safety Commission. In a little noticed speech to the conference, Simpson mapped out what union leaders such as he and Jack Jones thought should be done. This followed a speech by Harold Wilson, leader of the Party, calling for talks 'between the political and industrial wings of our movement on the voluntary means of strengthening industrial relations and eliminating the causes of industrial tensions'.

Although to a casual observer it might have seemed that all these speeches – from Jones, Wilson, Jenkins and now Simpson – were part of a carefully orchestrated campaign, the reality is that, like so many key political developments, they developed in a haphazard way. There had of course been formal working parties and more informal groups preparing policies for some years, but no one knew how these might emerge in general Labour policy. So the leading figures in the Party gathered in

Brighton for the conference aware of their own debilitating rifts but specially conscious of the place that Barbara Castle's attempted strike laws had played in causing their problems. Accordingly, when the Party's National Executive Committee met in Brighton's Grand Hotel on the Friday before the conference started, Simpson, who was both chairman-designate of the Party and the chairman of its Home Policy Committee, objected to Barbara Castle's speaking in the conference's industrial relations debate on behalf of the National Executive. Castle, he said (almost certainly with the backing of many union leaders), was 'no longer credible in this field'. After a bitter squabble, Simpson won and was given the job of making the speech himself.

Simpson's speech contained many ideas that had been put forward in a Labour Party working party report called *Industrial Democracy*, pro-duced in 1967 under the chairmanship of Jack Jones who was then a leading figure on the Labour Party's National Executive (see Chapter 14). In his speech Simpson called for a new industrial relations policy which would be implemented by the next Labour Government. This would provide basic statutory industrial rights with improved contracts of employment and redundancy arrangements, dismissal procedures, trade union recognition procedures, protection of shop stewards and disclosure of information to union negotiators. In addition, Simpson called for an Industrial Representation Act 'giving workers an effective say in de-cision-making and control of their working lives'. There should, he said, be a 'frontal assault on managerial functions' which would partly be achieved by institutionalising many of the shopfloor arrangements that already gave the shop stewards more informal power. He also called for new arbitration and conciliation measures.

Looking back, this speech was remarkably prophetic. The Trade Union and Labour Relations Act (1974) repealed the Industrial Relations Act. Then the Employment Protection Act of 1975 gave many of the points at the beginning of his list and backed up other legislation which had set up his own Health and Safety Commission by proposing that shop stewards should have new statutory powers over the management of factory safety. The Conciliation and Arbitration Service (set up in 1974 with Jones as one of its council members and later renamed the Advisory Conciliation and Arbitration Service) provided much of the rest along with another later institution, the Central Arbitration Committee. Then the Bullock Committee was created to look at what Simpson had called an 'Industrial Representation Act'.

It is here that the idea of industrial democracy in its widest sense, operating to extend trade union influence at national political level and at the level of shop stewards while also giving workers a better life–that is, embracing both the union power and worker participation dimensions–can be seen emerging from the level of debate into a political reality.

Liaison in the movement

After the 1971 Labour Party Conference, informal contacts were made between Labour and union leaders which were to lead to the creation of a unique institution in British politics. This was the TUC–Labour Party Liaison Committee which brought together parliamentary, party and union leaders in one policy body.

The Committee was formally set up in January 1972 following an initiative at the end of November 1971 when Sir Harry Nicholas, the general secretary of the Labour Party, wrote for the Party's leaders to Vic Feather, suggesting a meeting between representatives of the TUC General Council and Labour's National Executive on economic and industrial issues. This was discussed early in December by the Labour Party's Home Policy Committee where Jim Callaghan was chairman. Callaghan was already talking in terms of a deal with the unions being an essential general election gimmick to win over the electorate and had made it clear he wanted bridges built uniting the movement.

At the Home Policy Committee meeting some TUC people echoed what Jones had said at the Fabian tea party and said they thought that senior Labour MPs–that is members of the Shadow Cabinet who were not on the Executive–ought to be present too through the medium of the Parliamentary Labour Party. The National Executive members thought this raised major constitutional issues which one of their staff described as 'treading on a thousand principles'. Nevertheless, the union leaders on the TUC's Economic Committee, which met a couple of days later, were determined not to bother just with the National Executive members. They wanted a body that embraced members of the Shadow Cabinet– that is the people who would presumably be responsible for putting policies into practice when Labour was in government again. The last thing the top TUC leaders were interested in was agreement on the repeal of the Industrial Relations Act and on other measures with the not always very influential Executive members (who in any case include a lot of second-rank union leaders) only to discover their deal being bypassed by future Labour ministers.

There had in fact already been informal liaison between the TUC and the Labour parliamentary leaders in the Commons during the parliamentary passage of the Conservatives' Industrial Relations Act, and later in December it was agreed that six leading MPs and Shadow Cabinet members would be representatives on the new committee through the Parliamentary Party along with six members of Labour's Executive and six TUC leaders (who included Feather, Jones and Scanlon).

The relative power during the years of opposition of Labour's National Executive Committee on economic and employment policy-making was thus correspondingly reduced because many of the new policies emanated from the TUC through the Liaison Committee. The TUC therefore, for the first time in its history, had a direct line into Labour Party policy-making and thus into general election manifestoes. And when Labour was returned to power in February 1974, the Committee remained in existence with senior Cabinet ministers (including the Prime Minister, the Chancellor of the Exchequer and other ministers such as Michael Foot, Shirley Williams and Anthony Wedgwood Benn) attending as representatives of the Parliamentary Labour Party. It thus became virtually an arm of government in the heyday of the social contract.

The development of the Committee was also significant because it meant that ministers (or senior parliamentary leaders in days of opposition) no longer had to be elected to the Labour Party's normally left-wing National Executive by the annual party conference in order to have some direct influence on the Party's policy-making, although of course they still lacked the punch of the back-up bureaucracies of the TUC and Labour Party headquarters.

The Committee met monthly and within a short time, in July 1972, produced its first joint statement. Parts of this had been previewed by Jack Jones in a *New Statesman* article on 18 February 1972 entitled 'How to Build Industrial Relations'. It drew on his 1967 Labour Party working party report (Chapter 14) and called (like the earlier Simpson speech) for new employment laws. He also mapped out new conciliation and arbitration arrangements, plus 'democracy in management' through trade union representatives sitting on company management boards and 'social justice' to help the low paid. The Liaison Committee statement of 24 July 1972 added other items such as a National Manpower Board and broadened the industrial democracy idea by talking in terms of examining the 'role of the company in society'.

But the primary aim was to get rid of the Industrial Relations Act, and by the end of 1972 documents were produced spelling out, in a draft clause form, proposals for a 'short Bill' (which later became the Trade Union and Labour Relations Act (1974)), to repeal the Act, plus a subsequent longer Bill with new statutory rights. At the time this was being called the Rights at Work and Collective Bargaining Act or the Employment Relations Act, but it eventually emerged as the Employment Protection Act (1975). So, by the time the 1974 February general election occurred there was already a draft short Bill agreed between Labour and union leaders (including Harold Wilson) who were thus almost inextricably tied to doing away with the Conservative Act however much they might have been tempted, once they were returned to power, to try to salvage some of its restrictions on union activities.

The end of 1972 and the beginning of 1973 was an active time for such Labour policy-making. Not only did the draft employment laws pass through the Liaison Committee, but the TUC was also busy preparing its 50–50 worker director plan (see Chapter 14); and then, in January and February, the first major social contract document–*Economic Policy and the Cost of Living*–was agreed. It was launched jointly by Harold Wilson and Vic Feather on 28 February. Because of the mood of the unions over pay restraint, wages policy was not mentioned in any form at all in the document, which was therefore widely criticised at the time for showing how much the Labour Party leaders from Wilson onwards were in the pockets of the unions. In fact, union leaders like Jack Jones realised (as he had shown at the Fabian tea party) that wage restraint might eventually be necessary. But they were not prepared to admit this at the time when their initial priorities were to win from Labour leaders the concessions on industrial and social reforms that would have to be made first by a Labour Government. 'The problem of inflation can be properly considered only within the context of a coherent economic and social strategy–one designed both to overcome the nation's grave economic problems and to provide the basis for co-operation between the trade unions and the Government', said the document. The policy it then outlined covered all aspects of a government's programme (except detailed pay restraint) with only the qualification that final government decisions would depend on economic circumstances at the time, and added:

A new approach is needed also towards much greater democratic control in all aspects of our national life and towards a greater public accountability for the decision-making in the economic field. In the control of capital and the distribution of wealth there will be more economic democracy, and the growing range of functions of the trade union movement will bring about a greater extension of industrial democracy.

The social contract

Eventually the new understanding between the Labour leaders and the unions, together with their joint policy statements, became known as the 'social contract'. Where and when this title first became imported into Labour parlance from its French Revolution origins is open to dispute, with several people including Jim Callaghan and David Basnett of the General and Municipal Workers who was one of the first union leaders to use the term in TUC discussions, claiming original authorship. However as early as October 1970 Thomas (now Lord) Balogh, the economic advisor to Labour leaders, wrote a Fabian pamphlet called *Labour and Inflation*. Using Jean Rousseau's original French phrase, he said that 'a new departure, a new *'contrat social'* is needed'. Under it, unions would perhaps 'succeed in securing voluntary compliance with an effective prices and incomes policy on conditions in terms of social policy including taxation and social services'. Only in this indirect way, he said, could unions 'successfully influence and improve the distribution of income, secure advances in investment and obtain a restructuring of industry'.

Later, in February 1973, when launching the *Economic Policy and Cost of Living* Liaison Committee document, Harold Wilson called what had been produced a 'great compact'. For a time some people (especially Hugh Scanlon of the Engineers) preferred the slightly less legalistic sounding 'compact' to the alternative 'contract'. Nevertheless, 'social contract' it became, and it was mentioned in the Labour Party's February 1974 general election manifesto as being a 'central feature of the new economic policy of a Labour Government'. In June 1974 the TUC called its first and somewhat unsuccessful attempt at introducing some measure of wage restraint 'Collective Bargaining and the Social Contract', and the name was then well established – even though some union leaders were not keen on such a formal title. To many people it simply meant whatever form of wage restraint was agreed in the following months; but in fact it was a much wider development in the management of Britain's affairs, with the unions using their gift of compliance with pay policies to wrest social and economic reforms from a Labour Government.

Chapter 4

Social Contract Methods: Tripartism in Government

The sub-title for this second chapter on the social contract might be 'How the TUC Ran the Country'. Indeed, Labour had not been in power very long in 1974 when that seemed, for a time, to be the reality. This is because the unions, mainly through the TUC, brought together various initiatives in the wake of their defeat of the Conservative Government and had a major influence on Cabinet policies. As a result there was a relatively loosely co-ordinated, but still cohesive, onslaught on many bastions of British life. But to begin with there was no corresponding responsibility by the unions on pay, and union members became engaged in a series of outbreaks of industrial action for high pay rises.

On the broader political front, the unions turned their social contract relationship with the Labour Party into a vehicle of partnership with the new Government, so increasing their influence on economic affairs. Then they expanded their involvement in running government agencies and institutions, some of which had been conceived under the banner of tripartism adopted by the Heath Government. Next they made sure the Government forced through Parliament not only the repeal of the Industrial Relations Act but also new legislation such as the Employment Protection Act (1975), which both improved the lot of their members at work and also increased the organisational and negotiating powers of the unions themselves. At the same time they gradually started other initiatives to increase their influence and power in fields such as worker directors, pensions, the allocation of industrial investment and the distribution of wealth. All this was on top of their traditional collective bargaining role and their power of industrial action.

While the speed of the development of these policies flowed directly from the unions' social contract with the Government, the seeds for several of them had been sown earlier because some of the institutions, providing a framework for considerable TUC influence in Whitehall and elsewhere, had been founded by previous Conservative governments anxious to come to understandings with the union leaders. What was new however was the overall political dimension of the unions, through the TUC claiming the right to move nearer the core of government policy-making, even if the country's growing economic problems meant they did not always have their own way. In doing this they were reducing their traditional antagonistic attitude towards those parts of the Establishment with which they were co-operating. This attitude has always existed as the basis of union operations (despite the official line of the TUC that it is its job to do business with a government of any political colour) and had intensified during the years from Labour's *In Place of Strife* onwards, which made the change in 1974-5 even more marked. It inevitably helped to raise the question of whether it is the job of the trade unions collectively to shed some of the freedoms inherent in their traditional oppositional fall-back role in favour of influencing, and sharing responsibility with, the Government for the country's fortunes. Whatever the answer to this question (and it is unlikely to be clear-cut or permanent), the events that followed Labour's 1974 election victory amounted to a massive increase in central trade union influence, operating mainly through the TUC.

But it would be wrong to imagine that this was a carefully controlled and planned operation with a coherent TUC philosophy to pick off one British institution after another. The only link initially was that the unions realised they had the muscle to exert more influence in national affairs under a broad 'industrial democracy' umbrella and that pay restraint was something they could offer in a trade-off with the Government provided the restraint was achieved by consent. The social contract, drawn up with Labour Party leaders in opposition, provided the means for this to happen. In effect, the trade union leaders were saying it was no longer enough for them to have their own Labour Party in power; they must also develop a special working relationship so that the Labour Government developed and carried out its policies in partnership with the unions. The vehicle for this social contract relationship was the Labour Party–TUC Liaison Committee, mentioned above, in which top union leaders were brought together in regular monthly policy-influencing meetings with ministers, free of the trappings of the Civil Service.

The new union role of responsibility did not appear overnight when Labour gained power, however. First there had to be a period of bloodletting as workers and their unions celebrated the miners' victory and the removal of the Heath Government. To begin with, far from sharing responsibility with a sympathetic Government, some of the unions and their members appeared to be determined to cash in on the weaknesses of a Labour Cabinet in debt to them for the general election victory. Strikes broke out in key areas while pay rises soared to levels reaching as high as 30 or 40 per cent or more. This did irreparable harm to the economy, did little to enhance the public reputation of the unions, and indeed gave critics of the unions a permanent stick with which to beat the social contract. But it was arguably a period of government inaction which had to be lived through in the wake of the miners' victory because a tough restrictive line from Labour ministers would not have met with much success.

Gradually however the unions began to change and to adopt the responsibility implicit in their new industrial democracy-based social contract with the Government. Ministers persuaded the TUC of the seriousness of Britain's economic plight–wage earnings were rising at about 30 per cent a year–and eventually persuaded the unions to accept a measure of pay restraint and (later) also to accept, for a time at least, cuts in public expenditure and high unemployment.

The voluntary pay restraint deal that had eluded Heath was therefore delivered by the unions three years later in 1975 as a £6 a week pay rise limit. A significant constitutional sidelight on this deal was that extracts from the TUC's own policy document on the pay limit appeared in an annex to the Government's official White Paper (*The Attack on Inflation*, 1975) and in fact provided the details of how the policy was to operate. (Similarly the Government's July 1977 much weaker pay White Paper included a TUC annex.) The union leaders – notably Len Murray, the TUC's general secretary, and Jack Jones – thus emerged from the earlier legislative attacks on the unions' basic rights and adopted a new responsible guise under the social contract with Jones dominating the design and advocacy of the policy. They also eventually got to the stage of what some union leaders had called 'bargaining on the Budget' when, in 1976 and 1977, Denis Healey, the chancellor of the exchequer, made tax and other economic changes conditional on the unions accepting pay restraint. In this way the Chancellor was trying to make the unions face up fully to their social contract responsibilities; although he was criticised for pandering to trade union power, he was only underlining publicly the political point on which the social contract was based – that the Government's economic policies depended to a large extent on union co-operation on pay limits.

Wider industrial democracy

To the TUC policy-makers this change (despite its lack of permanency) formed a key part of the extension of trade union power through industrial democracy to the different levels of the economy – developments that a few top union leaders believe could also induce reforms in the unions' own outdated fragmented structures. It is in this overall context that the expansion of the unions' role in national economic affairs can be seen as part of the same drive for an expansion of trade union power that has enlarged the subjects on which unions bargain with employers, has led to Labour calls for company planning agreements, has helped to create the 1976-7 industrial strategy exercise of the Labour Government, and has provided the TUC demands for worker directors. It is inextricably linked with the socialist belief in planning economic and industrial affairs and in shifting the balances of power. It can also involve shop stewards, hitherto confined to shopfloor operations, moving up to positions of power at higher levels of the economy on, for example, company boards of directors and company or industry-wide planning committees. Equally, the Government, whose historic industrial role in Britain has been mainly limited to policy-making at the national economy level, spreads its planning tentacles into the lower levels of the industry and, maybe, the firm. This completes the socialist network in the policy-makers' eyes. The result, in theory at least, is that the risk inherent in a worker director system – that the shop stewards may have their primary loyalty switched away from the unions and towards the firm – is counterbalanced by planning agreements and other tripartite industrial strategies in which the focus of the shop stewards is redirected back to wider socialist targets as part of a tripartite government – industry – union planning network.

This is the background philosophy that has guided much that has been pushed by the TUC and Labour politicians and activists to the left of centre, and it is also a philosophy that, in some form or other, may survive any change of government unless there is a return to a total complete free-for-all approach to economic affairs.

The TUC philosophy on the total approach was spelt out in the TUC's economic review for 1975, an annual publication, which is a guide to advance trade union thinking over a wide field. Under a heading of 'industry and planning: four levels of the economy', it spelt out the theory that trade union activity is built at the levels of the economy, an industry, a company, and a plant:

Up to now Government action has only been at the level of the whole economy. Trade unionists naturally start from a different perspective. They start at the level of the workplace, the shopfloor or the office, the particular assembly line, plant or branch in which they work. They see how this relates to the firm in which they work and how this firm fits into the particular industry in which they work. The whole economy is an aggregation of these constituent parts. Trade unionists also see that there is an important regional dimension to these four levels of the economy. It is necessary to isolate these four levels, not only to improve the decision-making process but to ensure that trade unions are involved in the decision-making process at all levels.

Explaining that this is the basic TUC approach to the extension of 'industrial and economic democracy', the document continued:

The TUC proposal for supervisory Boards with 50 per cent direct trade union representation is concerned with the level of the firm. Other proposals on broadening the collective bargaining function will have effect at the level of the workplace and the firm. Trade union membership of industry training boards and economic development committees is concerned with the industry level, whereas trade union membership of regional industrial development boards and regional economic planning councils is involved with the regional dimension. Trade union representation on bodies such as the National Economic Development Council, the Manpower Services Commission, the Advisory Conciliation and Arbitration Service, and the Health and Safety Commission is concerned with industrial democracy at the level of the whole economy.

The document went on to explain that the creation of the National Enterprise Board, with TUC members on it, and the hoped-for development of planning agreements involving the Government, employers and the unions coming together to plan a firm's future, were further extensions of this.

Then it proposed fresh developments in company and workplace bargaining to help implement industrial democracy at the other levels of the economy. Among the suggestion was one that surfaced in a government White Paper in 1976–unions having half the seats on bodies controlling pension funds. 'The benefits from a pension scheme depend on the yield from funds and it is therefore vital that negotiators make major efforts to establish joint control of both schemes and their funds', said the TUC's 1975 document in a proposal that would also give the TUC an enormous influence over the nation's industrial investment because of the size of these funds (Chapter 17).

Planning agreements

Perhaps the biggest disappointment for the TUC in the social contract was the failure of planning agreements to become the major plank for trade union power that the TUC, along with the then industry secretary,

Mr Anthony Wedgwood Benn, had hoped. The TUC set out its ambitions in its 1975 document, in which it was said that: 'the development of a planning agreement system should lead to a recognition that all strategic decisions in large companies should be the subject of joint control'.

This would have supplemented the TUC's worker director proposal, possibly underpinning (although the TUC did not itself say this) the initial frailty of a union presence in the board rooms. They could also help new worker directors not to be subsumed by the systems of a major corporation because they would provide a wider socialist dimension outside the company. The TUC envisaged planning agreements covering three-year periods with annual reviews, and embracing financial planning such as company expenditure and pricing policies, productivity and investments and product development. However, industrialists and many government ministers, as well as senior civil servants, did not relish the trade unions being given this sort of role, so planning agreements became one of the few significant TUC failures of the 1974-7 period. This was first because, as the Government developed its policy, the trade unions were elbowed out into a sort of consultative status to a main game that was usually played in conclusively by civil servants and companies. In addition, planning agreements did not develop in any form at anything like the rate the TUC had hoped (Chrysler produced the first early in 1977), possibly partly because they could well be of limited benefit to either the Government or a company, whereas they could radically increase trade union power. So the TUC was reduced in its 1977 economic review to calling on the Government to 'take stock of planning agreements' because, it said, 'it makes little sense to have a policy which is completely inoperative'. Later it told the Government that any Bullock legislation should make the drawing up of planning agreements one of the functions to be carried out by a company board.

Industrial strategy and the Bullock Report
Not surprisingly the Bullock Report, published in January 1977, saw a link between planning agreements and worker directors and all the other aspects of the TUC's total approach to industrial democracy. By 1976 this approach also included trade union involvement in the Government's new 'industrial strategy' that was aimed at sorting out the micro-economic and industrial problems that might impede Britain's hoped for economic recovery. The Bullock Report based much of its justification for advocating trade union-based board representatives on the dynamic effect they could have in releasing new energies and responsibility which could be harnessed for the good of British industry. 'We believe that the change in attitude of the TUC and their willingness to accept a share of responsibility for the increased efficiency and prosperity of British companies offer an opportunity to create a new basis for relations in industry which should not be allowed to pass' was how the TUC-influenced majority group who wrote the majority report summed up their views.

Earlier in the report they had echoed the TUC's economic review of 1975 (plus the new 'industrial strategy' dimension) in a way that showed that there was more than an indirect link between the two documents. In fact there was such a link because David Lea, the TUC's economics secretary, and as such in charge of preparing its economic reviews, was a member of the Bullock Committee. He had been involved in the development of the TUC's worker director and wider industrial democracy policies (along with Jack Jones) for some ten years (Chapter 14) and his influence on the Bullock Committee was considerable, as it was in other areas of TUC–government business. The TUC's economic secretary has always wielded considerable influence on TUC affairs–Len Murray held the job before Lea–because the person doing it doubles up as being head of the TUC's research work as well as economic affairs. With the expansion of the TUC's role in national affairs in recent years, the scope of the job has inevitably widened.

Referring to the link between the industrial strategy and the introduction of worker directors in companies, the Bullock Report said:

Trade union involvement is seen as fundamental to forestall negative resistance to change, but also because employees through their trade unions have a positive role to play in combating industrial stagnation and in stimulating much needed changes in industrial structure and performance. This tripartite industrial strategy is likely to act as a catalyst to the further development of joint regulation of forward planning decisions at company level. . . . The emphasis of the industrial strategy on union involvement in company level planning, together with new concepts like planning agreements, are creating new pressures for the extension of joint regulation to higher levels of company decision-making. . . . The development of participation at national and local level has left a gap at company level, which some would argue can only be filled by employee representation on the company Board.

Such a view of the development of industrial democracy at various levels of the economy is however a peculiarly Labour movement approach, and it strikes chords of horror in the minds of industrialists when they realise that there are some influential trade union policymakers linking apparently innocuous developments like the tripartite approach to 'industrial strategy' with Labour's aim of changing society. One of the ironies of the development of the social contract and industrial democracy is indeed that the TUC is able to sell its radical ideas to those on the other side of the political and industrial spectrum because of the potential that, say, some forms of worker participation or the industrial strategy might well have for the fortunes of industry.

The institutions

NEDC and the Little Neddies

The Labour Government's 'industrial strategy', which emerged in 1975-6 as an economic palliative and then developed in 1977 under Prime Minister Jim Callaghan as a central–though still somewhat vague–plank of his overall policy, not only expanded the trade unions' potential impact on industrial policies but also gave a fillip to the oldest of Britain's tripartite organisations–the National Economic Development Council. Founded in 1962 by the then Conservative Administration as a tentative first step in national economic and industrial planning, the NEDC (or Neddy as it is known) acts as a forum for debate and as a catalyst for medium- and long-term reforms and is run from a headquarters known as the National Economic Development Office (NEDO). It has outlived many other organisations in the economic and industrial sphere that have been invented and killed off, usually for short-term considerations, by successive governments.

But Neddy survives, although its role sometimes changes depending on the economic problems and policies of the day. The tripartite Council includes ministers, industrialists from the CBI, nationalised industry chairmen, and six senior members of the TUC General Council. It meets monthly, normally under the chairmanship of the chancellor of the exchequer but occasionally—immediately after a major Budget, for example—is chaired by the prime minister. Generally it confines itself to examining and studying medium- and long-term economic and industrial trends. This helps it to survive because, by not sullying its hands with controversial short-term problems, it can more easily avoid the wrath of sectional interests who might then want to kill it off.

But the NEDC sometimes becomes more involved in immediate affairs. In the early 1970s it became the only forum where the Conservative Government ministers met the TUC and it was painstakingly nurtured by its then director-general, Sir Frank Figgures, for this purpose and became the umbrella organisation for the Heath tripartite talks. At one point during the 1974 miners' strike it even became the centre for talks on the national power crisis and was also used for the back-up work by the Heath Government on the tripartite preparation of details associated with possible pay policies. But this last part of its work mainly occupied the secretariat and was not normally an issue for open debate on the Council itself at its regular meetings.

Below the Council are the 'Little Neddies' covering individual industries, where top people—or their deputies—from both sides of an industry meet to discuss common problems, usually in the past to little effect. These 'Little Neddies' were adapted for use in the 1976-7 industrial strategy with working parties from both sides of industry being set up to cover different industrial sectors. The object was to involve both sides of an industry, with other experts to analyse what problems they would face when the national economy improved, and it achieved various limited successes.

In varying ways therefore—at the level of the national economy on the NEDC, and on industrial affairs on the Little Neddies—the trade unions can exert influence. But the influence is extremely limited because no government has yet envisaged giving the NEDC any real authority in economic policy-making or any executive role.

Tripartite-style commissions

So it is hardly surprising that the TUC should want to spread its wings elsewhere in Whitehall and move closer to both the formulation and execution of government policies. The way it has managed to do so has developed under both Conservative and Labour Governments on a somewhat haphazard basis over the past few years—namely, by gaining for TUC representatives a third or more of the seats on the governing bodies of new agencies hived off from the Department of Employment such as the Manpower Services Commission (MSC), the Advisory, Conciliation and Arbitration Service (ACAS), the Health and Safety Commission and the Equal Opportunities Commission. This gives the TUC, as the central organisation representing the country's workers, a considerable measure of influence. (At the same time ironically it turns the TUC representatives into joint employers of the agencies' staff. As a result, some of the agencies' civil service staff during studies in 1976-7 of public sector industrial democracy suggested they should have a seat for a staff union representative on the agencies' governing bodies, even though the TUC was already there!)

The degree of TUC influence exercised through these new agencies is potentially greater than through earlier organisations such as the old Prices and Incomes Board and the Commission on Industrial Relations, which were mainly advisory. This is partly because the new agencies have an executive as well as an advisory role and partly because the union leaders sitting on the agencies are often, though not always, in effect delegates of the TUC. They report back and gain their briefs from the TUC's specialist committees and so reflect TUC policy. There is therefore a degree of accountability, recognised as being desirable as will be seen by both Conservative and Labour politicians, straight back to the TUC from these agencies' governing councils. There is also of course the same degree of accountability back to the CBI but, because of the CBI's different nature, it is not so positive or effective.

As David Lea of the TUC told a Civil Service College audience in 1975:

I would underline the particular significance from our point of view of the creation of a new range of bodies in this country which are at one and the same time executive and representative. I am referring here to the Manpower Services Commission and the Health and Safety Commission. In different ways too, such bodies as the ACAS and, indeed the National Enterprise Board, are joining a list which includes such developments over the last decade as the NEDC and economic development committees and the industrial training boards. It is part of my thesis that the creation and extension of bodies of this nature does over time change the nature of the Governmental process itself and rightly so. The nature of accountability to which civil servants are accustomed in all their training and understanding of the constitutional process is of course quite clear – the accountability of the Minister to Parliament and Parliament to the electorate. But we are seeing the rapid extension of a perception of industry and society which adds a new dimension to the political and parliamentary perception. To the idea of political democracy one is adding the idea of industrial democracy. . . . In its broadest sense the whole area of trade union involvement in Government and involvement at the level of the industry or the enterprise or the workplace can be seen as an extension of industrial democracy in the broadest sense as conceived by Sidney and Beatrice Webb over 80 years ago. . . .

Some people still see trade unions as pressure groups, indeed this is one of the normal definitions of the sociologist. But increasingly the relationship which we are endeavouring to create with Government and with industry – albeit on the precept of two steps forward, one step back – is one of the growing involvement on a representational basis, combining your responsibility and your accountability with our accountability to our members, and indeed the accountability of industry to shareholders as well.

The work of agencies which are at one and the same time executive and representative represents an important innovation in the joint regulation of the economy. Civil servants will, I am confident, soon become accustomed to this new kind of administrative and executive animal: the zoological garden will soon contain more specimens.

Mr Lea did not list the other 'specimens' although others that followed in various forms covered equal opportunities, race relations and energy policy. TUC leaders have even been known to look wistfully at the Bank of England (at present there is just one TUC elder on the Bank's Court) and at the idea of an agency to direct industrial investment; while it would not be difficult for them to imagine organisations such as the Office of Fair Trading or the Monopolies Commission being reconstituted on a similar basis – especially if there were ever a widespread worker director system. Indeed, the Bullock Report suggested the creation of an Industrial Democracy Commission, as an independent agency with a tripartite governing council consisting of representatives of employers, trade unions and independent experts. A special significance of this idea is that, since such a Commission might have wide company management methods to watch over, it would, like the investment agency idea, be taking the unions into a new kind of area because all the early agencies apart from the Energy Commission were mainly limited to employment matters.

Each of these agencies has been set up for a different reason. The first ones were all hived off from the Department of Employment (or created to cover new legislation such as the Equal Opportunities Commission). And, despite the TUC's later rationale covering them all, they each gained their trade union representatives to meet different needs which often stemmed from a mixture of government political policies and Civil Service needs for reorganisation. But the common thread linking them all now is, first, that they have enabled the trade unions to develop their industrial democracy style of responsibility in areas where they have some expertise to offer, but have not yet exposed them far into subjects that are outside their traditional orbit. Second, the agencies have all been created in the hope that the co-operation of the unions – and of the other interests involved ranging from employers to educationists – will be harnessed at the policy formulation stage. This, it is thought, should make the execution of the policies more efficient. Obviously, these hopes have nowhere been fully realised and there are critics of the system in Whitehall who complain about the extra costs and wasted time of having hived-off agencies, especially when they sometimes compete for power and prestige with Whitehall departments. On the other hand, the Manpower Commission in particular has started to try to introduce cost-saving techniques often used in industry but rarely heard of in the Civil Service.

The Manpower Services Commission (MSC)

The MSC, a body of CBI and TUC representatives plus others such as educationists and local authority interests, runs the Government's employment and training services. Although this Commission has ambitions to develop a comprehensive manpower policy, its origins lie in more down-to-earth organisational problems within the Department of Employment at the end of the 1960s, by which time several attempts had been made over a decade or more to modernise the employment and training work. The problem was not only how to revamp the Government's labour exchanges and training centres, but also how to raise government money for them when successive ministers could rarely be interested in taking up such a financial cause themselves and in any case rarely had much success with the Treasury when they did.

One early idea was to separate the services in a managerial sense as directorates within the Department; but eventually the more radical solution that emerged was to hive them off into identifiable managerial operations which could also relate more closely with industry and act as a manpower lobby for government money. Coincidentally Robert Carr, the Conservatives' first secretary of state for employment in June 1970, had been talking about the idea of a national training agency even before the Conservatives were elected, and the Conservative Party's official policy for the election included the idea of a manpower board. It had become fashionable in the late 1960s, when wondering at West Germany's economic miracle, to admire that country's employment and training work which was run separately from the Government (admiration that also focused on Germany's strike laws and then in desperation moved on a few years later to worker directors). Sweden, another country visited by despairing politicians for its wage bargaining and worker director and job enrichment ideas, was also looked at for its employment services work.

So the decision to hive the employment agency and training work off from the Department was made under a Manpower Services Commission which would run two operational organisations – the Employment Service Agency and the Training Services Agency. The advantages of such an arrangement it was thought should be that the interested parties would be fully involved in working out policies instead of merely being consulted to varying degrees by civil servants. In theory at least this would mean that the different interests involved should shoulder the responsibility of making sure the Commission's policies were implemented in industry. For example, the TUC should ensure – or at least encourage – unions to co-operate with training arrangements and not let old craft prejudices interfere. The concept also fitted in with the political leanings of the Conservative Government towards the second half of its 1970-4 term of office when ministers were swinging towards tripartism in national pay talks, bringing union leaders into some form of national partnership. So both the Manpower Commission and the later Health and Safety Commission (which arose out of plans to rationalise authorities in its field put forward in the 1972 Robens Report on Safety and Health at Work) were designed by the Conservatives on a TUC–CBI–other interests shared-power basis.

Although not strictly tripartite in the conventional government terminology meaning of the word (that is, an assembly of government, employer and union representatives), the way in which the MSC fitted in with the eventual attempts of the 1970-4 Heath Government to solve the country's problems in what some would see as a 'corporate state' style were spelt out by Maurice Macmillan when the Commission's creation was being debated in the Commons. Mr Macmillan had taken over the Employment Department from Mr Carr and he soon emerged as an advocate of tripartism and worker participation – later to be bracketed together by the TUC under a Labour Administration as 'industrial democracy' but called the 'quality of working life' by Macmillan. During Commons debates on founding the Commission, Mr Macmillan stressed the ways in which the Commission differed from existing advisory and other bodies made up of different interest group representatives which did not operate any particular organisations. The Commission should, he said, also be distinguished from 'committees and boards which run important activities on which industrialists and trade unionists sit, but in a purely personal capacity'. Although the members of the Commission were not to be regarded as delegates of the interest groups, it was hoped that they would remain responsible to 'those bodies which proposed them'. They would not be required to refer back to their organisations on every major point, but in making policy judgements they should 'keep in mind the general views and interests of those who helped to put them there'. They would be running an important part of the Government's operations in the light of 'their own views and interests', said Mr Macmillan. In fact, one could go further and say that, while maybe in the softer world of tripartism Conservative politicians in 1973-4 might have assumed that the Commission members would have some personal autonomy, it has been shown in practice that the TUC's representatives behave like delegates especially in the manpower and health areas and follow the TUC line.

Mr Macmillan, who spoke elsewhere of the 'industrial responsibility' the unions and employers were shouldering, also did not duck the issue that such innovations reduced the power of Parliament: 'A body which has sufficient freedom of action to be really effective in this sphere should not be subject to day-to-day Parliamentary questions', he told a House of Commons which almost certainly (on the Tory side of the House at least) had little idea of the constitutional importance of the beast it was rearing.

However, one should not give the impression that the MSC or the other new organisations necessarily have an easy ride in Whitehall, especially when, like the MSC, they operate in an area directly linked with the politically sensitive subject of the country's economic policy. The MSC has been distrusted for two reasons by the entrenched ranks of Treasury mandarins and their counterparts in other ministries–first, it is a new institutional animal designed to take some power away from existing ministries and Parliament; second, it contains and represents vested interest groups such as the TUC. It tends therefore not to be regarded by the big ministries as an established part of government and often is not treated in the same way as an ordinary ministry or executive branch within a government department. It does not always receive confidential Treasury forecasts and is even denied some less sensitive government statistics–which effectively curbs its policy activities. Although the TUC may have moved into the government arena therefore, it is sometimes kept at arm's length by the rest of Whitehall. But relations have improved under a new chairman, appointed in 1976. He is Richard O'Brien, formerly a director of Delta Metal. He is also a former chairman of the CBI's Employment Policy Committee and as such was both a member of the CBI's team in the Heath Government tripartite and other talks and was also partially responsible for development of CBI employee participation policies.

So the MSC's effectiveness–and parallel tests could be done on the other agencies–can be judged on three levels. First, in its executive role, it is said to be able to do a better organisational job managing the country's training and employment services than could have been done by civil servants buried inside a big ministry. Gradually the staff involved have shed some civil service traditions; and, facing criticism from industry about training finances, Mr O'Brien has started to try to introduce some cost-effectiveness techniques into the Commission's work. He also prepared plans that emerged in the summer of 1977 to simplify the Commission's organisational structure by abolishing the confusingly separate employment and training agencies and merging them as separate directorates into one organisation. The object of this was to prevent them growing apart under their separate identities, to improve liaison between them, and to avoid confusion in industry and with the general public.

Second, also in its executive role, the support of the TUC and CBI is harnessed for the execution of policies – for example the commitment of both was gained in advance for the Government's school-leavers' work experience project in 1976. This helped to ensure that employers would take on the youngsters and that unions would not object either to seeing them in factories or to their being given low rates of pay. While no one would suggest that anything like every CBI and TUC member abides by and co-operates with the Commission's policies and work, both organisations say that their involvement, and the presence of educationists, helps, and that there is a two-way traffic on the preparation and execution of policies through the TUC's unions and the CBI's trade and employers' associations. The Commission has also benefited from the fact that there has been basic agreement between its constituents on the need to modernise the employment services, expand training and introduce special unemployment measures.

The third level of effectiveness against which the MSC should be judged is its influence on government policy-making and its ability to act as a lobby for government funds. One could argue that the MSC (and its counterparts in conciliation, health and equality) should stick to an executive role, leaving policy to governments, and that this should be enough to satisfy the industrial democracy ambitions of the TUC. However this is not a practical approach because the TUC is a policy-orientated animal and, therefore, instinctively aims for the policy centres of organisations it meets. So, despite the opposition in Whitehall, the TUC is likely to continue to press (unless it were to find a more potent vehicle) for the MSC to expand in the policy field.

The MSC has excelled as a lobby to raise government funds because of the TUC's social contract with the Labour Government at a time of high unemployment. The continuing success of the MSC's influence on governments will however depend primarily on the TUC's relationship with the government of the day and on the degree of consensus about objectives and priorities that can be sustained among its CBI, TUC and educationist interests.

The Advisory Conciliation and Arbitration Service (ACAS)
The ACAS was born for quite different practical reasons although the philosophy of shared responsibility was similar. Towards the end of the 1960s it became clear that there were major problems facing a government department that both tried to act as the country's main conciliation agency and also bore some or all of the government's responsibility for policing a formal or statutory incomes policy. Either the conciliation staff carried on with their work and helped to settle deals involving pay rises above the limits of the government policy (in which case colleagues down the ministry corridor or somewhere else in Whitehall had to decide

whether to freeze the rise and risk industrial trouble), or the conciliators had to shut their door (without the overall consent of unions or employers) on anyone trying to breach the policy. During the 1964-70 Labour Government's time the first alternative of both conciliation and freezing was operated, which did the reputations of neither the incomes policy nor the conciliation system much good. Under the Conservatives in 1970, the conciliators were strictly banned from handling claims above various official and unofficial pay norms. Even worse, arbitrators were also told by no less an authority than the chancellor of the exchequer (then Tony Barber) that they should not arbitrate above the Government's chosen figures.

This did a lot of harm to conciliation and arbitration, especially in the national area, and the Department of Employment's team of conciliators lost a lot of the trust union leaders had held for them.

This gave a new impetus to ideas that had been considered earlier for hiving the conciliation service off from the Department and therefore from direct ministerial control. Various alternatives were discussed and in several ways the debate was somewhat similar to the one about how to handle the employment and training service. One early idea put up by civil servants during Barbara Castle's and Robert Carr's periods was to hive it off from the Department but put only an independent director-general – as a sort of 'Mr Peace-Maker' – in charge, rather than have an employer–union-governing council. Another early idea was to form a directorate within the Department with a union–employer advisory or executive board. A third possibility was to hive the work off but to make the governing council a tripartite affair with government representatives included.

Clearly however any such direct involvement by the Government would only risk repeating the incomes policy problems, so when Labour was elected in 1974 the favoured solution rapidly emerged as a hived-off body run by the CBI and TUC on a council with some academics added to dilute the clashes (or maybe to improve the quality) of the council's deliberations. This owed something to an earlier conciliation and arbitration service set up in the summer of 1972 by the CBI and TUC on their own which, had it not been overtaken by the Heath tripartite talks and subsequent pay freeze, was scheduled gradually to take over industry's conciliation work.

Jack Jones, who played a key part in the design of ACAS, gained one of the TUC seats on the council (his deputy, Harry Urwin, took one of the Manpower Commission seats) and ACAS swung into action. It has rapidly proved its effectiveness by vastly increasing the amount of conciliation work carried out and has also rebuilt and expanded arbitration as a way of peacefully settling disputes, although there have been suggestions that it operates too much in the shadow of the TUC. It also has statutory duties to run some of the Employment Protection Act (1975) provisions on union recognition and these have led it into controversial areas with disputes such as the 1977 Grunwick film laboratory battle. The CBI representatives on its governing council even occasionally warned that they might have to withdraw because of what they regard as an anti-employer bias that has sometimes emerged in some staff documents.

During the social contract period up to mid-1977 it avoided clashing with the national pay policy limits because its governing council agreed that its conciliators should not help to settle disputes for amounts of money well outside the limits. But such an understanding can be harder to sustain if the TUC does not accept an incomes policy and therefore wants the ACAS conciliators to ignore the wage limits involved.

A side-effect of the creation of an agency like ACAS, as was envisaged by Maurice Macmillan in the case of the Manpower Services Commission, is that parliamentary control of the work of the agencies is considerably weakened. Since ACAS started, for example, there has been a sharp reduction in the number of MPs' questions in the Commons on individual labour disputes because ministers no longer have direct responsibility for settling them. (However, constant exposure to publicity does nothing to help the settlement of strikes, so the fact that the secretary of employment no longer has the direct resonsibility and so is not asked so many questions may be of practical benefit to the country.) But ACAS is still answerable to MPs because it has to compile an annual report for presentation to Parliament which was, of course, initially responsible for designing the organisation when it was debating the then Employment Protection Bill. Like the other agencies, ACAS is also run with money voted by Parliament (about £7 million a year at 1976 prices) on the Department of Employment's budget. The codes of practice that ACAS prepares on matters, such as disclosure of information and workers' time off for trade union and public duties, can also be debated by Parliament, which could throw them out. So the parliamentary accountability does exist over a broad front, while the industrial democracy dimension is provided by the CBI and TUC dominating the governing council.

This sort of system broadly applies to the other agencies as well as to ACAS. But ACAS has one special freedom which makes it more independent of Parliament than is often realised. This is a clause in the Employment Protection Act which says (in Schedule 1): 'The function of the Service and of its officers and servants shall be performed on behalf of the Crown, but . . . the Service shall not be subject to directions of any kind from any Minister of the Crown as to the manner in which it is to exercise any of its functions under any enactment'. It would of course be open to a government to remove this clause–perhaps as part of some incomes policy legislation–so that it could issue instructions to ACAS to keep to a pay limit in its strike conciliation work. But in practice such a move could hardly be taken without changing the basic concept of the ACAS and risking either or both of the TUC and CBI representative groups walking out.

Nevertheless, it should not be thought that ministers leave ACAS entirely alone. The nature of the Civil Service (most of the top officials of ACAS and of the other agencies are ex-senior Department of Employment civil servants) and the power of patronage and other indirect influences that can be brought to bear on public figures means in practice than ministerial will can still be exerted–up to the point presumably where it conflicts with the principle and style of ACAS. An interventionist secretary for employment, anxious to demonstrate his or her adeptness at handling trade unions, might also upset the success of ACAS by making the ministerial office a place of alternative conciliation, so weakening the authority of the agency.

So the influence of the TUC in ACAS–as in the other institutions–is that, within rules laid down by Parliament but without daily parliamentary or ministerial interference, the union leaders can exert a major influence on the way that industrial relations questions are handled.

Summary
The risk involved in the creation of such institutions is that the good they do may be dissipated if they eventually collapse under pressure of government policies or their own internal frictions. In practice, the hived-off agencies normally work well so long as the employers and unions are in accord on their own and the Government's policies. But once this accord breaks, critics will start arguing that such work would be better done within government departments under the direct eye of ministers. To argue that, however, is to turn away from the industrial democracy concept of making unions (and employers and others as well) face up to their responsibilities.

Chapter 5

Social Contract Methods: The TUC and the Industrialists

The actual impact of the TUC through government agencies and other institutions depends partly on the political colour, mood and priorities of the government in power. Even though Conservative governments initiated several aspects of the concept of industrial democracy in national economic and political affairs by inventing the NEDC, starting moves to set up the new hived-off commissions and agencies and, most important of all, starting the 1972 tripartite talks, the special relationship between the unions and the Labour Government arising out of the social contract gave the most significant increase in the overall power and influence of the TUC. Figure 1 (see page 50) shows the power structure under the Labour Government after 1974 when the social contract was giving such a boost to TUC influence in Downing Street and elsewhere, and this chapter explains the workings of that power structure. In the centre is the TUC policy, which emerges down through a string of TUC committees and, through monthly meetings of the TUC General Council, from the annual congress. The input for these key policy committees originates either with individual unions or in the Congress House TUC headquarters.

How the TUC works

But it is here that the current flaws in the operation of industrial democracy power can begin to be seen. Although there are 100 or so unions affiliated to the TUC, few of them make much regular impact on TUC policies. Generally it is the large ones that matter most–the biggest fifteen unions account for 80 per cent of the TUC's eleven million total affiliated membership–and of these it has been the TGWU, in the person of Jack Jones who has stood out above the others since the establishment of the social contract. Judging by his tactics in recent years, whenever Jones has wanted to influence a policy he has done one of four things. His first option is to make a public speech, circulated to national newspapers well in advance, in the sure knowledge that it will be widely reported and studied. Second, he can back this up with a letter or call–sometimes public, sometimes private–to the TUC general secretary requesting action in one of the TUC–Government policy-formulating arenas. Third, he can inject an idea into the relevant TUC committee, such as the Economic Committee or one of the industrial committees that the TUC has been setting up in recent years to bring it closer to day-to-

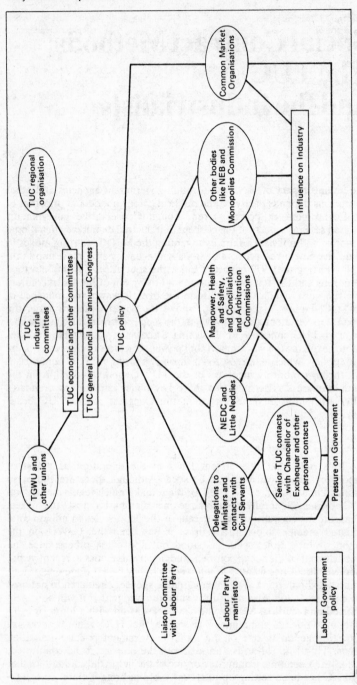

Conflict or Co-operation?

Financial Times

The TUC's channels of power

day industrial affairs. Fourth, he can work behind the scenes and use his influence to ensure certain ideas gain ground, or use his ready access to ministers, including the prime minister.

No other union leader has been in this position in the past decade and only a tiny handful of others could aspire to anything approaching it. It has been said that Jones's power goes with his job. However true this proves to be in the future, one thing is certain. Even if the immediate vacuum left in TUC affairs when Jack Jones retires in 1978 and hands over to Moss Evans, the TGWU's national organiser, were filled by several union leaders–with Len Murray at the TUC itself moving more into the forefront of affairs–the democratic aspect of industrial democracy would still be found wanting. This is because the great mass of the TUC unions have an extremely limited impact on decision-making at any level. Changes made in recent years–including the creation of industrial committees to study detailed problems and to bring unions more into the Congress House policy-making system–may help. But they are still likely to be swamped by the big battalions of Jones's union, the few others of the same size, or by the one or two with charismatic leaders.

Methods of influencing events
Once policies are decided at the TUC they move outwards in several directions–into the Labour Party, the government machine, the Common Market institutions, individual industry organisations or to the new bodies such as the Manpower Services Commission. With hindsight this can often appear to be a carefully controlled strategy pushing a TUC line, but in fact it is more often an *ad hoc* position with each attitude, tactic and policy being determined as events unfold.

For example, a policy statement approved by the TUC's General Council during the social contract on the high level of unemployment and the problem of jobs for school-leavers would have emanated from the TUC's Economic Committee, probably inspired by Jones and by David Basnett of the GMWU, both members of the committee. It would have been based on a policy document calling for rapid but orderly reflation prepared by the TUC's economic department, and might have been influenced on the fringe by the special problems of the television industry facing excessive imports and the construction industry trying to deal with both unemployment and a shortage of craftsmen. Left-wingers on the General Council might try to add calls for measures such as cuts in arms expenditure, wholesale import controls and a return to free collective bargaining. After the council meeting the document would be distilled by the TUC's office which might quietly drop some of the wilder Left-wing excesses which had only limited support. The main reflation drift of the policy statement would then be tabled for the next meeting of the TUC–Labour Party Liaison Committee. (This committee had emerged after February 1974 as a key institution for maintaining Labour movement unity, for allowing frustrated unions to vent their wrath over unemployment, and for ministers such as the chancellor to launch unpalatable pay and employment policies. Free of the Whitehall civil service machine, it allowed ministers, union leaders and representatives of the Labour Party's National Executive Committee to meet regularly, without the trappings of the formal Downing Street confrontations that bedevilled earlier government attempts to hold top-level consultations with the unions, and to produce joint TUC–Labour Government policy statements each year.) It would also be underlined at the next private meeting between the Chancellor of the Exchequer and the TUC's top six union leaders. These meetings were another innovation of the 1974 Labour Government and have played an essential role in preparing the ground for many of the more unpalatable policies that Britain's economic problems have necessitated. Over early evening drinks or dinner, the Chancellor would spell out in detail the facts and figures on the economy. This meant that the union leaders knew the worst and did not compound the Government's problems by challenging what ministers were saying in public. It also enabled them to be slowly eased into accepting the necessity of policies such as pay restraint and high unemployment, and generally backed up the Liaison Committee's work in de-fusing crises and maintaining Labour unity.

Government agencies
Elsewhere the TUC would meanwhile be pushing its General Council resolution in more detail. Its members on the Manpower Services Commission would be urging the introduction of special schemes to provide some form of temporary employment for the school-leavers and for special arrangements for training building craftsmen. Both these ideas would stand a good chance of being adopted by the Commission and they would then be urged on the Government.

Meanwhile the TUC would be peddling the same detailed ideas through its own channels to the Liaison Committee and the Chancellor. Then there might be a delegation to the Secretary for Trade on the problems caused by television imports while the TUC's members on other bodies like the Little Neddies and the 'industrial strategy' working parties and the National Enterprise Board would also raise the issue of television industry imports and building jobs where appropriate. At the same time the TUC's representatives on the European Trades Union Confederation and the European Community's consultative economic and social committee might try to generate political pressure within the EEC so that Britain's unemployment and imports problems were understood.

And while all this pressure was being exerted on the Government, the TUC's views would also be carried through organisations like the Manpower Services Commission and the Little Neddies into individual industries and companies.

Naturally this does not mean that the TUC could be sure that unemployment would be dealt with, school-leavers employed or television imports banned. But it does mean that the TUC has a fair chance of making its voice widely heard. Because they are political activists, union leaders are well used to this sort of work which means slogging away, slowly chipping at obstacles until they get their way.

The TUC in action – policies on wealth
In this vein, from the time Labour was elected in 1974, the TUC used its social contract and the emerging pay policy not only to help the Government deal with short-term inflationary problems but to move towards the

long-term social changes it wanted. These included the redistribution of wealth and income, and the way the TUC has operated on this subject illustrates how it has learned to flex its political muscles in a co-ordinated way across a wide front so as to affect the livelihoods of people in general and not just its own members.

Large incomes have been attacked since 1974 on three fronts. First, the initial social contract pay policies from 1975 were based on flat rate rises with the best-off being hardest hit (and with those earning above £8500 a year getting nothing in the first phase). This not only hit the highest earners in the country but also was of special importance to Jack Jones (who was instrumental in designing the policy) because it meant that his general worker members came off proportionately best.

The second front was the sharp increase in taxation on middle and high incomes introduced by the Government as part of the social contract. This rapidly narrowed the differences in salaries in the £6000–£30,000 + a year band, so hitting the rich. (The fact that it also hit the hard-worked middle-level supervisor, technologist and manager was regarded in TUC circles at that time as being 'just too bad'.)

The third front of the attack is even more significant because it tried to put this gradual shift in salary relationships between the average worker and the country's top-paid people on a permanent footing: the TUC started to argue that there ought to be a national consensus on all salary differentials and suggested £20,000 gross (1976 figures) as being a possible top figure for the highest earner in the country who, with a Labour Government in power, they loyally thought might be the prime minister. This was spelt out in the TUC's annual economic review early in 1976 when it was explained that 'the distribution of wealth and disposable income is the central feature of the TUC's policies on social equality but it also is necessary to examine the highest employment incomes'. The TUC pointed out that annual salaries of £50,000 or more then received by the highest paid executives were seventeen times the country's median or middle weekly wage of £55.90 and suggested that the top should be seven times the median–roughly the £20,000 a year figure. It submitted these views to a royal commission–the Diamond Commission, which was looking at questions of wealth and income and whose members included, significantly, David Lea, the TUC official in charge of preparing the TUC's policy. The TUC then backed an idea put forward by the Commission that 'a broad consensus over pay relationships would be a desirable goal, whether or not policies are in force restricting employment incomes, and that the consensus should cover the remuneration of those receiving higher incomes from their employment'.

Arguing that such a consensus did not yet exist, the TUC document underlined the way it thought that trade unions ought to influence salaries of high-earning non-unionists (or alternatively force these higher earners into unions). 'Progress towards a consensus on top salaries will require co-ordinated action over a number of years by trade unions, Government and employers to achieve a generally agreed bracket for top salaries', it said.

The TUC then explained its 7:1 target ratio to give the £20,000 top salary (while acknowledging that it would take some years to achieve, presumably progressively adjusted for inflation) and went on to say:

The target ratio could then be used for the fixing of top salaries by the Government in the civil service, the armed forces, the judiciary and nationalised industries. Firms should also be encouraged to use such a guideline of social acceptability for the remuneration of chief executives and directors. Many firms might be pleased to take the opportunity to opt out of the self defeating competitive spiral in bidding up top salaries and devote proper attention to the more productive task of training and developing a wider pool of managerial talent. . . . As unions become more involved in the joint determination of all aspects of company policy, they should also seek to ensure that top salaries do not exceed the national target ratio.

Here one can see how the TUC can use the trade union presence at different levels of the economy to thrust home its policies–in this case pushing an idea on national governments while at the same time hoping that its shop stewards would eventually push the same idea within companies. Such a pincer movement could prove most effective and is in effect an extension of what can happen with traditional union bargaining when the TUC pushes for statutory rights or freedoms on issues such as redundancies or wages after shop stewards have demanded the same things in their shopfloor negotiations. But the extra significance of the top salaries initiative is, as has already been said, that it uses TUC power at the different levels of the economy to affect the livelihoods of people who are not union members.

In this case, the TUC was in effect offering to trade some sort of wage structure orderliness among its own members–for example differentials between craftsmen and labourers–provided it had a say in the whole gamut of pay differentials. It was asserting that craftsmen and others would be more responsible in their wage claims if high earnings were curbed.

The corporate state partners–unions and the TUC

The increase in the TUC influence as it shouldered its social contract responsibilities not surprisingly led to criticism and jealousy both within the Labour movement and outside it. The feeling of helplessness as Britain's economic problems continued despite the TUC's pay restraint also fuelled the resentment because problems such as the size of the Government's public spending in 1977 could for example be laid at the feet of the unions who were opposing public expenditure cuts as part of their social contract wages deal.

In the national interest, the price that the unions exact for their co-operation therefore has to be balanced against the alternative of having no government–union compact, in which case the Government would not have to fall in with the unions' wishes. Margaret Thatcher, the Conservative Party leader, made the most of this point when at a Conservative trade unionists' conference in March 1977 she said: 'No Government should bind itself by any agreement with a minority sectional interest so as to lose its freedom of action on matters affecting all the people of the land.'

Thatcher was echoing here often-heard criticisms of the TUC's powers that it does not directly represent anywhere near a large proportion of the population. The total membership of the TUC's one hundred or so unions is only just over eleven million out of Britain's fifty-five million population, but the disparity is not so great when one considers that this eleven million is not far short of half the twenty-five million *working* population. Nevertheless Thatcher called this only a 'very important minority' and underlined that many people were outside the social contract or what is sometimes regarded as a corporate state style of government. She said a Conservative government would also listen to small businessmen, pensioners and the self-employed, so echoing Conservative Party sentiments of which Heath was well aware when he had only the CBI and TUC in the 1972 tripartite talks (the Retail Consortium was seen during the less formal 1973 pay discussions). In fact, Heath was considering during the tripartite talks setting up a new sort of economic council, and during the October 1974 general election campaign he developed his thoughts for what he called a 'national contract' which could have included the enlargement of the tripartite National Economic Development Council to take in leaders of other political parties and other interests. (He has also said that so long as there were only a limited representation of interests in talks with the Government, it is the Prime Minister's job to ensure that the views of those interests not present are taken into account.) The Conservative Party's policy document for its October 1977 annual conference, called *The Right Approach to the Economy,* also mooted an expanded NEDC.

Closed shops

The resentment that arises from the TUC's position as the sole central representative covering all sorts of workers is increased by the fact that unions have been seeking to consolidate their positions through the closed shop system. Although the closed shop is primarily an industrial rather than a political weapon, a direct link is seen by critics of the unions between unions extending their influence into new areas and at the same time underpinning this new power by making sure that only their members can be employed in certain areas.

Union leaders are of course scarcely likely to want to build new machinery for the operation of their worker power only to find that this power is vested not in TUC unions but in other organisations and in non-unionists. As Jack Jones said in 1976 in a document his union sent to the Government demanding industrial democracy in the country's defence establishments:

Industrial democracy is not just a debate about workers on the Board. The prerequisite for any radical extension of industrial democracy is the extension of trade union organisation and the right to bargain collectively at all levels. One of the first priorities should be that the Government should actively encourage 100 per cent trade union membership [another name for the usual sort of closed shop] in all its establishments. There is of course a very high level of union membership in the Government service. But pockets of non-unionists exist. We believe the time is now ripe for the Government to insist on all employees belonging to their appropriate union particularly on the industrial side.

Jones may not have got all he wanted, but the number of people in closed shops has increased considerably since the Industrial Relations Act's legal restraints on them were removed in 1974. Trade unions quickly decided to reassert their freedoms by consolidating their membership and killing off breakaway organisations that had made nuisances of themselves under the Act. Dr McCarthy, in the only major work devoted so far to closed shops (McCarthy, 1964), estimated that there were about 3.75 million workers in formal and informal closed shops, that is, in factories and other places of work where, because of written agreements or unwritten traditions, an employee had to join a union *after* he had obtained a job. (Such a place was dubbed by McCarthy a 'post entry shop'. It is also known as 'a union shop' or '100 per cent union membership'. The more restrictive and rarer type of shop–christened 'pre-entry shop' by McCarthy–is a place where a man must have a union card *before* he can get a job.)

A later book, *Industrial Relations and the Limits of the Law,* published by some Warwick University academics in 1975, suggested that by then the figure had changed little (Weekes et al., 1975). But by the end of 1975 demands for new closed shops were building up in some industries following the repeal of the Industrial Relations Act, and it was estimated in December 1975 (in the *Financial Times*) that claims were then either lodged or pending from some three million workers with more to follow. It was the size of this surge, accompanied by unions adopting a tough post-Act line against non-unionists plus some side issues such as the impact of closed shops on newspaper editors, that led to a considerable outcry in 1975-6.

These figures meant that as many as seven million workers either were in or were demanding closed shops. It represented a sizeable proportion of the TUC's membership and, consequently, a sizeable proportion of the nation's basic workforce, underlining the potential strengths of the trade unions.

The corporate state partners–industrialists and the CBI

Wherever the TUC is represented (except in its purely Labour movement operations such as the TUC–Labour Party Liaison Committee) there is almost always the parallel institutional voice of at least the CBI representing the other side of industry in all its aspects as investor, manufacturer, price fixer, employer and manager. But while maybe parallel, or even dominant in size, it is often not as effective a voice as the unions'. This has been most noticeable with an organisation like the Manpower Services Commission, where a well drilled TUC team can run rings round the more diverse and less well disciplined people from the CBI and other interests, who find it hard to mount campaigns against the TUC on items like alleviating unemployment, however well briefed they may be by their own back-up staff.

In addition, the TUC's campaigns have also been fairly well co-ordinated so that, as has been seen on unemployment for example, the TUC's moves in the Commission will be part of a fairly loosely organised series of initiatives in various quarters. While such moves are sometimes resented by the TUC's opponents, it should be remembered that what it really amounts to is that the TUC, which for many years has relied on formal negotiating and protest meetings with ministers in Downing Street and elsewhere, is learning for the first time how also to use the Whitehall machine effectively for informal persuasion sessions across a desk as opposed to a negotiating table, with a civil servant or minister. The CBI, on the other hand, while itself skilled at using the more informal Whitehall machine plus some informal contacts with ministers, showed itself in the 1972 tripartite talks to be amateur at the sort of formal negotiations at which the TUC excelled (Chapter 2).

Many employers' and trade associations and individual companies have been effective at informal lobbying for some time and actively use what political muscle they can in briefing friendly (normally, but not always, Conservative) MPs, lunching and entertaining senior civil servants, presenting detailed submissions and working for the ear of a senior minister.

Often, indeed, government policies may well be influenced far more directly by individual companies than by the political-level representations of the CBI. This is not to suggest that such CBI activities are unimportant. But the most telling influence may well be that exercised by the chief executive or chairman of a major multinational or key British company on the permanent secretary of a major government department. Backing this up both the CBI and individual companies (and the TUC) can have considerable influence on civil servants responsible for detailed drafting of parliamentary Bills and other government policies. The CBI and senior industrialists–along with top specialists in fields like taxation and personnel matters–will also have some influence on the advance policies being drafted in the Conservative Party's Central Office headquarters, though their advice is not always heeded.

Political lobbying

The political lobbying done by companies has increased considerably in recent years, mainly because industrialists and others have seen the need to fight the 1974 Labour Government's social contract legislation. The best organised companies have a political lobbyist paid to spend his time around the political parties at Westminster, and he or someone else will also monitor the detailed progress of parliamentary Bills. Then there will be senior staff in the company, part of whose job will be to maintain close contacts with relevant civil servants, not only at the top of a ministry but at the principal and assistant secretary middle rungs where much of the country's detailed legislation is prepared.

But few companies are so well organised yet in this field, and overall the private sector's political punch took a severe dent in the early and mid-1970s although it did climb back a bit in 1976-7. Part of the cause of this is that the CBI–the rough industrial equivalent of the TUC in national affairs–packs nowhere near the same clout as the TUC. In the first place, unless its members were to decide collectively to shut factories, refuse to work, emigrate, move their head offices abroad *en masse* (an idea that one or two big multinationals have considered recently) or refuse to pay their workers, they will never have the same industrial weight to throw around. And in any case, many of the members instinctively resent collective action of any sort and so do not run rapidly to the CBI's side, although this did start to change when they felt especially incensed at the policies of the 1974 Labour Government. But even then, any ideology that industrialists may have points to individual rather than collective action. The CBI has much more difficulty than the TUC in finding policies that satisfy both its large and small members but it did improve its overall base during 1977 by adding financial institutions, retailers and others to its hitherto manufacturing oriented membership.

In a book on the CBI, Grant and Marsh (1977) pinpoint the Confederation's lack of an effective sanction against the Government:

It can, of course, conduct a campaign against Government policies but . . . this is a hazardous course to follow. As an alternative strategy it could refuse to co-operate in the administration of any particular piece of legislation, but again such a sanction depends on the co-operation of the industrial firms directly involved. Such firms are likely to be reluctant to damage their own position with Government by withdrawing co-operation. The CBI might also recommend that its members attempt to influence the economy by withholding investment as a threat to Government. This is even less likely to be successful. Indeed, although throughout 1972 and 1973 the CBI was issuing glowing commentaries on the economy and urging industrialists to invest and expand, its exhortations had little direct effect on investments patterns. Investment decisions by companies are not taken at the behest of the CBI. The CBI's influence on the economy and the administration of legislation is thus indirect and hardly crucial. This is perhaps the most important point.

Another reason why the CBI's members do not wield the same political weight is because they are not an integral part of a political movement: there is no capitalist movement as such in the mixed economy of Britain of the 1970s and there is no immediate prospect of one developing, however much the CBI might try to follow TUC-style methods by publishing annual policy documents which it started in 1976 or even holding annual or biennial CBI conferences which began in November 1977. On the other hand, a more open method of drawing up CBI policies–for example through the overall policy documents and conferences–should help to marshal arguments. An annual public debate in a conference type of atmosphere might also help to give the policies permanency and credibility both to the Government, the public and the CBI's members, because one of the constant problems of the CBI has been that it has sometimes had to face situations without any established policy or creed. For example when the Labour Government was intervening during the winter of 1974-5 in ailing companies like Leyland, Alfred Herbert and Ferranti, the CBI for a time did not know whether to welcome the interventions because of their sheer practical financial necessity or oppose them because of the way they meant the State was wading into the private sector. Similarly, there is no overall philosophy–apart from a dislike of union power and a belief in profits–on how industry should react to the sort of TUC-designed moves towards industrial democracy described in this and other chapters. In each case–whether it is social contract pay policies, manpower business, labour conciliation, or the industrial strategy–employers and industrialists will see a clear practical advantage in co-operating so as to harness the goodwill of unions and employees in the formulation and execution of policies that affect their companies. They do not mind therefore helping to create and taking part in the necessary institutions. They may object instinctively when they feel that this trade union involvement is developing too far and, as they have shown in the Bullock debate, they will fight when it comes too near their own boardroom centres of power. But there is no overall ideological policy comparable with that which emerges from the TUC's headquarters.

There is in any case always a division of opinion within the CBI–especially when Labour is in power–over whether it should co-operate responsibly with governments in the hope of influencing their decisions, or sometimes adopt a policy of outright hostility. In their study, which basically stopped in 1974 but was extended in a limited way to 1976, Grant and Marsh said:

The CBI has had relatively limited impact on the major issues which have dominated British politics since its formation. As in other policy areas, it has been able to extract detailed concessions which are of benefit to its members. However the CBI faces the fundamental difficulty that it is operating in a political environment which is increasingly unsympathetic to its aims and aspirations. One does not have to accept the right wing view of a Left-wing media conspiracy to see that, with its limited resources, it is difficult for the CBI to win the support of public opinion for its policies.

The situation was changing as this study finished, however, because the 1974 Labour Government found increasingly that it could not ignore the CBI. For one thing a socialist government needing, for urgent economic reasons, to win foreign confidence cannot ignore its industrialists' lobby, especially when it has a thin parliamentary majority. And when that majority depends on the whims of minority parties (as happened in 1976-7) the Government cannot afford to upset the industrialists to such an extent that they will mobilise the Conservative opposition on an issue. So the CBI won a number of concessions from the 1974 Labour Government despite the TUC-oriented social contract on matters such as prices policy, corporation tax and planning agreements. But winning concessions is different from influencing overall policy, and on that the CBI is still at early stages, even with the Conservative Party. It has however also found the Liberal Party amenable to some lobbying and has even gone so far as to talk to the nationalist groups. It has also appointed its first parliamentary lobbyist.

The CBI also found in 1976-7 its best unifying issue for a long time – the growth of union power – and on that basis swung into action with an effective battle against the Bullock Report in early 1977. Its success in working against proposed legislation on this report will always be notched up as one of its main achievements, but it was hardly a difficult battle. For once the CBI found itself supported by many members of a Labour Cabinet (in increasing numbers as 1977 wore on), by almost every relevant senior civil servant in Whitehall, by an industrialists' lobby that was mounted in vast numbers in major company headquarters at home and abroad, and by a wide-ranging mixture of other interests.

On the other side of the arguments (see Chapter 16) stood a tiny and not very vocal group of union leaders. But the TUC was in such disarray generally that there were was no effective pro-Bullock lobby running. So the CBI was knocking on one of the most open doors of its life, and the Government's suggestions in 1976 that pension schemes might be subject to 50-50 union-employer control only fed the flames of fury. Indeed, if it had not won considerable gains from the Bullock affair, the CBI would have lacked credibility as a national institution.

It should also be said that the Bullock battle coincided with a new era in the CBI's own life, with John Methven, ex-ICI senior executive and former Director of Fair Trading, taking over as director-general from Sir Campbell Adamson. Around the same time Lord Watkinson became president. While Watkinson and Methven, both determined characters, did not always see eye to eye, they did together build a new credibility and new standards of efficiency for the CBI at a time when industrialists had just swung into a new, collective, mood for battle. But whether its successes were only a spin-off from the country's political situation or something more durable remained to be seen.

Mr Campbell Adamson had suffered almost throughout his period of office as director general of the CBI from 1969 to 1976 because he tried to bridge the widening credibility gap between big business interests and the general public. He was chosen as an antedote to his predecessor, Mr John Davies, who became a Tory Minister, and he understood better than many of his members the political and social changes taking place in Britain. But he shared the CBI's basic dilemma during his period – if he took a reactionary line the CBI was unlikely to win much sympathy from public opinion, but if on the other hand his stance appeared too 'progressive' he may have lost the support of the CBI's own membership.

A capitalist movement?

Generally the CBI lacks Labour-movement style ties to bind it to the Conservative Party with industrialists and entrepreneurs as a joint capitalist movement, however much the organisation of its institutions or the preparation and debate of its policies may improve. And the lack of that bond means the CBI is often much more wary of criticising a Conservative government than the unions are worried about attacking a Labour administration. Even if a capitalist liaison were organisable, there is another reason why it could not happen under the country's present electoral system. This is that a CBI-Tory link would make the Conservative Party firmly identified as 'the party of the bosses', which could alienate the millions of working class votes it needs to win a general election. But if the country's basic two-party system were to be changed, with some sort of proportional representation system being introduced which would allow for more and smaller parties, the sharp division that exists at present need not continue. Then, some industrialists believe, the CBI or some similar organisation could forge a link with a party that would form the basis for a capitalist movement.

For the time being, though, in any corporate state or social contract style of government, the unions have a head start because, however much the Labour movement may tear itself apart over issues like H-bombs, disarmament, Vietnam, pay and strike laws, unemployment or public expenditure, it has always emerged unified on its basic socialist beliefs. Its opponents meanwhile have been increasingly shamefaced about their role in operating within Edward Heath's 'unacceptable face of capitalism' and have had no unifying creed with which to fight back. The only major unifying issue to emerge by the mid-1970s – a distaste of trade union power – could not be a practical long-term platform because almost all the critics of such power were actively encouraging it in their own institutions (like those examined in this chapter), were endorsing it in their own companies, and in some cases were boosting it themselves as trade unionism spread into managerial and professional areas.

Conclusion

By the mid-1970s the trade unions of Britain were both confounding and angering their critics–growing more powerful, but with a new guise of responsibility. This showed itself in their social contract with the 1974 Labour Government, a relationship which then accelerated their representative role in a variety of institutions and national areas of decision-making. But even while these institutions were developing, the political social contract began to come under strain because the union's acceptance, within the social contract, of pay restraint was not yielding the expected benefits in terms of the level of unemployment and prices.

In 1978 there were still nearly 1½ million people unemployed, which would have been politically unthinkable a few years before. And while the rate of price increases had been cut from 16 per cent a year to under eight per cent between the middle of 1974 and 1978, workers did not generally feel that they had had a good deal, even though living standards had recouped earlier sharp·falls and wages were rising by over 14 per cent. Trade union conferences increasingly showed impatience with their leaders' relationship with the Labour Government, and the question was inevitably raised whether the trade unions ought not to protect their members by returning to an adversary role. Even Jack Jones (who retired at the beginning of 1978) was somewhat disenchanted: his members effectively rejected the social contract at the last national biennial conference of his union that he attended as general secretary in July 1977; he was also disappointed that the Government had not given more on its side of the social contract bargain since 1974–for example by introducing a wealth tax or refraining from public expenditure cuts.

Indeed the words 'social contract' were rarely used by this time, although the contract was still in existence because the partnership between the Labour Government and the union leaders continued. David Basnett of the GMWU, who was the TUC's chairman in 1977–78, proposed an 'economic contract' in an attempt to recover something from the disenchantment over the social contract and, in the pre-general election atmosphere of the summer of 1978, the Government and the TUC agreed a new joint policy document called *Into the Eighties: an agreement*.

What this showed was that the Labour politicians and the union leaders had not forgotten the lesson Jack Jones and others had learned at the end of the 1960s. Despite all their problems (including Labour being a minority Government in the Commons and so having both to water down its policies and to strike a political pact with the Liberal Party), the partnership was maintained and the conflict of the previous Labour Government was not restarted. Trade union fears of the policies that might be introduced by a Conservative administration helped to keep the relationship cemented.

But these chapters have ranged wider than the political relationship within the Labour movement, and it is important to remember that it would be quite possible for the close relationship between unions and Government to falter without causing too much disruption to all the institutions and to the practice of industrial democracy in companies.

Part II
The Path to
Industrial Power

Chapter 6

The Unions:
Traditions,
Roles and Policies

In recent years, the term 'industrial democracy' has come to be identified mainly with the issue of the mid-1970s over whether or not employee representatives–commonly called worker directors–should be appointed to the board rooms of British companies. As has already been seen, however, board representation is but one aspect of the growing ambitions of trade unions for industrial democracy at all levels of Britain's economic and industrial life. There is, therefore, a direct relationship between unions wanting to move into national decision-making through their social contract type of operation with the Government and their wanting to move into the board rooms and other decision-making areas of industrial life.

In both cases trade unions are claiming the right–as opposed to asking for permission–to have a say in the running of the country's affairs on behalf of their members and in the interests of progressively changing the structure of society. 'It is a basic function of the trade unions to obtain a degree of joint control through representation at the point at which decisions affecting workpeople are made', said the TUC in 1974 in its basic policy document on the subject called *Industrial Democracy,* which eventually led to the Labour Government late in 1975 setting up a Committee of Inquiry on Industrial Democracy under the chairmanship of Lord Bullock. This is a much wider ambition than the more limited concept of unions just being involved in issues such as the pay and employment conditions of its members. In industry it raises basic questions about the role of unions and how they can respond to the responsibilities involved in their having a wider say over company affairs such as investment, factory closures, takeovers, mergers and redundancies. Basically managements, in the private sector especially, oppose such an extension of union influence, whether it is to be wielded by shop stewards or by union officials. This is partly because they want to defend their own centres of power, prestige and authority; but they can also quite logically argue that trade unions have done little up to now to show themselves capable of shouldering positive responsibilities, even in keeping the deals on pay and allied subjects that they cover at present.

On the other hand the unions, in general highly critical of management, object to what they see as industrialists' primary motivation of making money, even at the expense of employees' jobs. They say that they ought to have a wider voice in order to be able to protect their members' long-term interests in a positive way instead of merely having to react to the results of boardroom decisions, taken some time earlier, over which they had no control. Such a role, some of their leaders argue, would allow them to make a positive impact on a company which would enhance its viability and so the livelihoods of their members.

This brings one to the central issue of the subject as it is seen by some but not all union leaders, by industrialists, and by politicians. It is whether or not industrial democracy provides a potential for unions to switch from their present negative and reactive role to one of positive and constructive responsibility in which they put aside some of their traditional tactics.

There is of course the parallel discussion within the unions over whether they should go for such increased powers through boardroom representation as advocated by the TUC, or through extended collective bargaining, because it is obvious that the former carries a greater aura of positive responsibility than merely extending the range of bargaining from a position of opposition.

But here the argument becomes even more complex because no union leader in Britain has yet suggested that his members should abandon the unions' primary adversary role when they enter the board room, however much they may be prepared to become involved in responsible participation when they get there. The reason for this is that the British trade union movement is not about to enter into Germany-style co-determination (and even in Germany the political and power-seeking nature of the unions can sometimes upset that country's co-operative system). The British trade unions will always – as far as one can see at the moment – be bargainers within a mixed economy. The question therefore is whether that bargaining can be harnessed positively and constructively in a board room without catastrophically upsetting the unions' overall credibility and the company's managerial efficiency.

It is possible that such a positive role, if it were feasible, could give the unions a new image of legitimacy in the eyes of both their members and the country in general as operators of positive rather than negative authority. This is not to suggest that the unions do not have a legitimacy at present: they do, but it is primarily, as has been said, a negative militant-based legitimacy which often gains little respect. It runs into trouble with shop stewards, who are the real centres of trade union power, not wanting to follow their leaders' agreements and often resenting union authority as much as management authority. Indeed, one of the attractions of industrial democracy for management should be that they could harness the energies and loyalties of these shop stewards as employees, without necessarily diluting any union loyalties, for the good of their companies. This could rationalise the position and authority of the shop stewards.

It was the deeply held doubts about the willingness and ability of unions and their shop stewards to adopt such a positive role, coupled with a fear of the unions' basic anti-capitalist political beliefs, that lay behind much of the industrialists' furore over the Bullock Report. Put simply, industrialists are not prepared to embrace union power in their affairs in the same way that governments have done for short-term gains such as co-operation in national incomes policies.

Reforms for the unions

The differences of opinion over the potential usefulness–as opposed to the question of rights–of an extension of union influence stem partly from despair among managements and governments about the way the unions operate. Too often unions have seemed to be cumbersome, unrepresentative, negative organisations dominated at the top by power-hungry autocrats and disrupted at the bottom by unruly shop stewards who have no interests in the wellbeing of the companies in which they work. Labour agreements seem to be made to be broken, and the officials who should take the responsibility for their members' unconstitutional action shrink from doing so. At the same time, union officials are under-qualified, underpaid and frequently overworked. They do not have sufficient expert back-up services to help them in their wage negotiations. There are also far too many unions, which leads to constant friction and, occasionally, to crises. And even where unions have merged, the old craft jealousies remain and shop stewards, who do not seem to be institutionalised in any formal way, use such problems to make management's life even more difficult.

Each one of these criticisms has some truth behind it, but the point that is often missed is that these failings are mainly sins of omission rather than commission. Union leaders and shop stewards rarely set out on a disruptive warpath looking for trouble and are not very often any more powerful than the collective will of their members. The real problem is that unions have failed to modernise themselves fast enough during the past half-century to technological and other changes and, as part of a grass-roots-based movement, cannot easily be forced to change, as the 1970 Conservative Goverment discovered. On the other hand their top leaders, as has already been seen, have been changing their attitudes in recent years and it is now realistic to suggest that the spread of industrial democracy could act as the catalyst to encourage the unions to modernise because of the new responsibilities they would have to shoulder, forcing them to adopt more positive and innovatory outlooks. Critics–and even some friends–of the unions would argue however that they would be more likely to break under the strain of their new responsibilities. They would add that there is no reason to expect that industrial democracy would induce positive changes any more than other advances given to the unions, such as the spread of closed shops, statutory organisations and employment rights and legal immunities, have done in the past.

A question of method

The immediate issue for the unions is the method by which they should try to obtain their increased influence over managerial decisions in industry. This issue arises because, as has been said, not all unions want to become embroiled in the radical change from their traditional conflict-based role implicit in the full-participation and worker director approach spelt out by the TUC in 1974. This does not mean that they want to remain in perpetual conflict, but it does mean that they do not want to lose their traditional strengths. Many unions would therefore prefer the alternative of extending the range of corporate affairs over which they negotiate with management outside the board room.

Both schools of thought want to reduce managerial prerogatives and the power of capital by obtaining laws that give them the right to joint control with management of the key strategic decisions affecting their members' working lives–although of course the degree of militancy or co-operation with which such joint control would be exercised would vary enormously from union to union.

The TUC says this can be done only by gaining seats in the board room, because bargaining systems, however much they might be extended, would leave some company matters uncovered. Unions that oppose the idea reject that argument and say they do not want to blur their roles by entering the board room and so instead want present employment laws extended and company laws changed to give them statutory rights to wide-ranging company information and to bargaining on company decisions. There are also doubts over whether union members themselves want to see their unions sharing responsibility for management either through shopfloor participation or in the board room. In fact, the nearer one gets to the shop floor with the concept of trade unions sharing responsibility with governments or industrialists, the more worried the trade union officials involved become about selling both the concepts and the results of such partnerships to their members and of maintaining the credibility both of their organisations and their shop stewards. This applies equally to a government social contract-style pay policy as to a factory closure in a company.

Shop stewards
Britain's 300,000 shop stewards (the figure is a TUC estimate) are the people who shoulder the burden of union organisation at the place of work. They are of course backed up and looked after to varying degrees by national, regional and local full-time union officers and, sometimes, by their unions' central research departments. But in the development of industrial democracy and especially of any worker director system it is the shop stewards rather than full-time union officials who will bear the increased responsibilities. This is partly because employers usually prefer to participate with shop stewards, who are employees of their company, rather than with trade union-employed full-time officials, and partly because there could never be enough full-time officials to cope with all the day-to-day aspects of a participation system. In any case, the essence of industrial democracy is the right of individual workers to exercise power over economic and industrial issues and the logic of this is that the power should be exercised from the shop floor, rather than from the trade union head or local office. But the corollary is that the shopfloor representative–the shop steward–then not only wields the increased power but has to shoulder consequential wider responsibilities.

Shop stewards in Britain are the hub of the collective bargaining-based system. Their role has expanded enormously in the postwar years, and the shifts from national wage bargaining to company and factory deals in the last decade or so have increased their importance and power because gradually they have become involved in the negotiation of full wage deals as well as dealing with traditional shopfloor matters such as piecework prices, productivity payments, assembly track speeds and other day-to-day affairs. But unions rarely define the precise functions of their shop stewards. They originated with the need for unions to have shopfloor representatives to recruit members, collect dues and act as a channel of communication, and were boosted by a militant Shop Stewards Movement during and immediately after the First World War. As unpaid volunteers, they now form the grass-roots base of both the individual unions and the whole Labour movement.

Only one thing has so far emerged to reduce their importance. This is the advent of incomes policies, which severely limit their freedom to negotiate shopfloor pay rises. Indeed, some union leaders have been heard to argue privately that, by giving shop stewards a role in the management of their companies through extended bargaining or board-room representation, industrial democracy is filling the vacuum left by incomes policies and is giving a new lease of life to shop stewards by channelling their energies towards constructive rather than conflict goals.

In effect, industrial democracy takes the shop steward, who has until fairly recently been confined to shopfloor affairs, up into the board rooms and even into national centres like the Government's industrial strategy working parties. This suggests that shop stewards will need not only training in new skills but also some basic education to help them accept the change in their role. Initial results of some research work being carried out by the Ruskin Research Unit at Oxford on British Leyland's participation scheme illustrates the problem of not enough attention being paid to the attitudes and beliefs of shop stewards when a participation system is introduced. This is not to suggest that shop stewards should be brainwashed by education techniques into rethinking their role and changing their traditional adversary tactics. But what it does show is that, like managers, shop stewards need to be given the opportunity to understand the concepts of participation–whether or not they then decide to accept them. One of the problems at Leyland was that such an opportunity was not given for the stewards to be taught about the concepts–let alone to be fully trained in the techniques. As a result many of them were confused about how the new way of life was supposed to fit in with their traditional operations.

A change of role

The problems borne by a national trade union leader who is only accountable every year or so to his ultimate authority–his union's conference–may be considerable; but they do not match the critical pressures that face shop stewards in a participation system. Such shop stewards firstly have to deal with a whole new range of company affairs and then have to return every day from their board room or participation committee meetings to the shop floor knowing secrets they possibly should not pass on to their members, bearing responsibilities for some decisions they know their members will not like, and probably feeling inadequately briefed on subjects outside their normal expertise. They could also have to straddle the long-term perspectives of many board-room discussions which can conflict with the shorter-term outlook of their members.

The point here is that in collective bargaining (these different terms are explained in detail in Chapter 10) the traditional defensive role of the unions allows the shop steward or union official to refuse to reach an agreement with the employer. He can then go back to his members and explain that he has failed to persuade the management to agree to terms he thought they would want to accept. His members can of course send him back and modify the terms they want, and, as usually happens in industry, an agreement may then be reached for which the union and its members share responsibility with the management.

But this is a voluntary responsibility based on either side having been free to abandon the negotiations. It is quite different from the situation where a union shop steward is locked into a participation forum, which should be based on co-operation rather than conflict, from which he cannot easily walk away too often without ultimately risking a break-up of the participation system. In such a situation he has to bear responsibility for the participation decisions, hoping his members will accept that, on balance, the long-term benefits gained make it worthwhile adopting immediately a new responsibile style of industrial life. (This is a problem sometimes known by academics as 'role conflict'.) Such problems apply both to participation committees throughout a company and to worker director systems – because both involve putting adversary relationships on one side – although the worker director board representation is the more onerous. (Chapter 10.)

The board-level dimension on this was discussed by John Lyons, general secretary of the Electrical Power Engineers' Association, who has been one of the unions' most implacable opponents of the TUC and Bullock worker director ideas. He wrote in *The Times* on 2 March, 1977:

That trade unions and the workforces they represent should participate in important decisions affecting them, and accept responsibility in a new way for actively promoting the efficiency and wellbeing of their firms and organisations, I personally profoundly believe. But there is all the difference in the world between achieving this through the extension of collective bargaining, under which in the last resort either side is free to make an agreement *or not,* and achieving it by putting trade union representatives on the board in such a way as to commit them to coming to an agreement, and taking full responsibility for it whether they want to or not. It is because employee representatives on Boards *à la* Bullock will tie the unions into the management decision-making process and simultaneously take away their ability to remain independent when they want to, that there is such a fundamental difference between collective bargaining and Bullock. In practical terms, if employee representatives on Boards agree to rationalisations, redundancies, etc, as they will be bound to do from time to time, then to that extent the trade unions representing the staffs in the company or companies concerned will be compromised in their collective bargaining positions. That is utterly unavoidable. . . . What is absolutely essential is that if trade unions accept the basic concepts of the Bullock Report, we do so with our eyes open, knowingly accepting the radically changed role which they will impose on us.

Another problem in this change of role, as past experience both in the UK and abroad indicates, is that where shop stewards are given some role in the management of an enterprise – in participation committees as much as on boards – they can easily lose their basic trade union approach. They realise the other conflicting pressures on a company's management and this dilutes the singlemindedness of their trade unionism. Such a watering down of potential militancy or of selfish worker-orientated claims might well be in the interests of the company as a whole and would be welcomed therefore by the management; but it might not be welcomed for too long by the workers who, ultimately, might decide to change their representatives (or even, in an extreme case, try to form an alternative independent union organisation).

Because of this risk of alienation, the TUC insists that any worker director or other participation system must be directly tied into the trade unions with the representatives being elected by union members (perhaps with other non-union employees having a limited role) to whom they must be directly accountable. This means the representatives must report back on their actions and submit themselves for re-election at regular intervals. The TUC's objective here is to ensure that the shop stewards (the same principle applies to any employee participation representatives, not just worker directors) are both strengthened and protected by their traditional trade union power. Ironically, however, partly because the participation aspect of industrial democracy implies some of that traditional power being put to one side, the link with the trade unions may not always be in the interest of the unions themselves if their representatives are saddled with the responsibilities for unpalatable decisions. To strengthen the union commitment of worker directors, TUC policy-makers have also pushed planning agreement ideas (Chapter 4) which they see as a way of preventing shop stewards being seduced away by employers from their Labour movement roots and interests.

A TUC lead

Len Murray, the TUC general secretary, does not accept that problems exist with a new union role or that responsibilities are a new phenomenon for the unions. Stressing that the aim of the TUC is to get trade union representatives into the decision-making areas of industry, he told the 1976 annual Trades Union Congress in a speech that marked the start of an effort to 'sell' the concept of worker directors on the basis of trade union responsibility:

We are not prepared to accept responsibility for the consequences of other people's decisions—which is all too often the case at the moment where workers end up carrying the can for management inadequacies. But we are prepared to accept our share of responsibility for joint decisions, as we do now in collective agreements .... In opening this new chapter in the history of our movement, we are taking on greater responsibilities. Collective bargaining itself carries such responsibilities. Every time you make an agreement you take on a responsibility in the interests of our members. That is our job. Now is the time to go forward.

This approach was based on a belief in some parts of the TUC that the crude adversary system in Britain can be shown to have failed to do much good for union members and therefore for the country. On the other hand, an extension of trade union responsibility into the board room would bring together the separate interests of capital and labour in a united effort to maximise the productive capacity of a company—so combining union power aspirations with commercial common sense. As Len Murray said in February 1977, in an introduction to the TUC's own guide to the Bullock Report, 'Its recommendations are based on a belief that the revitalisation of British industry is crucially dependent on the establishment of a new relationship of equality and co-operation between capital and labour, which provides for the joint determination of company strategy.' This development by Murray of the responsibility theme took the TUC's presentation a step away from the more militant tone of its original 1974 industrial democracy document, which called for legal rights to 'collective participation and control' in areas not covered by traditional labour relations. It did not appeal by any means to all unions. As an Institute of Workers' Control book *The Shop Stewards' Guide to the Bullock Report* put it later, the TUC had adopted 'a new emphasis on collaboration with management rather than the original stress on veto powers for workers' representatives'.

The Bullock Report itself however had said in its conclusions:

If such requirements as we have proposed are carried through, they will release energies and abilities at present frustrated or not used and thereby create a framework which will allow conflicts of interest to be resolved with greater mutual advantage . . . . We believe that the change in attitude of the TUC and their willingness to accept a share of responsibility for the increased efficiency and prosperity of British companies offer an opportunity to create a new basis for relations in industry which should not be allowed to pass.

The conflict tradition
This is of course the only argument that could be put forward to advocate such a development as worker directors and it was written at a time when, through the TUC and the social contract, unions were sharing responsibility on pay rises. The alternative 'truth'–that trade unions want to extend their adversary relationship into board rooms where they can indulge in unco-operative collective bargaining as part of a company's top decision-making process–would hardly have commended itself to the country at large or helped to 'sell' the Bullock formula. In any case, to be fair, union leaders like Murray genuinely do not want to extend destructive conflict into the board room; what they want is to create structures and procedures that enable trade union bargaining power to be harnessed constructively and positively in new areas, in the best traditions of positive union-based operation. And Jones wants to do just that through the shop stewards.

The problem with this however is that the traditional conflict approach does not stem simply from capital and labour having different interests within companies. It stems also from Britain's class conflicts and from the political base of the Labour movement, which is out to change society. Trying to lessen the conflict in the country's industrial life by maximising co-operation would not necessarily change the basic conflict within society as a whole, certainly not in the short term. Nevertheless, the TUC is still on strong ground when its leaders offer to try to dampen down the conflict, through industrial democracy, at all levels of political, economic and industrial life, in return for being admitted into the seats of power and invited to share responsibility for managing the country's affairs. In fact, this is in line with the traditional art of good and responsible adversary-based labour relations–to develop relationships and procedures that reduce the potential area for conflict as far as is possible while recognising the different interests of those involved.

Such an outlook is the basic philosophy on which trade unions and managers have operated–and learned labour academics lectured–for many years. It is however a philosophy that can be misinterpreted, and indeed it is sometimes resented by many union leaders because for most of the time the vast majority of Britain's work force and its shop stewards are co-operating with management. Union officials and shop stewards do not usually go out looking for conflict, and where the conflict does break out it is often the fault of poor management – that is of managers who have not been properly trained in labour management, who are not qualified to hold the posts they have been given, and whose horizons stop at the solution of the immediate short-term problems. It is then that militants in the trade unions move in. The history of industries such as docks, newspapers, motorcars, shipbuilding and building sites over the past decade or so is littered with examples of labour troubles thus exploited by militants – often politically motivated members of the Communist Party or of a Trotskyist faction.

One view of such industrial conflict at its worst was set out in *Working for Ford,* a book written by a sociologist, Huw Beynon, with a strongly militant and political tone (Beynon, 1973). Talking about life in the early 1960s when Ford had just opened its Halewood plant on Merseyside and was suffering from labour troubles, Beynon says:

The history of British trade unionism is built on various levels of factory class consciousness. Trade unionism and workshop organisation is, and always has been, a direct response to economic forces . . . . A factory class consciousness grew out of this; it understands class relationships in terms of their direct manifestation in conflict between the bosses and the workers within a factory. It is rooted in the workplace where struggles are fought over the control of the job and the 'rights' of managers and workers. In as much as it concerns itself with exploitation and power it contains definite political elements. But it is a politics of the factory, implicitly tied up with the day-to-day battle with the boss. Factory class consciousness finds its historical antecedent in syndicalism – the idea of workers' control of the factories, adhered to most strongly by skilled workers – which was most developed in Britain in the shop steward movement that occurred during and after World War One. While this was the high water mark of this tradition, strong elements of it still permeate the British working class. In its least developed form it is revealed in sporadic bloody-mindedness and 'malingering' – the 'fuck 'em' attitude that most managers are familiar with and find distasteful. The underlying structure of this view is not radically different from that which underpinned the consciousness of the stewards at Halewood. Their class consciousness can be seen as a high development inasmuch as they had worked out a sophisticated understanding of how they could best combat management there.

This is the British conflict tradition of labour relations at its most politically militant, and it is not this sort of area that is likely to respond rapidly to the inducements of co-operation in industrial democracy. But hidden behind these headline-catching trouble-spots are the basic social, political and hierarchical conflicts of industry that provide the basis for the adversary system. The real test for industrial democracy would be whether it could change the relationships in these areas. Here the conflicts are based on the old class structures and jealousies of Britain's society over the years, the traditional 'them and us' attitudes, which have not disappeared despite the educational and other social changes that have changed the balance of equality and opportunity in industry and commerce. The 'them and us' is still the manager and the managed, and especially between the shop floor and those whose job it is to run it, from the supervisor up to the company director. So career patterns and ambition – rather than inherited advantages – dictate the distinctions and divisions that fuel such shopfloor frustration and militancy.

On top of these long-running problems, there is also now a change in the basic attitude to life at work which lies behind the trend towards industrial democracy. This is a growing reluctance, embracing a far wider spectrum than just the militant Left, to accept the supremacy of capital and shareholders over employees. In industry this has sharpened the traditional conflict over the sharing of the proceeds of a business.

This leads advocates of industrial democracy to argue that, if the goodwill of the workers is harnessed by involving them in the management of the factory, the class and hierarchical divisions that can cause conflict during the creation of the wealth will be reduced and the business will be more efficient. The goodwill created will also help to minimise conflict over the sharing of the proceeds in wages to the employees and dividends to the shareholders. Critics of this approach argue – quite apart from the practical managerial problems of running businesses on a participative basis – that it is extremely unlikely that such a change could happpen. And even if it did, the wrangling over wages and dividends would so sour relationships that they would undo the good done by the participation in management.

The TUC and its dissidents

The orthodox TUC view that emerged in the Bullock Report was first set out in detail in the TUC's 1974 policy document, which opened with these words:

Throughout their history trade unions have generated a substantial measure of industrial democracy in this country. All of their activities have served to further this objective. The term industrial democracy cannot be considered outside that context. This report recognises that collective bargaining is and will continue to be the central method of joint regulation in industry and the public services, but there are a number of specific questions of close concern to workpeople, which are not being effectively subjected to joint regulation through the present processes of collective bargaining, and additional forms of joint regulation are therefore needed, particularly as capital becomes more concentrated and the central decisions of Boards of directors seem increasingly remote from any impact by workpeople through their own organisations.

The report went on to spell out other forms of trade union influence on companies and then returned to board representation and said:

It is a basic function of trade unions to obtain a degree of joint control through representation at the point at which decisions affecting workpeople are made . . . . The objective is to find a form of representation and participation in decision-making in the private sector which provides for participation in major decisions, but leaves the lines of responsibility of the workers' representatives to their constituents. The aim must be to give legal rights to workpeople of collective participation and control over decisions which the collective bargaining and consultative processes have not given them . . . . There would appear to be some merit in introducing into UK company law the division of the present powers of the Board of management into a management Board and a supervisory Board, thereby giving worker representatives on the latter a degree of trade union and social control over major management decisions . . . . One half of the supervisory Board should be appointed by the workpeople through trade union machinery, normally at company or combine level.

This was trade union-based worker participation, in search of extended trade union power, taken to its logical conclusion of board representation (albeit in a two-tier board structure which the TUC abandoned with the Bullock Report). Such ideas, as has already been said, have strong critics among trade unions where arch-left-wingers, opposed to having any truck with the capitalist system, are joined by other union leaders with practical worries about the wisdom of trying to blur the lines of conflict and about the strains that worker directors would impose on ill-equipped trade unions.

But, while those on the Left, including the Communist Party, which sometimes wields considerable direct and indirect influence on trade union policy-making, have opposed the idea of worker directors in the private sector because it means sharing responsibility for running the capitalist system, they do not mind worker directors in nationalised industries where the State is the owner, (a view that has roots in Labour movement debates earlier in the century–see Chapter 14).

The Communist Party expressed this view in its evidence to the Bullock Committee when it advocated extending bargaining and said:

The proposals we are making are for extending industrial democracy within the framework of capitalist society today. We believe that full workers' control can only be developed in a socialist society. There has been an extension of industrial democracy over the past 100 years in that the questions subject to some form of negotiation between the two sides of industry, management and labour, have been increased . . . . Bit by bit collective bargaining has been able to encroach on new areas, bringing what was hitherto regarded as managerial right under some form of control. We therefore see the major advance in industrial democracy coming through the further development of collective bargaining, with all major decisions being the subject of mutuality. This would cover negotiation on such matters as investment, location or expansion of the industry or enterprise, forward manpower planning, training etc.

Such developments, the statement continued, would need stronger trade unions and the maximum disclosure of company information. In the publicly owned industries however, where the 'principle of full social control is already accepted', there should be an extension of 'democratic control' which should be achieved both by extending collective bargaining and by introducing trade union-based worker directors.

This distinction between the private and public sectors of industry found some supporters in the trade union movement in the early 1970s, but among the large unions only the Communist-influenced Amalgamated Union of Engineering Workers still stood by the view in 1976. The breaking point for some of the others was first a disenchantment with the management of nationalised industries, which made them seem little different from private industry, plus the rapid growth of state financial holdings in the private sector through the National Enterprise Board and other means, especially during the country's industrial and economic crises of the mid-1970s. As Len Murray told the 1976 annual Trades Union Congress:

Those who argue that there should be a distinction between the public and private sectors are not saying that representation at Board level is an inherent contradiction of the basic trade union function. They are however arguing that the role and position of unions in publicly owned industries is basically different from their role and position in private industry. But I do not believe that that would stand up to careful examination. Is it a sensible distinction? How can we say that workers in British Leyland [now publicly owned] should have the right to parity Board level representation, but that Chrysler workers [where the Government had not taken a direct stake] should not? Such distinctions will become more and more meaningless as public ownership is increasingly extended into profitable areas of manufacturing industry through the National Enterprise Board and so on.

Murray here was mainly bent on whittling down opposition to the TUC's worker director plan on a wide front. His debating skill in blurring the distinctions between the private and public sector did not really meet the ideological distinctions adopted by the Communist Party and its supporters. Equally however, the Communist Party was only squaring up the reality of having to operate in a mixed economy and, if pushed, would be unlikely to hold that either British Rail or British Leyland, for example, are paragons of socialist virtue.

Left and right

The Communist Party had found itself ranged alongside some unusual allies from the right wing of the trade union movement–notably Frank Chapple, general secretary of the Electrical and Plumbing Trades Union, and (to a less permanent extent) David Basnett of the General and Municipal Workers Union. The Electrical and Plumbing Trades Union (EPTU) has held its view for some years. In 1967 its then president, the late Sir Leslie Cannon, listed the problems that would beset any worker director system in characteristically forthright terms, dwelling especially on the danger of blurring the lines of conflict between trade unions and management. In a statement advocating an extension of collective bargaining which he made to his union's national conference in Margate that year, Cannon said:

Inevitably there are conflicts within industry but the aim of a good system of industrial relations should not be to eliminate all conflict but to contain it within a framework so that it can be fought out without spilling into other areas. Where conflict is damaging it should be limited if at all possible, but it is neither possible nor desirable that all conflict should be eliminated. For properly contained it can be creative. Out of the many disputes the best agreements have been reached and the most efficient methods of working created.

This was an uncompromising line from a tough union boss who knew how to wield effective power and it has remained the union's basic philosophy ever since. Cannon told the conference: 'If workers' representatives are involved too deeply in management and are performing the task of management properly, they will inevitably be inhibited in their activities as trade unionists. In other words, if they act as managers they will no longer be acting as trade unionists.' Cannon's colleague and successor at the top of the EPTU, Frank Chapple, has stuck rigidly to this policy and the union has developed pace-making participative arrangements based on traditional procedures in the electricity supply industry and a special form of joint control in the electrical contracting industry.

With the General and Municipal Workers, the EPTU also believes, as do local officials of many other trade unions, that their members are not interested in taking over responsibility for management. In any case, they argue, trade unions are not equipped to cope rapidly with the burdens of widespread participative and worker director schemes because of their shoestring approach to the way they run their organisations with small research staffs and overworked officials.

The GMWU however, under their general secretary David Basnett, tends to be more pragmatic than the EPTU, perhaps partly because it has strong roots in the public sector, where consultation and bargaining are much more highly developed than in most private sector companies. In some nationalised industries therefore the GMWU sees the possibility for topping off a well-established substructure of joint management-union co-operation with worker directors and also accepted the Bullock Report during 1977 as one, but not the only, route to industrial democracy. It joined with other unions in the gas industry in a policy document in the summer of 1976 which was significant because it illustrated an early pragmatic approach to union power and industrial democracy. It bridged the gap between the TUC's worker director approach and the collective bargaining alternative by calling for both and was instrumental in swinging the TUC's annual Congress in 1977 behind both ideas.

Overall, however, the basic GMWU approach, based on an instinctive preference for extending collective bargaining rather than on worker directors, should not be construed as meaning that, with the EPTU and one or two others, it is putting forward an easy alternative. Industrialists and politicians who have seen a parallel with their own anti-worker director views are missing the point, because all the unions want to take power away from managements. However, with extended bargaining the union representatives would be able to pick and choose which company affairs they want to try to influence and so would not have either to sit quietly or to speak ignorantly when subjects are raised by management that are beyond their expertise and interest. This is one of the risks of the worker director approach – that it exposes trade union representatives to a whole host of issues such as complex financial plans or technical matters far removed from their immediate interests and to which they may well not be able to make an effective contribution.

Chapter 7

The Unions: Ambitions, Expertise and Organisation

The spread of trade union and employee influence raises the question of how far unions want to go in influencing decisions of companies and other employers. Do they simply want to extend their power as far as is necessary to guard the immediate interests of their members at work? And how far would the unions regard those interests as reaching? Do the editorial contents of a newspaper or the foreign investments of a bank for example fall within the range, or are the unions only interested in the organisation and printing of a newspaper and the opening and closing of banks because these are issues that have a clear impact on employment and pay?

Such issues affect the extent to which trade union influence will be felt by companies and other organisations as a result of the social and political pressures, the union ambitions and the possible institutional changes that have already been discussed. The issues to be faced start with how far the unions want, and might be allowed by society, to go outside their immediate interests and expertise on employment matters. This leads on to the question of whether, whatever happens, some areas like government policies, newspapers and financial institutions should be excluded from union influence.

Then there is the decision that employers must make about whether to respond constructively to their unions' and employees' ambitions and try to harness them for the good of their enterprises, or to try to thwart them and to nullify their chances of being effective. The widening areas of union and employee interest, and the unions' current lack of expertise in these areas, also raises the question of how shop stewards can be trained and given the research help they will need. There is the further problem of whether some unions' national and local policy-making bodies will try to impose their policy decisions through participating shop stewards on companies' internal affairs, what the effect would be on full-time union officials, and whether unions can co-operate together sufficiently to present coherent policies. Most of these issues would apply both to a worker director system or to extended collective bargaining.

Subjects for participation

The starting point for these considerations is the question of whether unions and their members should have a say in what a company does—that is, the purpose of its business—as opposed to how the business is organised. There is a considerable body of opinion among employers and politicians that argues that employee influence should be limited primarily to employment issues and should certainly not be extended to the purpose of the business, even though this may have an obvious bearing on employment prospects. But this issue vanishes as an argument of principle if worker directors are admitted on to the board of a company (although of course in practice the decision-making on the purpose of the business could be hived off to some other board or executive committee). But the essence of boardroom representation is that the employee representatives would have a right, through their seats on the board, to influence *any* decision, even though in practice they might decide at first to say little on matters outside their traditional expertise.

For the time being, however, while boardroom representation and allied subjects such as joint control of pension funds are not widespread, the question of how far workers' influence within companies should range will continue to be a controversial issue. It will certainly emerge whenever the shareholders' representatives and executive management consider that the worker representatives (whether they are board members or simply sit on consultative or negotiating bodies) are pursuing a policy that is not in the interests of the company as a whole–for example over redundancies, a factory closure or investment in a business in another part of the country or abroad.

There are also more emotive issues with sensitive political overtones, such as whether an armaments factory should switch to socially useful products (as shop stewards proposed in 1975 for Lucas Aerospace), whether gunboats should be built for right-wing dictatorships, or whether a bank should invest for example in South Africa.

Government policies

Such issues are most potently evident in national affairs where even people who might sympathise with worker influence in some of the examples above, would never expect to see Treasury clerks participating in making government economic policy, government dockyard workers deciding the nations' defence policy, or Foreign Office messengers helping to decide the future of Anglo-Soviet relations.

In government affairs however (as will be seen in more detail in Chapter 17), an obvious principle can be established. This is that ministers are answerable to Parliament for the policies of their departments and that industrial democracy must not be allowed to breach this electoral principle of parliamentary democracy. But even here it is not easy to draw a distinct line between what Parliament should decide and what should be left to the workers, despite a general principle that Parliament should decide the overall policies, with government employees being able to participate in how the policies are carried out–that is, in the organi·sation but not in the purpose of government business. Jack Jones however amply illustrated how obscure the dividing line can become when he submitted the TGWU's evidence to the Government's public sector industrial democracy inquiries in the summer of 1976 and showed how he might hope to muscle in on political decisions. He called for 50–50 joint union–management bodies to run defence establishments such as naval dockyards and suggested that the yards should be given increased autonomy by central government and should only employ union members under closed shop agreements.

He acknowledged that the Government should be responsible for the country's overall defence strategy and budget, but immediately qualified this by saying:

We do not wish to take away from Parliament the power to decide overall strategic matters but we believe the Government must always bear in mind the manpower implications of defence decisions. The cancellation and postponement of projects, or decisions to embark on a new project, should be matters that are discussed with the unions right at the beginning of the decision-making process, so that the Government will be well aware of all the implications of their decisions. We are not convinced that the needs of national security prevent any discussions on this. We believe that trade union representatives on the proposed Boards for the dockyards, ordinance factories and central ordinance depots should be closely involved in decision-making over the country's defence strategy while leaving the ultimate power to the Government and to Parliament.

Precisely what this might mean in practice was, not surprisingly, left unsaid by Jack Jones, who was indulging in the normal tactics of an expert negotiator–lodging contentious claims to test reactions. In fact, the white-collar civil service unions, when they submitted their views to the Government, made it clear that they were 'not seeking membership of bodies concerned with the formulation of Government policy'. Instead they asked, more realistically, for some limited experiments in staff representation on some management boards and then set out the limits of their interests when they said they wanted 'the fullest possible prior consultation regarding the make-up of estimates, including cash limits, imminent new legislation and the proposed location or relocation of work, *in so far as they affect the interests of staff'*. Even this approach–based on extended collective bargaining and consultation–could of course lead to a considerable incursion into government and parliamentary prerogatives. It could also impede civil servants' ability to manage affairs flexibly. But at least it was an attempt to come to terms with the realistic political limits for employee and trade union ambitions.

In the private sector however the primary issue is far less easy to define because there is no equivalent of the parliamentary principle. If one is moving into a situation where workers and shareholders have virtual equal rights in law, as is discussed in Chapter 16, then there is, logically, no reason why the workers' representatives should regard any subjects as being outside their orbit. But until British industry recently began to come to terms with the prospect of workers in the board rooms, it was often assumed that workers would not try to dictate what a company should do. They might, and some employers accepted this, gradually gain a larger say in how their employment was organised, how factories were arranged, and other matters to do with the production of their employers' business. But even the employers most advanced in this field would not automatically have gone much further towards the purposes as opposed to the operation of the business.

'Socially useful' Lucas
The best example of this attitude is the surprise and occasional horror that greeted a document produced by shop stewards at Lucas Aerospace towards the end of 1975. This document proposed a new corporate plan

which would take Lucas away from aerospace and into more socially desirable products. As an article in the *Financial Times* said on 18 February, 1976:

At a time when worker participation is becoming fashionable – at least among trade unions – such an attempt to get involved in a discussion on the company's future and to influence its production is not itself a remarkable phenomenon. But what distinguishes the Lucas Aerospace plan from most other attempts by workers to make their company change gear in order to save jobs is that it amounts to a fundamental political challenge to the way industry is operating at the moment with an attempt by the shop stewards to redirect Lucas production into new 'socially useful' markets instead of merely asking for a say in how the goods should be produced.

There were two important pre-conditions that made this exercise possible. The first was a genuine fear of redundancies among Lucas Aerospace's thirteen thousand workers, which meant that all the shop stewards were interested in trying to suggest new products which could keep their company in business and the workers employed. The second was the presence among them of a highly articulate far left-wing trade unionist, Mike Cooley. A past president of his union, the technical and supervisory section (TASS) of the AUEW, he is one of the most left-wing trade unionists to have held such a senior union office in Britain. Without Cooley, it is possible that such a plan would not have come about and his union, which is run on more central orthodox and Communist-influenced lines, while backing the plan, did not really regard it as a very effective method of social or industrial reform because it did not pack political punch. Nevertheless a combination of Cooley's political fervour and the fear of redundancies led to the production of the plan, which proposed a gradual movement away from aerospace. It suggested the development of 'socially useful' products such as medical equipment, cheap heating including the use of solar energy, and safer non-polluting transport. 'The aerospace industry is a particularly glaring example of the gap which exists between that which technology could provide and that which it actually does provide to meet the wide range of human problems we see about us', said the document. It wanted to demonstrate that 'workers are prepared to press for the right to work on products which actually help to solve human problems rather than create them'.

The Lucas exercise was also significant however for three other reasons, even though it did not lead to any positive action by the company, which thought the ideas were either unsuitable for its technolocial expertise or were in fact already being made or investigated elsewhere in the Lucas group. First, it enabled Cooley to suggest how workers in other industries might adopt a similar approach. He was reported in the *Financial Times* article, written by Lorelies Olslager, as having suggested that 'workers in the food industry, for example, could make sure that they were producing wholesome nourishing food instead of breakfast cereals of no nutritional value'. Second, the exercise showed the distaste in which the idea of worker directors has been held both by many far left-wing activists and by shopfloor workers. The shop stewards proposed that the work in their factories should be reorganised so that all employees involved on any product would be free to co-operate in its development and production. Such a breakdown of traditional factory hierarchies, the document suggested, could 'be far more significant in the long term than campaigns for worker participation or worker directors'. It thus also demonstrated how political activists could use participation of whatever sort to extend the ways in which they try to push their own ideological lines in industry.

Finally, the exercise illustrated how the limited interest normally shown by a work force and its shop stewards in participation can be galvanised when a crisis hits employment prospects – even though in this case not much was achieved and Lucas took little formal notice of the ideas. General experience in the UK up to now supports the theory that most workers have little interest in representational participation schemes until their own jobs are at stake – which means of course that relatively few employers are likely to find their employees quickly trying to change the nature of their business.

But as participation and shop steward expertise increases, this limited outlook may change. The sort of company-level shop steward committees proposed by the Bullock Report as the springboard for worker directors would put a company's shop stewards in a far better position to take an active interest in the purpose of the company than they are at present. In a fully developed system of participation reaching down from board level through the company stewards' committee (called the Joint Representation Committee – JRC – by the Bullock Report) to lower-level joint participation committees, the purpose and organisation of the business would be merged in a continual interchange and feedback of ideas based on extensive provision of information about the company. Indeed, if the system were operating co-operatively, it would probably seem illogical to exclude any significant subjects.

Possible exemptions: newspapers and finance
There are however specific areas where strong arguments are sometimes mounted against employees, and especially against trade union representatives, being given a say in all a company's affairs. The first is newspapers, television and radio where, in order to protect the 'freedom of the press', it is sometimes argued that workers' influence should be limited to how a newspaper or programme is produced, not what goes into it. Even this line is not that simple however because some would argue that journalists, who write the newspapers, do have a right to a wider say in the contents of their newspaper whereas the industry's printing and manual workers do not. This argument is mainly an issue of expertise but is also an élitist view – one that Anthony Wedgwood Benn exposed a few years ago when he suggested that the liftman in a radio or newspaper building should be given a say on the programme or paper.

The issue of the freedom of the press is too complex to be analysed in detail here. Suffice to say that it is a somewhat precarious freedom that has often in the past been wielded intolerantly by proprietors and editors. At present the editor of a newspaper is regarded as the guardian of the freedom and the least that this should mean is that trade unions and other vested interest groups should not take over and influence the editorial content of a newspaper. In the practical context of industrial democracy this means that the powers of any trade union-based participation systems, especially worker directors, need to be carefully considered. In theory however there is no reason why the employees should not be given an equal say in the running of the newspaper with the proprietors–who after all should already be delegating the responsibility for editorial content to the editor rather than wielding it themselves. Such a system could indeed help to separate the powers of the proprietor from the editor. A joint worker director–proprietor board could then choose the editor because there would be no justification under an industrial democracy system for the proprietor to wield any greater unilateral power over the choice of the editor than he would over any other business decision.

A second area that has been suggested as a possibility for special treatment is banking and insurance, where individuals' money is being handled in confidence and invested in what are judged to be the most productive markets. The confidential argument seems hard to pursue in depth however because the employee representatives in any participation system are bound to receive secret information. But the City of London establishment has tried to mount a special case for itself on the issue of worker directors through an appendix to the industrialists' minority Bullock Report, despite the fact that the Bullock Committee received some evidence that German and Swedish banks (admittedly operating in internationally less important financial centres than London) have experienced no special problems with their worker directors. The appendix was subscribed by Mr (later Sir) Norman Biggs, then chairman of Williams and Glyn's Bank, and a former chairman of Esso.

After acknowledging the employees' right to consultation on issues such as pay and conditions of service, opening and closing of branches, and mechanisation plans, the appendix said: 'It is simply not practical, however, to envisage collective decision-taking in relation to the multitudinous complex and highly confidential affairs of the banks' customers in the private, corporate and public sectors'.

The other potential problem area for worker directors in banking stems from the political aspects of investment policies. This is in fact merely a more potent version of the issue that can arise in, for example, a ship or aircraft manufacturing company over the manufacture of armaments for countries of which the Labour-oriented unions do not approve. Up to now the general experience is that workers are not much interested in allowing their unions' political beliefs–opposition to South Africa or some Latin American country, for example–to affect their livelihoods. Thus, although there have been exceptions, they normally continue to build ships or aircraft because to refuse to do so could put the livelihoods of their families and communities in jeopardy. Indeed, the experience so far in the UK and in some other European countries such as Sweden is that workers, given increased powers through participation arrangements or even through boardroom seats, do not try to interfere in these areas and are often conservative rather than radical in their views. This is partly because of their lack of expertise; as union representatives gain confidence and become more expert in fields outside their traditional employment areas, they are likely to become more ambitious to influence other policies.

Research, training and expertise

To cope with the new responsibilities of industrial democracy, however far they may or may not stretch, union activists will need rapidly to increase their research and training facilities to provide the necessary expertise. The responsibility for training is a sensitive political issue because the TUC is unwilling to allow anyone but the unions themselves to be responsible for educating and training trade union activists, and the same type of arguments may well arise over the servicing of worker directors and other employee participation representatives. The Bullock Report did not make any recommendations on the detailed provision of such facilities for its board representatives beyond recognising that they would be needed and suggesting that they should be looked at in detail by its proposed Industrial Democracy Commission.

The present lack of expertise among unions and shop stewards is however a serious impediment to the rapid extension of participation in general and of worker directors in particular. Experience in the British Steel Corporation's worker director experiments and in some companies' participation systems shows how difficult it is – especially where there are various unions with different interests involved – for the union officials and shop stewards to match the expertise of the management. First, they can be easily swamped by detail; second, they do not have the resources to counter management arguments; and third, they do not have the research help and leadership needed to amalgamate the various interests of different unions. Without expertise and inter-union co-operation, however, employee representatives become ineffectual or simply exert a negative influence. This means that special joint facilities may also be needed in companies where several unions have a significant voice, in addition to unions' own offices providing a service.

Shop steward education
The education and training of shop stewards and other union activists is a highly contentious matter which goes to the heart of the adversary tradition of British labour relations and is specially relevant to the development of industrial democracy. Basically, it amounts to the TUC having an official line, which it pushes and implements whenever possible, that the unions alone should be responsible for educating and training shop stewards in the art of trade unionism. The TUC considers that this embraces everything from basic trade union organisation to negotiating pay claims, reading company balance sheets, operating health and safety at work legislation, and learning how to be a worker director. On the other hand employers say that, while trade unions might want to educate their activists out of working hours in trade unionism, shop steward training during working hours should be agreed and administered jointly by the unions and the employers. In practice, the employers' view often prevails and joint training is organised, although the TUC successfully tries to stop it wherever it can. Not surprisingly, employers consider their joint-training argument holds special relevance with employee participation, and indeed the industrial democracy debate has made employers somewhat more energetically outspoken and critical of the TUC on the issue than they have been in the past.

The basic TUC view is that there is a conflict of interests between employers and workers and that this means that employers have different objectives from unions. Since no education can be carried out impartially, it would not therefore be realistic, they say, to expect employers to educate shop stewards to the satisfaction of the unions because they would slant their teaching with a basic management viewpoint. Equally, while it is the job of trade unions to turn the conflict between the two sides of industry into as constructive channels as possible, the way to do this in the workers' interest could not be taught jointly.

These TUC views have hardened in recent years from the time when the TUC reached an agreement with the British Employers' Federation (forerunner of the CBI) in 1963. This said that, while 'the aim of training must be to assist stewards carry out their functions as responsible officers of their unions', employers would be able to agree training courses jointly with the unions where they were paying the wages of the stewards on a day-release basis at local colleges. Now however the emphasis has changed, with the trade unions and especially the TUC, rather than local colleges, taking a central role in planning courses – an expertise that the TUC partially learned when it launched its first mass education exercise during the unions' battle against the Conservatives' Industrial Relations Act. The TUC is prepared however to share its training work load with those public educational bodies of which it approves such as colleges of further education, university extramural departments and the Labour movement-oriented Workers' Educational Association which runs a lot of the TUC's courses.

Such a restrictive attitude however is not peculiar to the British TUC. Its counterparts in some other countries, including Germany and Sweden, have the same basic policy. Like the British TUC, they fear the power and influence of managements to whittle down the singlemindedness of trade union representatives, and in Sweden, where some joint training has been agreed, a two-inch thick syllabus was negotiated line by line between national employer and trade union leaders.

A document prepared in 1976 by the TUC headquarters for its education committee on a subject that most people would instinctively imagine was relatively non-political – training trade union safety representatives – illustrates how strongly the TUC hold its views and how suspicious it is of employers' abilities to weaken the resolve and impact of shop stewards: 'That trade unions have the sole responsibility for the education and training of their workplace representatives in their trade union functions is an essential condition for maintaining independent trade unions and for conducting trade union affairs effectively'. The TUC added that it recognised an employer's responsibility for technical training of his employees in safety matters; but said that such technical matters should be seen as quite separate from teaching union representatives. As one union official put it during a dispute in 1976 over training responsibilities with an engineering company, 'We can't rely on the company to tell our people all they ought to know. Proper safety measures cost money which a company could be reluctant to spend.'

The TUC's viewpoint has received the backing of the Labour Government. In the context of the social contract, the TUC pointed out to the Government in 1976 that 'the success of any Government's industrial and economic strategy will inevitably involve the co-operation of trade unions', which would depend partly on 'the extent that trade union activists have a wide understanding of the trade union policy issues and improve their competence in those areas where new responsibilities arise for them'.

Under the Employment Protection Act (1975), employers now have to pay for shop stewards to have time off to take part in trade union duties, which are defined as including industrial relations training 'approved by the TUC or by a independent trade union of which he is an official'. In addition the Government in 1976-7 made available some £1 million for TUC and union-approved shop steward training, not only in the skills that might be needed by worker directors but also in other subjects raised by recent or proposed legislation on employment protection, safety and health, production and investment plans, and pensions. The scale of the TUC's educational work at this time can be assessed by the fact that in the year 1975-6 some 16,000 shop stewards and other union representatives attended 1200 regional day-release courses in co-operation with 150 local educational bodies. And on about one-third of these courses managers spoke as 'guest-lecturers' – under union control.

There were also 3500 students on TUC postal courses, plus a number of other educational projects including BBC television programmes and residential courses at the TUC's headquarters training college. The television programmes are part of the TUC's Trade Union Studies Project set up with the BBC and the WEA and aimed at bringing trade union education free into the homes of trade unionists. It involves over thirty half-hour television programmes spread over three years, backed up by free TUC postal courses. By the end of 1976 the TUC estimated that it had attracted about 20,000 students.

Now union leaders want to introduce a rapid expansion of all sorts of union training, backed with government funds, to meet the demands of industrial democracy.

Research facilities
Research facilities of most unions need to be expanded at least as much if not more than training arrangements because they are already fully stretched with their present work of providing information for pay claims and other routine labour matters. They could not cope therefore even with limited participation schemes, let alone servicing extended collective bargaining or worker director schemes.

Several unions amplify their own services by using a Trade Union Research Unit set up in 1970 at Ruskin College in Oxford under the direction of the College's vice-principal, John Hughes. But although this unit has grown so that it now helps more than thirty unions, plus some national and regional union groupings, it is not equipped to meet the needs of widespread participation. Indeed, the fact that it exists on a staff of only three or four plus some part-timers, with an annual budget of only £30,000 in 1976, illustrates the low priority traditionally accorded by unions to research. The Trade Union Research Unit carried out an investigation sponsored by the Social Science Research Council (SSRC) into trade union research in 1975 which illustrated this problem. The Unit surveyed thirty-eight unions ranging in size from 16,000 members (the Prison Officers' Association) to the TGWU which, with some two million members, is the largest union in Britain. It found that only half the unions with up to 150,000 members had separate research departments although the record was better among the larger unions. In all, there were 24 such departments in the 38 unions surveyed; but they had an average staff of only about 6 each (the actual numbers ranged from 1 to 17). The number of graduates employed ranged from nil to 8 – an average of only just over 2 to each research department.

In its report for the SSRC (called *Trade Union Support for Research)*, the Trade Union Research Unit noted that the broad areas of work covered by the research departments were collective bargaining subjects such as wages and employment conditions (embracing company financial information), general economic and industrial developments, legislative changes, and the preparation of evidence for government inquiries. Various union publications were also produced, including private research bulletins for the unions' officials and negotiators. It was also found that unions made only a limited use of external research facilities, in addition to the Ruskin unit, and then only for specific projects. For example: ASTMS used the industrial sociology unit at London's Imperial College in 1971 to study Rolls Royce redundancies; Warwick University academics have done work on the efficiency of the national executive of UCATT (the construction union) and on the organisation of the National Union of Public Employees; and USDAW (the shopworkers) used PA Management Consultants to look into the sugar confectionery industry.

But such external projects are generally rare, and the broad spread of the research facilities reported in the Ruskin survey demonstrated the unions' limitations. Now however unions are beginning to show a new awareness of the need for research help. This new interest springs partly from their lack of resources showing up glaringly on various occasions in recent years. For example, when Mr Wedgwood Benn, as secretary for industry, set up a series of inquiries in 1974 and 1975 into ailing companies such as British Leyland, Alfred Herbert and Ferranti, it quickly became clear that the trade unions involved could not always be relied on to put forward cogent evidence – partly because they did not have the research facilities needed and partly because they found it difficult to harmonise their inter-union differences and focus their attention on issues wider than short-term job and pay prospects. And now, under the Employment Protection Act, there is a Code of Practice on disclosure of company information to unions, few of whom have the back-up research help or expertise to make good use of the information.

Research carried out by the Trade Union Research Unit for the SSRC on the way trade unions acquire and use company information also points to a lack of comprehension among both shop stewards and union officials over what use can be made of such information. Ruskin researchers have looked at the use of information by the TGWU in Leyland Cars, by APEX (the clerical workers' union) at Lucas headquarters in Birmingham, by the ISTC (steel trades) in Ebbw Vale, and by the National Graphical Association at Odhams. First results indicate that, when faced with a company ready to hand over information, unions do not know what to ask for. Alternatively, if they are just given the information, they do not know what to do with it. Ultimately this boils down to unions frequently lacking strategies for dealing with situations outside their traditional bargaining areas: and without the strategies they do not know what information to seek. Hence, when one of the unions mentioned was given basic information about the future installation of a computer which would cause some redundancies, it did not know what strategic action to take and so had no idea what further information to ask for. Such a negative position often leads a union lamely to fall back on defensive tactics which finish up with the new machinery being boycotted for a time. So the problem is not only a shortage of researchers in union offices, but also a lack of sufficient general expertise among the unions for them to be able to move effectively and positively into the new areas that the TUC and other major union leaders are opening up for them in different ways.

Although on a slightly different level, the experience of trade unions with the Government's industrial strategy is also relevant. Union representatives – varying from shop stewards to experienced national officials – have sometimes found themselves outclassed on the strategy's individual industrial committees at the National Economic Development Office by the civil servants and trade association representatives. While the unions can sometimes provide a better drilled political force than the other interests, they often lack matching research back-up and expertise. The unions feel that they have less time on their hands than the civil servants and trade association representatives and that they therefore are not always so well briefed; also, the other interests are not always prepared to help by handing over relevant information. The union representatives on these committees are primarily serviced by the TUC headquarters economic department – which is however only twelve strong – and by their own union head offices. This severely stretches both the TUC and the individual unions, and new arrangements will clearly be necessary as participation expands. But many union leaders are not keen on research departments, partly because they can attract left-wing activists and emerge as alternative bureaucratic power centres, sometimes with a dominant personality in charge, vying for power with the union leaders themselves.

Harland and Wolff

One solution to the expertise problem, chosen by the unions and shop stewards at the Ulster shipyard of Harland and Wolff when they started to prepare their worker director plan, was to hire the services of a management consultancy, Compen (NI) Ltd of Belfast. This consultancy prepared a report early in 1976 on the training and expert back-up services – dubbed a 'resource centre' – which it considered would be needed by any Harland and Wolff worker directors. Its recommendations are significant because it was breaking new ground and because it shows the considerable amount of help needed by worker directors, with lower level participation committees, even in one compact shipyard with a labour force of only 10,000. The problems of servicing a company with many different subsidiaries, factories and other operations spread around the country would obviously be much more complex. Compen proposed facilities, funded mainly by the company (but with help from the Government) which owns the yard. Extravagant by normal union standards, Compen said it would cost approaching £40,000 in the worker directors' first year, including an estimated £20,000 fixed annual cost but providing a considerable amount of one-off training to launch the scheme. It suggested that the resource centre should comprise four offices including a library, a conference room and a committee room. The centre would be staffed by a secretary, clerk – typist and training co-ordinator, all working full-time, plus a possible research assistant and a two-day-a-week independent advisor. In addition, specific project research work would, Compen's report suggested, be needed on productivity and manpower planning. The company's newspaper would become the official communication vehicle for worker participation and would accordingly be run by a joint union – management editorial board.

One passage of Compen's report is specially significant because it sets the problem of trying to introduce participative style systems in a collective bargaining arena (see 'Confidentiality and the "balance of power"' later in this chapter), in the context of back-up services:

In identifying the nature of the information which will be required by workers' representatives it is important to recognise that the introduction of worker participation does not remove the right to collective bargaining in specific areas, based on the existing collective bargaining structures. Thus the extent to which information is processed before the unions enter into discussion with management will, in the initial stages of worker participation, depend upon whether or not the subject under discussion has collective bargaining connotations. If the subject under discussion has collective bargaining implications, then it is likely that the unions will want to collect and process the information, which may then not be available from the management, to a stage when they can assess the situation independent of management's views and, if necessary, formulate their own policy for discussion and agreement with management. However, if a subject has no collective bargaining implication, then the processing of the information will be a joint exercise with management to arrive at a mutually agreed policy decision. Thus the unions will, on occasion, require independent resources to assist them in assessing particular situations.

Two examples of the sort of special project work needed because of basic adversary relationships were productivity and manpower planning. As the report said:

All trade unionists in Harland and Wolff seem to believe that the future of the yard lies in significantly increasing productivity. At present they have no confidence in management's assessment of productivity levels nor in existing incentive schemes and therefore they are not in a position to: assess the scope that is available for increasing productivity; justify to their members that the productivity levels required to make the company viable can be achieved.

The report suggested that the issue of productivity pay rises would lead to conflict between workers themselves as well as with management and concluded:

We therefore believe that this crucial area of productivity improvement and its relationship to earnings must be objectively examined so that workers with the yard are able to take a constructive approach to this critical improvement area for the company's survival. It is critically necessary for the success of this project that the assessment is separate and seen to be separate from management resources or the key objective of achieving worker confidence will not succeed.

This view underlines not only the lack of expertise among the union representatives in the shipyard and their need for help, but also the basic atmosphere of deep seated distrust in which one would be trying to build a co-operative company board.

Such resource centres as those proposed for Harland and Wolff will obviously be needed in some form or other. But there are few unions or shop stewards that would trust their new-found strength in the hands of profit-making outsiders, and, significantly, the Harland and Wolff unions decided to have a former shop steward running their centre. Academics might also quickly fall from favour–despite the Ruskin Trade Union Research Unit's growing success and credibility–if it were suspected that they were cashing in on industrial democracy as a new source of personal income.

Sweden

One solution being developed in Sweden is to provide a system of part-time economic advisors–normally accountants. They are hired by the equivalent of a British shop stewards' committee and are paid for by the management. Their job is to advise the Swedish equivalent of shop stewards on company affairs, and they have the right of full access to all the company's books. Although only operating in a few companies at present, the system has been found by the unions to be effective, and in general those managements involved have also found it works well– although they prefer to see professional accountants rather than the alternative, occasionally chosen by a work force, of a more politically motivated union research official or academic.

Management initiatives

The provision of information is an essential feature of any participation scheme which means that managements have to decide how to react to their unions' present lack of expertise because ill-informed workers are likely to have little faith in the blandishments of either managements or shop stewards, and the employee representatives will have little chance of becoming a positive force.

On the one hand managements could adopt a negative stance and try to nullify the participating shop stewards' effectiveness. A company could either just exclude the stewards from effective participation by not allowing a debate to move down from a stratospheric level of specialisation, or it could flood them with so much complex specialist and technical information that they could not effectively master and argue their brief. (When organisations like the Trade Union Research Unit have prepared detailed economic and financial briefs for trade union wage negotiators in the past, it has sometimes been found that the union official can absorb the facts sufficiently to make his opening speech but cannot then cope with the details of the subsequent debate.) On the other hand, a constructive management approach to participation would be to take the opposite course and gradually ease the participation committees into corporate affairs, ensuring that they have the information the shop stewards require, in a form they can understand, and that the debate moves no faster and is no more technical than they can both absorb and take part in. This is an example of how managements can harness participation, including worker directors, for the good of a company.

Union influence and organisation

The question of how the participation representatives are serviced leads on to the issue of the involvement of external union interests in a company's affairs and the need for reform of union structures. Many companies quite understandably fear that their businesses may become the scapegoats of trade union policies and that their employees' representatives on boards or other participation committees may be mandated by their unions to follow certain policies. Such a line could be laid down by a union's annual conference, by its national executive council meetings or by occasionally powerful local union committees – none of which may have any significant interest in the wellbeing of a certain company. The role and policy-making of the AUEW is potentially significant here as an example because of the substantial impact it has across the engineering industry as well as elsewhere. At local level it has powerful district committees which, unlike some other unions, are not only based on a geographical area rather than on a single factory or local industry but also have a significant policy-making function. Thus an employer has often found such a committee laying down policies for the way his AUEW shop stewards conduct their labour relations even though there may be few if any members of his company's work force on the committee. Such a potentially disruptive influence clearly worries companies as industrial democracy spreads. The idea put forward in the Bullock Report for the 'joint representation committee' (JRC), a company-level shop steward committee embracing all the unions in a concern to be responsible for electing, hearing reports from, and mandating board representatives, would help to protect shop stewards on boards and other participation committees from direct control of their union – and would be resented by some unions for so doing.

Authority for shop stewards

This joint committee idea is important for three reasons, and it need not be applied only to Bullock Report ideas because such company-wide co-operation would be needed for any effective and responsible expansion of the unions' role. First, as has just been said, it could act as a sieve protecting companies from too direct an outside influence of individual unions. Second, it would in many cases provide union shop stewards with their first company-wide organisation and so could act as a catalyst for the reform and extension of bargaining and other arrangements. (Some companies do not have formal company-wide arrangements even for union officials, let alone for shop stewards.) Third, it could prove to be a most important catalyst in reducing inter-union friction and increasing co-operation to the benefit of the company. Sceptics could say that trying to put unions together on one committee would sometimes increase rather than reduce the friction between them and indeed, the record of unions trying to form such co-operative structures in areas like the post office, airways and Harland and Wolff has quite often been troublesome.

While managements would usually welcome being protected from too much external union influence and would also welcome any constructive inter-union co-operation, many of them would be less keen about the company-wide developments. This is because many companies often prefer to restrict their company or factory-wide union dealings to meetings with full-time union officials, while shop stewards are restricted to the business of their own individual factories or work areas so that they do not become collectively too powerful and demanding. Union officials often like such a limitation of shop steward power for the same reason. Consequently, several companies officially ignore the existence of company-wide shop steward committees–often called 'combines'. For example, Leyland formally recognised its 'combine' only when it came to set up its 1975 participation scheme.

Broadening the base of participation with shop stewards by whatever means could thus pose a dilemma for managements, who would have to choose between recognising their shop stewards on a company-wide rather than individual-plant basis, and so stand a chance of reaping the benefits of harnessing their combined support for company objectives, or continuing to rely on local and national officials, whose motives may be at odds with the company's interests. In addition, many companies may well prefer to take their shop stewards–who are their own employees–rather than full-time union officials into their confidence on a day-to-day basis. What this probably means is that a progressive management, prepared to try to harness shop steward authority, will see the advantages of legitimising the authority of shop stewards' positive roles in its affairs. The more old fashioned or conflict-ridden employer may try not to recognise the potential authority of his shop stewards more than he has to and will rely, probably somewhat less effectively, for his relationships with the unions on meetings with full-time officials.

For the unions however the more progressive management's initiatives might pose considerable problems of the sort that inevitably accompany the expansion of participation. For example, experiences of two major companies in 1976-7 show that involving senior shop stewards has helped them to introduce important changes. In one case an established policy was amended by the senior stewards whose prejudices on plant-level as opposed to company-wide wage bargaining had changed when their horizons were lifted as they moved from operating on the shop floor into corporation-wide participation affairs. In the other case, a local, hitherto all-powerful district committee of the AUEW was overruled by the stewards–a unique event for that committee. In both these cases the companies have gained, but the union organisation has been left with a problem that could rebound on the companies. In the first example, the problem is how the rest of the shop stewards, who still have only a plant-level rather than corporation-wide job to perform, will react to their senior stewards' new views which will reduce their shopfloor wage bargaining powers. In the other, it is what the AUEW activists would do if many of their district committees were reduced in power. In fact, some AUEW leaders, plus virtually all leaders of other unions, and every employer remotely affected, would welcome the reduction of the AUEW's district committees' powers, which are exercised often in such a way that they serve no one's purpose apart from the internal politicking of the committees themselves. But such a committee's spin-off resentment and attempts militantly to reassert its authority could lead to some major disputes.

So changing the balance of official power and authority within unions in favour of shop stewards would not be easy and could cause major problems. Some unions–on both the right wing and those with strong communist influence–would resent the change because of their primary interest in central control rather than developed shopfloor power. But there is no other easy alternative because there are not enough full-time union officials to operate any sort of industrial democracy procedures, and in any case employers would be throwing away a chance to harness co-operation if they did not decide to base any new methods on shop stewards, probably with full-time officials standing by as expert advisors.

Inter-union co-operation

Another primary effect of bringing shop stewards together on some sort of joint committee would be that the shop stewards from the different unions and factories within a company should co-operate among themselves.

The JRC would thus be a major challenge to unions to sink their traditional and often debilitating inter-union and internal battles in the interests of constructive co-operation. Indeed, if the unions could not show themselves capable of creating and sustaining such co-operation, then claims that they were prepared to, and capable of, adopting new responsibilities with management of whatever sort would sound rather hollow. On the other hand, effective co-operation could turn JRC types of organisations not only into springboards for board representation but also into catalysts for wider inter-union co-operation, starting with a pooling of information and then moving into joint ventures like some already tried in the research and pensions field and, later perhaps, for soundly based union mergers.

Often, in recent years, union mergers have taken place for political or personal reasons instead of being based on industrial logic. And even when they have been mainly industrially based–as in the printing, shipbuilding and engineering industries, for example–craft and political traditions have been carried over from the old unions and have slowed down or even prevented effective co-operation. But it is now possible that there may be a new spate of mergers or joint working arrangements among small and medium-sized unions which have suffered from inflation in recent years and which now will need to revamp their operations if they are to remain viable. This could involve financial costs that they will not be able to afford without raising their membership dues at a rate their members would probably be reluctant to accept, and so they might decide to pool their resources.

The union official

New roles for shop stewards put a question mark over the future function of trade union officials and could also reduce their relative expertise on company matters compared with the shop stewards, who live with the company's affairs every day. In some participation schemes union officials have no central official role to play, and so find it hard when they are expected by the employer or their general secretary to exert some authority over shop stewards because they are no longer as well informed as the stewards. This is a trend that the Ruskin researchers have noticed because of the growing complexity of wage bargaining in companies, quite apart from any growth of new participation in the board room or through extended bargaining.

But the conclusion from this is not that trade unions and their officials could become superfluous – even though any new joint-union structures in the biggest companies might develop over a period into mini-union federations with their own resource centres. The correct conclusion to draw is that, while a stewards' committee could be the catalyst for trade union reform within a company, it should also become the catalyst for union headquarters and regional and local offices to make themselves more expert and efficient so that they are used by shop stewards for research and other professional advisory help and also continue to be regarded as the mainspring of the shopfloor organisation.

Obviously, such a rational situation could not develop immediately; nor, because of the different traditions and situations of the unions themselves, would a uniform pattern emerge across the country. Indeed, there would almost certainly be some serious clashes, which could sour labour relations, between the conflicting interests of shop stewards from different unions as well as between what might sometimes emerge as the conflicting power centres of the shop steward organisation and the union hierarchy. In its report, the Bullock Committee acknowledged that there might well be such acute inter-union disputes among the shop stewards on a committee but added that the existence of its JRC type of body would be a 'catalyst' which would stimulate the changes needed in the machinery of trade unionism if it is to cope successfully with the new issues which are likely to be raised by representation on the Board'. In particular, it would 'fill any gap which might exist in trade union machinery at company level and encourage closer working between trade unions on a wider range of issues'.

Confidentiality

Linked with the problems of trade union expertise and influence is the question of confidentiality and commercial secrecy. Many managements worry that sensitive company information would leak when shop stewards broadcast facts and figures they had been given, not only to their members, but to union committees and research departments and, maybe, even to political and other pressure groups where it would be discussed with, and used by, people with no direct interest in the company.

The balance of power

But perhaps more important than the leakage of commercial information to competitors and other interests is the issue of confidentiality within and between a company and its union activists with the risk, in a board system, that a union-based worker director will feel bound to report back to his stewards. This problem arises from the fact that, however much shop stewards and union officials may participate and co-operate with a management in the running of the business, there will still be the eventual negotiations on wage levels and on other traditional collective bargaining matters for which the negotiators want maximum company information.

This is not therefore an issue of commercial confidentiality, on which most debate has been concentrated and which is examined below, or of the allied subject of whether shop stewards could pass company information back to their unions' offices and research departments for analysis and advice. Rather it is what might be called 'balance of power confidentiality', where the relative power advantages of either side of a negotiating table could be considerably upset – to the unions' advantage – if sensitive company information given to shop stewards in any sort of participation session were used as information on which bargainers prepared pay claims, resisted redundancies or other policies, and decided tactics. This would apply to any participation system, but would be specially relevant with worker directors where all a company's information would, or should, be made available equally to all board members.

It is one thing for a shop steward in such a boardroom situation to agree not to leak the information he has been given outside the company. It is also fairly simple for him to agree not to pass it on either to his fellow shop stewards or to his union researchers or members because of its commercial sensitiveness (though this is less easy when the news is bad and could affect his members' livelihoods). But it is quite another thing when either the worker director himself is involved, or his fellow stewards are involved, in preparing wage claims and perhaps also preparing tactics that could lead to industrial action. Some unions, to protect the integrity of their shop stewards, would prefer that, as has been planned for the Post Office, those who take boardroom seats should give up any negotiating role. In the same vein, some worker director systems abroad, including the union-based arrangements in Sweden, provide for the worker directors to leave the board room when wages are discussed. But these ideas would not entirely solve the problem unless the worker directors or other participators were to be separate from the union organisation.

The point is that any senior participation shop steward, and especially a worker director, will have sensitive information that could affect union negotiators' decisions. This could concern wage issues such as contingencies for high wage claims contained in a financial plan; or it could be the details of the timing of deliveries on a company's order book, which would show how vulnerable or otherwise it is to a strike: unions in the motor industry in particular are well used to finding that militancy suddenly lands them unexpectedly in a long strike because the employers' order book is low or there is a shortage of motor components from suppliers. Then there are especially sensitive areas such as redundancy and closure plans, and linked with this is the fact that a worker director should know whether or not the management is crying 'wolf' when it says a strike could force it to close a plant or switch investment or production abroad. He will also know what defensive plans the management is capable of preparing.

Now the advocate of worker directors will reply to these problems in two ways. First, if he believes in total co-operation, he will say that employee participation is intended to replace conflict with co-operation and that the characteristics of a company will consequently change, so that there is no longer a 'balance of power' issue to be faced. Second, the more political union advocate will say that it is only right that the 'balance of power' should be changed in the workers' favour and will point out that it is public policy, now contained in the Employment Protection Act's Code of Practice, for more information to be handed over to union bargainers. In any case, he will add, a company run in the joint interests of the shareholders and employees should not keep other than the most sensitive commercial secrets from either group. In practice however, while each of these answers has some validity, the bargaining base of British industrial relations will continue for the foreseeable future, so the 'balance of power' issues that it causes will make confidentiality a highly contentious issue.

Commercial secrecy

The more commonly discussed aspect of the confidentiality issue stems from leakage of information outside the company; for example, it has been suggested that union officials might pass on one company's secrets to another. Although most union representatives would dismiss this as so unlikely as not to be worth considering, some companies claim to have had experience of a local union official passing information to a rival concern. Usually this seems to have been done with neither a criminal nor a malicious intent – that is, the information was not being paid for and the union official was not trying to score one company off against another. It seems more likely to be a matter of a union official boasting about the amount of information that one company gives him, partly to boost his own morale but maybe also to encourage the other firm to give him similar information.

Clearly, the issue of the leakage of sensitive information is potentially most serious when facts are not being restricted to the company's own shop stewards but are being passed out for research help or as part of a policy debate within a trade union. This could happen for example if policies on redundancies within an industry were being considered by a union's leaders. It is a problem that arises whatever sort of participation or extended collective bargaining takes place but is obviously most potent with a worker director system. The Bullock Committee however was persuaded by evidence it received that such problems need not be too serious; and after some of its members had visited Sweden and Germany and had found that breaches of confidentiality were rare it reported:

We were told in Sweden that confidentiality had seemed a major problem when the experiment with employee representation on Boards started in 1973, but that management's fears had proved largely groundless. Most companies had developed a satisfactory and workable system for deciding what was confidential before employee representatives on the Board reported back to their constituents. The employee representatives and the chairman or managing director spent a short time after the Board meeting discussing and agreeing what could be reported back and what was confidential: both sides appreciated the value of such a system. At one company we visited the management and employee representatives distinguished three stages of confidentiality: information which could not be released out of the Boardroom; information which could be discussed with one or two senior officials; and information which could be passed on to the trade union committee and to the union members.

Although such a rational solution may stem partly from the fact that at shopfloor level the Swedish unions are not so conflict-oriented as British unions, it does point to a logical method of sorting out who can be given what information. In practice, many poor British managements hide behind the secrecy issue – and behind Stock Exchange rules about no one being allowed information before shareholders – in order not to have to hand over information which they regard as one of their weapons in the balance of power between the company and its unions. Such an approach would not be a sound base on which to build a new participative atmosphere, and in any case the Stock Exchange restriction would presumably disappear if the legal standing of employers' interests were changed (Chapter 16).

There would still however be a problem about too much potentially sensitive information ending up in union and academics' research departments because they could grow into the powerful position of holding secret information about competing companies. But shop stewards committees' own research arrangements – like the Harland and Wolff idea, could overcome this.

A company that uses such problems about confidentiality to limit what it discloses will risk wasting the co-operative mood that it could be harnessing. Any form of employee participation has to start with and be based on a principle of maximum disclosure of useful and relevant information by the company to its employees and their representatives (see Chapters 10 and 11). This is because, without such information, the employees will not understand the company's affairs sufficiently for their representatives to take a constructive approach to their new joint responsibilities with management – whether these responsibilities stem from boardroom seats or extended bargaining powers does not matter, because both forms of industrial democracy need well-informed worker representatives.

Conclusion

How companies, their employee representatives and the trade unions cope with the sorts of basic changes implicit in industrial democracy cannot be forecast. Much depends on the attitudes of industrialists and managers, which are considered in the next two chapters. What is already clear however is that some national union leaders in the TUC have pushed industrial democracy, and especially the worker director idea, so hard and fast that they have faced a credibility gap opening up between the policies of increased power and responsibilities that they are advocating and the interest, willingness and ability to cope of individual unions, of union officials, and of shop stewards.

Chapter 8

Employers:
The Industrialist, his
Company and the Manager

While the TUC and some union leaders have been pushing ahead in recent years with their demands for various forms of industrial democracy, Britain's industrialists have been slowly shifting their ground on how they treat their employees. In most cases they have done this because they have seen it as the only course for them to take against the background of political and social changes, including the EEC slowly evolving an employee participation policy, all three of the largest British political parties considering new participation ideas, and employees themselves no longer being prepared unquestioningly to accept autocratic management styles.

There is however an undercurrent of acute scepticism among managers about whether their primary job of running an enterprise will be made easier or more efficient if the people they manage are given a larger say over how their working lives are organised, particularly when the issues of trade union involvement and especially worker directors are included in the debate. The best of Britain's managers will approach the problem from the practical shopfloor aspect of asking which sort of management – worker relationship will produce their goods in the most effective way.

Legitimacy of management

Recently part of the interest in industrial democracy has stemmed from a lack of faith among employees in the abilities of management to manage. This has arisen against a background of poor management performance with a number of companies failing to cope with both large and small problems across a wide field stretching well beyond labour relations. There have been spectacular company failures resulting from bad technological, financial and general administrative decisions, and certain managements have deservedly got a bad name. So it is hardly surprising that, at the same time as companies have been recognising the need to take more account of their employees, managements have come under attack for their performance. Sometimes they have lost the confidence of their increasingly better educated and more acquisitive employees. They have been in danger therefore of losing their authority to manage because their lack of ability has also coincided with disenchantment over the workings of the mixed economy.

The Bullock Report not surprisingly seized on this for its own purposes and talked in terms of risks for the 'legitimacy of the management function'. It noted that in evidence it had received many employers had argued that worker directors would slow down decision-making, impair efficiency, and de-motivate managers. It then said:

At the other end of the spectrum is the view that employee representation on Boards would not only improve efficiency but is indeed essential to developing new forms of co-operation between labour and capital and a new legitimacy for the exercise of the management function which are needed if Britain is to overcome its current industrial and economic difficulties.

Something approaching this view was put to the Bullock Committee by British Leyland, which finished its evidence by saying: 'Appropriately nurtured not the smallest, although surprising, fruit of a natural growth of industrial democracy in the UK might be to relegitimise the job that managers do.'

The Bullock Report went on to endorse this view and argued for what might be called a new legitimacy of consent to be given to the workings of a company. This approach merged views held by Lord Bullock himself about the need to give a new and genuine respectability to the mixed economy, and by other members of his committee about the possibility of giving line managers a new basis for their authority. Management by consent would, it was felt, satisfy these needs by shifting the employees' representatives into the boardroom power centres of decision-making, so removing or at least lessening the shopfloor conflict about those decisions – an argument that can of course be applied to other forms of participation, not just worker directors.

It is hardly surprising therefore that the issue of giving positive power and responsibility to employees through the trade unions and their shop stewards strikes deep emotional chords in companies. This is because the whole subject impinges not only on the question of industrial efficiency but on traditional relationships and attitudes based on social classes and industrial hierarchies and on the relative powers and responsibilities of these different groups. These tensions have up to now been vented through industry's labour relations conflicts, a situation that constructive industrial democracy is intended to change because it involves the industrialists and employers and managers handing over some of their positive power to shop stewards, who in turn adopt new constructive attitudes towards the running of a business by co-operating in coping with day-to-day decisions and problems.

Management and conflict

But there is considerable doubt about whether such an ideal course is possible within a status-conscious industrial system. The significance of the tradition of conflict and the problems it causes are realised by some of the most competently managed companies just as much as by leading trade union activists. This was demonstrated by two companies' evidence to the Bullock Committee. Both, interestingly, were from powerful foreign-based multinationals which have proved themselves sometimes to be more competent than their British-based counterparts at facing up to the realities of Britain's industrial relations and at not fudging the issues involved.

First, Philips Industries said what many other companies would rather not admit:

We believe that the UK is a more 'class conscious' society than other countries in ways which are significant to industry. There is a real difference between the outlook and values of the so-called 'working-class' and the so-called 'middle class'. There is an identification in people's minds of the 'working class' with the trade unions and the 'middle class' with management (either as a self-perpetuating and, therefore, self-interested body, or as representatives of shareholders). Our experience is that this contributes to a 'them and us' mentality, and is largely responsible for the implicit assumption in industrial relations that in every situation a conflict exists which can only be resolved by 'antagonists'.

Philips said this as part of an argument that such a situation made it unwise to slap a worker director structure on to UK companies. The same point was made in a forceful way from a slightly different viewpoint by Ford Motor:

It is our experience that to achieve increased participation requires a fundamental change of attitudes all round. These attitudes–of hostility, and suspicion, of lack of confidence and trust–are not confined to 'management' or 'workpeople' but apply equally on occasions to sectional groups of management and sectional groups of workpeople, whether organised or not. We do not believe that these attitudes will be changed by any group vilifying or seeking to deny the legitimate interest or function of the other.

A few months before this evidence was presented to the Bullock Committee, Bob Ramsey, Ford's industrial relations director, was outspoken about the realities and historical perspective of shopfloor conflict in a speech (see next chapter) at an Institute of Personnel Management conference in Harrogate:

The 'them and us' division in Britain lies pretty deep. Although the industrial revolution benefited us enormously in giving us a head start on other nations in terms of economic progress, it gave us an appalling burden in terms of social relationships. This is because it produced an employing class with attitudes, at that time, so devoid of any social conscience that it developed amongst the working population a distrust of owners and managerial classes which has lived to this day and which shows no sign of disappearing. In the process it bred attitudes amongst working people of antipathy, not only to the men concerned, but to the objectives of industry and all that it stood for. These attitudes again have survived to the present day . . . . What compounds our British problem is that our divisiveness takes unique forms not met elsewhere . . . . Most nations do not see industrial relations as an hour-to-hour and day-to-day power struggle between representatives of management and labour, to be played out as a continuing dog-fight on the factory floor. They see industry ticking over to a highly organised and regular rhythm of production.

Property and managerial rights
Against such a background, many managements have not developed a confident basis on which to face up to such challenges of participation and do not know how to react to their unions' gradual assertion of what might be called the 'employees' right to participate'. Often, faced with this, management fall back on to their more traditional and defensive cries about the rights of ownership and management and the horrors of trade union power. The idea of 'managerial rights'–although often replaced now with the concept of 'the ability to manage'–is scarcely dead. Indeed,

the Engineering Employers' Federation, the biggest employers' industrial grouping in the country with about five thousand companies employing two million workers, had as the first clause of its trade union procedure agreement from 1922 right through till 1971: 'The employers have the right to manage their establishments . . . .'

The preoccupation with such an idea was explained by Eric Wigham in his history of the Federation, aptly called *The Power to Manage*. A major function of the Federation was, he said, the 'preservation of the power to manage', and he added:

It is not difficult to find reasons for the preoccupation of engineering with their management rights. Their industry above all other has been characterised by continual growth and change . . . . If an employer is hindered from rapidly bringing in new machines and techniques, or from using them effectively, he is at once placed at a disadvantage with his competitors at home and abroad. The problem has not of course been confined to engineering. Other industries have from time to time had similar struggles. But because of its size and importance, engineering naturally had to bear the brunt of the battle and over the years has set a pattern which others have followed. A factor in the background at every testing time, though its importance is hard to assess, is the fear that union intervention in the workshops is a stage on the way to socialism and the sweeping away of private employers altogether . . . . When the negotiations for a new procedure agreement [to replace the one quoted above] were begun in 1970, Labour Ministers had been talking sympathetically of workers having a share in control. Worker directors had been appointed in the steel industry and further experiments in the same direction were proposed for the ports. Employers noted with suspicion that Hugh Scanlon, president of the Engineers' Union, and Jack Jones, general secretary of the Transport and General Workers' Union, were prominent in an organisation called the Institute for Workers' Control . . . . [Wigham, 1973]

Eric Wigham here was embracing both the older reactions to traditional sorts of union power–spurred by the views of owners of businesses–as well as the fears of industrialists that the Labour movement ultimately would not only try to interfere with their right to manage but also with their shareholders' right to ownership. Originally the fear was of nationalisation only, but now this ownership factor–known sometimes as the property rights of shareholders–has arisen in the worker director debate.

The ownership worry emerged in some evidence submitted by companies to the Bullock Committee because the TUC's original claim for 50 –50 representation on a board holding a superior position to the shareholders' annual meeting would have meant that shareholders' rights of ownership of a company would be superceded by the power of the joint board with its worker directors. As Unilever told the Committee:

Supervisory Boards with 50 per cent trade union representation would create a situation where shareholders would no longer be able to exercise the degree of control over their property which up to now has been their right. This opens up a fundamental debate on property rights which we believe is far away from the realities of the next steps to be taken in this country to increase employee participation.

(The Bullock Report attempted to take care of this in its proposals, which in any case watered down the 50–50 formula for the board, by reserving for the shareholders certain rights to do with ownership.)

During the mid-1970s however this property rights argument has lost a lot of its punch with many but not all industrialists, partly because, as has already been said, the nature of company ownership has changed. A few companies even formally say that they base some of their main commercial decisions as much if not more on criteria such as the ability to stay in business and keep employees in employment than on the size of surplus profits and the next shareholders' dividend. Philips developed this point in its evidence to the Bullock Committee and emphasised that in a situation where employees as well as investors become involved in company decisions, the company's objectives may increasingly come to be 'defined as one of maintaining long-term employment opportunities consistent with a rate of return to investors commensurate with the risk involved'. Philips also illustrated its existing concern for maintaining employment as well as dividends when it quoted the first stated objective of its Dutch parent, N.V. Philips:

The objects of the company are to manufacture and trade in electrical–including electronic–mechanical, chemical and other products in the widest sense, and to do all legal acts pertaining thereto or in connection therewith, including participation and in rendering services to other enterprises. In order to promote the interests of those connected with it the company shall aim at a long-term welfare policy with maximum useful employment.

Philips (which has nevertheless been pruning its workforce in recent years) qualified this in its evidence by adding: 'This does not guarantee that all jobs will be maintained indefinitely, since ultimately the company's viability rests with consumers'.

But this does not mean that all industrialists or managers are yet ready to waive any or all of the issues hinging around the property rights arguments. This is partly because of the way that the job of representing the shareholders' interests has traditionally vested in the top management the right to exercise managerial authority (as the CBI's 1973 report on company responsibilities showed–see next chapter). Ford told the Bullock Committee: 'With management's responsibility for the business go the rights to make all the necessary decisions.' But Ford went on to recognise the reality of this when it said that on matters of employee interest, 'managements nowadays can only exercise their management rights unilaterally . . . at their peril'. However, its assertion of the principle of the basic rights would not remain valid if either or both of two changes often advocated are made–first if employees' interests were given equal rights with shareholders in company law, and second if employee representatives took up seats in board rooms. Even the first, which is far less controversial than the second, would change the statutory basis of 'management's responsibility for the business' on which the rights claim is based. Indeed, the basis of the Bullock legitimacy argument is pinned to changing the basis of ownership which in turn removes unilateral capital-based rights, which in turn (as Philips suggested above) changes the responsibilities and role of management.

Nevertheless, as has already been said, while such issues can be put forward to explain and justify changing the ownership and organisation of industry, the basic problems of managers overcoming the practical troubles of British industry's adversary system would remain for a long time, and little has been put forward in the theories surrounding the Bullock debate to appeal to industrialists or managers on a practical basis.

Hierarchies within management

The mixture of ownership and managerial interests produces differing attitudes among people who are variously grouped at present under the titles of the company, the industrialist, the manager–commonly termed 'employers' or 'management'. At one end of the scale is the self-confident, probably rich, owner–manager of an enterprise, and at the other end is the often financially squeezed, frustrated, status-conscious shopfloor supervisor. Like all other employees, each has his patch in the structure, his own pride, and his own real or assumed status to protect. And each feels increasingly under attack. But the spread of trade unionism in recent years plus the changes inherent in industrial democracy are making some of these groups of people rethink their loyalties even if they are all still united by a dislike of the union power overtones of industrial democracy and maybe of the 1974 Labour Government's social contract.

The different groups cannot be separated into precise categories because they overlap and because an individual can play different roles at different times. But it is still worthwhile looking at the attitudes in this corporate conundrum in order to illustrate the different stresses that exist in industry–stresses that may well increase if basic industrial democracy changes are made and the roles of those involved are consequently altered.

The company

First there is what is called the company. This up to now has been the sole property of the shareholders who, in theory at least, control it through annual and other meetings and by voting directors on to the board. In practice however companies are run by the directors, with little control, vetting or accountability from outside beyond the constraints–sometimes considerable–laid down by company and other laws and dictated by the markets and environments in which a company operates to hire its labour, buy its materials and sell its products and services. It is partly the result of this lack of accountability by board directors to anyone but themselves that has caused many of them to lapse, at worst, into self-perpetuating and often inefficient bureaucracies, showing little if any of the entrepreneurial talents that their supporters claim would be buried by industrial democracy. They have in fact laid themselves open for a takeover by another interest–their employees and trade unions. On the other hand, many of them have changed in recent years–in outward-looking attitudes if not in internal management–and do recognise their wider responsibilities towards society in general and towards their employees in particular (see next chapter). Such companies do not object in principle to the idea of changing the law so that company directors have to take equal account of their shareholders' and employees' interests –while leaving the shareholders in nominal charge. If that were done however (see Chapter 16) the nature of the company as a legal entity would change, and conflicting interests would emerge which, it can be argued, could only be restored by having employee representatives in the board room.

The industrialist

Companies are controlled by industrialists who in this context can best be described as the entrepreneurs, the owner–managers, the top managers of the biggest companies, and those who operate in the representational 'corporate state' world of the CBI and Whitehall described in Chapters 4 and 5. Some of them may be employees, but their instincts and attitudes will be those of employers. Their attitudes towards trade unions and employee participation will be partly governed by a belief that they and their managers, and not trade unions, know what is best for employees, and that managers should not be restricted by union power or hindered by slow moving participation. They will therefore stoutly oppose any institutionalised trade union role in the running of their company's affairs. And, while recognising that perhaps one day ways ought to be found of letting employees influence decisions, many (but not all) of them would foresee no significant place for employees collectively to take part in decision-making, both because they do not see any reason why they should and because, in any case, they consider it would be grossly inefficient. They will also be worried about the practical implications of boardroom or other participation arrangements. The impassioned outcry, violent at times, that was organised by leading industrialists early in 1977 to greet the Bullock Report was the result of this basically practical managerial approach and concern for industrial efficiency being magnified to almost hysterical proportions by a fear of the union power, class and ownership aspects of putting trade unionists in board rooms. The fear was centred on the consequences this would have for the power and success of the private sector shareholder system, its financial and other institutions, the industrialists' own lines and the managers' ability to manage.

The manager

The managerial approach has to do with the practical daily and hourly problems of running a company. It leads on to the third group-managers–who encompass the vast mass of a company's organisers, professional people, specialists and line management. They range from boardroom directors (where they will share attitudes with the industrialists) to supervisors on the shop floor (where they will share some of the attitudes of manual worker trade unionists). They will often quite probably have less confidence than the industrialist that they know what is best for the company and its workers, but, although they have probably not bothered to stop and think about it, their basic instincts will be those of employers rather than employees. Nevertheless, they will generally all be employees–whether they are a finance director or a shopfloor supervisor–and so will find themselves on both the company and employee sides of the fence at different times. But while they may be employees, they tend to view themselves in status terms as being apart from the usually unionised manual and clerical workers who make up the rest of the company's employed work force and with whom they may not easily identify.

Until relatively recently they will not have belonged to trade unions, at least not in the private sector (the public sector is more heavily unionised in these areas). Indeed, managers and their salaried counterparts would probably react against joining a trade union as part of their approach to the role of their job, and many of them will regard unions as negative and militant organisations that only have the effect of reducing people's ability to better their own individual rewards. There will also be resentment about the way industrial democracy can change the balance of power within an enterprise in favour of the hitherto 'lower' manual workers and their unions, who will often not have anything like the commitment to the success of the business felt by the more career-oriented manager. Many managers will also see this power balance change in terms of impairing their own efficiency because of their lack of faith in unions' and shop stewards' ability to shoulder responsibilities, and not in terms of potentially replacing some shopfloor conflict with constructive participation. Their detailed outlook on this however may depend on whether or not they deal with union representatives in their daily work.

At the same time they will be in the cockpit of experiments over Bullock's sort of legitimacy theories because it is they who will have to relearn and improve their techniques and test whether their job gains a new legitimacy that ultimately makes management easier, or whether they run into trouble with employees who become even less willing to recognise traditional sources of authority and whose shop stewards fail to accept new responsibilities.

There is indeed a danger of the manager being lost in the middle of a gradual carve-up of power between the industrialists, the shareholders and the unions. As participation committee systems grow within a company, the manager will have to perform a twin role as both the representative of the industrialists–that is as the agent of capital–and as a participating employee, which could blur his traditional line management accountability. And if a worker director system is involved, he will have to exercise his organisational authority in a new way over fellow-employees who are his equals in that he and they are partners in, and employed by, the joint board. There are likely to be very few managers at any level in Britain fully equipped yet to perform this dual general function effectively.

On the other side of the industrial fence from the unionised manual and clerical workers in the debate on industrial democracy, there are therefore proprietorial, hierarchical and managerial interests, mostly loath, for a variety of different but interconnected reasons, to embrace any catalytic reforms, and generally apprehensive about and jealous of any new industrial power. Despite the fact that some of them are joining unions, their basic instincts are similar to those of the Conservative lawyers in the pamphlet *A Giant's Strength* (mentioned in Chapter 2) because they will resent and want to curb the trade union barons. And if they cannot curb the unions by law–as they have learned they cannot–the last thing they want to have is laws that institutionalise union power into the board rooms and other power centres of industry. It is one thing, they would argue, to have unions operating at a high policy level in the once-or twice-removed stratosphere of government agencies like the Manpower Services Commission; but it is quite another to add a boardroom presence to the union's existing collective bargaining power in companies. Such an attitude does not contradict the general shift in emphasis away from curbing the unions by law and towards absorbing them by giving them responsibilities: it simply means that there are limits beyond which industrialists and many managers are not prepared to go quietly–hence the outcry early in 1977 against the Bullock Report. Nevertheless, almost all of them are employees, and as such are apparently increasingly finding a need for organisations to represent them despite the fact that this may dilute their corporate loyalties.

The manager as an employee

The traditional distinctions between the unionised manual and clerical workers on the one hand and the managerial groups on the other have become blurred in recent years when trade unionism has spread up the social, industrial and professional ladder. This has caused managerial groups themselves to become confused about how, faced with the growing power of the TUC and with their own declining status and living standards, they should assert themselves. As was discussed in Chapter 5, such people have found it impossible to counter the Labour movement with effective overall opposition. In the context of this chapter, which is primarily about industrial as opposed to economic or political democracy and power, they do not know whether to try to win through collectively by becoming trade unionists, or to remain professionally separate, operating as individuals.

A survey of a sample of some 150 Esso Petroleum managers working in the UK in 1976 illustrated this problem but showed that in general managers wanted to maintain their rights to individual expression through the company's line management structures–the traditional vehicle for communication between different management levels. The survey was carried out for Esso under the guidance of Kenneth Adams, director of studies at St. George's House, Windsor, and it embraced managers ranging from front-line supervisors to department heads just below board-level and earning (in the winter of 1975-6) between about £4000 and £20,000 a year.

The survey took place against a background of extensive formal and informal consultation systems within Esso which are being developed to allow employees to have a role in influencing but not making decisions. There are trade union-based joint consultative arrangements for manual workers and employee-based staff committees for non-unionised white-collar workers. The inquiry found that managers considered the manual committees worked well but that the staff committees were not well attended. Significantly, these staff committees did not effectively embrace managers because those earning about £5000 or more preferred not to be actively involved: they either considered themselves to be members of the 'management side', or feared that their careers might be jeopardised.

But the managers were not all satisfied with their lot. On the one hand the report said: 'Without exception, managers believed that line management should be the prime system for communication and consultation within the company. They saw the line system as the most important single management characteristic on which the success of the company depended.' They also believed that the concept of total accountability within the line was 'not only necessary but desirable'–so illustrating a preference for not clouding their responsibilities with new participative decision-making systems.

On the other hand, it emerged that junior managers did not always find that this line-communication system worked well up to their superiors. And the managers also realised that they were sometimes treated less well than other employees:

They saw the company as very ready to consult with hourly paid employees because it had to. They saw it as less ready to consult with non-managerial staff because the same compulsion to do so did not exist. They saw it as not aware of the need to consult managers because it did not have to. These observations were not made with anger or bitterness and were certainly not intended as an argument for the extension of union representation; but they did reveal a genuine need for improved consultation of staff and managers within the line system.

In short, the report concluded, the managers wanted 'a system which enables them better to represent themselves'.

Managers in unions

There have however been fresh pressures on managers in general to come off the fence and join trade unions. These pressures have come about partly because of the powers unions gained through the social contract, including the 1975 Employment Protection Act which gave a wide range of advantages to union members. There has also been the spectre of the unions gaining sole responsibility for exercising employee influence in the running of pension schemes and for operating worker director schemes. In order to have a say over such personal and company affairs, managers in many companies have therefore started to consider whether they ought to join a trade union. (Such ideas also received something of a boost when the Conservative Party took a new interest in trade unionism in 1976 and suggested that Conservatives should join their appropriate union and attempt to swing its policies.) It has not been unheard of even for some managers, in private conversation, to ponder whether (showing their employer instincts) they should join a union and try to steer it in the direction that the industrialists running their company would want. On the other hand groups of workers, notably in the white-collar area, have sometimes welcomed their manager members taking an active interest in trade unionism because of the expertise they can bring to bear in dealings with employers. In the clearing banks, for example, managers have sometimes been put up by the union involved as employee representatives.

Until comparatively recently there have been few unions in the private sector actively catering for managers, engineers and technologists. There have been some in the public sector, in industries such as coal and steel and electricity supply as well as in local government and the civil service, where trade unionism reaches as high as a ministry's permanent secretary or a local authority's chief executive. And even members of nationalised industry boards have recently felt sufficiently undervalued to form the Association of Members of State Industry Boards. But in the private sector, apart from one or two distinctive exceptions such as airline pilots, doctors and journalists, there has been little trade union activity above the ranks of clerical and other relatively low levels of white-collar employment.

Trade union expansion

The main growth of general white-collar trade unionism has occurred in the past fifteen to twenty years when unions have cashed in on both the technological switch within manufacturing and public sector industry towards white-collar employment and the changing social attitudes towards trade unionism. The term 'white collar' here embraces workers in technical, clerical, administrative and managerial jobs and it has been estimated that in 1974 there were about 10.4 million such people (including civil servants, who are heavily unionised) in Britain. Of these about 40 per cent (4.3 million) were in trade unions, according to research carried out by two Warwick University academics, one of whom (Professor George Bain) was a member of the Bullock Committee whose report quoted the figures (Price and Bain, 1977). But, since trade unions do not generally grade their members according to jobs, no precise estimate of the number of managers in trade unions exists. However, some government statistics suggest that there are about two million 'managers' in the country (again including civil servants), and it is generally accepted that trade union membership is less prevalent among this group than among the other white-collar employees. Even if one excludes the already unionised civil servants, the company directors (who would rarely be interested), and first-line shopfloor supervisors (who might well already be in unions), estimates still suggest that there are as many as 500,000 managers in the UK ripe for trade union recruitment.

So it is not surprising that, by the mid-1970s, the unions that had established themselves in the white-collar field saw opportunities for pushing upwards into the realms of managerial and professional grades. The Council of Engineering Institutions early in 1976 recommended members of its affiliated professional institutions, who are mostly chartered engineers, to join trade unions, and various unions threw their caps in the ring as the most suitable home for such people, who it is thought total at least forty thousand.

But the conversion to managerial and professional trade unionism has been far from complete, and the British Institute of Management (BIM) for some time has shrunk from advising its members to join unions. Instead, as the main managers' body, it has tried to start representing them within corporate-state types of operations by declaring in 1976 that it was to make itself the spokesman in political and economic affairs for Britain's managers. At the same time it was rivalled for this role by the somewhat more genteel and comfortable Institute of Directors, which decided that what the BIM could do for the employed manager it could do for the entrepreneur and businessman. (The fact that the same industrialists often belong to and head both organisations, while also helping to run the main institution involved, the CBI, was carefully sidestepped in the rush for status in Whitehall.)

To boost its position, the BIM in 1976 shed its charitable constitution, saying this would help it to do its representation job for its 52,000 members. But the dichotomy facing managerial groups remained. The BIM's ambitions illustrate on the one hand the belief that a manager is a somewhat different individual from other employees. This is thought to mean that he does not necessarily need an organisation like a trade union to negotiate with an employer collectively on his and his colleagues' behalf. But, learning from the influence that can be wielded in Whitehall and Downing Street on government decision-making by the CBI and TUC, he does need an organisation collectively to deal with governments.

On the other hand, there is an argument that is put forward by trade unions trying to recruit managers. This is that the manager, engineer and other professional worker does need a trade union collectively to deal for him with his employer and especially to provide him with an industrial democracy voice. And, if this trade union is part of the TUC, then his voice will be heard through that organisation in Downing Street. There are two problems here. One is that the TUC is and will remain oriented towards the interests of its lower-paid general worker members and its slightly higher-paid traditional craftsmen, not towards middle-level salary-earners. Second, membership of a trade union implies a willingness to strike. This argument about militancy has been a major stumbling block among managers and engineers who have traditionally thought they have codes of ethics that would make it unprofessional for them to strike.

There have been some new non-TUC management and staff associations emerging in industry to represent groups who see the need for a collective voice in their company but do not want to go so far as to join a TUC union with its connotations of links with militancy and the Labour Party. The problem for such organisations is that they meet strong resistance from TUC unions and can upset inter-union relationships within a factory because they are always suspect of being company-dominated. While this suspicion is frequently justified, there may be a case for some sort of collective voice to be recognised within a company for participation if not for ordinary trade union purposes. Managers do need a voice as employees in participation and worker director schemes, even though they will also be involved in their managerial capacities.

Their attitudes to trade unions may eventually change, however. The industrial action staged by doctors in the early 1970s proved a watershed on this issue because it showed how the profession perhaps most reliant on a code of ethics could nevertheless withdraw its labour. As a result, engineers and some other groups have sometimes been more willing to look at trade unionism with open minds, and it is partly this that has opened up the new potential trade union recruitment area of professional managers and engineers in the private sector.

But such developments do not change attitudes overnight, so the primary conflict between managers and unions remains. Some trade union leaders claim that clearly discernable changes in attitude are evident among managers once they join trade unions and become part of the collective labour movement of a factory. They say such managers drop some of their status consciousness and are willing to merge their interests with more traditional trade union collective groups. Conversely, it is also sometimes suggested that trade unionism has the opposite effect and makes the unionised manager more status-conscious because he does not want his union membership card to affect his authority.

Trade unionism would be the neatest method of sorting out in which camp the managers and their professional counterparts belong, unless one continues to rely on managers' own participation being through traditional line-management structures. But not all industrialists would welcome trade unions, and many managers themselves would resist it. So the conundrum of whether a manager is an employee or a 'boss' within participation schemes remains, further complicating the problems facing industry with industrial democracy.

Chapter 9

Employers: Company Views and Styles of Management

'A journey of a thousand miles begins with a single step . . . .'
Sir Arnold Weinstock quoting Confucius

Until the necessity to prepare evidence for the Bullock Committee concentrated their minds, there was a lot of woolly thinking in many companies on the issue of employee participation and the associated matters of the role of unions in corporate affairs and management styles. In the postwar years trade unionism spread across industry, and companies became more and more accustomed to operating in a world where the unions wielded a considerable amount of shopfloor power. But few companies gave much thought to a wider positive role for unions or their members, although some did gradually realise the need to try to communicate more with their employees about company affairs, while others had been driven by the conflict traditions of their factories to consider whether there were better methods of running their labour relations.

But generally it was the creation of the Bullock Committee in the winter of 1975-6 that finally jolted many companies into formulating policies. The purpose here, against the background of the different views and interests looked at in the last chapter, is to trace the development in company thinking on industrial democracy through the mid-1970s and then to set this in the context of the need for companies to adapt their management styles to absorb the pressures of participation – which brings one back to the question of the legitimacy of the function of management, in the eyes of employers, discussed in the last chapter.

It had taken some years for many employers to realise that they and the unions were talking about two quite different basic concepts of employee involvement. Put simply, the unions' ambitions to use industrial democracy to change the balance of power in industry are not compatible with industrialists' interests in using employee participation to boost company efficiency, while maintaining the *status quo* as far as possible. Between these two conflicting principles, as usually happens within Britain's system of industrial relations, there is of course a substantial area of potential compromise and co-operation for individual companies and unions to follow. This recognises that the economic and social balance of Britain is changing and that styles of management and union responsibilities also have to change faster than in the past, with both trade unions as representatives collectively and employees as individuals being given more rights and influence in companies. The potential bonus, in theory at least, for the employer in this is that a degree of conflict can be removed from his operations which should make them more profitable. As the

1969-74 legalistic period of industrial relations drew to a close, therefore, a large number of companies eagerly clutched at this new participative panacea for their problems and started to study how it could be implemented without too much upheaval.

Company accountability

At the same time, as has already been mentioned, companies have gradually come to accept in principle that the legal responsibilities of boards of directors should be extended so that directors would have to take equal account of the interests of employees and shareholders (Chapter 16). There has also been a growing feeling in some companies (and elsewhere) that the whole question of corporate accountability should be reconsidered as a general issue. Indeed, ICI told the Bullock Committee that any plans for changes in company law (which would be needed for a worker director system) should take account of the whole question of the general accountability of boards of directors, even though ICI added it thought there was more accountability already than was generally realised.

What seems to be lacking–and it is accepted that this is a cause of some general concern–is a way by which directors can be seen to be carrying out their duty to run the enterprise responsibly and well [ICI told the Committee]. A study is required of changes needed in company law and in the general accountability of Boards of directors (and of those who run other institutions which critically affect the community); this study will be complex and will take time, and it should not be confused with the issue of industrial democracy which is the subject of the present inquiry.

ICI here seemed to be trying (with no chance of success) to outflank the Bullock Inquiry by raising wider issues than the TUC's worker director plans–including possible inquiries into 'other institutions', which would presumably include unions. But the fact that it was prepared to say what it did about company accountability in its evidence illustrates that some companies realise that the trade unions–and others–are on strong ground when they argue that the lack of accountability of companies necessitates reforms.

Earlier, in 1973, the CBI had produced a report which, while far from radical in its proposals, acknowledged that company attitudes and responsibilities had to change. It was prepared under the chairmanship of Lord Watkinson (the former Tory politician, who had experience of employee communication systems in his company, Cadbury Schweppes, and who later became CBI president). Called *The Responsibilities of the British Public Company,* it started by noting:

The sociology of the company has changed. Most directors today are professional managers and have reached Board level through the ranks of management. More and more managers have practical experience on the shop floor and through membership of a trade union. The majority of employees in larger companies are highly organised in a complex structure of trade unions, demanding information and explanations before they consent to decisions to a degree unthinkable in the early years of the century. Shareholders too have changed and the institutional shareholders hold today a much stronger position in most large companies and many smaller ones.

But such a statement of awareness did not mean that the CBI was about to back down on either the ownership or the managerial rights issue discussed in the last chapter. 'None of these developments, in our view, in any way diminishes the authority to be exercised by the owners of the business, namely the shareholders. . . . Private enterprise must be capable of its own self reform,' said the report in a not surprisingly vigorous defence of the private enterprise system and its profit motivation.

The report went on in its section on the company and its employees to say:

We have a difficult inheritance in Britain in the notion fostered over the past century that the employer–employee relationship must be one of conflict and confrontation. This is no longer a viable industrial philosophy, if it ever was, but it will not be swept away until the majority of Boards are far more deeply involved in fostering genuinely constructive relationships with their employees than they are today.

This report was prepared by the CBI's company affairs committee and coincided with parallel work by the employment policy committee which produced, under the chairmanship of Richard O'Brien, then a director of Delta Metal and later chairman of the Manpower Services Commission, proposals for statutorily backed plant consultation councils. However, the idea of the CBI calling for legislation to require companies in some way or other to consult with their employees was too much for industrialists, who threw the idea out at a meeting of the CBI's council a week before the Watkinson Report was launched in September 1973. These were early days in the development of formal ideas on employee participation and worker directors (see Chapter 14), and the industrialists baulked at the idea, firstly because it meant using the law and secondly because they had conflicting loyalties within their companies. On the one hand there were their recognised trade unions–who would want consultation based on their organisations and, quite often, also would want it merged with collective bargaining arrangements. On the other hand the industrialists (as emerged again later in the Bullock debate) were often not willing either to give the unions this sole power or to exclude non-union employees. At the same time, the Watkinson Report came down firmly against worker director ideas of the sort then emerging at the TUC. It pointed out that the right way for workers to join a board was to be promoted on their individual abilities. This avoided the basic point of industrial democracy–to give workers influence over managerial decisions while remaining in their roles as workers, which is quite different from giving them access to be put into management positions on promotion.

Nevertheless by this time, as has already been said, industrialists were beginning to realise the need for a new approach to the role of employees in their companies. This meant that some large companies began to think through how employee participation could best be accommodated into their own styles of business. One or two companies, like British Leyland, were forced by pressure of outside events to embrace the subject more quickly than they might have wished; others were able to develop their ideas more privately and without being distracted by undue publicity. The hopes and philosophies of two of them–GEC and Ford– are spelt out here in detail to show the sort of detailed consideration that some companies were giving to the subject at a high level.

Arnold Weinstock's journey

The first is GEC, whose top eighty managing directors received an unusual and provocative private and confidential memorandum from their main board managing director, Sir Arnold Weinstock, in September 1975 which was aimed at generating a new approach. Weinstock was worried about the way his massive group of 206,000 employees (171,000 in the UK), could be beginning to drift because of its size. He was concerned about how individual factories were managed and accordingly he mapped out a vision of moves towards constructive participation, in a message that was something of an amazing statement from a man more renowned for having an autocratic and withdrawn managerial style than for believing in a participative approach (although none of his managing directors was deceived into thinking that Weinstock's personal style of managing them had changed.) But what his memorandum does show is how one of the hardest-headed and successful industrialists can be fired by the potential of employee participation for improving a company's performance in the interests of its customers, employers and shareholders.

The private memorandum followed a short article signed by Weinstock in his company's newspaper, *Topic,* which asked under the heading, 'Participation: What do you Think?' for views from the company's employees.

To his managing directors however, Weinstock went further and, having referred to the growing debate over worker directors, said:

Our objective is more substantial. We want to build a participative process right through the operations of the company, involving our employees in matters affecting their jobs and in methods, systems and procedures in the factories and offices. They have knowledge and experience, and they have much to contribute. Then we will have a basis on which to build upwards through the organisation in whatever way seems desirable. . . . Effective participation gives every member of the company the opportunity to make the optimum contribution to its well-being and his own. We want our people to be involved in their jobs, to be committed to the company's objectives and to be part of the process by which these objectives are set and reached. Of course, not everybody will want to be deeply involved, but everybody should have the opportunity. That is what participation is about. . . .

Very few working managers would find much with which to agree in the dicta of Mr Wedgwood Benn. But who would dispute his thesis that if the skills, experience and intelligence of workers can be harnessed constructively in the operation of industry, if the attitudes of management and workers can be brought together in effective co-operation, then there would follow a great upsurge in industrial efficiency and a general atmosphere of relative satisfaction. Unhappily, on that constructive basis is built the destructive proposition that the way to do this is by burying all classes except a 'working class' so defined as to exclude millions of working people. This approach masquerades under the label of 'industrial democracy' but there is not much democracy about it and, in the end, there wouldn't be much industry either. It will be a bad job for the British people if that is the best we can do.

Enlightened management and a wider spread of responsibility can bring about a better and more civilised evolution of our industrial society, one which will leave intact freedom of choice and enhance the dignity of the individual. GEC's policy is to strengthen and expand its business for the general good through the development of the new relationships which will provide that better alternative. Thus we may harmonise social advance and business objectives. . . . This requires that we should seek to add to the professional expertise of managers, supervisors and specialists, the vast fund of underused knowledge and intelligence in the company. It is reasonable and sensible to encourage employees to make their views known on every aspect of our activities. Whether sympathetic to our practice or not, we must treat their views constructively, with respect, and see that they are taken fully into account. We must consider their opinions, and consult with them in the formulation and realisation of company plans.

We must dedicate ourselves with renewed vigour to the service of our customers and the community, and, by the efficient use of our resources, maintain and build upon our industrial, commercial and financial strength. We must provide the worker with the best equipment to do his job effectively. By engaging his full interest and involvement in the job and in the wider aspects of the company's activities, we must encourage that personal pride in workmanship which will lead to ever increasing standards of quality, reliability and speed of delivery of the company's products and a greater sense of fulfilment for the worker himself. We must provide training of all kinds so that workers may fully understand what they are doing and why they are doing it; and we must give them every opportunity to play their part with management to get things done better.

Weinstock then looked forward to employees playing their full part in trade union and community affairs and to 'simple and uncluttered consultative machinery' being developed alongside separate wage bargaining machinery. New working methods would emerge, he said, and payment systems should be modernised with overtime becoming only an exceptional necessity. GEC should also aim to give people opportunities for greater satisfaction outside their work and in retirement. Weinstock ended his memorandum, having urged his managing directors to start local discussion on the issue, by saying:

This is the constructive way forward, through co-operation and the husbanding of mutual interest. It does not mean that there will not be continuing conflicts of interest. Such conflicts are endemic between groups in all societies. But they do not have to be obsessive and, as they arise, can always be resolved through negotiations by good sense and good will. . . By starting now, we can at least aspire to a more hopeful condition for the future. Confucius said that a journey of a thousand miles begins with a single step. We have taken it. Whether the journey be a thousand miles or a generation, we must see to it that we arrive at the destination of an intelligent and productive harmony.

Needless to say, not all of Weinstock's managing directors thought much of his 'journey' and, although a new detailed participation statement (see Chapter 11) was produced with their assistance five months later, Weinstock (in line with his usual devolved managerial style), did not try to force through massive changes in the way that GEC's factories ran their affairs. Neither did he specially change his own methods of running the business from GEC's Mayfair head office and indeed he pushed through proposals for a major financial reconstruction of the group sixteen months later without even informing – let alone consulting – either his eighty managing directors or the unions: the justification was that neither had the necessary expertise to be able to participate usefully, and that in any case there was a Stock Exchange requirement for secrecy.

The memorandum is significant however not only for its overall vision but because it illustrates some of the continuing views of industrialists over participation. It shows an industrialist's interest in harnessing the enthusiasm of employees direct to the company without at the same time explicitly accepting the trade unions' ambitions for industrial democracy, even though the unions would normally be the vehicles for consultation and participation in GEC. It also shows an interest in letting employees influence decisions, but not make them; further, it wanted to keep the consultation-cum-participation procedures separate from traditional collective bargaining–even though they would both normally still be based on trade unions. Weinstock also chose no single path to participation; nor did he rule any out (and indeed helped the Meriden motorcycle co-operative with £1 million and managerial assistance early in 1977). He would now not even totally reject the idea of worker directors in the future, even though he objected to the Bullock formula because it involved some statutory imposition and could slow up top management decision-making.

Realities at Ford Motor

There was in fact nothing in the Weinstock memorandum that could weaken management's ability to manage. Another company–Ford Motor–produced a similar mixture of vision about the role of companies and employees and hard-headedness about how this could be harnessed within the traditional adversary system of a British car factory. This came in the address by Bob Ramsey, Ford's director of industrial relations, to an Institute of Personnel Management conference in Harrogate in October 1975. First he discussed the legacy of class conflict in industry, and then said that shifts in the balance of industrial power should be accommodated in positive and not negative participation:

Management will have to accept that we are now fully in the age when the individual company is only going to progress, achieve objectives, play its full part in national revival, with the full and willing consent of its employees and their representatives. They must also accept the existence of the tiny but dedicated minority who see such progress as postponing the revolution. They will have to recognise, therefore, that their job as management is no less than a battle for men's and women's hearts and minds, to remove purely obstructive divisiveness and replace it with genuinely based co-operation so that we can play our full part in the world. . . . What we have to do is quite simple. First give employees and their representatives information on the progress and problems of the business. . . . Employees will not believe management just because management tells them what needs to be done. They will only believe management when they can check the facts for themselves. . . . Our second task is to delineate in our minds and in the minds of our employees the areas of future co-operation and conflict. This is most important and the subject of much woolly thinking. We will not eliminate all industrial conflict in a democracy in the next five years, maybe ever. . . . We must see the area of co-operation as all that concerned with getting the job done and the area of potential conflict, and I mean constructive conflict, concerned with the sharing of the wealth created as a consequence. Co-operation in getting the job done means employee involvement at the workplace.

Mr Ramsey saw this as a challenge to build primary working groups of people with common interests whose size could range from 50 to 250 people. The aim of continuing discussion between the supervisors, workers and their representatives in these groups would be 'full employee consent in getting the job done right, recognising that that consent will be obtained in many ways – sometimes by simple instruction, sometimes by instruction plus explanation, sometimes by consultation, sometimes by negotiation and sometimes by the establishment of respected departmental procedures for coping with regularly recurring changes of situations'.

These quotations, drawn from a long and somewhat provocative address, show both a mixture of optimism about the potential of new workplace relationships, and an acceptance that in the conflict-ridden traditions of a tough car factory it would be futile suddenly to introduce participative arrangements and expect the attitudes of workers and managers and shop stewards and trade union officials to change. This was underlined when Ford said five months later in its evidence to Bullock:

Whatever social system develops in the future someone will always need to make decisions and others at least acquiesce in their implementation. . . . It is our view that the facts of the industrial situation dictate that increased participation, apart from fulfilling social objectives, is a question of managing the realities of the distribution of power in industry so that the interests of the various groups involved are properly reconciled, thus ensuring the uninterrupted pursuit of industry's prime objective: that is the efficient creation of wealth in the interests of the community as a whole.

So Ford, rather like union leaders such as Frank Chapple of the Electricians, does not want to introduce procedures that might falsely be expected to replace collective bargaining but which in fact could blur relationships and cause chaos. What it would rather do, as Mr Ramsey said, is gradually to introduce a variety of changes aimed at improving workplace relations. Because of its tough labour traditions, Ford was also more outspoken than many companies about the problems of soft approaches to participation; but its sentiments have been echoed in various ways by other companies which are also prepared voluntarily to give their employees a greater say, but not at the cost of efficiency. However, Ford went further than most when it posed the question quoted in the introduction to this book about whether the unions wanted their role to be one of 'constructive opposition' or 'full coalition partner' – on the premise that nothing could be decided on industrial democracy till this answer was clear.

CBI policy develops

Various major companies made a series of policy statements about participation in general during the course of their evidence to the Bullock Committee, all of them containing sentiments and intentions about involving employees that would not have been aired a few years earlier. Their developing views were brought together for the first time in a policy document by the CBI in February 1976 which advocated what it called statutorily backed 'participation agreements' to be negotiated by large companies within a set period. This document in effect started where the CBI's earlier efforts had left off in 1973, but also was partially based on a British Institute of Management report called *Employee Participation: A Management View,* which was produced in 1974 by a working party under the chairmanship of R. E. Cotton, chairman of Samuel Osborn & Co. Ltd. Although the CBI document was hardly a trail-blazer in terms of employee participation practices, being something of a lowest common denominator of all CBI companies, it was important because it represented a collective view which all four hundred members of the CBI's council, plus its regional and small firms organisations, had been willing to accept. It thus showed how far opinion and a realisation of participation pressures had shifted in the two and a half years since September 1973.

The document condemned the TUC's worker director policy for being a set of 'extreme proposals' aimed at achieving worker control rather than employee participation. What the CBI favoured–and its views have been echoed since in varying forms by countless companies–was participation arrangements, probably involving special committees, and usually separate from collective bargaining with objectives far removed from the TUC's ideas. The objectives laid down by the CBI for example centred on only communication-style exercises aimed at 'promoting understanding' and making employees aware of the reasons for decisions that affect them–which is quite different from letting them participate actively in influencing or making decisions, let alone giving them an equal say.

Nevertheless, despite its limited targets, the CBI's stance was a major advance in collective employer thinking, especially because it envisaged (albeit without spelling out the problems of legal enforceability involved–see Chapter 10) legal requirements for large companies to negotiate participation agreements with their employees.

Styles of management

Whatever good intentions may be voiced by their top executives, however, many companies in Britain today are still run in non-participative, autocratic and paternalistic styles of management, limited in personnel terms only by the unions' bargaining powers. This is because, even in companies run by forward-looking industrialists, there will inevitably be managers who resent ideas of participation and want to be left alone to run their workers, and there will be many more managers at all levels who will not understand or willingly accept participative concepts, sometimes because of their past problems with the unions. It is in fact at the levels of middle and junior management, down to shopfloor supervisors, that participation will face its stiffest tests and is most likely to founder. There is a parallel here with the strains, already mentioned, on the shop steward in a highly developed participation scheme. Just as such a shop steward has to withstand conflicting participation and shopfloor pressures, so the nearer one gets to day-to-day or even minute-by-minute problems of decision-making and managing people, the harder it can be for managers to cope with the pressures of all the paraphernalia and changes involved in participation methods.

Despite all the shouts of horror from industrialists about worker directors, it may indeed be far easier for a company to assimilate (or even bypass through managerial reorganisations) industrial democracy into its once-a-month board meetings than into daily life on the shop floor. This is partly because, unlike in the board room, it is not very easy to divert decision-making away from the shop floor without anyone realising; and partly because of the often jealously guarded autonomy of the workplace manager who may resent participative changes, whether he is a supervisor on a factory assembly line or the manager of a local bank. In both situations companies report cases of men who have worked hard, possibly till approaching middle age or even retirement, for a job with some responsibility, prestige, power, and access to privileged information. Not surprisingly, these people resent having this authority whittled down by what to them is an unexpected and unwarranted change. They do not, therefore, want to allow their subordinates to participate in the decisions which they had always assumed would one day be theirs alone to make and execute, subject only to traditional trade union activities. Nor do they want union-led campaigns to change their workplace habits of a lifetime. Experience in British industry and commerce also shows that such managers sometimes do not willingly pass on information – partly because possession of information is itself a form of power and status. Such managers can in fact fuel the element of conflict in industrial relations by building their own versions of the 'them and us' on a hierarchical basis into their own areas of work.

A step at a time

It is extremely unlikely that the changes that would be required of managers could happen quickly, and this is in fact one of the strongest reasons for not pushing ahead too fast with compulsory changes towards industrial democracy, especially those that alter the nature of company operations. What 'too fast' is will of course vary from company to company. Some companies are fairly well advanced with communication and participation methods and could probably (although they would not admit this willingly) absorb statutory requirements, even on the Bullock pattern, without too much trouble. But this does not mean that they as companies are suitably equipped at all levels of management, and both GEC and Ford had passages in their evidence to the Bullock Committee that showed they realised the problems. GEC bluntly stated: 'Managers will need the goodwill of all concerned if they are to succeed. They need also to cultivate the humility and honesty to recognise this, and seek help from anyone who can render it.' Ford said: 'Management at all levels has to come to terms with the fact that it can no longer manage in the style to which it had possibly been accustomed for decades. Many supervisors, although trade unionists themselves, would find participation unfamiliar and uncomfortable'.

Education and training

The problem this creates for companies in the future has yet to be realised by many industrialists. It means that a widespread and detailed education and training exercise would be needed among all levels of management. It is no good simply telling a manager or supervisor that he has to deal with a participation committee, or negotiate with a shop steward before making a decision, or cope with the foibles of a worker director and expect him to operate efficiently. He may indeed not even carry out his operations willingly, let alone efficiently, because he may well not be convinced that such a dilution of his managerial autonomy is in fact a good idea. So the manager would need to be educated and persuaded, just like the shop stewards to operate in a new environment and to accept participative changes in his managerial style, whether or not there are worker directors in his company. At first this may not be a question of training him in new management techniques but rather a matter of expanding his knowledge and appreciation of the changing world outside the factory workshop or office block that may form the limits of his interest. This is commonly called management development, and a variety of money-spinning schemes have been developed by consultants and academics over the years to provide this sort of mind-broadening for the best managers who are potential candidates for promotion: the difference now is that this sort of exercise is needed for all levels and qualities of management, whether they are likely to be promoted or not. Only when they have been won over will they be anywhere near prepared to cope constructively and efficiently with the changes, because far more skills are needed to manage participatively than in an authoritarian or weak style. Detailed training may then be needed, ideally on courses run jointly for both shop stewards and managers, although the TUC's policy on shop steward training can make this difficult.

Leyland's troubles
Two experiences at British Leyland in recent years show the damage that can be done when worker-orientated reforms are introduced without sufficient prior preparation of shopfloor management. The first occasion was in 1971, when Leyland replaced a piecework pay system with measured daywork at its Cowley plant in Oxford to launch its Marina models. This meant that the cash incentive contained in piecework was to be removed. The company, desperate to make the switch in time for the launch, did not leave itself enough time to retrain its shopfloor management in the art of ensuring that production targets were met without the piecework 'carrot'. The result was that the shopfloor supervisors were not up to the task of switching from just being progress-chasers to being managers, so production targets were not met. The second occasion was very similar and involves Leyland Cars' participation committee system (Chapter 11), which was introduced after the Ryder Report had bailed the company out late in 1975. The bottom tier of these committees was based on the factories; but one of the problems of the scheme was that not enough was done to train the shopfloor management in the art of running their assembly lines alongside the new participation committees – or even to persuade them that such participation might be a good thing. As a result intense bitterness grew up in some plants.

One view of this was given in an article in the *Financial Times* on 17 December 1976 by Bill Roche, a senior Cowley shop steward who was also the joint secretary of Leyland's top-tier participation car council as well as being a national executive member of the TGWU. 'With the best will in the world, the management see their traditional role and authority eroded', he wrote:

Then participation came along and it is my belief that, after the initial burst of enthusiasm, a cold reality took over. Years of 'divine right to manage' were being challenged because a sharing of responsibility with shop floor workers, through the union representatives, could mean a reduction of management authority and status. This was coupled, I believe, with a general management view that participation cannot work. So the gradual process of entrenchment began, accompanied I regret to say, in some areas by a positive resistance to the principle and ideals of participation. The result was that some groups of managers opted out and reverted back to their traditional roles. We must therefore ask how one can expect the worker to respond to his supervisors' demand for change knowing that the supervisors are not prepared to do likewise. Because the expected change in management attitudes did not materialise, the workforce became disillusioned. . . .

A new 'legitimacy'

This account spells out quite clearly what is likely to happen in many factories if managers are expected to move too quickly from old-style conflict relationships, gilded with some limited consultation after the managerial decisions have been made, to anything like the full participation in decision-making implicit in a worker director system. It is in fact an excellent example of the problems that can ensue when one tries too quickly to clamp a participative framework on to a bargaining system.

However there is the alternative argument, propounded in the Bullock Report, which is based on the theory that participation gives the function of management a new legitimacy and therefore new effectiveness. It was expounded in December 1976, when the Bullock Committee was putting the final touches to its report, by Albert Booth, the secretary of state for employment. Addressing an Industrial Society conference in London, he went so far as to suggest that participation might actually make managers' jobs easier:

Increasingly it is a manager's role to lead and motivate his workforce, to gain their co-operation by explaining company policies, and to reach agreement with them on how these policies should be put into effect. At present this task is the more difficult because workers have no prior commitment to these policies. With workers represented on the Board and involved in policy formation, employees will be less suspicious of new policies and more willing to co-operate with managers in deciding how they should be implemented. . . . Managers should find their role less and less that of policemen. They will have a key role in establishing and maintaining the new machinery throughout their organisation. . . . Greater understanding and better decisions will promote a greater spirit of co-operation at all levels of the company. The workers will be more committed to company goals which they have helped to formulate and the authority of managers to operate towards these goals within agreed policies will be strengthened.

When this sort of argument started to emerge from the Bullock Committee supporters, some industrialists countered with a claim that British management was about to take a major leap forward in professionalism and competence. They suggested that a new breed of highly competent young managers were now working their way up company structures, and that these men would provide their own managerial revolution without the potentially de-motivating inefficiencies of worker directors and the rest, which would therefore be proved to be unnecessary and counter-productive.

On the other hand, because of Britain's changing social attitudes, it could be argued that the current generation of young managers may well be less hide-bound about union power and employee rights than their predecessors. They may therefore not regard worker directors and participation committees with the same horror as do their predecessors, although that is not to say they would welcome the overtones of union power. So if there is a new breed of highly competent managers now emerging, they may well not be de-motivated by industrial democracy and may indeed see the challenge in absorbing it into their factories. This could pose an interesting responsibility for older industrialists and managers because it is they who have the chance to help create the environment in which such new young managerial views can prosper, rather than encourage a continuation of their own generation's inheritance.

So the participation issue can be seen by management either as a perpetual stumbling block, forever impeding managerial rights and abilities, or as a catalyst for the changes that Britain's frequently poorly managed industries desperately need. One of the problems however of a subject like participation suddenly moving into the fashionable spotlight is that it is seized on by less efficiently managed companies as a panacea for all their ills – the debate about strike laws of the late 1960s served the same purpose. The result is that managerial time and energy can be diverted from real day-to-day organisational problems; facades are built on glib formulae which do not withstand practical usage; and the innovation – be it strike laws, participation or whatever – withers from over-exposure and misuse. In the context of the current grasping of employee participation, this means that many companies – egged on by consultants, politicians and others – may invent procedures and institutions like participation committees and even worker directors, that will not have been properly thought through. As a result, both established management structures and established employer–trade union relationships will be disrupted because effective participation will first change the way line-management operates and will second need, at least to begin with, to work alongside or in with established collective bargaining.

Badly designed and half-hearted participation systems foisted on companies by poor managements as tokens of advance or as hastily designed palliatives could do immense harm and create more problems than they could ever solve – in fact, instead of providing a catalyst for improvement, they could make bad management worse. But this is not an argument for managements to resist participation; rather it is an argument for companies constructively to do what the Weinstock journey called 'harmonising social advance with business objectives'.

Chapter 10

Methods of Participation

One of the practical problems about the debate on industrial democracy and employee participation is that the terms used to describe worker involvement in industry mean different things to different people. The purpose of this chapter is to try to sort out some of the definitions and to assess what they each involve in terms of traditional labour relations and in terms of more recent innovations under the broad heading of 'employee participation'. The potential influence and impact of these different aspects of participation – including worker directors in the UK and elsewhere in Europe – needs to be judged against the conflicting ambitions of British trade unions to extend their members' power over the making and implementation of corporate decisions and the industrialists' and managers' wish generally to slow down such a development.

There are sharp literal differences between terms such as 'participation', 'consultation' and 'bargaining', which become blurred in practice. This is well demonstrated by dictionary definitions. The *Oxford Dictionary* defines the word 'consult' as: 'Take counsel (with); seek information or advice from (person, book, etc.); take into consideration or do one's best for (persons' feelings, the interests of, etc.)'. This definition, emphasising the advisory nature of consultation, is in sharp contrast to the same dictionary's more challenging definition of 'participate': 'Share in by common action or position or by sympathy (Ip. your labours, suffering, joy); have a share (in things with people)'. The use of the words 'common action' is significant because it underlines the partnership nature of the exercise and has connotations of people sticking together, unlike the same dictionary's conflict-oriented definition of 'bargaining': 'Haggle, dispute (with persons over terms)'.

The wider implications of 'industrial democracy' emerge with a definition in an industrial relations dictionary as: 'An expression with a number of meanings and usages all concerned with the role and status of workers in industrial society and all implying, to a greater or lesser extent, the participation of those who work in industry in determining the conditions of their working lives' (Marsh and Evans, 1973).

General terminology

The two basic terms used in the current UK debate on the subject are 'industrial democracy' and 'employee participation', and both at least partially entail involving workers more in business affairs and improving

123

industrial efficiency. The first is generally preferred by trade únions and the Labour movement to indicate a sharing of power, with unions claiming a right for their members to what they regard as an industrial equivalent of the political democracy that runs the country. This means that they would have a right to elect representatives to run their companies, so that trade union activists would establish methods–through worker directors, extended collective bargaining or other means–of jointly controlling with management the corporate decisions that affect peoples' working lives. Sceptics however question whether workers would then respect the authority of the decisions reached in the same way as they broadly accept parliamentary authority.

There is an essential element of joint control involved in the concept, although in the debate of the mid- and late 1970s this does not usually mean full worker control. This is because it is accepted that the greatest power the unions would have would be for their representatives, jointly with shareholder representatives, to be able to make decisions for management to carry out. *Industrial democracy*, as it has come to be known, is therefore concerned with changing the industrial balance of power, especially in the upper reaches of companies. This is done by the assertion of workers' rights, which have already been established on the shop floor to varying degrees and which already include a statutory right to belong to a trade union.

Employee participation, in employer terminology, starts off as a much more limited concept and basically goes no further than the employer wanting to decide for himself, albeit often subject to union pressure, what company affairs he is prepared to let his employees hear about and influence. In this sense therefore it is based more on what industrialists think is in the interests of the company as a whole–maybe, but not necessarily, including the interests of employees–than on the wider political concepts of workers' rights, which industrialists will in general question.

The term 'participation' is however also used in a general and imprecise way by almost everyone on all sides of industry and politics to describe the general involvement of workers in their companies. Some people wrongly regard it as a new phenomenon of the 1970s, aimed at employee involvement quite separate from collective bargaining; others more accurately see it as an umbrella term which covers everything from the weakest form of employee communication through collective bargaining to some form of joint regulation or control. As the Bullock Report said,

Employee participation may take many forms, from improved communication to joint responsibility for decisions, to experiments in job enrichment and participative management, and it may range from unwritten but accepted codes of practice within companies to formal structures such as representative councils with constitutions, officers, etc.

Participation however can also have a special meaning–to describe the sort of co-operative relationship that employers and employee representatives are trying (or should be trying) to build when they set up participation committees or worker director systems. In such situations the unions should be shouldering new responsibilities in what should involve at least a lessening, though probably not a rejection, of the adversary system, and managements should be sharing some of their decision-making power. Both sides of industry in effect should be trying to accommodate their primary traditional conflict roles with less overt conflict, although there will still inevitably be clashes of interest. This is in line with the *Oxford Dictionary* definition quoted above and will be recognised by many industrialists and union officials as a state which, by some means or other, they can achieve, and have sometimes already achieved in various parts of their companies, to the benefit of the company and its employees.

So if one constructs a ladder of labour–management relationships in order of worker-influence, it starts at the bottom with *communication,* which involves management passing information to the employees (and maybe permitting a return flow back to them) about decisions that have almost certainly already been taken. It is the essential basis for everything else but is not an end in itself. Next up the ladder comes *consultation,* where management communicates information, listens to the feedback and may then discuss the issues. Often it takes place only after major decisions have been made by the management. Then there is *collective bargaining,* including what has come to be known as *extended collective bargaining*–where each side lodges claims and offers and where each, when they cannot agree, has the right to walk away in disagreement leaving the other side to do his own thing–the management to implement its decisions unilaterally or the workers to stage some form of protest action. Finally, at the top of the union and worker power ladder in traditional terms, there is *co-determination* or *joint regulation,* where neither side is expected to take unilateral action as a last resort, which means that only what is jointly agreed–or decided by a 'third party' arbitrator–can be implemented.

'*Participation*', including worker directors, fits in as a grey area between 'consultation'/'collective bargaining' and 'co-determination' and in fact represents a mixture of the two–which is why it can be a precarious business. On the one hand, both sides of the company are, at least subconsciously, bargaining according to their own interests, and they also know that in theory they could opt out as in ordinary bargaining. However, to opt out would defeat the co-operative style of the operation, so they both should be accepting tacitly that everything should be jointly agreed. This could be termed '*participative bargaining*', but 'participation' is simpler, if less precise.

This definition leaves *industrial democracy* to cover the wider, more politically oriented, rights of workers to a say in factors affecting their working lives. Therefore it covers all the terms that have just been discussed, although it centres on the concept of the sharing of power and responsibilities between management and labour. While not avoiding the issue of the conflicts of industry inherent in bargaining relationships, it would in an ideal world centre on 'participation' as just defined. Then, developed to its logical conclusion, the nature of the capital–labour conflict would change but not disappear, as would collective bargaining as it is at present known because the major employer–union bargains would be struck within overall corporate plans, either in the board room or outside it, through the extended collective bargaining methods.

Industrial traditions

In industry all these terms are interwoven into a network of relationships between a company, its work force and its trade unions, blurring the issue of the extent of union and employee power in the influencing and making of management decisions. How they are arranged and relate to each other in detail – and how they are expanded in the future – depends not so much on the protestations of TUC or CBI policy documents as on the historical traditions of different companies and industries. In some cases the style of management will lead automatically to participation; in the national newspaper industry, on the other hand, the printing trade unions are already effectively in partial day-to-day control of the production of the papers because of the way they have mixed closed shop arrangements with the militant negotiating power of a body of men who know their employers have a product that has to be produced on time or not at all. In other areas, such as various parts of the engineering industry, the car factories and the docks, there is also a dominant trade union voice achieving joint control through collective bargaining. As in the newspaper industry, the unions have taken over some of the functions of day-to-day management on the hiring of employees, their work rotas, the speeds at which they are expected to work, the machinery that is installed and even where work is carried out. But this is a negative form of participation, born out of conflict rather than co-operation, and will very often not be aimed at maximising the efficiency of the business.

At the other end of the scale, in industries like retailing, clothing manufacture, and white-collar areas such as financial institutions, there are few such militant trade union traditions and what rights the employees enjoy have often been handed down voluntarily by employers rather than been won through industrial battles. But in both types of case, and in the great mass of industry that lies between, the unions and their members have not got the *right* to joint control of the strategic corporate decisions that are their targets under industrial democracy.

The worker's shopfloor influence over his employer has also however sometimes been increased by industrial and economic developments. The productivity bargaining boom of the 1960s, for example, was specially significant in increasing the unions' and workers' say in management matters, as Eric Wigham notes in his history of the Engineering Employers' Federation, *The Power to Manage*. He points out that in 1968, when the productivity craze was in full swing, the then research director of the Federation, Eddie Robertson, wrote that productivity bargaining 'involves an acceptance not merely in intellectual but in emotional terms of the inescapability of shared responsibility with regard to efficient manpower utilisation and the effort-wage bargain'. For engineering employers, with their conflict-consciousness of managerial and ownership rights and prerogatives, this must have been something of a shock.

The terminology in practice

The terms that were mentioned earlier in this chapter emerge at varying stages of an employer's relationship with his employees and trade unions as the power and influence of the union over his affairs increase. Many employers offer a union trying to win recognition in a company for the first time some loose form of consultative 'chatting' arrangement before agreeing to the official sort of recognition that leads to collective bargaining. Equally, however, consultation frequently continues on certain fringe subjects in parallel with bargaining systems. It is easiest therefore to discuss collective bargaining in practice and the trade union strengths that go with it on traditional pay and conditions issues before moving on to 'consultation' and 'participation'. 'Collective bargaining' then re-enters the story along with 'worker directors' as ways of unions jointly controlling wide-ranging corporate decisions.

Collective bargaining

Bargaining normally covers a man's pay, hours of work and other conditions of employment, and can vary in its scope and the way it is included in an agreement, from a national deal covering a million or more workers (as has happened in the engineering and construction industries) down to a quick informal and unwritten understanding between a shop steward and a foreman covering, say, how much work a single man is expected to do in a given time. It is the major occupation of the country's 300,000 shop stewards and has become the basic operational reason for their existence. The TUC has been telling its unions for several years that it should be extended into areas other than wages and basic conditions of work as a preliminary to a major extension of industrial democracy. These areas are the subject of managerial prerogative until they are taken within the bargaining net, as they usually are. They include matters such as facilities for the shopfloor organisation and operation of the trade union; manpower planning items such as recruitment levels and training and redeployment arrangements; job and income security such as provision of guaranteed weekly wages, pensions, sick and injury pay, disciplinary and dismissal procedures; and the disclosure of company information to union negotiators.

Often in the past however there has been a gap in the bargaining arrangements of most industries at company level because agreements have been struck covering a whole industry at the top and then a factory or smaller shopfloor area at the bottom. This led to chaotic wage systems and started slowly to change after the 1968 Donovan Commission Report recommended that the situation should be rationalised with company-wide bargaining. This, it was hoped, would not only rationalise bargaining arrangements but also induce some reform of inter-union divisions. In the context of industrial democracy developments, such an idea is even more relevant because it brings the unions nearer the power centres of companies where they can get to grips with an enterprise's financial and other affairs instead of being confined either to the shop floor or to the distant offices of an industry-wide employers' federation. The Bullock Report gave such a trend a boost with its proposal that all unions in a company should have to come together on a shop stewards' Joint Representation Committee (JRC) before being admitted into board rooms.

As an offshoot of collective bargaining, trade unions and their members have sometimes shown their strength by negotiating further traditional inroads into management prerogative. The most controversial have been what is called 'mutuality' and 'the *status quo*'. 'Mutuality' is a term used in the engineering industry and involves what trade unions regard as the workers' right to negotiate piecework pay rates for individual items of work. The engineering unions have opposed occasional attempts by employers in national agreements to limit this sort of plant bargaining, which can be inflationary because it adds what is known as shopfloor wage drift to formal pay agreements.

Mutuality is especially powerful if accompanied by a *status quo* arrangement, under which existing working procedures are maintained until new ones have been agreed or until a disputes procedure or a set period of time has elapsed. This means for example that an assembly line would remain at a slow speed, or a modification could not be made to a product, till terms had been agreed or the procedure exhausted. This can constitute a major interference with a manager's freedom to manage without hindrance and has been a controversial issue in the engineering industry. It is being used in Sweden as a primary way of extending industrial democracy, within a statutory framework of labour relations, which could make managers negotiate almost any decision with their trade unions – and it is seen in these terms by the British TUC, whose 1974 industrial democracy document described it as an issue of 'management prerogatives'.

Backing up these forms and procedures of collective bargaining are the traditional methods of trade union protest strikes and lesser (though not necessarily less financially damaging) forms of industrial action such as go-slows, works to rule, non-co-operation and general bloody-mindedness, the latter being the least formal and often the hardest to correct. In addition, there is the 'sit-in', where workers stay in occupation of a factory instead of walking out of it but still do not work (Chapter 13).

Trade union power over management decisions has also been strengthened by new union-based laws such as the Employment Protection Act (1975) and the Health and Safety at Work Act (1974), which include statutory provisions on trade union recognition, the disclosure of financial information, notification of redundancies and joint control of safety affairs. There is also a provision that could allow collective bargaining and recognition to be extended to new areas within a company (which the TUC might one day try to use as a vehicle for 'extended collective bargaining'); and there are specific advances for individual employees covering some matters that it could be hard for a union voluntarily to persuade an employer to concede through collective bargaining. This is partly because, while the items are important, they are not the sort of issues over which a union negotiator could viably threaten a strike. They include paid time off for maternity cases and for people engaged in trade union and public duties, improved guaranteed wage arrangements, and help for employees hit when their employer becomes insolvent.

Consultation
Trade unions are highly suspicious of consultation systems, which are sometimes dismissed as 'employers' tea parties' and are specially resented because they are based on the assumption that management's right to decide will in the end prevail. The cynicism stems partly from early

postwar experience, when private sector employers used consultative committees only to communicate decisions already made to their employees (separate from any union organisation). Even today, many employers still regard consultation as a means of propping up autocratic or paternalistic management styles (especially in hard times) with an illusion of involvement, and the TUC reflected the unions' view on this in its 1974 industrial democracy document:

Either the consultative machinery acted to inhibit the development of local negotiating machinery, or at least to limit its sphere of competence, or the consultative committees themselves tended to be reduced to a formality discussing only trivia.

Since the traditional approach to consultative committees does not envisage their reaching decisions (although they have sometimes been delegated certain powers in fringe welfare areas such as canteen or sports facilities), they rarely raise much controversy within companies. They are tolerated by unions, who often regard them as necessary evils, because they at least make companies hand over some information about their operations. Generally the employees' representatives (now increasingly often the unions' shop stewards) will not have to become involved in matters outside their expertise and there need be no potential clashes with the conflict-based collective bargaining of the company because the exercise is purely consultative, based primarily on the communication of information.

Participation

Gradually consultation systems can be developed and extended into more positive methods when they would qualify to be described as 'participation' (or 'participative bargaining') and would involve the employee representatives beginning to take responsibility for, and have a major influence on, a growing number of management decisions. This can be done in a variety of different bodies such as company councils, which are primarily consultative, or advisory bodies, whose views have a major impact on management thinking, or various tiers of participation committees linking the shop floor with top management. Some of these different styles emerge in the following two chapters on private and public sector practices, and ultimately they involve a change in the trade unions' traditional role as they move towards joint responsibility with management of the sort involved in a worker director system, even though the background of the bargaining relationship will remain.

Critics of the Bullock Report have suggested that all these sorts of procedures need to be built before boardroom representation could be considered because, they say, at present there is no 'infrastructure' for such a 'bottom-up' approach. The infrastructure is in fact already in existence through all the shop stewards and their committees, which exist in unionised companies. What is missing however is the harnessing of this infrastructure by management for constructive purposes and the recognition of shop stewards' committees as the basis for participation.

'Single channel'

It is at this point that the issue becomes controversial and begins to embrace the unions' growing interest in only having one channel of communication between employee and management—that is, the unions' bargaining channel, which means both merging consultation and bargaining and excluding non-unionists. The Bullock Committee took this union approach to its logical conclusion and said in its report that statutory rights to its worker director system should be firmly based on the union representative channel, which would tie it into the unions' bargaining arrangements.

This is called the 'single channel' approach and is an essential feature of the unions' attempt to extend and consolidate their influence within companies. But it raises a lot of anger elsewhere because of the way it can militate against non-unionists.

For some time many trade unions have tried to create such a single channel by merging their consultative arrangements in companies with collective bargaining machinery because they are suspicious, as has already been said, about the employer orientation of consultative machinery. Merging the two can also enable unions to put some bargaining power into the discussions which may otherwise become bogged down by consultative inertia. Furthermore, they have a chance to negotiate an immediate price—maybe a pay rise—for concessions agreed without having their power weakened by transferring the subject from one lot of employer—union machinery to another. And there will also be a set bargaining-based disputes procedure into which they can slot issues when they fail to agree.

The TUC's 1974 industrial democracy document indicated its firm preference for this, although it built in some reservations to cover those unions that do not want to disrupt moderately effective consultation systems for fear of losing what they have already gained. It echoed an earlier 1967 Labour Party document on industrial democracy (see Chapter 14) and said:

It is important that all improvements in industrial democracy should be based on a single channel of communications.

Not surprisingly, employers generally oppose such an idea because it can mean that the unions gain formal bargaining power over matters—say factory closures and redundancies—on which employers really only want to consult them. (Equally, it is a union fear that employers might stop even giving information on such matters that prevent them adopting a policy of total opposition to consultation.) Quite often this is what academics call 'bargaining creep' which is a sort of twilight area where managements agree to 'talk' but not to 'bargain'.

The Bullock Report, reflecting the unions' view, commented:

It has been customary to draw a distinction between consultation on the one hand and negotiation or collective bargaining on the other, but in practice the distinction is blurred and there has been a gradual trend in recent years towards the fusion of consultative and negotiating machinery. The purely consultative system, where it is clearly understood that, however much influence those consulted may have, any decisions taken are those of management, is becoming less common. Consultation is being developed to the point where those consulted acquire a *de facto* power of veto over certain actions of management. The term has indeed become so stretched that its usefulness must be doubted, as must the neat categorisation of participation into communication, consultation and co-determination which some witnesses have suggested we should adopt.

It was of course essential for the Bullock Committee to follow this line of argument in order to develop its advocacy of trade union-based worker directors forming part of a single channel bargaining-cum-board representation system. To allow such a system to develop separately from the union organisation, from the unions' point of view, would not only negate the power-changing aspect but would increase the risk of the unions losing a primary role as their activists move into the new system and become distracted from the unions' aims.

But the argument can equally well be used to develop the alternative trade union route to industrial democracy – that is, to merge consultative arrangements into extended collective bargaining on key corporate decisions without going so far as to obtain seats in the board room.

One way in which a compromise on a single channel approach can be reached to retain a distinct bargaining forum separate from any participation emerged at British Leyland, where there are separate structures but union-based shop stewards sit in both.

Extended collective bargaining

As was explained in Chapter 6, the extended bargaining alternative to worker directors has been preferred by unions such as the Electrical and Plumbing Trades Union and by the General and Municipal Workers as well as by the Communist Party. It is probably also the instinctive preference of the vast majority of union members, who do not want to be put in a position where they might have to share management's responsibilities – or at least who want to maintain the right to walk away from such responsibilities. It involves unions expanding the orbit of their traditional negotiations on pay and employment conditions, first into the list of other manpower items advocated by the TUC and then into a wide range of company business such as the location of new factories, redeployment, mergers, redundancies and changes of products. The law would provide an overall legal obligation on companies to negotiate on such specific 'corporate strategy issues' (as they are called by the unions), and the negotiations within the company involved would be voluntary, not legally binding. This would however be linked with a legal requirement for companies to disclose a wide range of information to the unions (far outside the range envisaged by the Employment Protection Act), and there would be provision for arbitration where companies either failed to hand over enough information or refused to negotiate company-wide issues.

One of the most resolute proponents of this line among the ranks of Britain's academics is Dr (now Lord) McCarthy of Nuffield College who set out his ideas in *Management by Agreement* (McCarthy and Ellis, 1973). The book advocates a system of what it calls 'predictive bargaining', in which future management problems are analysed and their solutions negotiated between management and union:

One way of symbolising this concept would be to say that within a system of management by agreement there would no longer exist any area of management decision-taking where management itself could claim an absolute and unilateral right to resist union influence in any form.

There would therefore, say McCarthy and Ellis, be nothing left of the

131

'sacred garden' of managerial prerogatives.

These authors' views are firmly rooted in the conflict tradition of labour relations expounded earlier by their friends and tutors, Professor Hugh Clegg and the late Allan Flanders. McCarthy firmly believes that bargaining is an inevitable and basically unchangeable relationship between employer and employee–inside or outside a board room–and he stresses that management by agreement is not intended to lead to the disappearance of industrial conflict. The McCarthy–Ellis ideas are therefore intended to maintain the distinct responsibilities and loyalties of management and unions. For this reason, the authors are highly sceptical about the usefulness of worker directors except as a back-up to collective bargaining, possibly exerting some influence in the board room on subjects that bargaining could not reach, but not carrying any responsibility for management decisions.

This alternative of extended collective bargaining is sometimes regarded by industrialists as a softer or at least a preferable option to worker directors because it keeps the unions out of the board room and also makes it easier to compartmentalise the subjects on which they have influence and, correspondingly, those confidential and other matters on which they will have no influence and no knowledge. It may also be possible for industrialists to undermine or even ignore the details of a collective agreement on, say, investment plans unless the agreement is precisely drafted. Recent experience in Italy, where there has been some extended collective bargaining on corporate plans especially in Fiat, has illustrated the problems unions can face in monitoring the implementation of agreements on subjects outside their traditional employment areas with the apparent result that investment agreements have not been kept.

So it is not hard to understand why the industrialists might be tempted to opt for extended bargaining, at least as a short-term expedient, because it could well lead to a much slower incursion of effective union influence into their affairs (and save company directors the embarrassment of shop stewards invading their executive suites). On the other hand, if one stretched the logic of the idea to the same extent that the Bullock Committee stretched the concept of worker directors, one could finish up with unions having statutory rights to a potentially stifling stranglehold on managerial decisions, which could lead to negotiations on every aspect of a company's business. This is because all corporate plans and decisions might have to be negotiated in good faith and, presumably, recorded in agreements that, presumably again, could not be varied without further negotiations. Every important management decision would thus be subject to formal horse-trading between conflicting interests. This could turn out, if a sanction to enforce it by law and a method to organise such negotiations were discovered, to be managerially far more rigid and demotivating a strait-jacket than worker directors. It would not involve the participative approach implicit in boardroom representation.

From the unions' point of view however extended bargaining has the advantage that they are clearly not tied to a participative framework of the board room, that they can choose which subjects they have the will and expertise to try to influence, and that there is no conceptual blurring of their role. They would however still have to shoulder some extended responsibilities in practice because, as Len Murray has pointed out,·

unions are supposed to be responsible for making collective agreements stick (even though this does not always happen in practice). In this situation, a corporate plan collectively negotiated between company directors and union officials involving factory closures, redundancies, a merger or the purchase of new machinery would involve the unions in making sure that these possibly unpleasant changes were not opposed by their members. This would be a similar responsibility for the unions to that stemming from worker directors. But the unions would still have maintained the right, under extended collective bargaining, to opt out of negotiations on a company policy they did not like and to refuse to reach an agreement, so leaving the company free to go ahead on its own and the unions free to organise protest action or simply to make it clear they did not agree to the decision.

There is however one basic snag with unions wanting the law to give them a statutory right to extended collective bargaining as opposed to, or in addition to, boardroom representation. This is how the law could be enforced to make an employer keep to the agreed plans or, for example, to reopen a factory on the instruction of an arbitrator. The problem arises from the unions' traditional insistence that there must not be any laws restricting their organisations or their negotiating power (as opposed to laws giving them collective and individual rights, which they welcome). There is therefore, unlike the situation in Sweden for example, no framework of labour bargaining law on to which could be added a requirement for employers to bargain in good faith on a range of corporate matters—with statutory arbitration to solve disputes (which itself would hardly be a good way to decide on how to manage a factory).

There is of course nothing here to stop a statutory right being written into legislation. But to be enforceable it would presumably have to finish up with legally binding arbitration, which would rapidly lead the unions into the area of the sort of legally binding labour contracts they fiercely and successfully fought under the Tories in 1970-4. A legally binding arbitration on, say, a company's financial plan or a modernisation project could, like an old Tory-style legally binding contract, statutorily restrict the unions' ability to fight for pay rises or to oppose redundancies (as well as giving the management an unreal lack of flexibility). Similar enforceability problems have been found with the CBI's original plan in 1976 for its participation agreements to be enforced statutorily. The CBI proposed, in order to emphasise the seriousness of its plans, that such agreements should be required by law. But then it realised this statutory backing would be worth little if there was no statutory means of making companies abide by such a law—simply penalising them would not force them to obey and could be counter-productive.

But no such problem need exist with a worker director system, which would become part of the country's established and respected company law, not its employment law. The only way a problem could arise would be if worker directors were made legally responsible for the implementation of board decisions (which would kill the system off because the unions would never accept such a legally binding restriction of their freedom of action) or if some frantic industrialists decided to bolt the boardroom door against a posse of employee representatives.

Worker directors

Worker directors are the most radical and most highly contentious of the various sorts of participation. This is first because they involve employee representatives moving into the top policy-making levels of a company's hierarchy and decision-making areas and second because they are regarded as implicitly involving a change in the role of the employees' trade unions.

Their advocates among the unions regard them as essential on the grounds that they would enable shop stewards to get to grips with company decisions that could probably never be caught up in a collective bargaining net, however far it was extended. Such advocates argue that there need be no change or blurring of the union role if it is understood that the bargaining basis of British industry will remain even if it changes. On the other hand, the presence of union-based workers in the board room would bring a measure of consent to top management decisions which would percolate down to the shop floor and so ease management's job and boost industrial efficiency.

The degree to which worker directors would have any significant impact on either the management or unions in a company depends on several points (Chapter 16). Basically, they involve whether the system is union-based, what proportion of the boardroom seats the workers have, whether the board on which they sit is in a one- or two-tier company structure and what responsibilities it is given, and how much residual power is left to shareholder meetings and votes.

Whatever the arrangements however, union-based worker directors ought, in one way or another, to mean the unions changing many of their styles of operation and adopting a participative approach–an approach basically against the nature of their bargaining traditions, which are unlikely to change quickly.

As a result any group of worker directors (unless they controlled the board) might rapidly have to decide whether to adopt a full bargaining approach to their boardroom role, fighting every decision to the last and then returning to the shop floor to continue their protests and whip up opposition when they had lost–so opting out of the boardroom responsibility.

Alternatively, the worker directors could adopt a passive role, arguing their case but accepting when they lost that that was the end of the matter and that they should respect the board room's confidentiality and not return to the shop floor and lead their privileged information in order to continue the battle.

The problem with the first alternative is that the board room would no longer be a viable policy-making body. This could prove to be to the detriment of both the shareholders and the employees, unless the management was astute enough to devise means of overcoming the problem by taking its major decisions elsewhere–for example, where the worker directors were not present on boards and committees at home and abroad or in informal settings. In such a situation the board room would become the place where management argued through decisions already reached.

The problem with the second alternative (which superficially might seem the most attractive to management) is that the worker directors could rapidly lose credibility with their fellow shop stewards if they did not brief them on the problems brewing in the board room (see also Chapter 7). They would be seen as 'management men' and would probably no longer hold the respect of fellow shop stewards and workers as their representatives. Whether they were then simply ignored or replaced, or the system was abandoned would of course vary, but whatever happened they would no longer be effective employee representatives. Workable compromises might be found, but there would still be the traditional bargaining backcloth reflecting the different interests of capital and labour, against which worker directors would have to operate. This would apply whether or not they decided to separate themselves from traditional bargaining activity so as to try to keep their new role clear.

The problems would arise because worker directors would find themselves constantly faced with decisions on matters such as shareholders' dividends, investment policy such as where factories should be sited or expanded, the run-down of old plant, the purchase of labour-saving equipment, and even the salaries of top management, where their sectional and other basic interests would clash with boardroom harmony. This is not to suggest that board rooms do not at present have to make executive decisions weighing different conflicting viewpoints and interests, not that worker directors could never cope. But the boards normally operate without too much of the overt sectionalised conflict.

Foreign experience

Foreign experience has only a limited amount to teach Britain on these sorts of issues because of the vastly different traditions and legal systems of other countries. Nevertheless two countries–Sweden and Germany–provide important examples of how worker director systems can operate with the qualification that both, unlike the UK, have a legalistic labour relations environment.

Minorities in Sweden

Experience in Sweden, where there is minority union-based employee representation in the board room, indicates that a minority presence need not have any significant impact either on board decision-making or on the attitude of the employees to board decisions–even though in Sweden the worker directors are sitting on a company's main single-tier management board. The system is recognised by the Swedish unions as a useful back-up however to a broader-based programme of industrial democracy, and is regarded primarily as a means of collecting company information and checking on management. The broader programme includes extensive disclosure of company information, the availability of financial advisors to help the unions (see Chapter 7), legal rights to bargain on a potentially wide range of managerial decisions, and a proposed controversial worker share-ownership scheme (see Chapter 13), which if implemented would gradually hand the finances of companies over to the union-controlled central funds.

Introduced in 1973, the Swedish worker director system is union-based (more than 90 per cent of Sweden's manual workers and 70 per cent of white-collar workers are in unions) and to begin with provided for two worker seats (plus two reserves standing by) on single-tier company boards which traditionally have about six to eight directors. The National Swedish Industrial Board prepared a report on their effectiveness in 1976 and concluded:

The Board Representation Act is regarded as a useful supplement to other measures aimed at the improvement of industrial democracy. Although one may question whether the reform in itself has done very much to increase the influence wielded by employees, it has undoubtedly improved their opportunities of insight. In the long run it should also strengthen their influence. The reform has also had a salutory effect on relations between management and employees.

Since then a new law in Sweden has tried to ensure that employees are not excluded from key decision-making areas by providing for an employee representative to sit on any special committee set by the board and also to sit on the boards of conglomerates and other group boards of companies. In addition, the two reserve worker directors can sit in and speak during board meetings but may not vote, so underlining the main purpose of this system, which is for employees to gather information and have a little influence on decisions rather than to wield power. And to underline that this is an adjunct to, but not part of, the collective bargaining system, the Swedish worker directors often leave the board room when industrial action or wage bargaining is being discussed–although they are present when the company's financial plans, which inevitably include an allocation for wages, are on the agenda.

One-third in Germany
In Germany too the minority system of one-third employee representation, which has existed since 1952 (outside the coal and steel industries, which have been 50–50 since 1951), has given employees only a limited impact. It has recently been changed to give something approaching 50–50 everywhere, but with provisions that leave management in an ultimate majority.

But the system has never been regarded as providing much worker power, partly because it is not union-based (although in practice the worker directors often are union activists) and partly because the representation is only on a supervisory board, with fairly remote powers, in a two-tier structure. The co-operative success of German industry, indeed, contrary to some views in the UK, stems mainly from the history and traditions of the country, the system of labour law, and national and industry-wide pay bargaining, and from the outlook of the unions (they are committed to, and work for, the immediate wellbeing of the company and usually leave issues about social changes that are the mainspring of the British adversary system to their political activities). In any case, the real power within Germany's rigid and complicated statutory labour relations system is wielded by all-employee works councils, which have rights of consultation and access to information on personnel, social and economic matters, plus rights of co-determination on manpower issues. The works councils in fact provide the industrial democracy teeth in the German system and are widely regarded by companies as significant institutions with effective power to curb managerial prerogatives–in the same way as shop stewards are often regarded in the UK on shop floor issues. However, they are not admired by British union leaders because they are not based on the unions and are therefore quite separate from bargaining arrangements. This means they can develop what is called 'company egoism'–which the Bullock Report defined as 'too much concentration on the internal affairs of the company and too little regard to the wider context in which companies have to operate'.

A gloomy view of the lack of effectiveness of the worker directors put forward by a leading German labour lawyer, Professor Daubler, was quoted in a research paper, *'Industrial Democracy: European Experience'*, commissioned by the Bullock Committee from two British academics, Eric Batstone and Paul Davies:

In practice the representation of employees is reduced to a mere right to be heard. As the majority formed by the shareholders almost always votes unanimously, there is no chance whatsoever to carry through staff interests in the supervisory Board. . . . Many employee members . . . claimed that their activities on the supervisory Board were less important than the representation of interests in the works council.

Since this was written the worker director scheme has been revamped, following a report by the Biendenkopf Commission (1970), with a system which at first glance looks like a 50–50 'parity' split but which in fact gives the shareholders a built-in majority. This is because the employee board representatives include one nominee from senior management, and because of the way the chairman is chosen and is given the casting vote when deadlocks occur.

Conclusions

It has been shown that employee influence on company affairs can be extended in several different ways. It can be done through low-key communication and consultation exercises of the type generally favoured by management, which do little to change the employees' balance of power in industry but might marginally help job satisfaction and industrial efficiency. Alternatively, consultation can be extended into participation where, without necessarily reaching formal agreements and without all the connotations of boardroom representation, managers share some of their decision-making power with workers in the interests both of boosting industrial efficiency and of recognising workers' rights to a say in their working lives. The primary problem with this (as will be seen in some of the following company examples) is defining the differences between traditional collective bargaining and the new procedures and making sure that the shop stewards and workers, and the foremen and supervisors, understand and accept what is being done. Carried out effectively, such exercises could lead to a new level of co-operation in the running of the business, with union representatives shouldering new responsibilities and management benefiting from sharing its decision-making role.

Next there is the extension of collective bargaining into new areas without any overt dilution of the traditional attitudes of British industry. In one way it is the safest of the options (apart from simple consultation), because it blurs no one's role; but it is also the least likely to have any catalytic effect on industrial relationships. Like worker directors, it could however gradually change the nature of industry-wide and shopfloor pay bargaining because the main bargaining agreements would be taken at a different level on, for example, a financial plan, which would leave less room for manoeuvre by union negotiators elsewhere. Extended collective bargaining also has the disadvantage from the company's point of view that it could be unduly restrictive on managerial flexibility, while from the unions' point of view it might be impossible to make managements bargain in good faith and stick to their agreements.

Finally, there are worker directors, which take all those involved into a new arena of relationships and which, while having the greatest potential for reforming management and union relationships and traditions, also carry the greatest risks. There would be problems about how the boardroom policy decisions were related and inter-linked with other management executive-level decision-making and union bargaining in the company, and there would almost inevitably be a progressive change in the way that unions traditionally bargained on matters such as wages, a problem that the TUC has not yet fully faced up to. This is because it would be a nonsense, for example, for the shop steward employee representatives to vote for, and therefore accept, an annual financial budget in the board room and then go back to the shop floor and a few months later indulge in collective bargaining aimed at making the management pay more in wages than had been allowed in the budget. (This, it should be noted, is a different issue from that where a shop steward might 'opt out' in the board room and say he will continue his fight on the shop floor.)

Even worse problems could arise over board decisions on factory closures, mergers and redundancies, and the freedom for shop stewards to 'opt out' could not be limitless or the credibility of the board as a decision-making body would suffer.

So the traditional freedom of shop stewards and union officials to negotiate pay rises (subject to pay restraint policies) and other matters on the shop floor would have to become curtailed. Ultimately this could lead to the end of so-called 'free collective bargaining', as it has been known, because the major bargains would be struck in board rooms in a viable worker director system. This would also affect industry-wide pay bargaining covering many companies (as for that matter would fully developed extended collective bargaining), and would also restrict shopfloor activity on pay, although in a fully developed system the shop stewards would presumably be kept busy in participation and other committees helping to run the factory.

Such issues underline the need for the relationships between new-style participation and old-style bargaining to be established clearly in a company's employee and management structures. They also put a large question mark over how ready either side of British industry is for such developments.

Chapter 11

Participation Trends: The Private Sector

Communication and consultation

Ever since the TUC started to push its ideas of industrial democracy at the start of the 1970s, it has had to contend with the fact that relatively few of its one hundred or so affiliated unions and an even smaller proportion of the eleven million TUC union members have shown much positive interest in taking a major role in the running of employers' businesses. Equally, those employers who have been far-sighted enough to foresee social and industrial trends and realise they ought to try to involve their employees (with or without their unions) in the running of their enterprises have often met with little enthusiasm. The inertia among employees has been matched if not exceeded by a reluctance among many unions to become involved in anything very far outside their traditional employment areas for fear of the upheaval it could cause to their patterns of often not very energetic or expert operations. So a consideration of the extension of employee and union influence into company affairs would have seemed somewhat unreal even as recently as the end of the 1960s. Some employers at that time were thinking about how to cope with both their industrial problems and their social duties by, for example, setting up advance redundancy consultation schemes; and there were also preliminary moves towards the world of Bullock with the appointment of worker directors in the British Steel Corporation and with some consideration of similar ideas elsewhere in the public sector. But these were not regarded as very urgent topics in the late 1960s and early 1970s for two reasons: first, attention then was concentrated on legal controls of labour relations; and second, Britain's economic problems had not developed to the state that, in the mid-1970s, helped to start the sort of heart-searching that eased the way for the Bullock Committee's inquiries.

The result is that by the mid- to late 1970s, Britain has established no significant track record of formal participative employee involvement, let alone significant pace-making experiments in union-based participative industrial democracy on which future national policies could be built. What Britain does have is one of the largest trade union movements in the world, with half the country's manual workers belonging to unions (compared with about 80 per cent overall in Sweden and 25 per cent in the United States) based on a powerful shop steward system. The 300,000 shop stewards in the UK provide the shopfloor strength and worker participation (albeit often in a negative, defensive form) that other countries' unions have sought through statutory enforcement of innovations such as works councils, worker directors and the right to bargain. There have not therefore been the employee or union demands in Britain for industrial democracy on the shop floor that have emerged in other countries with less highly developed shopfloor bargaining arrangements. Now, however, this is changing because economic, industrial and technological developments have made national union leaders, particularly in the UK and Europe, want to track down the sources of corporate power up to, and maybe into, the board rooms so that they can influence decisions that affect their members–even though their members, primarily interested only in life on the shop floor where they spend their daily lives and earn their pay packets, may not be very excited about such a long-term prospect. Because this development is a recent phenomenon, there are few examples of its operation in the UK. The purpose of this chapter therefore is to explore the far less radical notion of employee consultation, which has been developed by industrialists as the other side of the industrial democracy equation to improve industrial efficiency, and to show how this and other limited involvement in individual companies in Britain has developed voluntarily, with little of the legal enforcement more common abroad.

Communicating the facts

The most widespread development in the past few years has been an acceptance by employers of the need and usefulness of giving their employees information about their companies. Until relatively recently most employers have regarded company information as something that should be withheld in order to strengthen their hand in collective bargaining with the unions. Gradually this has started to change on two main fronts. First, since Barbara Castle's ill-fated labour law proposals of 1969, it has been public policy that employers should hand over company information to union negotiators. Gradual progress has been made towards enforcing this in recent years, culminating in an ACAS Code prepared under the 1975 Employment Protection Act. This involves disclosure of information for bargaining purposes and is seen by the unions as an essential tool if they are to be able to increase the strength and scope of their bargaining, especially at company as opposed to shop-floor level. But it is often a reluctant form of communication, born of the adversary system, and has been a hotly disputed subject since the former Commission on Industrial Relations produced a report (CIR Report no. 31) in 1972 which trod a careful path between on the one hand recognising the logic of unions being given certain information while on the other resisting any blanket disclosure provisions which might unduly upset the balance of power in collective bargaining. The subject was made even more controversial by provisions for the disclosure of more general information linked with planning agreements in the Industry Act (1975) which, after long political battles, turned out to be fairly ineffectual. Now however the Employment Act disclosure provisions are going ahead, and unions can force employers to provide information on a relatively wide range of financial and other matters. The provisions in this Act could also be extended to cover a wider range of company planning and other matters as bargaining expands.

The second front is the more positive aspect of giving employees information so that they understand more about their company. Its proponents prefer to give it the more constructive title of the 'provision' of information rather than the more secretive and reluctant sounding 'disclosure' It is in this area that there has been a major breakthough in the past few years with more and more companies providing information in a variety of ways. Popular versions of companies' annual reports to shareholders have been prepared in an attempt (often only partially successful because the presentation is too complex) to make them understandable to employees. A further new development for some companies has been the preparation of the figures so that they relate to the factory or unit in which an employee works rather than covering a complete group of companies to which he cannot relate.

A variety of other methods of disseminating information in the hope of promoting understanding of, and involvement in, a company's affairs have also been developed. Some companies prefer to tackle the problem through managers briefing small groups of employees while others favour written reports for employees, slide and video tape presentations, and annual or more frequent presentations by a company chairman to mass meetings of his employees. The Industrial Society, the employer–union body which has taken a lead in these matters, has a general programme in which it recommends an annual one- to two-hour mass meeting of not more than five hundred employees, briefing groups of about twenty people every one or two months in sessions lasting about thirty minutes, and participation seminars every few months lasting up to a day and including maybe eighty people from a cross-section of managers, employees and employee representatives. Information passed on at these meetings would range from a broad-brush approach to company problems and successes in the mass meeting, to routine reports in the briefing groups, and analysis of how to solve problems in the seminars.

Because of the lack of employee or union interest until relatively recently, however, most such initiatives have stemmed from companies and have therefore mainly depended on the styles in which the companies are run–often dictated by the interests of the company chairman. Esso Petroleum, which prides itself on what has been described by the late Professor Allan Flanders as the 'habit of discussion' of employee–employer relationships in the company, has a long history of formal and informal communication and consultative arrangements. This company has developed various communication methods including a special issue of its company newspaper when its results come out and a visit by the company's chairman at around the same time to plants where he addresses mass meetings. Video tapes of his address are sent to plants he cannot reach and, when they are shown to employees, local managers answer questions. Other large companies carry out similar exercises; while they may seem at first glance to smack of old-style non-union paternalism, one usually finds that the most effective big companies have built such exercises effectively into their traditional union-based industrial relations systems.

Such exercises form a basis for consultation and participation of any sort because, without sufficient information, there is no chance of involving employees or of them or their union representatives understanding the broader areas into which industrial democracy will take them. But – and maybe this is the most difficult part of the exercise – the information needs to be the sort that is understandable to the employee. It needs to relate to his own working life and to be provided and discussed by sympathetic and able managers. When this is done, and no attempt is made to gain an advantage because of the employee or union representative's lack of expertise (see Chapter 7), companies have found that they can build a sound base for whatever participative path they, their unions, and their employees, decide to follow. This in fact is the most important aspect of the 'bottom up' debate which grew out of the Bullock Report with opponents of worker directors arguing that industrial democracy should be built from the shop floor upwards and not from the board room downwards. This was often a fairly sterile general debate because it was frequently initiated only for anti-worker director reasons. But the positive aspect of the 'bottom up' issue is that no employee's representative, whether he is involved in the smallest and most obscure maintenance shop consultative committee or is on the board of an international conglomerate, can work effectively without either relevant information or the substrucure to be able to communicate with, and be accountable to, his members.

Consultative developments – three surveys

Until relatively recently it has been rare for consultative systems in companies to deal with much more than welfare and personnel items such as the provision of tea machines, rest rooms and sports arrangements and, sometimes, safety issues. They have therefore not come to grips with the central issue of a company – that is, the way that it goes about its business and the way that an employee's daily work fits in with the company's efficiency. Historically, managements have preferred to keep such sensitive subjects to themselves and so have not given their employees a chance constructively to influence the way they do their work – let alone to move on to the next participative stage of jointly making business decisions. Changes are now taking place in some of the most advanced (and often the biggest) companies in Britain; but progress has been and remains slow.

There has been no recent comprehensive survey to show precisely what British companies are doing, although the poor record is illustrated by the fact that most experts asked about participation can roll off the names of companies with such schemes in a few seconds. One attempt to review current practice however was carried out by the CBI early in 1977. It found that acknowledged leaders in the field such as ICI and United Biscuits, which have long-established communication-oriented consultative procedures, are being joined by companies such as GKN in ways that suit their own styles of management and labour relations. But, apart from the collective bargaining type of traditional shopfloor joint control discussed in the last chapter, these new schemes are predominantly either post-decision exercises or, if they involve consultations before decisions are made, often do not have much impact on the outcome.

Companies such as Reed International, United Biscuits and Scottish and Newcastle Breweries have made advances in laying down groundwork for employee involvement. This is based first on managers being accountable for involving the employees through whom they have to achieve their objectives, and second through organising employees into small work groups wherever possible. Such companies have also tried to involve their employees in improving their efficiency by adopting a three-part approach according to the CBI survey. First they involve employees and their representatives in discussions about their own jobs and the decisions that affect them directly as individuals. Second, with shop stewards present where they are recognised, broader-based meetings are held every four or six weeks. Some companies have occasionally found that matters may start as topics for discussion before decisions are made and end up as matters that are finally decided by negotiation, which means that shop stewards involved with the company's bargaining process have to attend. This is in sharp contrast with many managements' traditional dislike of their direct consultative arrangements with employees being sullied with shop steward-based bargaining.

Third, management takes the initiative and feeds in topics for discussion that affect the job that the employees are carrying out. This expands the discussion outside traditional employment issues and moves into the quality of the work produced, ways of saving costs, changing methods and introducing new machinery.

Another survey was carried out around the same time by the Industrial Society of forty-one companies, three-quarters of whom each employed more than two thousand employees (2000-plus is normally regarded as the starting point for legislation in industrial democracy). This exercise illustrates both the variety of ways in which participation is interpreted in industry and the limited way in which it has been applied. In answer to a question, 'Is there a formal system or scheme for employee participation in your company?' several companies provided details that show how existing consultative machinery could be developed. But some regard it as only relating to matters such as inquiries into industrial accidents, or merely as joint 50–50 management–employee panels on grading jobs, while one even cited a joint 'campaign against increase in income tax for people with company cars'. Few companies, said the survey, show many signs of intending to develop their systems beyond consultative arrangements, so falling far short of involvement in decision-making.

But the lack of widespread and radical developments in companies does not stem only from managerial, employee and trade union inertia: it may well also be a product of a company's adversary industrial relations system. Such a system can lead to either a tough, but productive shop-floor relationship or to near anarchy. The negative problems associated with it were put by one company, which told the Industrial Society: 'Trade unions are very much involved in everything the company does, but involvement is nearly always obstructive and destructive, rarely constructive.'

Hardly any of the companies had plans for worker directors early in 1977 and a sample of their answers adequately summed up industry's general attitudes after the Bullock Report:

We believe participation at Board level is only a sop . . . . We cannot envisage how union nominees at director level could operate without prejudicing their functions as union representatives at local level . . . . Putting trade union representatives on

Boards is purely political pressure to give power to full-time trade union officials
. . . . We must have strong representation from both unionised and non-unionised
employees . . . . The real pressure is for information and consultation to improve
collective bargaining rather than decision making . . . . From our feedback with the
union there is no demand for worker representation with the Board.

Another survey has produced examples of how some of the country's
largest companies have been adapting their practices. This came in a
private research project for a European client commissioned in 1976 from
e Institute of Personnel Management. It covered ten companies, some
mentioned elsewhere in this chapter, with work forces ranging from 11,000
to over 200,000. Although certain issues are regarded as largely a management prerogative (investment, products etc.), even on these issues
information is invariably provided and consultations frequently take
place', says the report, noting that to compare practice fairly with those in
Europe one has to add in Britain's comprehensive shop steward bargaining arrangements.

On investment plans, while there were no signs of negotiation, six of
the ten companies passed on investment information and three fairly often
entered into consultations. There was a similar spread of practices on a
company's products. Pension schemes also had a high degree of involvement, with two being jointly regulated (where both sides must agree on
what is done), two being negotiated (where management goes ahead if it
cannot get agreement), and three more involving consultation. But on
promotion of employees, while seven companies said they informed
employee representatives of what was to happen, there was no evidence
of involvement in the promotion decision-making.

There was of course a high degree of negotiation on matters that are
traditional bargaining areas in the UK such as pay (all ten companies)
and manning levels, piecework, job evaluation, job mobility and disciplinary action (about half or more of the companies in each case). Apart
from pay, these are matters that in Europe would often come under the
scope of statutory works councils.

The likelihood of the role of the full-time trade union official changing
(see Chapter 7) as companies and their shop stewards build their own
participative structures also emerges from the IPM report. It showed that
full-time union officer involvement in negotiations was not echoed in consultations that sometimes also embraced non-unionists:

In four companies employee representatives for the purposes of consultation were
identical to those for negotiation purposes. In three other companies, the same
representatives were supplemented by a staff consultative committee representing
non-unionised employees. In two of these companies full-time officials never or
very rarely were involved in consultation and in all cases the main union representatives were shop stewards, either as individuals or meeting as a shop stewards'
committee. In two companies lay employee representatives with formal consultative rights were elected through trade union machinery. Although these representatives were usually shop stewards, they were not invariably so and they were
consulted in their capacity as elected employee representatives rather than in their
capacity as shop stewards.

Consultative developments – some company examples

A considerable number of companies took the opportunity of presenting evidence to the Bullock Committee to set out in some detail how they have developed their own labour relations and consultative systems. The fact that such evidence was not very often relevant to the primary Bullock question of how power could be shared in industry by the election of union-based worker directors did not deter the companies. The evidence revealed two things. First, as has already been said, British concerns have developed forward-looking employee involvement schemes or are drawing up plans to do so covering complete companies as well as the shop floor. Second, these schemes have been based primarily on disseminating information (itself a worthwhile advance) and giving employees a limited influence.

Significant aspects of some company policies and schemes are outlined here. In some cases the examples show how the unions, for expediency, will accept far less involvement in a company's affairs than TUC leaders of either the worker director or extended bargaining schools demand. A system being developed in ICI, including new high level consultation in investment plans, is significant because it is based on one of the oldest private sector consultative processes in the country. Unilever's plan for consultative councils in its subsidiary councils, on the other hand, is a more recent development. Ford is firmly basing its developments in the adversary system of British industrial relations, and GEC is now enlarging its consultation following the Weinstock Memorandum (Chapter 9).

ICI

ICI has a tradition of consultation with its 100,000 UK employees going back to 1929 (three years after the company was formed). It has a four-tier system of formally constituted consultative committees, which have been based on unions for manual workers for five years and include some union representation in the white-collar committees. They link individual plants with the company's main board, and there are more recent investment committees as well as informal arrangements.

Plant committees are at the lowest level within the formal four-tier structure and comprise managers, shop stewards and other employee representatives. The next tier up are the works committees, which in turn send shop steward representatives to divisional consultative committees, where the chairman and directors of the division are present (ICI is divided up mainly into divisions, not subsidiary companies). Above this is the central committee of some four hundred people comprising the chairman and main board of ICI with shop stewards elected from the works committees.

Like many employers, ICI prefers to keep its consultative arrangements as employer – employee-oriented as possible, and its system falls well short of joint company policy-making, although the unions do claim that they have affected major ICI decisions and the management say they would not take a major decision, affecting employment prospects, for example, without doing their utmost to carry the unions with them.

Guidelines for the company's main consultative committees were issued by the ICI board in January 1975 and they illustrate ICI's interest in making sure that, while encouraging plants to develop their own experiments, its relatively open policy is kept within strictly understood limits. It presented the guidelines under the twin but distinct titles of 'communication and consultation' and said that subjects usually appropriate to be covered by them would be: plant closures, manpower plans, recruitment and promotion policy, quarterly results, productivity, cost control, competitive conditions, customer complaints, research policy, achievement of capital expenditure estimates, forward capital programmes, acquisitions, mergers and divestments, and major organisational changes.

The ICI board made it clear however that this was not to be an opening to unlimited free-ranging discussion before decisions were taken. It said that what it called 'consultation' would occur only at or near the place of employment itself and would involve, where possible, employees being given the opportunity of discussing and making known their views before a decision was taken. 'This can only apply in cases in which the management decision is still open and would be adjusted where possible to take employees' views into account', said the statement.

ICI then went on to bolt the door a little harder by introducing its lesser concept of 'communication':

There are however cases where consultation with employees before decisions are taken is either impracticable or is harmful to the company. In these cases, management should inform employees as soon as possible after the decision, should disclose as much as possible of the reasons for the decision, and should consult with employees on the detailed implementation of the decision.

The rest of the board's statement was mainly devoted to explaining the advantages of consultation and of passing on as much information to employees as is commercially practicable.

Since these guidelines were produced, the system has been developed further, notably by the creation in 1976 of a new central business and investment committee which comprises about twenty people including about eleven employee representatives, three main board members and other top management. The objective of this committee, which has about two formal meetings a year, is:

To enable a group of employee representatives to achieve a sufficient understanding of the company's investment planning, financial planning, and manpower planning policies at company level (and other special subjects which arise from time to time) for them to be able to appreciate how these policies affect them in their own day to day activities within their own divisions, and to contribute to the formulation of such policies. It will do this as part of a communication process involving all employees.

This puts ICI well in advance of most other companies and the committee's work is accompanied by similar investment meetings with full-time national officials and by joint discussions on investment in the company's divisions.

The idea for setting up such a central investment committee (some divisional committees had existed earlier) arose from the report of a joint employee–management working party on consultation and participation in ICI. Other issues arising from this report included the need for greater shopfloor understanding and involvement to back up the shop stewards, for better communication, which meant managers having more knowledge and commitment to consultation, and for supervisors to be involved more. Shop stewards also needed better facilities.

Generally, the shop stewards covered by the report made it clear that they wanted, through regular discussion and consultation methods, to be able to influence general company decisions before they were made and, especially, to share in the making of decisions affecting employees (so claiming a bigger say over employment issues).

Many of the problems associated with participation were apparent. There was a problem of making sure that shop floor employees knew what was happening within formal consultative systems because without such knowledge they were unlikely to feel involved or committed to its affairs. One way ICI attempts to solve this is to create work groups as a means of communication. Problems were also found in differentiating between consultation and negotiation, and workers were sometimes disappointed when matters being handled through the consultative process failed to produce as quick an answer as might have emerged from a negotiation forum. On the success side however there were examples of the formal committee structures and informal arrangements helping to solve problems such as health hazards, the run-down of a plant, communications with widely dispersed work groups and advance preparations for expensive new equipment.

Shop stewards were conscious of the potential problems associated with their close liaison with management decision-making and with their possession of business information. There was concern that, while this was expanding their role in the representation of their members' interests, it could lead to a danger that they would be seen to be holding élitist positions which separated them from their members. It was recognised that shop stewards would be vulnerable if this happened, especially if their members did not understand and accept the value of consultation and its relationship with a steward's more traditional negotiating role. The problems of élitism and severance from the shop floor were felt to be specially acute, for example, in committees that had been set up to bring a chairman of an ICI division together with a small group of senior shop stewards with whom he might share highly confidential information.

Overall, the report did not suggest any major changes in the company's consultative systems although it did look forward to gradual evolutionary change. Top managers in ICI now consider that the attitude of the company to practical involvement of shop stewards and others has developed radically in the past few years. So far few of the national union officials involved with the company have shown much interest in the worker director concept and so they point to the virtues in the ICI system. But in the future they may well try to tie the consultative arrangements more firmly into trade union structures and to bridge the gap between consultation and negotiation.

Unilever

Unilever is a multinational company with two parent companies, in London and Rotterdam; it employs 90,000 of its 321,000 worldwide work force in the UK. In its evidence to the Bullock Committee it said it

147

planned to expand existing local consultative arrangements with new company councils in all sizeable subsidiaries and it explained how it saw such a development relating to existing employee arrangements including traditional bargaining:

We recognise that a great deal of co-determination already takes place on the shop floor in the course of collective bargaining with shop stewards. We have no wish to interfere with these established practices. Our aim is to build new structures which bridge the communication/consultation gaps between not only the unionised groups and non-unionised, but also between the separately organised union groups – to recognise in fact their common characteristics that they are all employees of the company.

Unilever said it hoped its company councils would both create participation at the company level and stimulate further participation in local units. Significantly it also grasped the problem of what to do about the role of the manager (see Chapter 8) and said that it hoped the developments would lead to 'more involvement of managers in their role as employees'.

Unilever was also frank about how far it had really got in employee participation:

Basically we are still at the consultative stage, improving communications, providing opportunities for dialogue, ensuring that issues are fully ventilated before decisions are taken. These stages of development are important in providing a base of data, knowledge and understanding necessary for further progress. When all parties to these discussions are ready we must and will be prepared to define very specific areas of co-determination.

The principles for its proposed company councils were that all employees, not just union members, should be involved; that outside union officials could not become representatives; and that all matters subject to collective bargaining should be excluded from discussions. The councils' objectives would be to provide continuous consultation, to discuss company results, to promote job development and to provide information about long-term plans. The councils, while not having any decision-making role, would be informed about and have authority to discuss and express opinions on economic and marketing questions including budgets and investments, production questions including re-organisation and technology, personnel issues such as manpower planning and labour turnover, and special issues such as safety, health and hygiene.

By the middle of 1977 these company councils had been set up in some Unilever subsidiaries, although occasionally unions were either loath to move too far till their unions had adopted policies on the Bullock Report or were unwilling to sit down with non-union representatives. In one Unilever subsidiary employing twelve thousand people in factories scattered around the country, a central company council has been set up and has sprouted a smaller liaison committee which prepares the way for the council meetings. The company council has fifty members. Most of these are union representatives but they also include non-union representatives of such groups as head office staff, senior and middle management and salesmen. To begin with basically a communications exercise, the council discussed the company's five-year plan and influenced some changes in the plan's product manufacturing proposals. The attraction for the unions, which apparently outweighed the fact of having to sit alongside non-union representatives, was that they were gaining information and having a limited potential impact on some decisions covering their company as a whole, not just their own individual factories and shopfloor areas.

Ford Motor

Ford takes a rather different approach from many other companies in its attitudes to the current debate because, while it is developing communications exercises with its 66,000 employees in the UK, it puts its primary emphasis on its collective bargaining machinery rather than on new participative councils. It has a tough labour relations tradition and a determination not to blur existing arrangements by clamping participative methods on to conflict-based systems, so its detailed policy is of relevance here (see also Chapter 9).

Ford runs highly centralised wage bargaining and labour relations systems based on a thirty-year-old national joint negotiating committee for manual workers covering the whole company, plus factory level works committees, also set up thirty years ago. The national committee now comprises union officials and shop stewards and serves both as a consultative and negotiating forum. (Parallel arrangements exist for white-collar workers.) Its business over the years has expanded from negotiating wage issues, developing employer–union procedures, to reviewing business plans and company prospects. The joint works committees cover some grievance procedure problems and act as consultative bodies (there is no local pay bargaining in Ford) on matters such as market penetration, quality, costs and production schedules. This is backed up by twice-yearly meetings when Ford UK's managing director and other senior executives meet about 150 hourly paid and salaried employee representatives to review a range of company issues. At one meeting in 1975 for example these issues ranged from Ford's share of the car market and its marketing strategies and sales forecasts to exports, future model programme, investments, including why Ford was investing in Spain, profitability comparisons, and manufacturing efficiency. (A similar exercise is mounted for other groups of people including MPs representing Ford factory areas.) These information exchanging sessions are then repeated by local senior management throughout all Ford's twenty-three UK factories where work is stopped for mass meetings each attended by about five hundred employees and lasting perhaps one to two hours.

Now, without turning its back on its basic bargaining approach, Ford is looking for new ways of developing plant-level systems for reviewing and discussing important issues. It will be doing this with the knowledge that its employees' shopfloor power already prevents it from having a unilateral ability to manage on many matters. At the same time it knows that the unions' adversary traditions mean that up to now there are many management decisions in which they have no wish to participate and show no willingness to accept wider responsibilities for company affairs. A combination of these viewpoints means that, despite an awareness of social changes, Ford sees no industrial logic in radically changing its practices. It will not therefore be looking for any early changes in its basic managerial systems, especially since it already has its company-wide and works committees straddling bargaining and consultation.

GEC

Following the Weinstock Memorandum of September 1975 (Chapter 9) GEC five months later circulated its subsidiaries with a participation document which set three broad objectives:

To improve business performance by developing opportunities for growth and eliminating inefficient practices, in the interests of all employees; to increase the involvement and commitment of all employees, especially at the workplace where they have most to give and most to gain; to ensure proper regard for the dignity of every individual employee.

The document then went on to outline 'essential preparation and development' which concentrated on the education and involvement of all managers from managing directors to foremen in the preparation of consultation and communication processes. It said: 'In particular senior managers should not underestimate the importance of being seen on the shop floor, in offices and at sports and social functions.'

It also gave a shopping list for consultation:

Business performance: To enable employees to have an understanding of the business in which they are involved management should, consistent with the need for commercial security, report regularly (possibly once a quarter) and discuss such items as: sales including exports, orders received and in hand, output levels, capital employed, inventories, employee numbers, costs, investment spent and projects, quality, reliability, service, other aspects of customer satisfaction, state of the market and competition, profit levels and cash flow–as and when these can be understood and usefully discussed, and performance as against budget. Other business matters which should be considered and then reported and discussed as and when appropriate are: management's commercial objectives and plans; training and manpower plans; non-financial objectives; budget preparations; methods of improving productivity and effecting savings; marketing policy and problems; particular cost problems–e.g. fuel consumption and material conservation, new products, changes in organisation, production methods, factory layout designed to improve business performance and/or job satisfaction, power restrictions, procedures for dealing with disciplines, disputes, absenteeism and time off.

The document then emphasised that such consultation should not be confined to formal meetings–other informal methods such as briefing groups and house magazines should also be used. Employees and their representatives should also be involved in health, safety and welfare subjects.

As with other companies, however, all this was basically to do with communicating information and encouraging limited consultation rather than introducing any participation in decision-making. It was of course written to be broadly applicable to all GEC's 130 companies in the UK. Developments within a large group inevitably occur at varying speeds, and the carefully calculated terms of the document did not stop some GEC companies from making considerable strides forward, including the creation of joint shopfloor–management teams to plan new operations. One small GEC company in south London for example has had twenty such teams preparing for a move to a new factory. The teams have worked out varying aspects of how the factory would function (putting job design ideas into practice) within an umbrella management–union deal on pay and productivity which was agreed in advance. This GEC subsidiary's experience illustrates how a participative approach can be grafted onto collective bargaining methods, given the right traditions, attitudes and incentives (in this case the employees not being made unemployed).

Towards power sharing

In general these examples underline the fact that even some of the most advanced organisations in this field are only now developing the sorts of communications and consultation systems that allow employees an extremely limited and far from consistent opportunity to air their views. There are however some instances of employers going a little further. There is for example the relatively new participation scheme in British Leyland which operates at all levels in the company. Chrysler has also developed participation arrangements which bring union operations and management decision-making close together.

Such innovations are still relatively rare and other companies which have begun their own experiments have generally been loath to publicise them for fear either of upsetting the success of the achievements or of laying themselves open to union claims for similar treatment elsewhere in their companies. But some of the country's biggest organisations, like GEC and GKN in the engineering industry, have started down this path. Some companies have taken the ICI investment consultation a stage further and given shop stewards a degree of influence over local invest- ment and production matters; still others, like GKN, have set up factory councils to embrace bargaining and consultative issues. There are no major worker director schemes in the private sector of British industry, however, although there are one or two limited small company examples.

Charters for workpeople in GKN

A handful of smallish companies within the large Guest Keen and Nettlefolds Group (73,000 employees in the UK) have developed their own special style of participation schemes during the past decade. While appearing on the surface to smack of the benevolent paternalistic attitudes that have inspired other better known arrangements (such as those in Cadbury Schweppes), they in fact involve what their managers regard as a hard-nosed commercial approach. This is based on a belief that operating in tough industries and often in militant areas, co-opera- tion can be based only on workers being given all the economic facts possible about the running of the business. This is different from a company's management paternalistically or autocratically deciding what it thinks it would be good for the employees to be allowed to be told. In addition the GKN examples, while they do not give anything like the sort of full power-sharing that the most radical union leaders are seeking through industrial democracy, illustrate how collective bargaining and consultation can effectively be merged and conflict traditions diluted.

Five of the schemes are covered by what are known as 'charters for workpeople' which are in effect enabling agreements that provide a way for day-to-day arrangements to be worked out. The first such experiment was started in 1968 at Vandervell Products of Maidenhead which manufactures components for the motor industry and employs about two thousand people. Another was at GKN Shotton, which is a foundry in Halesowen near Birmingham employing three hundred people. Following some success in these first two agreements, other similar arrangements were introduced at Scottish Stamping and Engineering of Ayr in Scotland, with 1800 employees, at the BRD Company in Walsall employing 1500, and at the Bromsgrove division of Garringtons, where there are over two thousand workers. All these companies supply parts and components to the motor industries.

Each agreement has relied on special styles of management–employee relationships developed from scratch, which means that managers can have a major influence by introducing methods on their own terms rather than having them dictated by entrenched union-developed traditions. The Shotton scheme was set up in 1969 when the foundry, shut down earlier because of intense racial and labour troubles, was reopened with new management and a new labour force. The Vandervell scheme was set up around the same time, when GKN introduced trade unionism into the company, which had been a non-union family firm till GKN bought it in 1967.

In an attempt to stress the role and importance of GKN's customers and its eighty thousand shareholders and to dilute the worker–management conflict, the charters stress that GKN is a 'British Public Enterprise entrusted to the direction and control of professional managers who are the servants of the company'. Customers, it points out, need quality products and investors want fair returns. So productivity must be high with employees being given 'equitable treatment and fair reward' and trained to 'develop their full potential at work'.

Within these high-sounding aims, the charters lay down a practical consultation-cum-bargaining system based on the trade unions and designed by the employees and management involved. It is headed by a factory and productivity council which, in the Vandervell manual workers' case, comprises twelve elected shop stewards and twelve appointed managers. (Vandervell has a separate charter and structure for manual workers, salaried non-managerial staff, and supervisory management. At Shotton the three groups come together in one scheme with a factory and productivity council of six appoined managers, eight shop stewards, two elected staff representatives and one elected supervisor.)

These councils have the authority to discuss and agree 'any matters affecting the interests of workpeople', which is generally interpreted as being limited to employment and workplace matters as opposed to wider company affairs. Beneath them they have four or five individual committees dealing with agreements, factory manning arrangements, safety and health, discipline, fringe benefits and disciplinary matters. These committees have a mixture of negotiating-style or joint regulation powers on normal labour relations subjects, and rights to advise or recommend decisions on issues such as manpower budgets, redeployment and training policies and other employment issues. The company considers that the shop stewards involved have shown no signs as yet of wanting to extend these consultative advisory and recommending roles into the management area of joint decision-making.

A similar style of system exists in another GKN company, Ionic Plating, which employs a total of 450 people at three factories in Edinburgh and in the Midlands at Smethwick and Dudley. The participation in these factories revolves round the running of a plant-wide added-value bonus scheme. The operation of such a scheme can in itself be regarded as a method of participation because of the way it involves employee interest and co-operaton in the wealth-creating success of the business. The scheme is watched over by a council of appointed managers and elected employee representatives who are changed every year so that as many employees as possible learn the economics of their factory. Shop stewards, if not elected, are co-opted on to the committee, which considers the factories' performance, recommends production improvements to the management, and acts as a general consultative force.

These particular schemes are not typical of GKN establishments, but they serve both as effective ways of running the factories involved and as test-beds for methods that might be copied by other companies in the group. Their experiences for example influenced plans that have been considered for employee councils to be introduced across GKN. But the main participative advance in the group has been a communications exercise based on a 'provision of information to employees policy' that is being implemented by all GKN companies. This includes education and training schemes aimed at providing employees with a wide range of company facts. In addition, companies are reviewing their employee involvement practices.

Chrysler

After a rather shaky attempt at introducing industrial democracy during its financial crises of 1975, Chrysler emerged by the start of 1977 as one of the more progressive new entrants to the participation arena. Its mistake two years earlier had been suddenly to offer the unions some boardroom seats and a full scale committee system for participation in management. These proposals sounded at the time more like the last throes of a dying company than a constructive participative proposal. Chrysler said when it made the offer, early in May 1975, that it was 'acknowledging that the world has changed, and will continue to change, and was offering its assurance that it was ready to proceed with new concepts and ideas since it was obvious that the old ways have not done the job'. While few people who knew of Chrysler's sad UK record in the preceding years would query this statement, the offer of creating worker directors seemed a mere gimmick. Accordingly, when combined with general uncertainty among some unions over the worker director concept, it fairly quickly faded into the background, to be replaced by a far more wide-ranging and pragmatic participation approach.

This new approach has been based on a communications exercise involving the company's nineteen thousand UK employees, plus arrangements for union representatives to participate, without detailed formalised structures, in management decision-making where they wish. Alongside these exercises, Chrysler has also worked out the country's first planning agreement with its shop stewards and presented this to the Government in February 1977.

Three main participative devices were developed during 1976 by Chrysler. The first two are similar to techniques already discussed. They involve conferences being held four times a year between 250 union representatives and senior management, echoed at local level by other conferences, plus a quarterly company bulletin issued to all employees detailing items such as production targets and financial results.

The third element however is more radical and moves union representatives into the area of management decision-making on an *ad hoc* basis by letting them take part in normal management meetings. This allows them to retain their right to opt out of decisions that they think might blur their basic trade union role. The emphasis has been on relative informality without too much concern for detailing precise powers. An added significance of this Chrysler development is that it takes the employee representatives directly into the management structures instead of having them operate in the sort of parallel but separate structures associated with normal consultative or bargaining machinery or with the sort of participation committees set up at Leyland (see below).

The planning agreement process provided a corporate-level umbrella exercise above these plant-level operations and enabled thirty-five shop stewards to come together in a working party with nine senior company directors to produce a document mapping out how the company's future should be secured. The main working party sprouted sub-committees dealing with finance, sales and product planning, manufacturing and supplies, and employment and productivity. Inevitably, most of the expertise came from the management side, which also dominated a lot but not all of the decision-making; but the exercise did provide a major communications forum where the shop stewards could scrutinise management plans and try to influence the decisions. The result was that the shop stewards, and to a lesser extent some outside local union officials, became far more involved in the company's affairs and helped during 1976 in the efforts to ease the company's troubles. In the future however it may be difficult for Chrysler to maintain the informality that it successfully engendered during 1976, and it may well find, if the experiment continues successfully, that the unions want to institutionalise their influence and the power-sharing. The involvement of employee representatives directly in management structures (as opposed to operating alongside them) could then confuse the executive functions of management as well as raising questions about the traditional role of unions.

British Leyland

A more formalised and structured approach was introduced around the same time in British Leyland (BL) and involved the creation of three tiers of participation committees, separate both from management structures and from traditional collective bargaining machinery. This scheme was proposed by British Leyland's management in December 1974, just before the Government set up the Ryder Committee to map out the company's future.

British Leyland's first attempt to set up a central consultative council to discuss company affairs with the unions away from the bargaining arena had been made in 1970, two years after the company had been formed by the merger of British Motor Holdings and Leyland Motors. The 1970 initiative was rejected by the unions, who were worried both that such a consultative committee might be used to organise redundancies among the company's 168,000 employees and that it could provide a platform for central wage bargaining, so removing some autonomy from shop stewards in the company's fifty-eight factories.

In May 1974, in an attempt to recover something from the 1970 debacle, BL held its first-ever company-wide conference, which was attended by four hundred shop stewards and managers. Then, in December 1974, it drew up its participation committee plan. This was adopted in full by the Ryder Committee apart from the fact that a proposed top-level company-wide joint council was dropped in line with the Ryder Report's preference for the company to be run on a divisional rather than group basis. Two main and quite separate participation structures have therefore been developed for the cars division and the truck and bus division as well as a less wide-ranging structure in the company's special products division.

Proposals put forward by some unions and shop stewards to the Ryder Committee for worker and government representatives each to have one-third of the seats on a nationalised Leyland board (with management 'specialists' having the other third) were not taken up, and the Ryder Report also made it clear that participation did not mean joint regulation or control when it said that participation committees should 'seek as far as possible to reach agreement . . . while recognising that executive responsibility rests with management'. This limits the potential for real power-sharing by giving the management the executive power to go ahead if there is not a consensus on a participation committee. But it also raises the problem of what shop stewards then do, because in theory at least they are locked into a co-operative participation framework – although, again in theory, they are as free to walk out and protest as the management are to go ahead alone. In practice it has emerged that when they have lost an argument the shop stewards have sometimes gone away and just let events take their course but have occasionally staged industrial action in protest. (An early and major example of the latter militant course occurred in 1976 over the siting of a big paint shop in the Midlands. This was however something of a special case because it arose from a management decision taken before the participation system was set up.) Such a participation system could not survive as an effective co-operative forum if such protest action were taken often.

The participation schemes set up for both the cars division and truck and bus division were agreed in October 1975, only six months after the Ryder Report appeared. In Leyland Cars this led to the system that started to come into force the following January. It consisted of a top-level car council of eleven shop stewards, four staff representatives and some ten management representatives (it was an achievement in itself to get the manual worker and staff representatives to sit down together). The employee representatives had been elected from six middle-level divisional committees, which in turn sprang from more than thirty factory committees. The top and bottom levels are the most important in this structure, with the middle rung usually only acting as a channel of communication, while the top level's work has become so complex that it has set up its own specialist sub-committees on subjects such as productivity, quality and safety.

Subjects handled by the committees cover almost all Leyland's affairs from long-term ten-year plans to detailed plant business. For example, the company used the cars council in 1976 and 1977 to obtain advance commitment on productivity targets for its projected new Mini, to harness support for production of its Allegro model to be shifted from Birmingham to Belgium, and for other production changes.

In a highly unionised company such as BL it would have been fool-hardy to have tried to set up a system separate from the unions. The company's rationale on this and on the single-channel issue (discussed in the last chapter) was explained in evidence it sent to the Bullock Committee. It said that it had set up a separate structure from the collective bargaining machinery but that the same employee representatives sat on both systems:

The company thought it undesirable to combine a new participation system with the traditional collective bargaining system. At the same time employee representatives were reluctant to allow a completely new system to be established which might become a rival and conflicting power grouping. Equally the company had no wish to be confronted with the task of reconciling the interests of yet one more power group with those which it already has the duty to harmonise. It made good sense to keep the institutions and the roles separate but the membership common so that industrial relations realities are observed.

But, the company added,

Undoubtedly the participation representatives will at times act as negotiating representatives to protect the interests of those employees who elected them and to whom they remain accountable. If they did not do so on those occasions when a conflict of interests has to be reconciled, they would cease to enjoy the confidence of their members who might see them as no more than a duplicate and unnecessary set of managers.

The company went on to note (prophetically) that conflicts of interest would emerge between shop stewards themselves as well as between the stewards and management; but it hoped that the participation committees would be a place where such inter-union difficulties could be sorted out. It also hoped that facts learned in the participation process would make the shop stewards be more 'constructive' in their negotiation, so improving the use of manpower. 'In this way the participation system and the negotiating system can interact beneficially', said the company, which also acknowledged (as the Bullock Report suggested later) that, 'appropriately nurtured', the natural growth of industrial democracy might 're-legitimise the job that managers do'.

In practice however, as BL recognises, all its early hopes have yet to be fulfilled, at least in its car factories. As has been mentioned elsewhere this is partly because of the speed with which Leyland Cars introduced the system when it was accepted in individual factories (four plants raised objections and stayed out to begin with, including the Triumph factory in Coventry). Problems have also arisen in practice because managers and employees have not fully understood either their new roles or the relationship between traditional bargaining arrangements and the new participative exercises. In addition, because the employee representatives are not sitting Chrysler-style in the actual management decision-making structure, they often have not felt that they have had much real power.

Opportunities for employee influence to be felt should however increase within a Leyland-style system the longer the system remains in being, because major corporate decisions that the top employee representatives have influenced, for example on the controversial new Mini project, should gradually work their way through till they arrive on the shop floor. Certainly the Mini project was influenced by the shop stewards and staff representatives on the top tier in 1976 and 1977, by which time management proposals on other topics had also been altered and employee suggestions accepted, particularly in specialist sub-committees. But the long lead time for major projects means it can be years before a major project originated entirely under such a participation system reaches the shop floor, and in the meantime it is inevitable that the growing pains of participation will be accompanied by frustration and scepticism.

In the early months of this scheme, one was hearing that while the shop stewards thought they could exert some influence on the top car council, they found that the major decisions were being taken elsewhere by management. They were then passed down the management line where, to complicate matters, there were usually six executive levels compared with the basic three participative tiers. By the time the matters reached the bottom tier, the key decisions on how the top-level policies should be executed had, the shop stewards complained, already been made: so there was apparently little chance for the shop stewards at any level to have a major impact on day-to-day affairs.

At the same time it has become clear – as was expected from the start – that there has often not been enough shopfloor involvement and that the bottom third tier covered too wide an area to be anything but remote from employees. Some factories have therefore created a lower fourth level, which might cover a thousand employees, instead of the six thousand in the third level covering a whole factory. It was thought best, to begin with, not to create too many formal tiers, but simply to start with three and then let individual plants see what else they needed – the giant Longbridge plant for example has even moved to a fifth lower tier. The involvement of full-time local trade union officials, accustomed to playing a major role in the affairs of their local car factories, has created further problems and also some jealousies because full-time officials have no role in the participation system.

In its evidence to the Bullock Committee, Leyland illustrated the sheer weight of work involved in such participative exercises. Interaction between the six executive and the basic three participative tiers on a matter passing through them meant, the company estimated, that the matter would be considered on a minimum of twenty-four occasions, which meant planning for decision-making had to start earlier. But Leyland saw an advantage in this:

Although there is no doubt that decisions of a kind that could previously have been taken and put into effect without adverse consequences will now suffer delay, decisions of a kind that were previously taken in hope and perished in effect will not now be attempted. Instead, the decision will be made more slowly but the results will be achieved more rapidly.

Leyland emphasised the need carefully to organise who is to be consulted about what and illustrated the size of this problem by pointing out that, taking its car, truck and bus divisions together, there are a total of fifty-five third-tier committees, twelve middle-tier and two top councils. In a normal year, it estimated that this would lead to some 760 joint meetings with each group of participants presumably having an equivalent number of preparatory and de-briefing sessions in addition. This led BL to estimate that something like 260,000 manhours would be used up in the course of a year at a cost of approximately £650,000–which however, even with travelling expenses included, represented only 0.14 per cent of British Leyland's total UK pay and employee benefits bill, an investment that the company not surprisingly thought should 'ultimately produce a return greater than the cost'. While the cost might be relatively small, however, the organisational problems illustrated by these facts are immense and show the problems involved in trying rapidly to introduce a full participation system.

One of the main problems that BL–now basically a state-owned company–has suffered for several years because of its political and economic importance to the UK is that it is rarely allowed the luxury enjoyed by some other companies mentioned in this chapter of introducing its reforms slowly away from the public gaze. Pat Lowry, the company's industrial relations director, said in 1975 of worker participation in general:

Employee participation is a delicate flower and it is my worry that unless we are all careful it will either wither in the frost of managerial suspicion and mistrust or, more likely in my view, will perish through over-exposure to the hot house of our political system.

One of the problems that Leyland had found itself facing in its car factories is that these managerial and political factors have sometimes put the credibility of its own participation scheme at risk, especially when too much is expected of such innovations too quickly.

Worker directors

There are no major worker director schemes in operation in the mainstream of the private sector of British industry. What does exist however is a growing number of schemes in the public sector, while workers' co-operatives and common-ownership enterprises such as Meriden and the John Lewis Partnership have workers on their boards and governing councils. But in the private sector, Chrysler's surprise offer not having been taken up in 1975, no major private sector company has a significant number of worker directors. Where they do exist in smaller concerns they normally form only a part of a broader employee participation programme and have been introduced because of an employer's benevolence, not through trade union or employee initiation. They thus often amount to what is sometimes called 'sham democracy' because the worker directors have no real power.

One of the largest private sector companies with such a system is Bristol Channel Ship Repairers, a subsidiary of the C. H. Bailey Group and the company that made much of the running against the Labour Government's shipbuilding nationalisation Bill in 1975-6 with the result that ship-repairers were left in private hands. Another is the Felixstowe Dock and Railway Company, which runs one of the most successful ports in Britain and was also coincidentally the subject of a state control versus private ownership row around the same time. It appointed a TGWU shop steward to its board in 1975. But the union asked him to give up his shop steward's role, and he is now the director in charge of health, safety and welfare.

Bristol Channel Ship Repairers, with about a thousand employees, mixes its worker director system with a share ownership scheme (see Chapter 13), under which employees hold 20 per cent of its shares. Communication conferences take place four times a year between management, employees and union officials, while small group briefing sessions are also held for employees on the company's finances. Two or three worker directors are elected in ballots of all employees to the boards of subsidiary companies but not to the main group board because the company believes that employee directors should be involved only in their operating companies.

Another company with a worker director, in this case chosen by the management, is Bonser Engineering, a forklift truck manufacturer with 350 employees. The scheme was introduced at the end of 1975 and the worker director sits on a supervisory-style board. Describing the company's views a few months later, an Industrial Society booklet called *Democracy in Industry* reported that the company had said:

Though Bonser's employee director is an active member of the AUEW, he carries to the Boardroom the viewpoint of all employees, including non-union workers, members of two other unions and, of course, office workers. He does not 'represent' any union block and so does not pre-empt any of the functions of the stewards or of supervision. He must have – and be seen to have – integrity, maturity, judgement, intelligence, independence of view, and contact with those about him. The company believes, and the employees agree, that this can be accomplished only by selection – not election – of someone of suitable attributes; but after full consultation with local union organisers and subject to *post facto* approval of the entire organisation.

There are two worker directors at the Computer Machinery Company of Hemel Hempstead which has 450 employees, only about 6 per cent of whom are in a trade union. It introduced a system in 1974 for two worker directors to be elected annually to its management board – the lower level of a two-tier structure. The worker directors have found that they broadly fulfil a welfare and communications role rather than serving any major decision-making function. The management board meetings are also attended by nine managers who are department heads and appear to perform a consultative role on subjects such as production, sales and cash flow.

Other companies, including Berry Wiggins (Bitumen and Refining) and Steel Engineering Installations of Sunderland, have experience of worker directors. But generally, like the examples briefly described above, they primarily only provide a form of two-way communication between management and employees in relatively small companies. As such they are found to be valuable by those concerned, but few if any of them (by early 1977) had had to withstand problems such as a major pay dispute or widespread redundancies (although Bristol Channel had laid some men off); nor had they come to terms with the key issue of the accountability of a significant proportion of a board's members to a trade union organisation.

A different solution was introduced in 1978 in the operating subsidiaries of a medium-sized engineering company, Grundy of Teddington, where the employees hired (with management help) an outsider called an 'employees' director' to be their board representative.

Conclusion

It is clear from all these developments that relationships between companies and their employees have started to change in the past few years. To begin with the initiative has come from employers aware of the need to try to keep their employees happy and motivated, especially at a time when Britain has been going through industrial and economic difficulties which can affect workers' pay packets and job prospects. At the same time, industrialists have wanted to counter political trends and persuade their employees of the validity of the role of profits – and therefore industrial efficiency – in the running of their businesses. This has meant they have wanted to consult employees more in order to persuade them of the wisdom of management decisions.

But this efficiency-oriented employer-led movement has now run up against a union trend moving diagonally across its path, with the TUC and some top union leaders saying that this employer interest in telling workers about companies' fortunes and giving them a very limited new say in their working environment is not enough. What these union leaders want is to see the balance of power – not just the balance of financial knowledge – in industry changed so that they can influence today those major corporate decisions that will affect their members' lives tomorrow. 'I am tired of having to cope with shopfloor problems affecting my members' livelihoods which are the result of management decisions taken hundreds of miles away in some board room two or three years ago. I want to be able to influence events when the decisions are taken, not years after when it is too late to do much more than protest and make the best of it' is a typical viewpoint of a union leader seeking this increased power.

But the blunt fact is that, without legislation, the unions will not gain this power. This is because private sector industrialists have different traditions and more to lose personally than their public sector counterparts and do not believe the unions are prepared or ready to shoulder full responsibilities. They also distrust the political aspects of industrial democracy and are worried about the conflicts of multi-unionism being given more scope to develop. So they are not prepared to hand over that much of their decision-making autonomy. What some industrialists, worried therefore about the catalytic 'leap in the dark' aspect of industrial democracy, are prepared to do is to move slowly down the paths mapped out in this chapter – gradually telling their employees more about their company and only later letting employee representatives in on the outer fringes of decision-making.

What companies should be aiming for fairly quickly, of course, is to develop some form of participative system. While not always actually giving employees a formal role in the final decision-taking, this would involve them in discussions sufficiently for them to play a significant and growing part in the decision-making process in the hope that this would remove some of the conflict over how industry operates.

Chapter 12

Participation Trends: The Public Sector, from Whitley to Worker Directors

The public sector of employment, embracing areas such as nationalised industries, the public services and the Civil Service, has different traditions of management–employee relationships from the private sector. More emphasis has traditionally been placed on communication and consultation with employees, and managements do not always hold the almost instinctive view of private sector industrialists that trade unions are primarily organisations based on conflict, able and willing to exercise only negative powers.

Nevertheless, the increasing state ownership of the past thirty years has not proved to be the socialist panacea that had been hoped for, let alone a commercial success. The result has been the emergence of massive and often inefficient and unprofitable bureaucracies. The traditional British conflicts of industrial relations between the manager and the managed have not disappeared either, despite the communication and consultation traditions. Indeed, the conflicts have sometimes been more bitter than in the private sector when groups of public employees (notably the miners, but there are several others) have been at the centre of national pay disputes stemming from the political policies of their ultimate employer, the Government.

On the other hand, the traditions of consultation and communication do give a firmer base in the public sector on which to build new methods of industrial democracy and to recognise the legitimacy of unions as sources of positive actions. This is now emerging, especially in the nationalised industries, in innovations ranging from new national consultation systems in the electricity supply industry to a worker director experiment in the Post Office.

The traditions are partly the result of the ability of the unions to persuade governments (especially Labour) to improve their employees' rights. This dates back to the First World War and to what has now become called Whitleyism, and to the founding statutes of nationalised industries which have provided a legislative requirement for employees to be consulted. The philosophy of Whitleyism was aimed at reducing conflict by providing associated bargaining and consultative procedures so that both sides of industry would meet to sort out their problems. Initially intended to cover all areas, the Whitley tradition is now mainly, but not exclusively, apparent in the public sector. Furthermore, Labour governments, when they have intervened to provide state cash in ailing industries, have also occasionally started industrial democracy experi-

161

ments. So it is not surprising that the public sector is ahead of private industry in worker director and other participation ideas. There is one stumbling block, however. This is the potential clash between industrial democracy and parliamentary democracy, including a minister's responsibility solely to Parliament for his public services and industries (see Chapter 7).

Some of the more notable developments have emerged in four main industries – electricity supply, coal mining, the post office and steel – each of which have been pace makers in their own ways, as well as in Harland and Wolff. While there have been developments in other areas, such as the railways, gas supply, the health service, local government and education, these are specially representative of the trends, along with the Fairfields Experiment of the 1960s. The electricity supply industry has strong consultative traditions springing from nationalisation in the 1940s; but it shows little current interest in worker directors and is developing its consultation systems with new arrangements. The coal industry is now trying to come to terms, through new participative arrangements, with a recently highly successful militant work force which is clinging to old adversary traditions. The Post Office is carrying its consultative traditions, started when it was part of the civil service and enlarged into participation in management decisions when it became a nationalised industry in 1969, forward into the area of worker directors. The steel industry, which provided Britain with its first major, but limited, experiment in worker directors in the 1960s, is now considering fresh developments. The innovations introduced and planned at the Belfast shipyard of Harland and Wolff show how one relatively small part of conflict-based industry with private sector traditions has moved into State ownership and is now trying to cure some of its problems through participation.

In each of these cases, the managements involved have accepted and designed systems tuned to the views and traditions of the unions involved. None of the unions has been coerced into accepting responsibilities it does not want; but in each case the managements are trying, through different forms of industrial democracy, to coax the unions to change some of their traditions and to co-operate with management in the interests of their members' and their industry's efficiency.

Whitley traditions

The Whitley traditions date from 1917 and 1918 when a government Committee on Relations between Employers and Employed under the chairmanship of J. H. Whitley, MP, produced for the then Ministry of Reconstruction a postwar framework of labour relations in five reports. The reports recommended three levels of employer – union organisation based on joint industrial councils covering a whole industry with lower-level joint district councils and works committees (which could, but need not, be union-based). The objective was to achieve 'the better utilisation of the practical knowledge and experience of workpeople'. As Professor Hugh Clegg says in his book – *The System of Industrial Relations in Great Britain*:

The Whitley Committee thus established three important principles of joint consultation as it subsequently developed in Great Britain: that there are many topics of concern to employers and trade unions, and to managers and men, which are not suitable for settlement by negotiation and collective agreement; that these topics should be handled by co-operation; and that relations within the plant should be predominantly or entirely confined to co-operation over issues outside the scope of collective bargaining. *(Clegg, 1972.)*

This system was to be operated with industry-wide pay agreements which, while reducing the power of shop stewards that had built up during the First World War, enabled the divisions between negotiation and consultation to be neatly drawn within a common system. But the proposals worried union activists rather like worker directors worry some now, because, as Clegg puts it, 'Although they were presented as an extension of industrial democracy, these principles were in fact a retreat from the position which many war-time works committees and shop stewards committees had established.'

The Whitley reports were accepted by the Government. It recommended them to employers in the private sector, although much of their initial works committee impact was swept away during the period of post-war unemployment. Some national joint industrial councils however still exist and companies like Rowntree, Cadbury and ICI set up consultative works councils on the Whitley model in the 1920s.

Once it had recommended Whitley-style union recognition, negotiation and consultation to the private sector, the Government found it hard to resist union pressures to do the same for state employees (then of course in a much smaller public sector, mainly based on public services, than today). Whitley councils and their equivalents were set up in the Civil Service, which then included the Post Office, in 1919, and also in other branches of the public services. So by the time the Labour Government was returned in 1945, all the public sector had Whitley style negotiating and consultative arrangements.

The 1945 and 1964 Labour Government's waves of nationalisation also added new but limited extensions of a trade union presence in the boardroom. After an intensive debate within the Labour movement (Chapter 14) various retired and other union leaders were given nominal Boardroom seats and there was also the wider steel industry scheme. In 1968, the Labour Government also ordered an inquiry from the Tavistock Institute on railwaymen's interest in participation in British Railways' management decision-making–a study which appeared to show that workers were more interested in participation around their own jobs than in any high-level power sharing on boards.

But, more importantly, the nationalisation schemes of the 1940s and 1960s expanded the Whitley traditions of consultation, and of white collar unionism, into hitherto private sector industries such as electricity, coal, gas, steel, and rail. So, although it started out as a system of industrial relations for all sorts of private and public sector employment, 'Whitley-ism' is now often regarded simply as a system of employee consultation. In this guise it served the public sector well and has provided the groundwork on which a scheme like the post office's worker directors can be built.

In recent years however the Whitley tradition has begun to come under strain as unions have tried to move beyond its traditional confines of employment and welfare issues and to institutionalise nationally and locally the growing influence they have sometimes developed through informal arrangements on wider policy matters.

The Whitley tradition has however meant that some public service-based unions have developed their research and expertise more than is usual among private sector unions, as Geoffrey Drain, general secretary of the National and Local Government Officers' Association, told the Institute of Personnel Management conference in October 1976:

Public service unions have developed over the years in a way which enables them to play an effective part in the wider development of the services in which they are involved. At national level they have equipped themselves to participate authoritatively in discussions relating to all developments in their services, whether legislative or otherwise. At regional and local level they expect to have the same degree of participation in the framing and carrying out of policy against the national background. This degree of participation has been reflected in the growth of research, education and legal staffing within unions, and the development of administrative expertise over a wider field.

Electricity supply

The impact of the Whitley tradition on the newly nationalised industries of the 1940s was illustrated by the Electricity Act (1947), nationalising electricity supply in the 'public service board' traditions of Herbert Morrison (see Chapter 14) and specifying that unions should retain their independence and not formally enter the board rooms but should be involved in Whitley-style negotiations and consultations, with only a nominal union 'worthy' having a board seat. The principle was put into practice by Lord Citrine, the electricity industry's first chairman after nationalisation in 1947 and TUC general secretary from 1926 to 1946, who played a major part in the development of Whitley-style ideas. It is explained in a book on the industry's productivity schemes of the 1960s written jointly by a former chairman and a personnel chief of the Electricity Council, Sir Ronald Edwards, and R. D. V. Roberts:

The industrial relations machinery in electricity supply is cast in the classic mould: it has a lineage that goes back directly to the thinking of the TUC in the thirties and forties, to the Whitley Committee Reports of the First World War and the writings of the Webbs. The philosophical assumptions are twofold: that over pay and conditions of employment, conflict of short-term interests is bound to arise, and a representative body of employers and unions is necessary to reach orderly compromises on these issues, with provisions for [binding] arbitration when necessary; but also that employers, unions and employees have underlying interests in common–the prosperity of the industry and the wellbeing of its employees–and that some joint machinery (whether separate from or as a part of the negotiating machinery) should exist where these issues of common interest may be discussed. But here the procedure is essentially consultative: the final decisions on these matters are made by the employers. *(Edwards and Roberts, 1971.)*

This was a clearer statement of a nationalised industry's joint interest than would often be possible in the private sector of industry with its capitalist ownership overtones to the traditional employer–employee conflict. But this is not to say that there is no conflict in nationalised industries, as Edwards and Roberts made clear: 'Collective bargaining was appropriate to the area in which the interests of the employers and the trade unions were in conflict, but joint consultation was concerned with the area of common interests.' Even in 1947 however the unions, while seeing the practical force of the argument for separate negotiating and consultative machinery, argued strongly for the joint consultative machinery to be given 'teeth' so that their consultations had some authority. In the 1960s, when the industry became a pace maker in the negotiation of sophisticated productivity agreements, and when trade union interest in national and local policy and management issues widened, it became less easy precisely to define clear differences between consultative and negotiating issues.

By the mid-1970s the consultative systems in the electricity industry (and less highly developed and more secretive consultation in the gas supply industry) had therefore begun to come under strain. It was regarded by unions as only giving the illusion of participation in management decision-making, as not relating sufficiently to shopfloor workers, and as impeding the development of bargaining. While acknowledging that the electricity system may have been in advance of its time in 1947, union leaders and others also felt that it had become top-heavy and cumbersome, that it excluded key subjects because it had been designed primarily to deal with employment issues, and that the sharp official organisational split between bargaining and consultation was impractical with some subjects not falling clearly into either category. Taken together, these problems had meant for example that emergency consultative arrangements, extending existing arrangements for twelve-month advance notification of closures, had to be devised to discuss urgent power station closure programmes. As a result of these problems, discussions were initiated by the Electricity Council in 1974, and by the end of 1976 fresh consultative arrangements were being set up. These were formally announced in May 1977. While not satisfying all the nine unions concerned with the industry, they provided a new national consultative committee called the National Joint Co-ordinating Council. Discussions then started on what sort of network of similar consultative arrangements should be built below it.

The interest of public sector managements in gaining increased employee support for their policies while at the same time meeting the unions' demand for increased powers, was demonstrated when the Electricity Council announced the development. It said the aim was both to make unions and employees 'more fully involved in influencing the industry's decisions' and to gain 'full understanding among staff for the industry's policies'.

The Co-ordinating Council started work on an interim basis in July 1976. It was welcomed by some of the industry's senior union leaders, who are among the most vociferous opponents of worker directors, as showing how industrial democracy could be built outside the board room. Its first jobs were to design the way in which it would itself operate on a permanent basis, to set up a new national health and safety committee for the industry, and to advise the top management on current policy issues such as the power station ordering programme and long-term corporate plans.

Its long-term job is to try to extend participation discussions on a wide range of policy and management subjects separately from, but much more closely linked than before with, the industry's negotiating procedures. The subjects include matters affecting the efficient operation of the

165

industry and its corporate plans, financial matters including capital allocations and profitability, energy and appliance sales and trends, plant closures and openings, manpower trends and forecasts, organisational and technical changes including the choice of generating plant, fuel policies and relevant national economic matters.

The final shape or participation in this industry depends on the outcome of the Plowden Report, published early in 1976, on its reorganisation And the actual potential for the unions to share power with the top managers of the industry also depends on how crucial they are to the balance in the country's energy policies. But by the middle of 1977 the unions (backed by the Plowden Report) were resolutely sticking out against the introduction of worker director systems, following the purist lead of the Electrical and Plumbing Trades Union (see Chapters 6 and 17). Not all the union activists however were convinced of this and some, in NALGO and elsewhere, felt that their shop stewards or local officials could be more useful at least on the industry's regional boards than the semi-retired local MPs and other 'worthies' who were usually appointed. Nevertheless, as became clear at a consultative conference NALGO held of its electricity supply members late in 1976, there was a lot of grass-roots feeling, as there is in other industries, that, while employees and their unions should be consulted and have the power to influence decisions, they should not shoulder the job of management–even in state-owned concerns. On the other hand, there was a high level of exasperation with the industry's management and an undercurrent which could turn at least NALGO (which favours worker directors in the gas industry) towards board representation in electricity supply, if the new consultative arrangements do not provide an effective employee voice.

Gas supply
New arrangements were also being introduced early in 1977 in the more backward gas supply industry with the creation of a national planning liaison committee. This did not however go far enough to satisfy the unions, which have developed their own policy for moving via extended collective bargaining to worker directors (see Chapter 6). The new consultative arrangements specifically exclude detailed discussions on the industry's corporate plan but do permit consultations on two- to five-year trends for subjects such as work load, markets and manning levels under a broad brief to 'discuss and consider planning and objectives of the British Gas Corporation'. When it held its first meeting in January 1977, this committee expected to meet about four times a year and was considering whether to set up regional organisations. The gas industry is therefore considerably behind electricity and others such as the Post Office but is significant because it is probably still in advance of many private sector companies in the way it consults its employees. It is also developing local arrangements which are sometimes being based on special management–shop steward committees created over the past few years to implement a new wage structure. Having done their wage structure work, these committees are being turned, where shop stewards want such a system, into grass-roots participation organisations.

Coal

In the coal industry also major changes have been taking place to give miners' representatives a more positive say in how their industry and its pits are run and to build a four-tier consultative system linking the Government and the National Coal Board (NCB) to individual pits. Coal mines are of course a classic example of the adversary system at it strongest with the members of the National Union of Mineworkers (NUM) effectively using their strength to control what happens, from the rate at which a coal seam is dug to the fortunes of a government's national pay policy. This militant tradition has continued even though coal was nationalised at roughly the same time as electricity and had the same statutory consultation provisions, and even though the NUM has one nominee on the NCB as board member for personnel.

Nevertheless, since the national miners' strikes of 1972 and of 1973-4 (which coincided with the oil crisis), new efforts have successfully been made to introduce more positive participation, involving the unions in the realities of the business, with the intention of harnessing their positive co-operation and commitment. This is in fact a good example of a business trying to devise methods to increase participation and reduce conflict, within a strong adversary system, on those matters that might be jointly agreeable without trying to force the unions to dilute their traditional freedoms. None of the parties would therefore expect what they are doing to have more than a fringe impact on a future 1973-4-style clash over a basic conflict issue such as pay, although obviously there is the hope that, one day, increased business awareness might help curb high pay demands.

Left-wingers have naturally been suspicious of the new attempts at a participative approach and the miners oppose formal worker director ideas. But while the participation arrangements effectively mean that the NCB does not take any major decision without the agreement of the NUM leaders, the autonomy and loyalties of the NUM are in no way jeopardised. This is because the participative power is not institutionalised in a formal boadroom way—so union representatives are free to walk away from any issues or decisions they do not like. They have therefore generally co-operated while, ironically, it is the management unions, aware of the consequential change in the status and role of their members, that have been most worried.

The latest series of developments of the coal industry's systems of communication and consultation started after the 1972 miners' strike when a national joint policy advisory committee was set up with representatives of the National Coal Board and top leaders of the coal unions. This discusses, and tries, without any formal voting, to reach agreement on, the industry's broad budget, investment, new projects, manpower and other such issues. It is therefore the main board-level industry-wide forum and gives the miners the major powers over NCB decisions mentioned above.

After the 1974 strike, a new higher-level body was set up by the new Labour Government on a tripartite basis. Called the Coal Industry Tripartite Group, it brings in the Government, alongside the NCB and the unions, through the secretary of state for energy and ministers from other departments such as Employment and the Treasury. (Significantly, this was used as a model by the National Economic Development Office when it prepared its report–see Chapter 17–in 1976 on relations between nationalised industries and the Government. But the miners, horrified at the idea of institutionalising their arrangements in the way the Office suggested, rejected the NEDO report while continuing with their own arrangements.)

This Tripartite Group is now the supreme joint body in the decision-making area and, for example, issues reports on the industry's prospects. But again, it stops short of full decision-taking–which is formally in the hands of the Government and the board–and so need neither weaken the unions' independence nor break down itself with split votes. This was well illustrated in 1974 when there was broad agreement on the need for an incentive scheme but the NUM still fought the NCB over how the scheme should operate, which delayed it for years.

Lower down the scale, area policy committees and colliery policy committees have been planned to complete the four-tier structure and echo the national NCB–unions body in the board's twelve areas and 240 collieries. There has been some dispute however about the miners' union's interest in an equal say on colliery committees–an issue made more controversial in this industry by its safety problems, for which management are at present statutorily responsible. The new committees would develop from consultative bodies to provide participation in decision-making and would discuss the same sort of business problems dealt with nationally–in principle, deciding the policy issues, while leaving the management job of executing the policy decisions to managers. They should be a major advance on the older consultation machinery, which has officially been limited to employment, safety and welfare matters and domestic job-oriented colliery issues such as the working of a coal face.

Worker directors

Fairfields

The Fairfields shipyard at Govan on the Clyde in Glasgow was the scene for an experiment in participation after the Government intervened to save it in 1965-6 under the ebullient ministerial guidance of George Brown (now Lord George-Brown), then in charge of Labour's new Department for Economic Affairs. Unions and industrialists joined the Government in trying out new management and participation methods; and, spurred by the need to save jobs, some of the unions in the yard put in cash and agreed to join the board. This led to what became known as the Fairfields Experiment, which continued till 1968 when the business was swallowed up by a shipbuilding reorganisation into the ill-fated Upper Clyde Shipbuilders, which itself earned a place in the history of industrial democracy with its 1971-2 work-in (see next chapter).

During its relatively short life the Fairfields Experiment set out to overturn traditional shipbuilding attitudes on matters such as production management, demarcation and pay structures. Its innovations included shop stewards being given new recognition with seats on management committee meetings, and there was a joint non-voting management union council. Other communication and consultation methods were introduced, but there was no question of there being any system of joint-control. Indeed, the trade unionists in the shipyard did not apparently want to extend the communication–consultation system into any form of full-fledged industrial democracy power-sharing beyond the power they already exerted through their traditional militant approach to bargaining relationships. The shipyard workers were in fact showing a not un-common reluctance to change the adversary system.

The two union leaders who joined the board included Lord Carron, then president of the Engineers (some other unions, including the Electricians, refused to join). But they were in no way directly account-able to the workers. Indeed, their limited but still potentially useful contribution was well summed up by another member of the board, Professor Ken Alexander, in his book *Fairfields*. What he says is probably as good a summary as any of the limited impact that a nominal trade union presence can have on such boards in nationalised industries and elsewhere:

The presence of trade union directors enabled the executive directors to take soundings on trade union attitudes which prevented the presentation of policies which would have been rebuffed or proved unworkable in practice. What was remarkable was that neither the workers in the yard nor their stewards sought to bring pressure on these trade union leaders who were influential in the company's councils. One might have expected lobbying when the Board met at the yard, but nothing of the sort took place. It would be wrong to believe that the presence of these trade union leaders on the Board gave the workers at Fairfields any sense of 'participation' at the top and this was never suggested as a reason for their presence. But it did create a certain confidence that the top management had nothing 'up their sleeves' which could be seriously damaging to the interests of the workpeople. That top trade unionists were privy to the key papers and influenced company policy made some contribution to the general atmosphere of security and co-operation which infused industrial relations at Fairfields most of the time.
(Alexander and Jenkins, 1970)

British Steel

The British Steel Corporation's worker director scheme–covering in 1977 some 210,000 employees–was started with somewhat less general high-level enthusiasm than the Fairfields Experiment, although it has survived far longer and has developed considerably. But to begin with, when it was introduced with the renationalisation of steel in 1967, there is little evidence that it amounted to much more than a larger version of the paternalistic, small, private-sector worker director schemes described in the last chapter. The Labour Government itself showed little interest in increasing the industrial democracy of a nationalised industry beyond the nominal one or two union 'worthies' on the main board, and this was all the nationalisation statute provided. But the first board member for per-sonnel and industrial relations was Ron Smith, who had made his name as the general secretary of the Union of Post Office Workers. This union had in the past been more interested in the Guild Socialists' worker control ideas than many other unions (see Chapter 14), and Smith, who brought his ideas with him, found a receptive colleague in Lord Melchett, the Corporation's first chairman.

The result was that a worker director presence on the Corporation's four group boards was introduced. Ever since, however, there have been disputes about its effectiveness and it has always been overshadowed in the Corporation by more primary policies of building participation upwards from the shop floor through extending union bargaining and consultation. In 1976 four academics produced a critical study made during the first few years of the scheme (Brannen *et al.*, 1976) based on work they had carried out for the British Steel Corporation (BSC) from 1969 to 1971. This book helped to provoke a personal defensive, but more up-to-date, reply from the worker directors themselves a year later (BSC Employee Directors *et al.*, 1977). Now there have been fresh plans to extend the scheme as part of the trade unions' operations with a significant proportion of union seats on the main corporation board.

When Melchett and Smith pushed the initial scheme–they were the two full-time members of the 1966-7 Organising Committee in charge of preparing for the re-nationalisation–they found scepticism and often indifference among unions, and opposition among industrialists and managers. Both managers and unions were concerned about blurring the unions' role; but the unions also wanted to protect and support any worker directors by tying them into the union system in a single-channel style. One idea put up by some unions was for the unions to nominate five out of the thirteen members of the national board of the Corporation; but this was not taken up and only one ex-steelworker (who had been president of his union) was appointed to the national board alongside Ron Smith.

The main worker director scheme was pushed down below this board under an agreement eventually reached between the embryo Corporation and the TUC Steel Committee (a committee created by the TUC at the request of Melchett and Smith to bring the steel unions together in one industrial body for the first time in their history). Three steelworkers were appointed to each of the Corporation's four group boards for three-year periods from May 1968. But it was insisted that they should be chosen by the Corporation from a list submitted by the unions; that they served in a personal capacity without any accountability back to their unions; and that they relinquished any union office on appointment. This separation seriously undermined the efficiency of the worker directors and indeed blighted their reputations for many years. The situation was worsened by Sir Michael Milne-Watson, one of the Corporation's deputy chairmen, while he was standing in as acting chairman early in 1968 for Lord Melchett who was recovering from a heart attack. He made it clear to at least one worker director that not only should he relinquish his union posts, but he should also sever all his connections with his old union and not even attend its meetings. This illustrated the considerable fear there was in some parts of the Corporation about the risk of importing union-based power into the higher reaches of management.

But the fear need not have existed, because the worker directors had to fend for themselves with little help from the TUC, the individual unions or management, and they had little chance to be of much influence. Although an early idea that they should be appointed only to parts of the Corporation away from their normal place of work was dropped, they were still effectively contained and restrained by the management systems of the Corporation. They were appointed to the group boards which themselves had no policy-making or executive authority since they only advised the group chairmen, who then went away and made their own decisions. Their lack of effectiveness was summed up in the academics' study:

The worker directors had no effect on the decision-making process because the Board was not really the place where it occurred. Even if it had been, things would have changed little. Management have a monopoly of knowledge, of language, and of authority; the worker directors were individuals with no sanctions and no power. Nor did the scheme lead to the representation of shop floor interests at Board level or a feeling of involvement in the organisation on the part of the workforce.

The initial reception of the worker directors by senior and middle management varied from opposition (50 per cent of managers opposed the scheme in a survey conducted by the academics) to nullifying paternalism. As the worker directors' own book reports: 'I think you've got to admit that for the first few years it was really a bit of a sham. People made you welcome, were very nice to you, but in many ways we were only a rubber stamp. I think that was to be expected'. There was, the book reports, a group chairman who benevolently 'never turned from one page of the agenda to another without enquiring of the worker directors whether they were satisfied'. The same man stressed that 'you were at liberty to ask questions'. Even worse though was the director who bluntly said 'I don't believe in this scheme and I don't want you at the Board.' Lower down the management ladder it was little better, and the status jealousies of managers emerged:

Management below Board level couldn't understand how we could have a relationship. These men were the ones I had dealt with as a union representative. They became unsure of themselves, realising that I now had access to levels of information they didn't have. They resented this and felt they had an equal right to have this information, possibly a greater right. They gave me a real hammering. . . . I admit it's a bit awkward. One day the department manager is my boss and I have to carry out his instructions like other workers. The next day I'm off to a Board meeting, and it's a meeting he'd love to go to. . . . I didn't allow for envy, jealousy, bitterness.

But there was also jealousy and envy from fellow workers and trade unionists, who would say 'He's a big boy now and he's bloody lost touch with us.'

Following the academics' study, the scheme was reviewed and (after some modifications in 1970) was in 1972 put on a permanent basis (until then it had officially been an experiment) and improved. But the Corporation continued to show little public enthusiasm for the scheme and there were even arguments, once the experimental stage was over, about when and how the worker directors should meet together and whether they should have joint access to the BSC chairman and the TUC Steel Committee.

The worker directors were however allowed to hold union office (twelve out of the total of seventeen had been elected to posts ranging up to union president by 1976) and to participate actively in the industry's consultation procedures. Unions were involved more in selecting the candidates through the TUC Steel Committee, which could—but never has—asked them to resign on fundamental issues of confrontation between the Committee and the Corporation. They were also given specialist subjects to watch over. And, the Corporation reported in a statement announcing the changes on 2 March 1972: 'More managers are now becoming aware that the employee directors are not a challenge to their authority but can help managers to obtain a better understanding of shopfloor feeling and can also help them in resolving their difficulties.'

But the boards on which the worker directors sat remained advisory, although the influence of the worker directors did increase in 1973 when the functions of their boards and lower-tier management executive committees were merged and they gained seats on manufacturing division management committees – the bodies identified by the academic study as being key decision-making bodies – and other subsidiary committees covering items such as planning, capital expenditure and personnel matters. Later they also started to sit on individual works management committees.

The worker directors spent a lot of time seeking out the real decision-making centres in the Corporation. They realised there was little point in sitting on bodies that only considered matters that were more or less finalised. As two worker directors said in their book:

I felt that, if they're only going to have us working once a month on a divisional Board, the BSC is wasting its money and our time. We wanted to be involved at all levels, and we wanted to see the whole system operating. . . . When you only attended the divisional management committee you sometimes felt you were just rubber stamping because the decision to put in planning forms and so on came from the groups. So we asked to go onto the group management committee and then found that the group had its own planning committee and that we were actually rubber-stamping that. So we moved to the planning committee within the group to get to the source of decision-making.

Some of the worker directors accepted that there should be a continuing limitation of their powers in order not to interfere with the traditional union role. Ward Griffiths, a veteran worker director from Ebbw Vale, who was one of the first appointed and who joined the national BSC Board in 1970, explains the position:

It should be clearly understood that in the view of the employee directors and the Corporation, the official representative voice of the employees are the trade unions through collective bargaining and joint consultation. The employee director scheme is in no way a substitute for these critically important traditional methods of participation but it is a useful supplement which enables a trade union view to be expressed at the policy formulation stage which precedes even effective joint consultation and collective bargaining.

This is an inevitable attitude for a union activist and worker director to take, given the fact that his board representation system was not tied directly, with positive accountability procedures, into the union machinery. Using the labour relations jargon, it was not a 'single-channel' operation because it was divorced not only from the main union bargaining procedure but also from the union consultative process – indeed, it was really a 'third channel' operating formally, as Ward Griffiths explains, separate from both the bargaining and consultative procedures. Outside union officials would therefore criticise the system as it emerged from the 1972 review for not putting the worker directors in general on the major decision-making board, for not making their right to the seats statutorily enforceable, for not allowing a full accountability procedure to operate between the board representatives and their union members, and for not giving them some form of parity of representation – generally they have been in a minority of 25 to 30 per cent of the seats. These criticisms arise from the fact that, however competent and determined the worker directors may be, in the eyes of many union activists they will still become 'management men' unless they are made accountable to the union organisation.

The main problem as far as accountability is concerned is that the worker directors were not directly accountable to the steelworkers who they represented, and therefore did not always gain the briefing on workers' views or detect the strength of feeling that a more direct system could engender – although this is not to suggest that in the later years the worker directors were out of touch with the members. The problem stemmed mainly from the election system which has been highly complex, with a procedure which starts with 'favourite sons' being nominated in individual steelworkers' union branches, then moving up through the unions themselves and the TUC Steel Committee till eventually the seventeen or so men to be appointed would be chosen by a joint 50–50 BSC–TUC Steel Committee meeting. Reporting back is also less formalised – and therefore accountability is weakened – than it would be if there were direct elections. (It is only fair to add however that, even if one had a full Bullock-style system with shop stewards being elected direct to the board, the direct accountability could inevitably be watered down in a larger company or one with scattered and varied products and operations – especially for example in a conglomerate.) However there was a lot of union contact after 1972 between the steel unions' branches and the worker directors, who sometimes, most unusually in the trade union movement, would even attend local meetings of unions other than their own.

The worker directors themselves did not see the problems so acutely. They resented the Bullock Report echoing the TUC's view that the 'relative lack of success' of their system stemmed from the fact that they were neither 'truly representative' nor 'properly accountable'. The worker directors said in their book that after 1972 they did act as representatives and they saw themselves as being 'accountable to the employees in general, the particular trade unions which had nominated them, all the trade unions in their constituencies and, in a special way, to the TUC Steel Committee'.

But this did not mean that they were entirely satisfied, and they included in their book a charter to solve their difficulties, although they did not agree with the TUC on the need for 'parity' of representation. They thought it more important to have the right man on the right committee or board because powerful influence could be more important than numerical voting strength.

They wanted the scheme improved to give them initially a statutory minimum of one-third of the seats on the main corporation board (where in mid-1977 they still only had one seat – with no statutory back-up – out of a total of sixteen on the board). They also wanted the same proportion on the main board's policy-formulating committees and on the divisional board management committees. The need for worker representatives to be on the committees where the real management decisions are made, as well as on the top showpiece board, is probably one of the main lessons to be learned from the steel experience.) They thought that the employee directors on the top board should be drawn from those on the lower levels through the TUC Steel Committee. They wanted to be provided with expert advice by both the unions and the Corporation and to have the same status and facilities as other directors. They also wanted to have their dissent to decisions recorded (an important proviso for the union activist who wants to be able to reserve the right to opt out so that he and his union can continue the battle on the shop floor).

By early 1977 the steel unions themselves were drawing up their own ideas in the post-Bullock era when nationalised industries started to prepare new board representation plans (see Chapter 17). As a result, an idea produced by the Corporation to have three worker directors on the main board was shelved by the TUC Steel Committee.

The national board itself was in line for changes under a new chairman, Sir Charles Villiers, who had taken over in September 1976. In a speech to the ISTC conference in May 1977, he showed how he wanted to harness the concepts of industrial democracy within a 'steel contract'. This would not just give the unions more power over management decision-making, but would also set out to gain their co-operation for badly needed industrial efficiency. This in turn meant the unions not only signing agreements in national headquarters, but pushing through consequential redundancies and cuts in wasteful over-manning in individual steelworks. Not suprisingly, he found the unions less than enthusiastic to embrace all aspects of such responsibilities, including trimming some of their craft and inter-union pride and conflicts.

But, whatever problems he was to run into, his remarks went to the heart of the issue about industrial democracy involving unions and their members in shouldering positive reponsibilites and so winning respect for their legitimacy as sources of constructive as well as negative powers. He explained his 'steel contract', which involved unions sitting both on a top consultative steel council and a steel policy board (see Chapter 17) by telling the conference:

It is a system for the settlement of problems at all levels. It would be a way in which the industrial democracy which I – and you – believe in could be made to begin to work. It would therefore mark a change in our affairs – one in which we could build on the good co-operation we do have between us to make the industry better: working with all who work in it.

For their part by this time, the unions were considering going initially for one-third of the national board seats and then to move on to 50–50 with parallel union-based developments at lower levels. They had learned the lessons of having neither sufficient numerical strength, despite the lack of interest in parity among the worker directors, nor the right powers to share in decision-making. They realised how the success of the worker directors had depended too much on individual personality rather than institutionalised power.

Indeed, the BSC experience shows how easy it can be for a minority employee representation to be reduced in effectiveness by a partially indifferent and partially hostile management and by a less-than-enthusiastic union system. It also shows how difficult it can be for worker representatives to seek out, and gain a foothold in, the real decision-making areas of management. On balance, however, the scheme had done some good by 1976, at least in increasing management–employee communication and understanding. There was however no real power-sharing, and there was little if any feeling among the steelworkers that, since they had worker directors on some boards, they were bound into the welfare of the industry.

Benn and the Bullock era

By the time Labour was re-elected in 1974, the steel industry's worker director experiment, started in 1967, was generally regarded as a somewhat irrelevant hang-over from an earlier era because of its lack of punch. Innovations started in various industries after 1974, which led into the era of the Bullock Report and its allied inquiries in the public sector, however broke considerable new ground. Again it was the areas where the Government could influence events by being the owner of an industry or where it gained influence or control through financial intervention that produced the initiatives.

Several of the initiatives emanated from the fertile mind of Anthony Wedgwood Benn, secretary of state for industry from 1974 to 1975. Benn never really made it clear whether his primary interest was in unleashing unfettered shop steward power (as in his earlier support of the Upper Clyde Shipbuilders' work-in) or in grass-roots workers' co-operatives where unions might hold little sway (as in Meriden and others) or in shop stewards committees helping to save industrial giants through participation committees (as in Alfred Herbert), or in national union officials negotiating planning agreements with civil servants and industrialists (as in Chrysler), or in worker director solutions as in the Post Office.

What he did however was to encourage all these forms of participation and to use the financial collapses of companies like Leyland, Herbert and Ferranti during his period in the Department to encourage shop steward and national union official involvement in the rescue attempts. In so doing he quickly exposed the unions' weaknesses, such as inadequate research facilities, disparate inter-union voices and shop steward-union official power conflicts, which can make industrial democracy a risky business. The inability of the unions to cope effectively with masses of statistical information that emerged in some of these situations even led one or two left-wing academics to ponder in the spring of 1975 whether Benn was consciously intending to expose the unions' inefficiencies! But while his motives may not always have been clear, the activities in the companies involved during the run-up period to the Bullock Committee (plus provisions for industrial democracy being written into statutes nationalising the aircraft and shipbuilding industries and setting up the National Enterprise Board) at least showed the beginnings of a new era and fresh arrangements were considered in a number of industries, including steel.

Two schemes in particular that followed mapped out a fresh approach while the Bullock and allied inquiries were still in operation and while industries like electricity, gas, coal and airways were improving or introducing below-board level participation arrangements. They were in the Belfast shipyard of Harland and Wolff and in the Post Office. While

similar in that they both provide for an effective and accountable proportion of worker directors, they each have distinct characteristics. One has
been planned on the shop steward system of a compact but troubled
multi-union shipyard, while the other is based primarily on the national
organisations of two rarely militant but highly expert single-industry
unions which, with other smaller unions involved, are well used to somewhat advanced Whitley-style consultations.

Harland and Wolff

The scheme at Harland and Wolff has been born out of the problems of
this loss-making shipyard in Ulster. It owes much to the energy and
commitment of Stan Orme while he was minister of state for the province
from 1974 to 1976. (He then returned to London to become minister for
social security and produced a 50–50 plan for the union-management
control of pension schemes–see Chapter 17.) Like so many participation
innovations, the spur at Harland and Wolff has been the fear of
redundancy and unemployment and the need to boost productivity and
reduce militant strikes, rather than any primary interest among the
work force in industrial democracy; and it was this fear of the shipyard
closing during Ulster's political troubles that led Mr Orme (a left-wing
supporter of industrial democracy) to launch his experiment in 1975.

With Dr George Quigley, a leading Ulster civil servant, Orme prepared a discussion paper (Department of Manpower Services, Belfast
1975), which set out the options. But first he had had to persuade his
colleagues at Westminster that the situation in Ulster and the financial
problems of the shipyard, which the Government took into full public
ownership in August 1975, meant that the experiment should be launched
immediately to harness the workers' co-operation. He thus overcame
Whitehall sceptics who were trying to slow down any government
initiatives in the public sector till the Bullock Committee (by then still not
formally set up) had reported on what to do in the private sector. But
Orme's hope for speed foundered in a mass of inter-union and other
problems and the proposed scheme was still only nearing finalisation by
the end of 1977.

The ideas put forward for discussion in the Orme–Quigley document
included a two-tier board with worker directors on the top tier, the continuation and extension of traditional collective bargaining, the development of joint consultation, the creation of joint executive committees to
discuss and jointly regulate subjects such as accident prevention, training,
discipline and job evaluation, joint working parties for special projects,
and participation by the yard's 9500 workers in their individual jobs.

What emerged from lengthy discussions was a proposed fifteen-man
supervisory board made up of three equal sectors: trade union representatives, management, and government nominees; the shop stewards believed it was in their interests to tie the Westminster Government, on
whose financial help their livelihoods depended, into the yard's management in this way. This board structure was designed as the top level of a
four-tier scheme. Just below the board would be a 50–50 joint implementation council of twenty people aimed at ensuring that the board's joint
policy decisions were turned into operational decisions–an institution
partly borne out of mistrust among the shop stewards that management

would actually do what the top board decided. (It is quite possible therefore that this council might disappear or change its nature once a system were working effectively.) Lower down were the tiers that came into action fairly quickly and helped to build a participative approach. They comprise five departmental joint councils covering areas such as hull production, shop outfitting and ship repair; below this are productivity committees.

While these two lower tiers of the departmental councils and productivity committees have been helping the shipyard improve its performance and have begun to build the participative basis on which a joint board depends, the board-level representation foundered for some two years in a mass of individual union scepticism, inter-union rivalries and electoral muddle. And because the joint board was not operating, the joint implementation council was not set up either (although the new government nominees were appointed in 1975 and included Alan Fisher, general secretary of the National Union of Public Employees, and Dr McCarthy, a leading Labour academic and sceptic of worker director schemes). Ironically, therefore, the self-generated reluctance and inability among the yard's shop stewards to rush into their five vacant boardroom seats meant that the scheme has proceeded along a more logical and efficient path by leaving time for participation to be built first at lower levels. The shop stewards may well not have minded this delay for the added reason that, until it received orders for two large ships in April 1977, the yard had not had a new order since 1974 and there was a risk of serious redundancies. Indeed, the fear that they might well have to take responsibilities for redundancies was undoubtedly a deterrent to the shop stewards.

The electoral problems stemmed from an electoral college developed for the shop stewards by a management consultancy which also advised the stewards on the training and expertise they would need to function as worker directors (see Chapter 7). The scheme was based on four areas of the yard–steelworkers, other craftsmen, ancillary workers and staff–each electing its own board representative on a complicated alternative voting system, with an extra seat being open for election by all 9500 workers. It thus ran into a log-jam of incomprehension and tensions among the yard's thirteen unions and seven negotiating groups.

This shows the pitfalls that other companies and industries may face in the future, although the Bullock Report's structurally simple concept of setting up a joint representation committee of all shop stewards as a base for board representation could save the electoral college problems. At its best, this stewards' committee would expose the inter-union tensions and allow them to be sorted out. But, judging by the experience at Harland (and similar experiences elsewhere, including British Airways, whose unions ran into internal rivalries problems on a planned joint committee covering the airways early in 1977), there would be a lot of trouble first. The problem at Harland hinges around craft and general union jealousies and especially around the proud and élitist craft attitudes of the Amalgamated Society of Boilermakers, Shipwrights, Blacksmiths and Structural Workers (usually referred to simply as the Boilermakers). To add to the confusion, the Electrical and Plumbing Trades Union continued its established policy of opposition and refused to nominate stewards for the board. The Boilermakers at one stage potentially reduced the authority of their board representatives by falling back on traditional Labour movement philosophy and saying they would have to give up other union and shop steward positions in order to protect the integrity of the independent bargaining power of shop stewards. The result of this was that, in the spring of 1977, the yard's three senior Boilermakers' shop stewards were loath to stand for the board, although they were considering a plan to let those who were elected continue to sit in on stewards' meetings but not vote.

Nevertheless, despite these problems, the innovations started by Mr Orme in 1975 had by 1977 helped to build up participation in the yard and to prepare the ground for a worker director system–moves that the rest of the UK's freshly nationalised shipbuilding industry watched closely because it had been instructed in its own nationalisation legislation to prepare plans on industrial democracy.

Post Office

The worker director system in the Post Office was created for quite different reasons from the self-survival motivation of Harland and Wolff. It started as a continuation of established interests of post office union leaders in industrial democracy and was one of the innovations launched by Mr Wedgwood Benn during his time at the Department of Industry. He asked the post office unions to build on their effective consultation systems–which bordered on joint regulation of management decisions on some matters–and to prepare ideas for increasing industrial democracy. He was thus rekindling Guild Socialist worker control ideas which had interested postal union leaders earlier in the century (see Chapter 14) on the base of the consultative system they had inherited from the Whitley traditions up to 1969, when they stopped being part of the Civil Service and became a nationalised corporation.

Early in 1975 the two main post office unions–the Union of Post Office Workers (UPW) and the Post Office Engineering Union (POEU) –finalised their proposals. They envisaged the Post Office Corporation being run by a two-tier supervisory and management board structure. Half of the supervisory board would be elected by trade unions and the other half would be appointed by the Government with the consumer interest being taken into account. Parallel joint organisations at regional and local level would carry the participation down into individual post offices and telephone exchanges and so turn the existing consultative arrangements formally into joint decision-making procedures.

This was the first trade union worker director plan to be broadly in line with the 50–50 worker director two-tier board proposals contained in the TUC's 1974 Industrial Democracy document. The supervisory board would, the UPW and POEU suggested, be responsible for laying down policy decisions such as corporate plans, investment, future planning, equipment manufacture and pricing. But, in order to try to avoid a clash with traditional collective bargaining, the two unions proposed that no union official with negotiating responsibilities should stand for election to this board.

Eventually these proposals were adopted by the Council of Post Office Unions, which embraces all the unions involved, and it slowly received backing from the Labour Government – although ministers' first priority was not to allow anything to happen that could pre-empt the slow development of overall government policy in the light of the then-awaited Bullock Report. There was also opposition from the Post Office Corporation which told the Government that, while it would not mind one or two worker directors being appointed to its board as an experiment, it had no enthusiasm for the unions' full-blooded power-sharing ideas. On the other hand, the unions had no interest in what is sometimes called the 'sham democracy' of a nominal boardroom representation – they already had considerable powers of joint regulation through their consultative system, which was not so rigid as the electricity system and so did not inhibit consultative issues becoming bargaining topics. Eventually in July 1976 Gerald Kaufman, minister of state for industry (serving under Eric Varley, who had replaced Mr Wedgwood Benn as secretary of state), held a tripartite Government – Corporation – union meeting and formally launched talks between the Corporation and the unions aimed at working out a solution. This was the first such industrial democracy conference called in any industry by the Government and Mr Kaufman was outspoken about the implications: 'Industrial democracy means participation in decision-making and this is absolutely crucial. Anything less is no more than a shadow', he declared.

By early 1977, shortly after the Bullock Committee produced its '$2x + y$' single-tier board proposal, agreement was reached on a two-year experiment. This showed the same shift in union thinking that had happened at the TUC during the life of the Bullock Committee because the 50–50 split and the two-tier idea was dropped once the Corporation had persuaded the unions that a third element was needed. In its place, it was agreed that a single-tier post office board would be made up of three groups comprising up to six full-time management and six union members plus four outside members. A seven–seven–five formula emerged later to enable consumer interests to be included in the third group. The chairman would be additional to these three groups unless he was also formally designated chief executive or given some other executive function, in which case, having lost his 'independence', he would form part of the management group. The size of the board was initially dictated basically by the Post Office insisting that it needed six management directors to ensure that its top specialists were represented in the board room. It then grew when the Government's liaison with the Liberal Party raised the issue of consumer representatives but there were, significantly, inter-union rows over who should have the seats available. The formal position agreed was that all board members would continue to be appointed by the secretary for industry so that he could still fulfil all his ministerial responsibility to Parliament for the industry (see Chapter 17) – although in practice it was realised that the unions would leave him little choice by only providing sufficient names to fill their seats. The names would be produced by ballots within the unions concerned and would be appointed for two-year terms. A potential conflict between parliamentary democracy and industrial democracy was therefore glossed over in the hope that it would not emerge into a major issue with the unions putting up a name the minister felt unable to accept.

Formally it was also agreed that independent directors would be chosen by the secretary of state so as not to produce either a management or a union bias. But after consultation with both parties, he would not make an appointment against the reasonable objection of either side. In practice, the co-operative spirit within this industry means that genuine independents or mutually accepted people might well be appointed. But the careful choice of words also meant that at the worst the Government would have to let the two sides choose at least one each. The Post Office was therefore showing how the Bullock '$2x+y$' formula could be adapted for use by a nationalised industry, including the absorption of a consumer voice in the 'y'. It showed a skilful balancing act between the interest of the unions in producing a genuine industrial democracy board, while at the same time not setting any precedents that might positively water down the principles of parliamentary responsibility or ministerial prerogative, although some points remained vague.

This balance was also evident in an agreement that all board members would have equal responsibilities and that the worker directors would not be mandated on policy by their unions; although it was recognised that they would be accountable and would report back to their 'constituencies', which could remove them, which in practice would mean they would have to balance their board and union interests. The original POEU and UPW idea that the worker directors should not hold negotiating positions in their unions, so as to try to lessen the risk of conflict between boardroom representation and bargaining roles, also remained.

More controversially, at a time when the emphasis in TUC thinking was in favour of shop steward rather than union official involvement in board rooms, the agreement also effectively ruled out lay shop stewards becoming worker directors by saying that the union nominees would be of the standing of union national executive council members or full-time officials. Since virtually all the unions involved are concerned only with post office affairs and have no responsibilities in rival companies or industries, this does not raise the potential problem of conflicting involvement and commitment that could arise with union officials or executive members being involved on the board of, say, an engineering company. But it has led to allegations that the Post Office would be raising a breed of boardroom participators far removed from the realities of branch post office or telephone exchange life. The fact that no negotiators could have boardroom seats (or, if they were negotiators, would have to give up this role in order to be acceptable) lent weight to this argument because it would mean that people like research and finance and medical officers of unions would gain the seats. The postal unions' answer to this in mid-1977 was that they were experimenting with an idea that would produce people with the necessary expertise who, while not being negotiators, could and would hold other major union posts which would keep them in touch with their members' views.

Other activists, it was also intended, would be able to participate in the industry's regional and local organisations where it was planned to mirror the national board arrangement—so as to ensure that the participation in national decision-making was repeated with participation in the operational executive decisions down the line. The intention was that, where there were boards in the post office's nineteen regions, the national formula would be repeated with the primary insistence on parity between management and union representatives. Below the regions, it was also agreed that there would be 50–50 management–union committees to take care of operational decision-making in the Post Office's area organisation.

By the time all these details had been agreed early in 1977 the Post Office–which, with 420,000 employees, is Europe's biggest employer–was set to pave the way for a major experiment in industrial democracy. Legislation was then passed by Parliament in July 1977 making the necessary statutory changes to laws governing operation of the Post Office Corporation and the size of its board despite the fact that a Government Inquiry on the Post Office (called the Carter Committee) had opposed a worker director system.

Some people in Whitehall tried to use the Carter Report's opposition, and a recommendation it made that the Post Office's postal and telecommunications businesses should be split into separate organisations, as an excuse to delay developments. But the Government pressed ahead and on January 1, 1978 a two-year experiment was launched. It was agreed that there would be a joint review after two years, without any commitment from the Government or the unions about an extension.

An explanatory booklet, *The Industrial Democracy Experiment and UPW Participation*, was published by the UPW in April 1978. In it Norman Stagg, the union's deputy general secretary who had been a major influence throughout the debate, stressed that the experiment 'will not impinge in any way on the traditional function of the trade union as the protector and defender of its members' interests'. This rapidly proved to be true because the UPW board representives soon became embroiled in a row over Weekend postal agreements while the POEU took industrial action later in the year over working hours.

Stagg estimated that by the time the experiment was under way at all levels, more than 1800 trade union representatives would be actively participating in management.

Summary
The experiences of both Harland and Wolff and the Post Office in framing their proposals show two things. The first is the need for well established procedures and well understood attitudes to be developed before a new participative worker director system could be expected to operate effectively. The second is the need for time for the parties involved to work out precisely what suits their own needs. Overall, the varied developments in the different parts of the public sector also show how individual traditions, political attitudes and degrees of militancy can lead different groups of unions to choose their own forms of industrial democracy with Government encouragement.

Chapter 13

Shopfloor Democracy

All the chapters in this book up to now have been concerned primarily with what might be called representative industrial democracy: that is, employee participation in national, industrial and company affairs through representative organisations. Inevitably, since the politically oriented TUC-affiliated trade unions are the established representative organisations in Britain, there has been a constant overtone of trade union power out to change society. With shopfloor representative and collective power already established (to varying degrees) across British industry through the country's 300,000 shop stewards, the unions have been seen seeking higher levels of corporate and political power in which to spread their influence. And industrialists and managers in the private sector in particular have been seen defending these centres of power against what they regard as the politically inspired, power-oriented and potentially inefficient ambitions of the unions.

Power to the individual

There is however a further dimension to industrial democracy in its broadest sense of giving workers a share in the control of their places of employment. This is to give them an opportunity partially or wholly to have a say in running the immediate area in which they work so that they can have a direct as opposed to a represented voice in their working lives. This can come through a worker directly owning or controlling his company through a workers' co-operative or other system of common ownership, or through his part-owning it through a profit-sharing scheme which will give him a stake in an otherwise traditional free-enterprise company. In the workers' co-operative he may also share in the overall policy-making of the concern. Finally, his company may have so organised its management structures that workers have a high degree of autonomy in working groups about the way their immediate working environment is organised – a practice more common in Scandinavia and America than Britain.

In all these cases there will of course still be a representational element present because the workers' co-operative will need a governing council, the company profit-sharing scheme may well be administered by a management–worker committee, and even the most autonomous shop-floor work groups will need some representative co-ordinator to act as their spokesman. But the difference between these techniques and the types of participation described earlier is that the commitment and activity of the individual can be harnessed directly and thus become the primary issue. The representational element–and therefore the issues of trade union power–is therefore secondary.

So it is hardly surprising that such forms of industrial democracy are often favoured by industrialists, politicians and others who do not like union power and socialist change. The Conservative Government was showing considerable interest in them when it was considering employee participation in 1973 (see Chapter 14), and various sorts of policies on share ownership are emerging now. The methods in fact form a sort of 'soft participation' alternative to the 'hard' union power ideas of the TUC. They are thus unlikely to have much impact on society as a whole although they may help to reduce the alienation to work. Even worker co-operatives, despite their overtones of an alternative form of industrial society, can be looked on with favour because, as will be seen, they are unlikely to upset the industrial establishment and structure of Britain.

The collective alternatives

Equally, it is hardly surprising that, in the traditional Labour movement-based system of British labour relations, such schemes are often either opposed or regarded as irrelevant by trade unions. They usually regard profit-sharing schemes as risky paternalism, shopfloor autonomy as a way of employers improving productivity without paying for it, and workers' co-operatives as interesting but somewhat irrelevant small by-plays aside from the main industrial stage.

Significantly, the unions have their own versions of these developments, which turn what have so far been seen as individually based soft participation into vehicles for changing society or at least for making the employer pay for what he gets. Profit-sharing, where individuals hold a small number of their company's shares, evolves into British unions sharing the running of company pension funds (see Chapter 17) or, in Scandinavia and elsewhere, into unions collectively holding the shares on behalf of their members–matters to do more with the redistribution of wealth and the economic power of trade unions than employee participation. In a less dramatic vein, the TUC has also given its blessing to factory occupations such as sit-ins and work-ins (sometimes the starting point of a co-operative), dubbing them an 'appropriate trade union tactic in certain circumstances' in its main 1974 Industrial Democracy document. Finally, the union official faced with an employer interested in improving the 'quality' of his employees' working life will either discourage the idea or will quickly try to negotiate a productivity deal to cover the innovations, so providing his members with some extra cash and establishing the union role in the development.

Experience abroad

Some of these individual-based forms of industrial democracy are far more common abroad, for example in Scandinavia and America and also in countries such as Yugoslavia and Israel, which have their own types of worker–co-operative-based systems. These countries have developed according to their own political and industrial traditions. The fervour of a community working together to build a nation, led to kibbutz co-operative industries in Israel. The wish to show a break from communist centralism has led to co-operatives in Yugoslavia, while the spirit of Basque independence has helped to inspire co-operatives in Spain. The absence of primary political and class conflict allows America's business-oriented unions to be interested in individuals having a stake in the share-holding of companies whose profits they are out to maximise, while the liberalism of Scandinavia has partly led to an interest in the quality of the working life of the individual.

There are two other trends relevant to this area of industrial democracy. One is the 'small is beautiful' school of thought, which favours small work groups in small factories and is specially prevalent in Norway and Sweden. The other trend embraces the various theories on the motivation of workers and managers developed by consultants and others such as Herzberg, Rucker and Scanlon, which basically try to sort out relationships between the manager and the managed at different levels of a company both as individuals and as members of working groups.

The relevance of all these different styles of job power to the UK debate of the mid- to late 1970s is that, while the issues of the Bullock era have inevitably centred upon unions and the structural aspects of representative democracy at work, other systems have often been developed to a greater extent in other countries. Some of these may well be looked to by British industrialists as ways of avoiding or diluting the union power issue. However, they all provide potentially useful methods of participation for use in any country and can help to increase employee involvement in his work.

Employee share ownership

Until relatively recently the financial participation method of involving individual workers in the fortunes of their companies has held little appeal for most British industrialists, who have rarely been interested in sharing the ownership of their companies with employees. This attitude, which is hardly surprising in the British political and industrial system, has been matched on the other side of industry by scant trade union interest either in individual workers holding shares or, indeed, in the more socialist solution adopted by Labour movements abroad of advocating centrally collectively held employee share funds. The primary trade union objections to workers holding shares in their own companies are first that they are doubling their insecurity when the company fails, (an argument that is refuted by companies which say that profit-sharing means workers are receiving *extra* cash), and second that companies rarely if ever allow the shareholders to carry any corresponding influence over management decisions. In any case, the TUC pointed out in its 1974 Industrial Democracy document, 'they do little or nothing to reduce the inequality of wealth and they do not include the public sector.' Further union objections to all such types of schemes are that they use employees' money as cheap investment and that the shares saved can in effect amount to a backdoor approach to incomes policies and wage restraint because some money that otherwise might have been added to the pay packet is taken out of the economy.

Abroad however there has tended to be more interest, and schemes have been introduced by people as disparate as the Shah in Iran and De Gaulle in France; the main enthusiasm is to be found in the United States, where they are sometimes linked with pension arrangements. The British Wider Share Ownership Council has estimated that at least 197,000 American companies have set up such share schemes (Wider Share Ownership Council, 1977). This growth has mainly been during the past ten years and has recently been encouraged by legislation which boosts them as cheap ways of raising capital. Compared with this figure, there were early in 1977 barely 100 schemes in the UK (although there were 1000 for top executives alone) and most of them only involved about 10 per cent of the employees.

'Sharing wealth' at ICI

The best known of these schemes is one run since 1953 by ICI. Its 95,000 monthly and weekly paid staff receive a profit-related annual share allocation–worth in 1975 for example an average of £112 each after tax–which they can either keep or sell. Over the years a lot of the stock has been sold (about 60 per cent at the last count in 1971), but ICI still feels that the amount retained is significant. The company does not overplay the employee participation importance of the scheme, however, and would not suggest that it has a major motivational role among its work force, although some of its managers would like to see it play a larger role in factory-level incentives. The official ICI view however is that, within its overall policies (see Chapter 11), it helps to build a company-wide identity and corporate image quite separate from the company–trade union pay and productivity bargains. A report prepared by an ICI working party late in 1976, which approved its continuation subject to some reforms, put this view clearly:

The effects on employees of a broadly based profit sharing scheme, no matter how well designed and implemented, in such a large company as ICI, are necessarily limited. It is very doubtful if it can by its own nature have a direct effect on their motivation. Its contribution is more likely to be to the background of the feelings of employees about, and their interests in, the company. There is no doubt that the existing scheme is valued by a large majority of employees. It is something distinctive about the company which helps to give many employees a sense that ICI is a good company to work for. It helps as one of the background factors to give employees a feeling of cohesion with others in the company and to encourage co-operation.

This statement of interest is specially significant because the report was produced by a joint management–employee committee that included twenty-three elected shop steward and other worker representatives. The shop stewards were therefore backing a form of direct employer–employee participation that their unions usually dismiss–sometimes dubbing them 'grace and favour' handouts. Indeed, revisions proposed for the ICI scheme in its report were aimed at removing some of the paternalistic overtones, especially by replacing the ICI board's right unilaterally to fix the annual bonus rate with a permanent formula (based on the company's results on an added value or wealth created concept). But ICI is not interested in raising the proportion of its employees' income provided by

185

the scheme. This is partly because it feels the pay-out should not be large enough either to cause hardship when it is cut back in bad years (for those who cash it in immediately) or to attract the attention of trade union negotiators as a significant item.

Industrialists become interested

The general lack of enthusiasm among industrialists in the past was expounded, with overtones of the proprietorial preoccupations of top management, in the CBI's 1973 report, *The Responsibilities of the British Public Company*, prepared under the chairmanship of Lord Watkinson (see also Chapter 9). The report said the CBI approved of voluntary schemes in certain circumstances but opposed their mandatory imposition and added: 'We dislike a situation in which an individual other than a director has the bulk of his savings in the company that employs him.'

By 1977 however the CBI was changing its stance and had set up a working party which was moving towards a position just adopted in a Conservative Party 'green paper' that such schemes should be encouraged by the Government. The Conservatives' idea was that workers selling their shares should be taxed for the profits made only on a sliding scale with the amount of tax being reduced the longer the shares had been owned. The renewed CBI interest stemmed not only from this Conservative Party initiative (which itself had been encouraged by the Wider Share Ownership Council) but from results of a survey it had commissioned in 1976 on employee attitudes. Industrialists interpreted the survey as showing that employees were far more interested in profits than was often assumed (only 8 per cent said they thought profit a 'dirty word') and that more than half those questioned (58 per cent) thought that less profit ought to be distributed to directors and shareholders and more distributed to themselves.

By the middle of 1977 several major companies were introducing share ownership schemes for the first time. It seemed indeed that the changes that were beginning to emerge in the attitude of industrialists towards participation in management affairs were also being reflected in a cautious new approach to employee financial participation through share ownership. Up to this time ICI had been almost the only large company to have such a scheme, and its early experiences with workers selling off their first shares allocations in 1953 at its factory gates had helped to build up a mythology in the City and elsewhere that workers did not want to own shares.

There are however still very few companies at the heavy manufacturing (often militant) end of British industry with schemes and some of the new companies in 1977 reflected the underlying attitudes involved. Among some of the largest for example, one (Marks and Spencer) is non-union while another (British Home Stores) has only a tiny minority of unionised employees. A third (Barclays Bank) is white-collar and largely non-militant and in any case does not give shares to its most junior staff who receive profit-related cash handouts instead. Another company – Joseph Lucas – was partly motivated by the fall-off in managers' living standards when it introduced its scheme for white-collar staff, not for its heavily unionised shopfloor workers.

So while it may seem attractive to industrialists to try with company shares to lure their employees away from joining or reflecting the views of their unions, and towards involving themselves in the fortunes of their companies, not many heavily unionised companies have decided to run the risk of clashing on the subject with their unions, who would probably want the money spent in other ways. There is also great scepticism among many industrialists and personnel experts about whether share schemes really help employee–employer relationships. On the other hand, in a more liberal and ideological vein, a few companies may be deciding that it is illogical of them to perpetuate the class divisions of company owner-ship when they are allowing employees increasing democracy in manage-ment affairs. But the more down-to-earth reason for the increased interest in such schemes has been the growing employer concern to make employees understand the realities of company affairs through increased communication. There has also been a realisation that, since the growth of industrial democracy might well lead to worker director systems, there is likely to be an advantage in encouraging financial awareness among shop stewards. Some optimists even hope that such financial awareness and employee share ownership might reduce boardroom disputes about the size of shareholders' dividends in the days of worker directors.

Meanwhile, on a more political level, Conservative interests (partly looking early in 1977 for employee participation policies that a future Conservative government could implement) and organisations like the Wider Share Ownership Council (anxious to bolster up the credibility of the City) have been lobbying industrialists about the value that an in-jection of worker–shareholders could be to the survival of the mixed economy. Then, in the late summer of 1977, the Liberals persuaded the Labour Government to draw up its own proposals for profit-sharing including tax concessions to encourage it.

Ownership and co-operation

The central issue about industrialists' favoured forms of share ownership is that they are not a method of redistributing existing wealth and changing society (which is the Labour movement interest); instead they aim at involving employees' interest in the fortunes of the company by sharing out the new wealth created. ICI now uses the words 'wealth created' extensively to explain that the workers are getting a share only in the pro-ceeds of the value that ICI *adds to* the goods it buys and sells. There is also no intention in such schemes for the workers to gain enough shares to be a dominant force in a company–American companies rarely have more than a 25 per cent worker shareholding after many years.

The other main point about the new industrialists' and Conservative Party viewpoint is that it is individual, not collective, accumulation of capital that is often involved. They are therefore not only going against the trade union collective fund ideas described below and the forms of workers' co-operatives, which rely on a collective or 'common wealth' approach rather than partial or total individual forms of ownership. They are also sometimes going further than old-style profit-sharing schemes which gave the illusion of financial participation without any actual share ownership because they only involved cash handouts.

Those who take such a purist individual share ownership approach should therefore prefer the ICI scheme, where the worker finishes up with some financial property to sell, to the partnership system of for example the John Lewis Stores group, which mixes what its critics regard as 'sham democracy' as far as real participation in management is concerned with collective ownership of the firm by the employee 'partners'. This is because the individual John Lewis employee does not have any personal stake in the company to sell when he leaves.

It is worth noting here that there is sometimes only a rather thin and vague borderline between some of the more paternalistic worker co-operatives (see below) and some share ownership or partnership schemes operated within the legal framework of statutory companies. John Lewis is a good example of this, while another well-known concern started by two Quaker philanthropists in 1898 is Kalamazoo, which straddles the ideas of a collective partnership or co-operative with a form of participative management. Kalamazoo is a successful office equipment concern, whose 1700 workers in Birmingham own 52 per cent of the company's shares through a collective trust. This trust is primarily a vehicle for allocating the company's profits in bonuses that are calculated according to an employee's seniority, length of service and salary, so that a director of the company may receive ten or more times the few hundred pounds paid out to a shopfloor worker. Combined with consultation committees which give some participation in decision-making, it has led to a successful co-operative spirit. The Quaker traditions of concern for the welfare of employees still live on but are now being questioned by a work force that has shown signs of wanting a more egalitarian division of the profits, while the management is preparing now for more participation.

Labour's collective fund alternative
The industrialists' concept of profit-sharing was roundly condemned by a Labour Party study group report published in 1973 which went on to recommend the creation of a national capital-sharing scheme based on a national workers' fund not unlike that proposed or adopted by socialist governments elsewhere in Europe. But first it reacted to the distaste in the Labour movement for internal company share schemes by condemning them as a 'threat to workers' interests', adding:

We believe that profit sharing can all too easily encourage workers to accept the ideology of management that they are somehow part of a company 'team' with their role being simply to carry out the orders handed down from their management 'team-leaders'. What is more it can also encourage the belief that the interests of managers, and those of workers, are 'when you come down to it' really identical.

It then went on to say, in a passage that goes even further in underlining Labour activists' political and adversary views of industrial democracy and ideas of shopfloor teamwork or co-operation: 'This kind of approach, we believe, is the very antithesis of industrial democracy. For there is surely no such identity of interests.'

The report (Labour Party, 1973) was prepared by a study group whose members included Lord Diamond (later to become chairman of the 1974 Labour Government's Royal Commission on the Distribution of Income and Wealth – see Chapter 5), David Lea (the TUC economics secretary and member of both the Diamond Commission and the Bullock Committee), Barbara Castle and Derek Robinson (an Oxford academic expert on the subject who had been economics advisor to Barbara Castle at the former Department of Employment and Productivity, and a deputy chairman of the Conservative Government's Pay Board).

The report received only a lukewarm reception within the Labour Party, however, partly because it was treading relatively new ground, so it did not emerge as front-line policy when Labour was returned to power in 1974. Instead, worker director systems of industrial democracy, which had been included in an earlier 1967 Labour Party report (see Chapter 14) gained a higher priority along with the labour law reforms of the Trade Union and Labour Relations Act and the Employment Protection Act. The report, which put the subject in its socialist setting–sometimes called 'economic democracy'–of the redistribution of wealth, has not been forgotten, however. It can be expected to re-emerge in both Labour and TUC policy statements in some form or other to take its place alongside the ideas that have been floated in the 1974-7 period for trade unions to influence the management of company pension schemes and the direction of industrial investment (see Chapter 17). The ultimate aim of such plans taken together is not only to redistribute wealth and give workers through their trade unions a growing control over the capital ownership of firms, but also to give the unions considerable influence over major investment decisions made and thus over the course of the economy.

The precise proposals put forward by the 1973 report partially followed ideas being developed in Denmark and envisaged the creation of a national workers' fund, to which companies would be required to transfer each year 1 per cent of their equity shares, creating new shares for the purpose. Certain types of company would subscribe in cash. All workers in both public and private sectors would participate in the fund, which would be run by a governing council with TUC-nominated representatives having a clear majority of the seats alongside government nominees and specialist advisors. There would be a seven-year running in period for the fund, after which workers could cash in their first year's entitlement and so on subsequently year by year. In 1973 terms, the report estimated that the fund would grow by about £600 million a year. The fund would be free to exercise full ownership rights through its shareholdings, including the right to nominate workers to attend shareholders' meetings. It would operate as a sort of workers' unit trust and would, said the report, be governed by rules that emphasised its social role, including safeguarding prospects for employment.

A slightly different approach to capital accumulation was produced in 1976 by the Swedish trade unions' confederation (the LO) in what is known as the Meidner plan after the name of its author. This un-ashamedly aimed at giving the unions real instead of possibly illusory power over the economy and proposed that 20 per cent of a company's profits should be put each year into a central fund controlled by the trade unions; but there would be no individual involvement of employees. The Swedish employers' federation (the SAF), horrified by the implication of such economic power in union hands, countered with a proposal that 1 per cent of company's profits should be put into employee-controlled funds which would buy shares in their own companies. There has been a

189

similar sort of split in the views of unions and employers elsewhere in Europe including Germany, where there have been government and union proposals for both a central fund and a decentralised scheme while employers would prefer company-based arrangements. The EEC has reflected the interest around Europe in such ideas by its members' proposing, at a tripartite conference of governments, employers and unions held in June 1976, that steps should be taken to promote the participation of employees not only in management decisions but also in 'capital accumulation'. The EEC's fourth medium-term economic policy programme predicted (rather optimistically) in October 1976 that 'concrete reforms along these lines should be in force in all Member States by 1980 at the latest.'

Sit-ins and co-operatives

There has been a limited but growing interest among workers in Britain and other European countries during recent years in the occupation of factories and the creation of alternative co-operative ways of owning and running them. Such workers' occupations and co-operatives are however not a new phenomenon. They go back at least to the middle of the last century in Britain and in France when workers, often encouraged by some social reformer such as Robert Owen, banded together to provide and run their own places of employment.

Few have survived in the UK, however, and it is only in the last few years that they've sprouted again, spurred by the country's economic and industrial problems leading to financial collapses of companies and to redundancies. This has coincided with changing attitudes among workers to the rights and abilities of both owners and managers of their factories—especially when the interests of the employees involved seem sometimes to have been of little account. This occasional questioning of traditional sources of managerial authority and unilateral rights of the providers of capital has led to a spate of workers' actions ranging from short-term protest occupations of factories to attempts to set up permanent working co-operatives. So far, however, the trend is more significant for the underlying changes in social attitudes that it reflects than for any effect it may have on the industrial organisation of Britain. Judging by the record, the inherent conflicts of capital and labour in Britain's mixed economy and conflict-oriented industrial relations system generally prevent co-operatives from growing to any size. While there may soon be many more of them around the country, they will generally be small and so will avoid the conflicts that can accompany both massive capital investment and wide-ranging managerial authority. Nevertheless, they must be regarded as a radical and theoretically viable (if, on political grounds, unrealisable) alternative to the present systems of private sector and state-owned industry.

Labour disputes

There are various forms of protest worker occupations. First there is the sit-in staged by workers as part of an ordinary collective bargaining labour dispute, where occupation of the factory—or maybe even just part of it—is chosen as a specially potent way of hitting at the employer. Sometimes dubbed 'picketing from the inside', this has become a popular form of protest in the 1970s but is not new. Miners used to stage 'stay-down strikes' in mines during the 1930s and motor assembly track workers and others habitually down tools for an hour or so without leaving their work area. In other parts of Europe, and in America, there have been occupations during the past fifty years.

The main British development in this area came in 1972, when more than thirty factories in the Manchester area were occupied by sit-ins during a series of local strikes staged over an engineering industry national pay dispute. Since then there have been many more such protests; one management consultants' study has estimated that in the first six months of 1975, some eleven thousand workers were involved in fifteen industrial sit-ins with the largest number of workers occupying the factories of companies such as Massey-Ferguson, Ford Motor and the British Aircraft Corporation (Metra Oxford Consulting Ltd, 1975).

There are three main areas of possible advantage for workers in this type of action over the traditional walk-out. First, there might well be more publicity given to the dispute than would otherwise be the case (although this is not always true – the novelty of the 1972 Manchester events having been blunted). Second, and most important of all, the employer's business is disrupted far more than it is by 'picketing from the outside'. The workers can paralyse the business within the factory – especially its paper work, if offices are occupied as well. Indeed, sometimes only key parts of a factory – say its access gates and offices – may need to be occupied to ensure maximum effect. The third area of advantage is more political, and really only applies to activists who know that sitting-in gives workers a first, if small, taste of worker power (tinged perhaps with frustration once the initial euphoria has worn off), which might be harnessed later for wider aims.

Broadly the sitters-in are committing the civil wrong of trespass and ultimately can be evicted, and faced with civil actions for repossession of land or goods. There might in some cases be a basis for an allegation of criminal theft; employers do not often take legal action, however, especially if the sit-in is over a labour dispute where those involved have got to live together afterwards. In 1975, at the TUC's Annual Congress, TUC leaders agreed to look into a union demand for a law to allow workers freely to occupy their factories, and the TUC told the Government in 1977 that factory occupations should be treated as accepted forms of industrial action and should be immune from legal proceedings. Such a change in the law however is unlikely to be introduced by any government because of the issues of ownership involved and the tacit encouragement it would be seen as giving to such protests. The Labour Government refused the TUC's request in July 1977.

Redundancy sit-ins and work-ins
Most of the advantages and legal implications that apply to labour dispute sit-ins are equally relevant to redundancy sit-ins and work-ins, where the primary aim is to stop an employer shutting his factory permanently and putting people out of work. The difference between a redundancy sit-in and a work-in is simply whether the workers only occupy the factory or whether they try to prove its commercial viability by continuing to turn

out its products. The most famous of all such actions, and the one that inspired the other redundancy and labour dispute occupations, was the occupation and work-in at the Glasgow shipyards of Upper Clyde Shipbuilders which lasted for fourteen months from July 1971. This successfully kept the company's four shipyards open under new conventional owners with both private sector and government help. Less successful, but equally famous, was a worker's takeover in 1973 at the Lip watch factory in France, while later occupations in Britain led to the creation of workers co-operatives at a small leather factory, Fakenham Enterprises in Norfolk, and to the famous three co-operative projects backed with state aid by Mr Wedgwood Benn when he was secretary for industry–the Meriden motorbike factory, the Kirkby Manufacturing and Engineering concern (KME) on Merseyside, and the short-lived *Scottish Daily News*. Many other occupations followed, some of the most recent taking place at factories of Plessey and Courtaulds in the North-West.

The primary aim of redundancy occupations is to preserve jobs (although it might on occasion finish up with the workers simply getting better redundancy terms), and those involved rarely have any ideological commitment to a co-operative solution. The element of industrial democracy is therefore contained in the initial protest action and possibly in the final solution, for which there are several options: the existing owner can give in and agree to reopen his business, which in practice rarely happens, or to reduce the number of redundancies; the workers can sit it out till the Government or a new private sector owner appears to run the business on conventional lines (as happened at UCS); alternatively, under political pressure to save jobs, the Government can fund a co-operative with state aid (as in the Benn enterprises), or one of the existing common-ownership enterprises can help the workers to turn themselves into a co-operative (as happened at Fakenham); finally, funds can now be made available for co-operatives from other sources including provisions in the Industrial Common Ownership Act (1976) and (so long as it lasts) the Government's job creation programme.

Relatively few sit-ins and work-ins however are successful in leading even to temporary, let alone permanent, solutions, and financial problems that have dogged the Benn enterprises have increased the scepticism with which worker co-operatives' claims are met by potential backers.

Workers' co-operatives

British workers' co-operatives in general can be divided into three groups, some of which involve a significant degree of financial participation by the workers. First there are those sit-in types mentioned above where a militant work force packs enough political and industrial clout to find a financial backer–as at KME and Meriden for example–who will provide the capital for them to salvage their company and run it themselves. Somewhat similar, in that they also stem from the unemployment problems of the late 1970s, are others backed under the Common Ownership Act and the job creation schemes which have just been mentioned and which are explained later. All these co-operatives have been born in the 1970s out of industrial failure of one sort or another and thus originate in defensive workers' reactions.

Second there are about twenty older co-operatives embracing nearly two thousand workers, mainly in the shoe and textile industries. With a total turnover in 1973 of £5.6 million, they are the sole survivors of producer co-operatives formed in the latter part of the last century, at a time when it was not clear whether working-class solidarity would polarise around trade unionism or co-operatives, or whether the then-emerging co-operative movement would become a consumer or producer movement. As it turned out, the trade unions and the consumer co-operatives won the day, partly owing to the dominating influence of Sidney and Beatrice Webb, the socialist theoreticians, who backed trade unionism, consumer co-operation and state ownership rather than the worker co-operative notion of merging the interests and authority of the industrial employer and employee.

The third group–and now the mainstream of worker co-operatives in Britain–is centred around an organisation called the Industrial Common-Ownership Movement, which has evolved from the initiatives of Ernest Bader, formerly the owner of Scott-Bader, a Northamptonshire chemical concern. With his family, he gave 90 per cent of the company's shares to its employees in 1951 and the balance in 1963. Scott-Bader has also helped other co-operatives including Fakenham Enterprises and Sunderlandia, a north-east building contractor, and the Movement, which emerged in 1971 from an earlier Scott-Bader foundation, now embraces thirteen member companies. Scott-Bader, with four hundred employees and an annual turnover in 1976 of £15 million is the largest, while Bewlay Cafes of Dublin with four hundred employees and a £1.8 million turnover is the second.

There is a certain similarity between some of these concerns and the John Lewis Partnership stores group, which has 25,000 employees and operates much like a paternalistic co-operative with participative committees and councils and profit distribution. They often stem from a charitable, Christian (Quaker), and paternalistic attitude on the part of their former owners, who decided for themselves to hand over the ownership to the workers–or even to found the company on common-ownership principles. Rarely if ever has there been any initial grass-roots demand from the employees involved for this or any other form of industrial democracy. Some of the former owners however would now rationalise what they have done as a preferable alternative to the prospect of sharing power with their employees as Bullock-style worker directors; indeed, while they have given up the rights to ownership, many of them have remained in effective managerial control.

A further sort of co-operative has emerged abroad, mainly in America and France, where large companies have sometimes sold off distant and often smaller factories and subsidiaries to employees who can make such enterprises operate more profitably without the overheads of a large empire.

New enterprises

Now the Industrial Common Ownership Movement (ICOM) has been given a fresh role, which could lead to a new generation of co-operatives that have neither the militant nor the paternalistic traditions of those already mentioned. This is the result of the Industrial Common Ownership Act (1976), which emerged from a private member's Bill and was backed by the 1974 Labour Government. In effect, the Act commits the Government through the Department of Industry (which is interested because it is concerned about the de-motivational effects of large corporations) to give some moral and practical support. A limited amount of cash–initially £400,000–was made available under the Act for the development of co-operatives, and there are plans for a co-ordinating Co-operative Development Agency. To test the mood of this new area of government operations (large-scale support given to co-operatives such as KME and Meriden is classified separately under general state industrial aid), the small firms division of the Department even held a conference at the Co-operative College in Loughborough in April 1977. It was addressed by junior ministers from the Departments of Industry and Employment–Bob Cryer and John Golding–and was attended by about 150 established and would-be co-operators and representatives of other interests ranging from the Labour-controlled Wandsworth Borough Council (which wanted to use its ratepayers' money to fund co-operatives) to the Friends of the Earth (which was concerned about the environmental aspects of what co-operatives make). Although sometimes more evangelical than realistic in tone (and hindered to some extent by confusingly rival orthodoxies and organisations), the conference showed the possibility of a series of small co-operatives springing up around Britain. They would be helped by ICOM, which was being given £250,000 of the new Act's £400,000 to spend in revolving loans to would-be co-operatives through a spin-off organisation, Industrial Common-Ownership Finance.

Another £1.3 million was being made available by the Government in 1976-7 for the Manpower Services Commission's job creation unemployment programme to spend on workshop projects, including co-operatives, which had a prospect of becoming self-financing within a twelve-month period. These projects, often in the woodworking or plastics business and usually not employing more than twenty or so people at first, would (unless further government funds were made available) either have to become profitable, find another backer–maybe ICOM–or go out of business after a year, thus demonstrating the problems faced by those co-operatives that are not blessed by a paternalistic benefactor.

Capital needs
Indeed, lack of capital–along with trade union lethargy bordering on opposition–has been a major stumbling block to the development of worker co-operatives in the past century. By the early part of 1977, for example, the Government had paid out at least £5 million in grants to the KME multi-product engineering co-operative on Merseyside, which works out at more than £6000 for each of the enterprise's 775 employees. Meriden has been helped on the same sort of scale by the Government (plus £1 million along with managerial help from GEC), which means that these are primarily state-financed, rather than worker-owned, enterprises because the actual shareholding of the employees themselves is either non-existent or is nominal–about £1 per person.

So what does being a workers' co-operative or a common ownership enterprise mean? Does it involve a sizeable personal financial stake so that the workers *do* actually own at least a significant part of their place of work instead of relying on the State or some other benefactor or investor? Or does it simply mean a place where (whatever the presentational or actual financial arrangements may be) the workers run the enterprise for themselves on co-operative lines? And in either case, who is actually in executive day-to-day charge – the co-operators or hired management? These questions, which have yet to be resolved, stem from the usual industrial conflicts surrounding the providers of capital and managerial authority in any political or economic system. They lie behind the fact that there are no self-sufficient large genuine co-operatives in Britain today. Those that do exist are either very small, or have been created out of successful businesses (like Scott-Bader), or are relying on state or other aid (like KME and Meriden).

The meaning of common ownership is that an enterprise should be controlled by and run in the co-operative interests of those working in it, not in the interests of those providing the capital or (as has been proposed in the Bullock debate for ordinary companies – see Chapter 16) in the joint interests of shareholders and employees. Such a principle, when there are plenty of other more conventional homes for investment, inevitably does not attract capital. This is a major problem for larger industrial co-operatives in a highly geared technological world, especially since any provision of capital would almost certainly, over time, change the balance of power away from common-ownership principles and might well rebuild traditional capital–labour conflict.

There is also a further dimension to this issue of investment within the smaller existing ICOM type of co-operatives and it involves the degree of financial participation by employees. This is whether the shares of the company should be fully bought and held individually by those working in it or merely held collectively on their behalf – on payment of a nominal small sum – by a co-operative organisation. Scott-Bader (through an organisation known as the Scott-Bader Commonwealth) and the other ICOM co-operatives have opted for this collective ownership. But the problem here is that there may be no incentive for the workers to maximise profits enough to expand the business as well as paying their wages and keeping production at existing levels once debts have been paid off.

An alternative route has been used by another philanthropic co-operative founder, David Spreckly, who sold his business of manufacturing mobile offices – now called Landsmens Co-Ownership – to his work force over a period of years in the 1960s. He chose to sell his shares to the workers as individuals who now each have a financial interest in the company and in its expansion – an interest they can cash in when they leave. So, unlike the ICOM formula, they have significant financial participation. The problem here is to find fresh would-be co-operating employees with enough cash to buy their way into the co-operative when existing employees wish to leave or retire. Sometimes the only answer may then be to let traditional capitalist investors back in. Ideally, co-operatives therefore need a mixture of individual and collective ownership, plus other means of raising loans.

Mondragon in Spain

For this reason some co-operative activists favour trying to develop something similar to the community of industrial co-operatives that have grown up with their own bank since 1956 in the Basque area of Spain. They are centred around a town called Mondragon and there are now some sixty industrial and other co-operatives employing thirteen thousand people who have each invested about £2000. The combined annual turnover is roughly £200 million, (according to an independent report prepared in 1977 for the Anglo–German Foundation for the Study of Industry). But the most interesting thing about these co-operatives is the way they have dealt with their financial problems of raising capital. As part of the co-operative community there is the bank, called the Caja Laboral Popular, which acts as a savings bank for the local community and provides 60 per cent of a co-operative's capital – the other 40 per cent comes half from the State and half from the workers. It has sixty-four branches with deposits totalling roughly £95 million and capital and reserves amounting to £15 million. It also acts as the co-operating centre of the group, providing management services and assisting with short- and long-term planning and monitoring the progress of the co-operatives. The authors of the report on Mondragon proposed a solution such as this for the UK to create 'a democratic worker ownership sector as a third alternative to private and state ownership in a multi-institutional economy'. Their idea was that the Government, industrialists and unions should together help to launch such an enterprise, all of whose employees would have to invest £1000 themselves (which most workers would find hard to raise).

Management expertise

The Mondragon example is significant also for the fact that the bank acts as a management consultancy, because lack of skilled management expertise is the second of the three problems that hit co-operatives in Britain – the other two being lack of capital and the trade union lethargy bordering on opposition. While the ICOM pioneering industrialists have provided their own entrepreneurial and managerial skills after changing the status of their businesses, organisations like Meriden and KME have suffered from a lack of managerial expertise. Meriden, indeed, relied first on some short-term factory management help from GKN in 1976. It then received some longer-term expert managerial help from GEC executives and sales assistance in America from Lord Stokes, former chairman of British Leyland, as part of the Government–GEC rescue of the co-operative put together in the winter of 1976-7 by Harold Lever, chancellor of the Duchy of Lancaster.

Several other large companies around the country have also helped embryo and established co-operatives in the past few years by loaning specialist management in technical, marketing and other fields. (It is noteworthy that a co-operative almost always meets with a sharp division of opinion within the business community. On the one hand there are companies anxious to help for a mixture of practical, personal and emotional reasons. On the other hand there are companies – usually in the same area of activity as the co-operative concerned–that do their best to undermine it through their contact with banks, customers and suppliers.)

But the main problem for new co-operatives is attracting permanent expert managers—first because of the usually dubious stability of their business, second because they are often trying to follow an egalitarian path and level-down their salary differentials, and third because the mood of newly created co-operatives does not blend well with management authority.

Summary

While such problems may de-motivate managers, they can motivate workers, which means that co-operatives can sometimes provide a valid and radical solution to the basic problem of how to remove the alienation to work that lies behind some of Britain's industrial problems. Up to early 1977, both Meriden and KME could produce examples of how the changed nature of their shopfloor relationships had boosted productivity, reduced industrial action and curbed wage demands. On the other hand, it has to be remembered that this is the least one should expect in the early days of businesses where survival is the main objective and at a time when pay demands have in any case been restricted by national pay policies.

In both KME and Meriden, the longer-term problem of operating in industries and areas of active militant trade unionism (Merseyside and Midland engineering) have yet to be faced. Indeed, the trade unions themselves have yet to come to terms with how they treat co-operatives. While they back them at the stage of their creation as a useful way of saving jobs, they do not see them (and never have, from the time of the Webbs onwards) as the right path for the British Labour movement, especially if workers have to invest their savings as well as their working hours. The shop stewards in these two co-operatives have operated in a variety of mixed roles as governing councillors, managers and union or employee representatives. In most of the ICOM enterprises, on the other hand, the unions and their activists play no significant role and all the co-operatives want from them is assurances that, although the workers may in effect be non-union, their products will not be blacked elsewhere. From the union's point of view there is always the fear that, were co-operatives to be successful, there should in theory at least be no job left for the unions to do.

On top of this lack of interest from the trade unions, there is a lack of interest from most investors, which starves would-be co-operatives of capital.

Satisfaction at work

The third area of shopfloor democracy is concerned with employees being able to have a degree of autonomy and freedom over the way that their daily working lives are ordered. It travels under a variety of titles (which all roughly amount to the same thing): the quality of working life, job satisfaction, autonomous work groups, group technology, job enrichment, job design, job enlargement, job rotation and work restructuring. Broadly all these ideas (and the specialist management and motivational techniques such as the Scanlon productivity plan and the Herzberg theories that go with them) are aimed at removing the drudgery from boring work, increasing the worker's involvement and the quality of the life he leads at work, and thus at improving efficiency. Often they are therefore trying to re-create some of the freedom of initiative and job satisfaction removed by the past decades of mechanisation.

Trade unions, especially in Britain (and sometimes even in America), greet such ideas with a mixture of scepticism and opposition because they do nothing to change society in socialist terms but can enable an employer to make productivity gains without paying for them. On the other hand, as one of the most famous experiments of all at Volvo's Kalmar car factory in Sweden has shown, the quality of the workers' life may be improved when autonomous work groups replace a monotonous efficiency-oriented production line, although the change in production techniques may well reduce productivity and so raise rather than reduce overall costs.

'Descending participation'
The theory of this sort of employee participation was dubbed 'descending participation' by Kenneth Walker in the January 1977 edition of the *Bulletin of the International Institute for Labour Studies*. First he defined workers' participation in general in a non-political way as something that happens 'when those below the top of an enterprise hierarchy take part in the managerial functions of the enterprise'. He then divided this up into 'ascending participation', which provided, through structures such as worker directors and participation committees, 'some means whereby workers can exert influence on the performance of managerial functions at levels above their own'. Compared with this, participative shopfloor supervision and job enrichment schemes were 'descending participation' and involved 'managerial functions being pushed down the hierarchy and carried out at the workers' own level . . . the worker helps to manage his own job and to control his immediate work situation'.

This definition is specially helpful because it can be used to underline the different approaches to participation. First there is the TUC–Bullock and the extended collective bargaining approach of trade unions claiming the right to search upwards into the higher corporate decision-making areas of management. On the other hand, descending participation is normally, because of its nature, inspired from above by management and involves the delegation of decision-making towards the shop floor and eventually down to the individual worker. In organisational and managerial terms, both forms can disrupt middle and supervisory management and foremen, who can find themselves left behind searching for new roles whichever way the trend is moving. But from the individual worker's point of view (as opposed to his unions' more power-oriented interests on his behalf), his own life can be specially enlivened by the new responsibilities and freedoms that descending participation gives him. (It must be added however that not all workers want the extra responsibility and effort that this involves, and some will opt for the simple but un-demanding monotony of the production line.) It is also worth noting, in the context of ascending and descending participation, that one of the unions often found to be most interested in the job enrichment sort of exercises is the Electrical and Plumbing Trades Union, which is also the most opposed to the summit of ascending participation – worker directors in the board room. Some forward thinking managements also see the introduction of shopfloor job participation as a good way of mobilising a worker's interest in his immediate environment and then progressively extending this into other matters.

From Scandinavia to Britain

The current spate of interest in removing the monotony of work and giving workers the freedom to decide how they do the work started in Norway in the 1960s and then spread to Sweden where it was eagerly taken up both by industrialists and politicians concerned about high rates of absenteeism and by unions worried about the impact of technological developments on their members' working lives. In Saab and Volvo, the two Swedish companies best known for their experiments in removing the assembly tracks, labour turnover figures were reaching 100 per cent in 1970 with absenteeism running at more than 20 per cent. Elsewhere in Swedish industry, absenteeism in 1976 ranged up to 30 per cent with an average of 11 per cent, while Volvo's experiments at its Kalmar plant had cut its own figure to about 14 per cent.

While Sweden developed job-enriching autonomous work groups to try (only partially successfully, as it turned out) to cure its absenteeism problem, the Norwegians have been more interested in the idea for its own sake and tend to see the development of small factories with small work groups as an end in itself. The British motivation, on the other hand, is usually to remove the alienation to work, improve industrial relations and boost sagging efficiency, and much of what impetus has been achieved has come from the Department of Employment. Other countries such as France, Germany and Holland have also started what they sometimes call 'humanisation of work' for a variety of reasons including, in Germany, growing interest in health and safety. (Shopfloor involvement in such matters in Britain is provided through trade union organisation under the Health and Safety Act (1974).) America has probably the most straightforward aims of all – to increase efficiency. Job enrichment and similar schemes are of course virtually the only basis for what industrial democracy does exist in America, with its business-oriented unions, although the US motor industry provides some of the strongest opposition to Volvo-style ideas. Its giant multinational motor companies, with mass-produced high production runs, find little of relevant interest in the Volvo and Saab slower and more specialist form of car production.

Indeed, the lack of spectacular success in the highly publicised experiments of Saab and Volvo has made it easy for a mythology to grow up that job enrichment and autonomous work group types of schemes cannot work efficiently and therefore can safely be ignored. This is far from the truth, as experience in a variety of businesses in Scandinavia and elsewhere in Europe, including Britain, show.

Volvo's scheme

The point about the Volvo experiment at its Kalmar assembly factory is that it tried to involve all aspects of the work environment, including a specially designed factory built on a ground plan of interlinking hexagonal shapes (to allow the production run to be split up into clearly-defined self-contained small workshops along the sides of the hexagons). This proved unnecessarily costly, because Volvo has now decided that small workshop environments can be created less expensively in conventional buildings. But the other three main parts of the experiment are being tried elsewhere by the company including at its Skovde engine plant. These are: splitting up the assembly process into areas of group working; allowing considerable freedom within these groups for workers to rotate their jobs, design and change the layout of their working area and vary the pace of their work and the frequency of their rest periods; replacing constantly moving assembly tracks, which dictate the speed at which a man must work, with computer-controlled mechanical trolleys which run round the factory at variable speeds dictated by the workers within overall limits. These ideas combine the two basic ingredients of job satisfaction schemes—first, making a worker's job more interesting in itself, and second, giving him a chance to a considerable say in how and when he carries it out.

Elsewhere, encouraged by the Americans from their Detroit headquarters, motor manufacturers generally have often tried to stress that Volvo is a special sort of motor manufacturer in a special situation. They also point to the fact that some US car workers visited Saab, where the system is similar to Volvo, and said they preferred their Detroit assembly tracks. They also point to an independent report on the Volvo experiment prepared by the Swedish union and employers' federations (the LO and SAF) in 1976 which shows that the Kalmar experiment has been only a qualified success because it has not recouped the 10 per cent extra investment that Volvo said it had had to spend. This is partly because the quality of the work produced is not as much improved as it ought to be.

Nevertheless, motor manufacturers elsewhere are using some of the Volvo ideas; Peugeot has some limited group working and Fiat, while abandoning a full group assembly experiment, has a mixture of group assembly techniques together with mechanical trolleys plus some robot machines along with normal assembly tracks at its northern Italy Miafiori plant. Even in the UK, British Leyland has been conducting small experiments and has also designed its new Rover plant at Solihull so that the monotony of jobs can be relaxed with group working if workers demand it in the future. Such ideas can be introduced only in the right environment, however, and one limited experiment at Ford's Halewood plant failed.

Experience in Britain

Elsewhere in Britain a limited variety of successful schemes has been introduced in different industries. One of them has been operated by United Biscuits, one of the most advanced British companies in adopting different types of participation techniques, at its Manchester factory. Without changing its technology (and therefore in a more limited way than Volvo), United Biscuits gave its process workers the authority to start up and shut down production lines as necessary and to carry out their own simple maintenance work, organise their own meal and other breaks, and work out their own job rotation arrangements. In day-to-day working, management is involved only when the operators cannot solve a problem.

Such ideas can be applied to clerical and other white-collar work as easily (and sometimes more easily) than to the assembly track. One example of this is a system introduced nine years ago by the South East Electricity Board, which had broken its work down into highly specialised compartments so that a variety of clerks dealt with different aspects of a client's account. When the work was computerised, it was rearranged along job enrichment lines so that each clerk deals with all work and queries to do with a customer's account, thereby, it is hoped, improving the interest of her job, the efficiency of the operation, and the service to the customer.

Critics of job enrichment as a subject may well argue that such changes do not deserve any grand-sounding descriptive titles because they are simply the sort of good management organisation that companies ought to be carrying out either through normal modernisation or through productivity schemes. The difference is the attitudes of those concerned, because the sort of schemes described here involve a positive willingness on the part of management to allow individuals to participate in managerial decision-making. A company that does this may well find that this participation in a limited part of a company's activities gradually makes employees become interested in wider areas of management decision-making.

In Britain, however, there has been little general interest in such developments. A report by the Department of Employment's Work Research Unit (Department of Employment, 1975) was able to trace only 111 examples of work-restructuring in Britain – a figure that had probably reached 200 by mid-1977. Most of the 111 had been aimed at enabling workers to rotate their jobs among themselves and thereby to enlarge and enrich their work. They had been introduced since 1950 with an acceleration of interest from 1970 onwards, and most of the workers involved were employed on assembly lines and process production in industries such as chemicals, food and drink, engineering and other manufacturing businesses.

Government interest
The first official British government interest in this subject came in 1972-3 when the Conservative Government was trying to mend its relationships with the trade unions. It was aware of the Volvo and other developments and realised during the Downing Street and Chequers talks of Heath's tripartism period, when it was looking for non-contentious union subjects of discussion and possible co-operation, that what it called the 'quality of working life' was an ideal candidate. Then, faced with the EEC's moves towards worker directors and the need for it to draw up its own policies (see Chapter 14), its interest increased. The 'quality of working life' title was indeed being used in 1973 by the then Conservative secretary for employment, Maurice Macmillan, to embrace all aspects of employee participation and industrial democracy even to the extent of including the TUC's involvement in proposed new institutions such as the Manpower Services Commission and Health and Safety Commission.

As a result, a tripartite steering group on the specific subject of job satisfaction was set up by Mr Macmillan in 1973 with representatives from the Government, CBI and TUC. This led on in December 1974 to

Michael Foot, then Labour's employment secretary, setting up a small Work Research Unit within the Department of Employment with the task of trying to persuade industry and other government departments to consider introducing job enrichment schemes and then to give advice on how it could be done. And in May 1976 Mr Foot's successor, Albert Booth, echoed Mr Macmillan's views and said in a speech:

There is a good deal of evidence to show that one of the principle means of improving job satisfaction is to provide scope for employees to organise their own work and participate in day-to-day decisions which affect them. This is why the Government's job satisfaction programme should not be seen in isolation but as part of its wider industrial democracy programme.

But for all the official backing, the subject has been a slow starter in the UK even though it received recognition in the post-Bullock Report debate as one part of below-board-level participation. Only the most advanced and keen managements have been able to overcome the fear among middle managers and foremen about the change in their status which accompanies workers being given more autonomy. Shop stewards also often oppose the ideas because they may, but need not, undermine their shopfloor authority. But most important of all in the 1970s has been Britain's economic problems. First, profitability and investment problems have not made many managements keen on expensive capital experiments. Then consecutive pay policies have prevented, or at least have hindered, the productivity and wage structure payments that might be needed to coax a work force into new styles of operations. Third, and most importantly, workers' fears of unemployment have made them less than interested in co-operating with anything that might reduce job prospects.

Conclusions

There is little sign however that the individual (as opposed to representative) forms of industrial democracy are likely to make any major impact on their own in Britain in the near future, although some companies will encourage them as a stepping-stone into other means of employee participation.

In order to achieve a real individual interest among workers for the financial success of their companies – beyond the payment of wages – one needs worker co-operatives with workers subscribing some of the capital. But because of the British traditions of capital, management and unions, this is likely to remain an experimental – albeit laudable – fringe area in the foreseeable future in which the main successes are the Scott-Bader type of somewhat paternalistic but participative smaller enterprises.

The expense and scepticism associated with the 'quality of working life' approach and the limited financial participation involved in share-ownership schemes means that neither can be regarded as a primary way of extending industrial democracy. On the other hand, both can help to improve the participative elements in companies – especially job satisfaction, which can help build shopfloor involvement. Both methods are also likely to move further into the foreground of debates on participation when Conservative and Liberal Parties hold political power.

Part III
Bullock and the Future

Chapter 14

Britain's Road to Bullock

One man and one international political event primarily lie behind the shifts in thinking during the years 1966-77 which led Britain to the brink of a statutory worker director system in all companies employing more than two thousand workers. The man is Jack Jones, the country's leading trade union figure for much of the period. The event is Britain's accession to the European Economic Community on 1 January, 1973, which made British union leaders, industrialists and politicians consider how Britain should react to the EEC's harmonisation of trade policies on the reorganisation of company laws. Because Germany has a two-tier worker director company structure, this reorganisation embraces the quite separate subject of employee participation or industrial democracy. Jones took the impetus created by this event and used it both to harden his own views on the value of worker directors and then to try to have it adopted in the UK, even though it meant over-turning many cherished concepts of the Labour movement.

First steps in the 1960s

The story starts in the mid-1960s with the creation of two inquiries into trade union affairs. The first, the Donovan Commission on Trade Unions and Employers' Associations was set up in 1965 (see Chapter 2) by the Labour Government to map out new relationships between employers and unions. The second, a Working Party on Industrial Democracy, was set up in May 1966 by the Labour Party under the chairmanship of Jack Jones, who was then a senior national official of the TGWU, a member of the Labour Party's national executive committee, and who was already beginning to be regarded as heir apparent to the then general secretary of the TGWU, Frank Cousins. So this working party effectively marks the beginning of Jones's influence in Labour Party affairs, an influence that in the following decade was to help to lead both to the 1974 Labour Government's social contract with the unions and to the 1975-6 Bullock Inquiry on worker directors.

Back in the mid-1960s however there was little active interest in the concept of worker directors, and the Labour Movement was still wedded to the doctrine of industrial democracy handed down at the turn of the century by the Webbs which was based on the tradition of collective bargaining between unions representing workers and management and the representatives of capital. This doctrine was so deeply established that even in the nationalised industries the role of the trade unions and any sort of worker representative on the board had been kept completely separate.

Despite this there were Labour activists who were interested in board-room representation of some sort or other and there was also considerable, if somewhat ill-informed, interest in the German system of co-determination with its worker directors introduced in the early 1950s (see Chapter 10). This flickering of interest emerged through the Donovan Commission which reported in 1968 and the Jones working party, which published its report in May 1967 just a year after it had been set up. But both reports were heavily based on traditional collective bargaining and only regarded worker directors as possible areas for experiments, whereas the developments that ultimately led to the Bullock Report were based on a belief that collective bargaining outside the boardroom was inadequate for trade union purposes.

The Donovan Commission

The Donovan interest was sparked by the evidence given to it by the TUC (written in the TUC economics department by a new young recruit, David Lea, who was to follow the subject through for a decade to the Bullock Committee–under the supervision of Len Murray, then economics secretary and from 1973 TUC general secretary). This evidence showed the first glimmerings of the argument that, through the extension of industrial democracy, unions and their members should be given the opportunity to shoulder a greater degree of responsibility at various levels of economic and industrial affairs:

Workpeople form trade unions to assert their right to have a say in matters which are of close concern to them. . . . They have a continuing interest and experience in all matters affecting their employment and together have potentially the competence to make an essential contribution to decisions affecting the enterprise in which they work. The extent of this contribution has hitherto been limited by the nature of the master and servant relationship. Workpeople, through their trade unions, can play no responsible role in such circumstances as there is nothing that they can be responsible for. If all decisions affecting the running of an enterprise are made unilaterally by the employer there can be no basis for mutual respect.

The evidence went on to acknowledge that such industrial democracy issues raised problems about the function and organisation of trade unions but nevertheless called for legislation that would 'allow companies to make provision for trade union representatives on the board of directors'. The objective would be to 'encourage companies to recognise and take advantage of the mutual benefits to be obtained from more active participation by trade union representatives in company policy and day to day practice' (TUC, 1966).

This idea of *allowing* companies to have worker directors (and so leaving the initiative in the hand of management) was of course a far cry from the ideas that were to develop in the 1970s of giving unions the statutory *right* to introduce worker directors without any corresponding countervailing management power. Nevertheless it was a start, even though it failed to raise much interest in the Commission, whose members received little if any other evidence on the subject. The Commission was concentrating on the issues of company and industry-wide employer–union bargaining and it was only through the efforts of a handful of its members, notably Eric Wigham, then Labour correspondent of *The Times,* that anything was said about it in the report at all.

The majority of the Commission felt 'unable to recommend' the appointment of worker directors to the boards of companies, and the main reason that they gave in their report published in 1968 is worth noting because it is still at the centre of the debate a decade later:

Such an office might expose its holder at times to an almost intolerable strain when decisions unfavourable to workers (for example on redundancy) had to be taken because they were in the interests of the company as a whole. A concurring vote by the workers' director [sic] might be unavoidable if he is to do his duty as a director; and yet could easily be misunderstood or misrepresented. The result might be to open a gap between the workers and the workers' director which it would be extremely difficult thereafter to bridge. In effect he would cease to represent them.

Three of the Commission's members (including George Woodcock, then TUC general secretary) wanted to encourage and facilitate voluntary experiments, partly by introducing legislation to relieve worker directors 'of those legal and financial responsibilities which it would be wrong to ask them to share with other directors'. Only Eric Wigham and one other member (Andrew Shonfield) wanted to go further. They said the Government should prepare for legislation to make the largest companies with five thousand or more employees have not less than two directors appointed by unions after consultation with the TUC. They would 'act as guardians of the workers' interest'. This was quite different from TUC ideas that were to emerge later for shop stewards to be elected to the board, as Wigham and Shonfield explained: 'It is envisaged that those chosen would be more likely to be men with industrial or financial experience or knowledge, or trade union officials, than workers from the bench.' But these ideas, although relevant now in an historical context, made little impact at the time.

The Jones working party
Meanwhile far more radical ideas for increasing the power of trade union members at work had been produced by the Jones working party and presented to the Labour Party's national executive. This working party had been created partly out of a fear that the Donovan Commission would concentrate on the problems of strikes and other such aspects of the country's industrial relations (as indeed it did) and would design new structures to deal with these problems rather than looking on to an expanding role for unions.

In general terms the working party was significant because it produced a report called *Industrial Democracy* which gave the broad subject a boost within Labour circles. More specifically it mapped out a path, mainly followed by the 1974 Labour Government (but partly implemented earlier), for legislation to give union bargaining and shop stewards more statutory rights and powers of the sort contained in the Employment Protection Act (1975). The list included subjects such as union recognition, disclosure of information, protection against unfair dismissal, time off and facilities for union duties, shop steward training, and trade union-based safety representatives.

But perhaps its main general contribution apart from this legislative shopping list was firmly to launch the 'single-channel' union-only policy. It first showed what little regard the Labour movement had for the sort of low-key consultation committees, operated separately from union and bargaining structures, which were favoured by employers, and went on to pinpoint the need for a 'single channel of worker representation based on trade union organisation' in which there was no separation between bargaining and consultation and no provision for non-unionists. (Ironically, ten years later to the month, in June 1977, the TUC was to fall out seriously over this single-channel concept with Labour ministers, many of whom did not see why rights for statutory Bullock-style worker directors should be given only to union members and not to non-unionists.)

The Jones report also acknowledged the possibility of worker directors but, as far as the private sector was concerned, only as a somewhat distant possibility:

The question of worker representatives 'on the board' in the private sector gives rise to a number of difficult problems and we cannot see it as a suitable starting point for the extension of industrial democracy. We think it is likely to arise in the main after the further extension of the scope of collective bargaining and of statutory protection.

That the report even said this much was due mainly to the dogged insistence of Jack Jones who, while at this time far from firmly committed to the idea, could not see any real reason why ultimately shop stewards should not sit in board rooms. His views on this stem from his conviction of the value of shop stewards to the unions and to industry and his firm belief that, on a practical level, they have expertise and skills that would make management more efficient and that such a positive involvement would also improve industrial relations. But there were few if any other worker director enthusiasts on the working party whose members included Professor Wedderburn, later to form part of the Bullock majority group, and Dr Bill McCarthy, Donovan's research officer and a worker director sceptic. The report did however go on to call for worker director experiments on the boards of publicly owned companies and industries and this kept the subject firmly alive in Labour policy-making.

Government consultations

So by the late 1960s there was little major impetus behind the worker director idea. Labour Party leaders were aware both of the company law and the union role problems involved in such a step. But Jack Jones did not let go of his idea, and his growing influence in Labour Party and government affairs emerged again in April 1970, when, having lost her labour law battles with the TUC, Barbara Castle, secretary for employment and productivity, published a short consultative document she had circulated a month earlier to the TUC, CBI and other organisations. This was a direct result of the Jones working party's report and subsequent pressure from Jones for some action, and it posed four main questions. (1) Should company law continue to give shareholders a final choice of all directors (including any worker directors), or should a German-style supervisory board structure be created? (2) How compatible would worker directors be with the development of company-wide bargaining, and was there a danger that the same worker representatives would appear in both roles and 'thus be forced to serve two masters'? (3) Should worker directors be full-time with executive responsibilities or part-time, and if so with what responsibilities? (4) Should the system in the nationalised industries be changed so that union representatives could sit on boards of their own rather than other industries?

Within a couple of months however Labour was defeated in the June 1970 general election and ideas for unions to expand their roles through worker directors or any other form of industrial democracy were pushed into the background for a year or two while they concentrated on defending what powers they already had against the Conservatives' Industrial Relations Bill.

Morrison and the public sector

Up to the late 1960s when the Donovan and Jones reports appeared, the worker director debate within the Labour movement had been concentrated on the nationalised industries and was still dominated by the earlier influence of Herbert Morrison, the former prominent Labour politician. The main debates were in the 1930s and concerned how Labour should run the industries that it would nationalise, and they polarised, as they still do, over whether or not it was the job of unions to risk losing their identity by involving themselves in the policy-making and organisational functions of management.

These arguments go back beyond the prewar years to even the First World War when Guild Socialism was making a mark on the thinking of Labour activists, especially encouraged by the economist G. D. H. Cole. The main issue then was whether state-owned industries should be handed over to representatives of the workers, or run on more conventional lines by state-appointed directors with only a nominal trade union presence. The Guild Socialists, pre-dating in some ways the impact that Bullock-style thinking has been having on the nationalised industries, wanted the workers' own representatives to sit on the boards. But, in a development of the syndicalist worker control ideas, they wanted this done tidily in a way that would almost gladden the hearts of some 1970s employers because all workers in an industry would belong to one union (or guild, as it was called). These industrial-union guilds would run the industry, negotiating on its behalf with the Government which would finance it and represent the consumer and other public interests.

These ideas eventually had little practical influence on Labour policy-making although they gained considerable support in the Post Office (then part of the Civil Service) and in the privately owned coal mines. But the more establishment-minded Labour and TUC leaders, led by Herbert Morrison, opposed such radical ideas. So when the London Passenger Transport Board was created, initially by the Labour Government but finally by the National Government, in the early 1930s, the alternative policy of merely appointing a nominal trade union 'worthy' to the board won the day. This tradition, set by Morrison before the Labour Government fell in 1931, was backed by the TUC in 1944 which wanted unions to 'maintain their complete independence'. It has continued through to the present day and is only now being changed. For example, in the 1940s nationalisation era, coal and rail received their nominal trade union director–the first one in the nationalised railways was W. P. Allen, former general secretary of ASLEF, the locomen's union. When they joined a board–where they were intended to contribute knowledge and understanding on employees' view–they gave up their union posts.

Union leaders who were given posts while continuing with their union jobs were–and still are–normally appointed from other industries in order to 'protect' their independence. This has operated under a TUC nomination system which has been the subject of understandings between the TUC and successive prime ministers. Effectively the TUC general secretary and other key union leaders have had the right to nominate, or have a major influence over, those chosen for many but not all types of public appointments. In 1947 this was privately formalised between the TUC and Mr Attlee, then the Labour prime minister, and it was ampli-fied in private correspondence in 1966 between Harold Wilson and George Woodcock, then respectively prime minister and TUC general secretary.

The result has been, for example, that the General and Municipal Workers' Union has sent union directors to the boards of the Post Office, the railways, and bus industries, while the Public Employees' general secretary has gone into airways, electricity and shipbuilding (at Harland and Wolff). The general secretaries of the textile and clothing workers have gone to coal and gas, and the civil service unions to atomic energy, the engineers to gas, and the shopworkers to airports. Such appointments could hardly rate as major aspects of industrial democracy although the system was sharpened in the late 1960s and early 1970s with union leaders sometimes being appointed to their own industries–so that the Transport and General Workers and the Railwaymen now have seats on the National Freight Corporation. In the coal industry, the National Coal Board has also taken its personal board member from the mining unions while at the British Steel Corporation, alongside its lower-level worker director experiment, the general secretary of the Post Office workers became the personnel board member in 1967 and remained on the board till he retired in 1977.

When Labour was returned in 1964 it continued with the same main policy apart from its cautious experiment with the nationalisation of steel, the railways participation study, some appointments to passenger trans-port authorities and the broader-based Fairfields Experiment, despite attempts by Jack Jones to persuade ministers to go for more radical experiments.

By the time Labour had been returned to power in 1974 the TUC was determined to change the system, which had little if anything to do with employee participation and which had often meant that right-wing and elderly trade union leaders, who were regarded as 'safe bets' by the Civil Service, industrialists and ministers, did well and boosted their income both before and after retirement to the tune of a few thousands of pounds a year (£1000 a year was the going rate for a part-time nationalised industry board member in the early and mid-1970s). With its new interest in industrial democracy, the TUC started urging the Prime Minister in 1975 to recognise that shop stewards and local union officials with experi-ence of an industry could have more useful impact on a board's deliberations than a time-served and maybe retired TUC general councillor. What the TUC wanted at this stage was a Bullock-style shop steward election for up to one-half of a nationalised board with the TUC centrally having an influence on the choice of some of the other government-nominated board members–so potentially giving union sympathisers a majority in nationalised industries.

Impetus from Brussels

Despite the minor changes in the nationalised industries, little had happened by the beginning of the 1970s to indicate that Britain–or even its unions alone for that matter–was moving towards a worker director system, especially in the private sector of industry. Jack Jones had apparently been the only senior union leader seriously interested in the idea by the time the Conservative Government arrived, and the basic problem for the union movement about its proper role had not been resolved even in the nationalised industries, let alone in the rest of the economy. All that happened in the meantime was that the TUC in 1970 set up a small working party to look at the subject. This had been largely at the instigation of Jones, who had moved a resolution at the 1968 Trades Union Congress, following his Labour Party report, calling for wider industrial democracy moves with participation in management in all sectors of trade and industry, plus legislation in the nationalised industries. But the working party, with Sir Sidney Greene of the Railwaymen as its chairman, made little if any headway and hardly met for nearly two years even though Jones was a member.

But Jones was not letting go of the subject and, in a *New Statesman* article on 18 February, 1972, which mapped out the industrial relations aspects of what was to become the social contract (see Chapter 3), he showed how his ideas were developing. Having described Labour ministers who had refused to experiment further in the late 1960s as a 'few small minded men in the Government' with little experience in industry or understanding of workers, he stated that 'a major involvement of trade union representatives on management boards' was vital to the success of industry, particularly nationalised concerns. Pushing the Morrisonian traditions aside, he said that 'this direct trade union representation should be from within the undertaking and based upon a proper system of election and reporting back through the medium of the shop steward system.' Without bothering with the two-tier board ideas that were to emerge later from the TUC, Jones was here moving straight to the eventual TUC–Bullock position of single-tier management-cum-policy boards with 'single-channel' union based representation. It was one of the first signs of his growing interest in the subject on a broad front, although he still fell back on the idea of having nationalised industry developments first. A few months later, in July 1972, the first embryo social contract statement from the TUC–Labour Party Liaison Committee (see Chapter 3) said it would 'work on a programme to promote the widespread development of industrial democracy' including looking into the 'role of the company in society'.

Britain joins the EEC

With the Conservative Government still in power and the Labour Party showing few signs of being a viable alternative government, there the matter of worker directors might well have rested for a long time had it not been for Britain's accession to the Common Market on 1 January, 1973. This event was approached by many institutions (including the Government) from a position of, with hindsight, amazing ignorance. Fear about the power of the EEC's bureaucratic German- and French-dominated Commission in Brussels filled traditionalists with fear and reformists (sometimes) with enthusiasm. The impression grew that unless it moved quickly Britain would be swamped with alien policies in a number of areas.

Accordingly an under-secretary in the Department of Employment wrote on 29 November 1972 to David Lea at the TUC and to Alan Swinden, the CBI's deputy director-general in charge of employment affairs, asking for their initial views on the EEC's harmonisation of company law plans for two-tier boards and worker directors–which were likely to be considered in their latest forms by the EEC's Council of Ministers early in 1973.

TUC goes 50–50

Within a matter of weeks the Department, much to its surprise, was told the TUC's hitherto virtually dormant industrial democracy working party wanted these worker directors to have half the seats on a 50–50 basis with shareholder directors on the supervisory board of a two-tier company structure that might even displace the shareholders' annual meeting from its traditional position as the supreme policy-making body of a company.

This comprehensive policy, overturning both company law practice and apparently even the basic conflict traditions of the British trade union movement in favour of some co-partnership German style of co-determination, amazed not only Whitehall but the industrialists and even many European bureaucrats. Despite the surprise, the policy was approved by the TUC's hitherto virtually dormant industrial democracy working party on 24 January 1973 and was sent in a memorandum to the Government in February.

What had happened in the meantime was that Jack Jones and David Lea had taken the opportunity of Britain entering the Common Market and of the Department of Employment's letter to put a new impetus into the industrial democracy working party whose secretariat in Lea's TUC economics department had been attending meetings on the EEC's plans with other countries' union officials in Europe and so had done much of the ground work ready for the rapid moves in December and January. This was the turning point in the TUC's policy but it took place with even some members of the working party itself not fully understanding what was going on around them as Jones, with Lea doing the drafting, seized the initiative and shifted the debate from its Labour movement sticking point in the nationalised industries into the private sector. So little understood was the subject that one respected member of the TUC working party even said, privately, 'They've got these worker directors in Germany you know and it works very well so we want them here.' There was of course, despite the confusion, no question of Jones wanting to sink the British unions' tradition into German-style co-determination. As he said at the time, 'This is not the old idea of detaching a man from the shop floor and putting him in the boardroom. This is industrial democracy based on an extension of collective bargaining and on direct trade union representation.'

What Jones as an expert negotiator was in fact doing, as one admirer of his puts it, was 'taking up a position on the Left of the field so as to be able to negotiate effectively both with the Tory Government and the EEC'. The rationale for this is that on the one hand there was the EEC, heavily influenced by the German industrial democracy model where worker directors, not based on trade unions, held only one-third of the seats (apart from a 50–50 split in the coal and steel industries) on a relatively weak supervisory board in a two-tier board structure. Beneath them were works councils, also not based on trade unions. On the other hand there was a Tory government wanting to find itself a policy that would not boost trade union power. Such a policy might also have to fit in with the EEC because Britain might not want to start upsetting EEC policies too quickly.

Jones's distaste and contempt for non-union works councils had emerged in his 1967 working party's report with its rejection of consultative committees which he later described as 'tea party committees'. So what could be more natural than to over-bid and so head off the whole non-union and worker director question till a more sympathetic Labour government was in power? The way to do that was to turn the one-third all-employee basis of the German and European ideas into a demand for a 50–50 trade union-based system. And if at the same time British unions were seen by their counterparts in Europe to be setting out on radical policies, so much the better. How much of this is a rationalisation with hindsight is hard to say; but it certainly fits the Jones style of operation, and it succeeded, because the Conservative Government had still failed to come to terms with the problem by the time it was swept from office early in 1974.

Conservative indecision

At the Department of Employment during this period, as secretary of state, Maurice Macmillan was already interested in the profit-sharing aspect of employee participation, through the Wider Share Ownership Council of which he had been founder chairman, and in job satisfaction programmes. He coined the phrase the 'quality of working life' to cover the whole subject of employee participation and prepared a variety of draft Green Papers for his Cabinet colleagues, who were however too busy in the 1973-4 period to face up to the issue and who were also opposed to giving way to the unions.

By the middle of 1973 it was becoming clear in any case that the EEC did not move in Brussels with quite the dominating teutonic precision and efficiency that had been feared, and the worker director scare could therefore be allowed to cool off. But by this time the subject had gained a momentum of its own in London. The CBI and TUC were developing their own policies and the Heath Government was loath to interfere with any industrial interest that might help its new tripartite approach of bringing both sides of industry and the Government together. The

Conservative Government, however, if it was moving anywhere, was not moving towards worker directors although some younger Conservatives were in favour of more nationalised industry experiments (Cassidy, 1973).

A ministerial sub-committee of the Cabinet was set up consisting of a handful of ministers including not only Mr Macmillan but also the two main architects of the Industrial Relations Act–Robert Carr, by then home secretary, and Sir Geoffrey Howe, who had become minister for trade and consumer affairs with responsibility for company law reform on which the Conservatives were also working. If this committee was moving in any direction, it was towards a statutory obligation on employers to consult with (but not necessarily agree with) their employees. This would have operated through unions where they were recognised but would have involved employees generally where they were not, and so would have been a halfway stage between a single-channel union-only and a non-union approach. It would have involved consultation on a specified list of company issues, mainly to do with employment matters. Even this might have meant too much union involvement for the more die-hard Conservative back bench Tory MPs who would have preferred German-style non-union works councils (although in practice in Germany the works council members are usually also the trade union activists).

Initially Mr Macmillan, who was keen to produce a positive useful contribution in this area, had hoped to produce a Green Paper or consultative document by the summer of 1973. But this date constantly slipped so that nothing was agreed by the ministers by early 1974. This was demonstrated in a letter written by Sir Geoffrey Howe to John Garnett, director of the Industrial Society on 29 January, 1974. The purpose of the letter was to refuse a request from Mr Garnett and others to change employees' legal status in company law (an issue in the later Bullock debate–see Chapter 16) beyond proposals in the then embryo Companies Bill. This Bill proposed only that company directors should be permitted but not forced to take employees' interests into account. But Sir Geoffrey also used the letter to stake out what he regarded as the 'real questions' to be faced on participation in general, and the way he did so showed how far the ministers were from conclusions:

First, what rights employees should have to be consulted about day-to-day management decisions which affect their working lives or to share in the making of those decisions; second, how far they should be involved in strategic decisions taken at higher levels, whether through some form of company council, by direct representation on company boards, or in some other way; third, whether there is scope for extending participation in ownership, whether by profit sharing schemes or by schemes with wider coverage going well beyond the securities of the employee's own firm; and fourth, what can be done to make work more satisfying and to give the individual employee a more effective voice in the content and organisation of his own job. It is by means such as these that we can hope progressively to change the position of the employee in an industrial economy and turn him into a partner of the employer in a way that recognises the difference of interest between the two.

If the Conservatives had not been swept from power in the general election of February 1974, presumably they would have ultimately produced a Green Paper. Instead, in opposition they hardened their position. In June 1974 when James Prior, who had been appointed Conservative spokesman on employment, spoke on the subject, he picked up the Macmillan–Howe discussion papers and announced that it was Conservative policy to 'impose upon large and medium-sized employers a general duty to consult employee representatives upon a wide range of subjects'. Meanwhile the Liberal Party had also entered the debate with a private member's Works Councils Bill from its later leader, David Steel, in the spring of 1973. This called for statutory works councils covering subjects such as takeovers and redundancies, and working and holiday and overtime arrangements.

But the CBI's leaders had been turned down by their council in September 1973 when they tried to push through a policy for statutory plant consultative councils. This idea was too much for industrialists, and it was not until February 1976 that the CBI adopted its participation agreements policy and so had a positive firm view on this subject. Meanwhile industrialists were totally opposed to worker directors of the TUC type, which the Engineering Employers' Federation, for example, said would mean admitting to board rooms people who were 'politically motivated to destroy the market economy'.

Summary to 1974

By the beginning of 1974, despite the lack of a Conservative Government policy, Britain's membership of the Common Market had turned what had been really only an issue of debate among a select group of Labour Party activists into a positive TUC policy. This had been confirmed in June 1973 when the 50–50 worker director ideas were set out in a policy document called *Industrial Democracy* which was approved by the September 1973 Annual Congress with little debate. They emerged again in July 1974 with some minor revisions as the TUC's 1974 *Industrial Democracy* document, which has been mentioned and quoted throughout this book and which remained the TUC's policy up to the time the Bullock Committee was set up. Although opposition from key unions opposed to worker directors was already beginning to build up, the policy document stressed that worker directors were an optional extension of collective bargaining–not an alternative–which muted some of the opposition. In any case, general inertia about the subject among many medium-sized private sector unions, coupled with enthusiasm among those operating in the public sector, had prevented a significant opposition ever being built up in the annual Congress debates which have been, in any case, normally squeezed into the spare moments between debates on more immediate major issues such as economic affairs and pay policy.

Battles in Whitehall

When the Labour Government regained power in 1974 its first priorities as far as unions and industrial relations in general were concerned were to repeal the Industrial Relations Act with the Trade Union and Labour Relations Act (1974). Next, many of the ideas contained in the 1967 Jones working party report on statutory union recognition and bargaining rights were contained in the Employment Protection Act (1975). Industrial democracy was seen as the third leg of this series of reforms, and the Labour Party's general election manifesto in February 1974 summed it up by saying a Labour Government would: 'Repeal the Industrial Relations Act as a matter of urgency and then bring in an Employment Protection Act and an Industrial Democracy Act, as agreed in our discussions with the TUC, to increase the control of industry by the people.'

While the first two priorities steamed ahead, however, little was heard about the third, and what was to be a long battle against the whole worker director concept began to build up in the power centres of Whitehall, especially the Treasury and the Department of Trade (which is responsible for company law). When the TUC published its revised Industrial Democracy document in July 1974, it said in its introduction that 'it is now expected that there will be a White Paper on *Industrial Democracy* later this year.' No one else seemed to expect such a development, however, although the October 1974 Labour Party general election manifesto repeated the pledge for legislation (albeit dropping a specific title for the Act): 'We will introduce new legislation to help forward our plans for a radical extension of industrial democracy in both the private and public sectors. This will involve major changes in company law and in the statutes which govern the nationalised industries and the public services.'

These were the days when the TUC was wielding most power in Whitehall through the social contract. Slowly the Labour Government was edging the unions towards a wages policy and for this it relied heavily–if not almost totally–on the leadership and co-operation of Jack Jones. So there was no way that his special subject of worker directors would be removed or forgotten, and the pressure on the Government to start doing something on industrial democracy remained. Anthony Wedgwood Benn, who in 1974 was the secretary for industry, advocated planning agreements and also experimented with other forms of shop steward involvement in company affairs. But the primary responsibility for worker directors lay with the secretary for trade, Peter Shore, who showed little interest in getting to grips with the election manifesto pledges.

Few Labour ministers understood the subject, and those that did were often either put off by the union power aspects or did not see much point in pushing the matter when a fair number of unions were opposed to the Jones ideas. In short, it was too controversial and complex a subject for a government, beset with many more pressing problems, to face up to voluntarily. So by the end of 1974 ministers were being persuaded by senior civil servants to plump for a Committee of Inquiry into industrial democracy in general, which would delay matters, rather than moving straight to legislation.

The Radice Bill

Then, thanks to a parliamentary muddle, the tables were turned, and the TUC suddenly discovered early in 1975 that it had been given the lever it needed to force some action. The occasion was a private member's Bill launched by a Labour MP, Giles Radice, a former research officer of the General and Municipal Workers' Union, who had had some influence on the preparation of the TUC's policy. He told part of the story in the *New Statesman* on 4 March, 1977:

On 15 January, 1975, I requested leave under the Ten Minute Rule [devised to enable back benchers to ventilate issues] to introduce a Bill to establish employee representation on the boards of large companies. After I had made a short speech in favour of my proposed legislation, a Tory MP spoke against it and divided the House. Fortunately it was one of those occasions when a large number of MPs were in the House expecting an early vote–and over 250 MPs, mostly Labour, supported me and we won the division.

Normally that would have been that. But almost miraculously, at 4 p.m. one Friday a few weeks later the Industrial Democracy Bill, as it was called, suddenly became a serious proposition. Because of a slip-up, it got an unopposed second reading and went into committee. This gave my colleagues and myself an unexpected bargaining lever. Two busy Ministers had not only to attend Committee meetings but also to express the Government's view on the issue. And there was always the chance that we could finish the Committee Stage in time for the Bill to come back to the floor of the House. In the end we accepted a proposal to set up an inquiry into Boardroom representation and I withdrew my Bill. . . .

In fact, in the early stage of this story, Radice did not have a Bill at all– only a title for one. When he realised it would go ahead he went to two colleagues–Professor Wedderburn and David Lea (both subsequent Bullock members)–who drafted a twenty-three clause Bill along the lines of the TUC's 50–50 policy over one weekend.

Cabinet rows

Then started months of endless bickering in Whitehall, where the battle that raged between Cabinet members, government departments and union leaders is regarded by some of those concerned as one of the most bitter involving outside interests that they have seen. The initial task for the Cabinet was to get itself off the Radice Bill hook, so most ministers wanted to offer to set up a Committee of Inquiry if the Bill was withdrawn. The TUC camp, led by Jack Jones–and by Michael Foot, employment secretary, within the Cabinet–wanted a government Bill without delay. It felt on strong ground because it knew the Government could not allow the Radice Bill simply to become law–it would therefore either have to do a deal to have the Bill withdrawn or back the Bill itself and insert amendments.

On the other side were Peter Shore, at Trade, enthusiastically backed by his own civil servants, the Chancellor of the Exchequer, Treasury mandarins and many others, who argued passionately for a delaying Committee of Inquiry with as vague terms of reference as possible. Their primary worry was over the impression that would be created abroad if Britain, in the middle of all its economic problems, suddenly rushed into a system that would seem to be putting militant trade unionists into board rooms. Foreign confidence would suffer and inward investment might be frozen, they argued. There was also a feeling among some ministers that the TUC had already been given too much within the social contract. This was a view that was fuelled during 1974 and 1975 by bitter rows over the Trade Union and Labour Relations Act's closed shop legislation (which had to be amended after the October 1974 general election), and over its impact on the freedom of the press. These battles scared the 'moderates' within the Cabinet away from any further union power legislation and meant that they linked up with the hostility emanating from the main economic and trade ministers and civil servants. On the other hand, the social contract wage policy and the backing of Jack Jones were still essential for the Government's survival, whatever foreign and other opinion might say about union power.

Eventually Foot and Jones lost the first round of the battle, in that the Cabinet decided (after the matter had been considered for some weeks by a Committee of Ministers) that a Committee of Inquiry would be set up. The next stage of the battle lasted right through to the middle of the summer and concerned the terms of reference because, having been forced to have a committee, rather than immediate legislation, the TUC was determined to neuter it by loading its terms of reference and its membership so that it had to produce a report backing TUC-style worker directors. Eventually the TUC won – although at one point it only just managed to make enough last-minute noise in Downing Street and Whitehall to stop terms of reference, of which it did not approve because they were too open-ended, being announced to the Commons. Throughout this period the matters went to the Cabinet several times with the Prime Minister frequently being lobbied by the different interests.

Terms of reference
Eventually, on 7 August, months later than had been planned, Mr Shore announced the terms of reference to the Commons. They were heavily weighted in the TUC's favour although the last section did provide an opportunity for some criticism to emerge:

Accepting the need for a radical extension of industrial democracy in the control of companies by means of representation on boards of directors, and accepting the essential role of trade union organisations in this process, to consider how such an extension can best be achieved, taking into account in particular the proposals of the Trades Union Congress report on industrial democracy as well as experience in Britain, the EEC and other countries. Having regard to the interests of the national economy, employees, investors and consumers, to analyse the implications of such representation for the efficient management of companies and for company law.

They covered the private sector only – other internal inquiries were to be set up by the Government for the public sector.

Search for members
Then started a long four-month search for a chairman and members of the Committee, a task that lasted much longer than had been intended and involved extensive horse-trading, with Peter Shore constantly sending proposed lists of names back to his department's civil servants (and to the TUC) for changes. The bitter battles over the terms of reference continued in a different form with the TUC wanting to underpin its position by flooding the Committee with union and 'independent' sympathisers. At the same time the way the terms were phrased meant that it was not easy to find either a chairman or industrialists. The Departments of Trade and Employment received formal nominations from the TUC and ideas from the CBI and the political parties, and some people even wrote in nominating themselves.

Lord Rothschild, former head of the Central Policy Review Staff (the Government's think tank), who was also then the chairman of his family's merchant bank, N. M. Rothschild, was the only person early on formally invited to be the chairman. But he refused in August. Other names, including some leading academics, were considered but were discounted, often because of pressure of other work.

Ultimately the Government found Lord (then Sir Alan) Bullock, master of St Catherine's College, Oxford, and the university's vice-chancellor from 1969 to 1973. A distinguished historian, he was widely known as a biographer both of Hitler and of Ernest Bevin (the former TGWU general secretary and Labour minister). He had also been a member in the 1950s of the BBC Brains Trust and the chairman of a government committee of inquiry on the reading and use of English which was set up in 1972 by Mrs Margaret Thatcher when she was secretary for education and science. (He had also been a trustee of the *Observer* newspaper in the 1960s and of the American Aspen Institute. After the Institute became involved in saving the *Observer* late in 1976, Bullock was made a director of the newspaper and, as critics later enjoyed pointing out, so became the only company director among the signatories of the majority Bullock Report.) A business-like academic, well used to committee work, he was later to use all his skills to try to keep the Committee together. But first, towards the end of 1975, he took a hand in trying to achieve a credible balance of interests on the Committee so that the ultimate report would carry authority.

Various industrialists and industrial relations experts from the ranks of the employers had already been considered and eventually, without the CBI demurring, two men were chosen. One was Barrie Heath, chairman of GKN, a company that had had some experience of worker directors in Germany and had also pioneered some 'worker charter' participation ideas (see Chapter 11). The other was Sir Jack Callard, a former chairman of ICI, which had also pioneered consultative systems (Chapter 11)–he had also been president of the Industrial Participation Association. It was decided that a City of London figure was also needed, and government consultations with the Bank of England produced Mr (later Sir) Norman Biggs who, although his main industrial experience had culminated in his being chairman of Esso Petroleum from 1968 to 1972, had held various banking appointments and had been chairman of Williams and Glyn's Bank from 1972. All three of these men were assumed to be sympathetic to the notion of some employee participation and, indeed, to have accepted appointments on the terms of reference could not have been wholly averse eventually to the idea of worker directors. Of them Biggs was the most sympathetic to the TUC position and Callard the least, as will emerge in the next chapter.

Also from the City came one of the 'independents', Nicholas Wilson, a partner in the law firm of Slaughter and May and a member both of the Capital Markets Committee of the Bank of England and of the Department of Trade's companies consultative group which advises the Government on company law reform. Wilson turned out to be the truest independent of them all and worked closely on company law aspects with one of the two academics on the committee, Professor Wedderburn, of the London School of Economics, a Left-wing academic lawyer. Regarded widely as an expert in both labour and company law, Wedderburn had forecast in a Fabian Society pamphlet, *Company Law Reform,* in 1965 that 'the wires' of company and labour law reform would soon cross. He had won an influence in TUC affairs often denied to most of his academic colleagues and had in the past worked closely with David Lea, the head of the TUC economics department. He had also been a member of the Jack Jones 1967 Labour Party working party, and was one of the first people whom Shore decided had to be on the Committee.

There were two other independents along with Wilson. One was John Methven, who at the time of his appointment was director-general of fair trading. As a lawyer and a former member of the Monopolies Commission he brought special knowledge to the Committee. (He was also a former deputy chairman of ICI's Mond Division, and helped to supplement the indirect influence of ICI thinking paraded by Sir Jack Callard on the Committee. Peter Shore's successor as the secretary for trade, Edmund Dell, was also ex-ICI.) Methven was rated highly by all members of the Committee but resigned in July 1976 after he became director-general of the CBI, where he rapidly donned the mantle of a leading critic. (Eventually all three ICI men were to emerge in this opposition role.)

The other independent was a Canadian, Professor George Bain of Warwick University, an expert on trade union recognition and white-collar unionism and, then aged thirty-six, the youngest member of the Committee (Biggs, then sixty-seven, was the oldest). It was clear from early on that Lea and Jones would be members of the Committee. There were a lot of problems about who the third TUC nominee should be. There was after all little choice for the TUC among the ranks of private sector union leaders because hardly anyone, apart from Jones, had come out positively in favour. The trio of Len Murray, TUC general secretary, Jones, and Lea handled the matter privately among themselves and ultimately, just two days before the names were finally announced, chose Clive Jenkins of ASTMS. The offer came as a surprise to him as much as anyone else because no one could remember his ever speaking on the subject, although he himself remembers having proposed a resolution at the TUC's Congress in 1962 calling for a reappraisal of the worker director concept. Like Jack Jones's TGWU, Clive Jenkins's union was and still is far from united on the issue and in fact rejected the Bullock Report at its annual conference in 1977.

The names were announced on 3 December, 1975 and the Committee was told to report within a year.

Conclusion

Just ten years after the TUC and Jack Jones had started toying with the idea in the Donovan Commission and Labour Party working party, an official Committee of Inquiry was charged to produce a worker director plan for the Government. It seems certain that this would not have happened had it not been for Britain's need to react to the EEC's interest in harmonising European company laws so that companies from different countries could trade and compete on equal terms. It is also virtually certain that the TUC would not have got such precise terms of reference for the Committee if it had not been for the parliamentary accidents of the Radice Bill. And none of it would have happened without the interest, determination and political muscle of Jack Jones.

Chapter 15

The Bullock Committee and its Report

It took just a year plus a few days for the Bullock Committee of Inquiry on Industrial Democracy to prepare its report on how the TUC's 50–50 worker director plans could be turned into practice. After the months of haggling in Westminster and Whitehall described in the last chapter, the Committee was formally set up with an announcement by Peter Shore on 3 December 1975 and the Committee held its first official meeting on 12 December. A year later, on 14 December 1976, the main report and its dissenting note and minority companion were signed by the relevant authors and delivered to Edmund Dell, who had succeeded Mr Shore at the Department of Trade. The report was then published on 26 January 1977. Lord Bullock and the TUC contingent on the Committee, and especially the dominant figure of Mr Jones, kept the work going at a fast pace so that it could be completed in a year. This would give the Government time, it was thought (as it turned out somewhat forlornly), to get legislation under way in at least the form of a White Paper or a draft Bill by the time the 1976-7 parliamentary session ended in the autumn of 1977, so that legislation could be enacted before the next election.

Partly as a result of this speed, and partly because the main TUC supporters were loath to include anything in the main report that might damage their case, the report did not turn out to be always well argued and arranged and it did not establish itself as an authority on industrial democracy and employee participation in general. It tended to move on some key issues from an assertion of a need for change, to a statement of the TUC solution, to a little-analysed report of opposing views, to an assertion that the TUC solution was right. It did not therefore always do its own case justice. For example, the report was so concerned to ensure the ascendancy of its own worker director ideas over the rival union view of extended collective bargaining that it did not analyse sufficiently how the two could be married together. Nor did it come out into the open and admit that it would in fact be shifting bargaining–albeit maybe of a participative style–into the board room, although it did propose an important new sort of shop stewards committee. Equally, its speed of preparation meant that it did not analyse how boards and subsidiary management structures operate in practice and so did not adequately explain how a worker director system could be fitted in on a day-to-day basis without major disruption of a company's operations, or how the board policy decision-making could be married in with lower levels of employee participation.

These and other similar shortcomings were not all the fault of the individual committee members. Rather, they were the almost inevitable result of the TUC's official central stance which had led to the terms of reference in the first place. However, the way the terms of reference did eventually dictate the content of the report meant that the opponents of the TUC's ideas had plenty of ground on which to stake out principled, philosophical and practical criticisms and objections. Equally however, the minority report produced by the three industrialists on the Committee goes in for little more analysis or debate of its assertions. Again, this was partly, but not wholly, the fault of the terms of reference.

Evidence to the Committee

A vast amount of evidence was sent to the Committee in a total of 337 submissions ranging from the biggest companies and the National Consumer Council to City of London financiers and workers' co-operatives. But it produced few surprises, and much of it went into far wider participation and other issues than the Committee had been told to examine. The TUC put in its own 1974 document proposing 50–50 worker directors and subsequently expanded some points. It issued a letter which discouraged individual unions from submitting their own ideas (they might often have contradicted the TUC line), and eventually only leaders of the extended collective bargaining school did so. The CBI submitted its statutory participation agreement policy together with a somewhat vitriolic introduction attacking the whole basis of the Inquiry because it was only asked 'how', not 'whether', the TUC's ideas could be statutorily implemented. This CBI submission–supplemented later with a description of how one could have worker directors voluntarily–set the scene for a flood of evidence in similar vein from employers' federations and individual companies. All of them generally proclaimed their faith and good intentions about employee participation, in an attempt to show how progressive they were and therefore how little they needed chivvying or bullying by the law. But they also almost all opposed the political and power dimensions of industrial democracy and attacked the TUC's statutory worker director ideas as power-oriented proposals which would not be democratic and would make management inefficient.

At the same time, with the TUC going for a 50–50 split on a supervisory board, the CBI opted, in its evidence as a last resort if there had to be legislation, for a minority of worker directors on a single-tier board, although a few companies veered in favour of a two-tier structure. Within a year however, as will be seen later, the main emphasis had changed, with the TUC switching to a preference for a single-tier (or unitary policy board, as it became known) and industrialists (with the CBI remaining somewhat ambiguous) beginning to see benefits in two tiers.

Political parties

The Labour Party, along with the Fabian Society, put in evidence broadly along the same lines as the TUC. The Communist Party submitted its known objections to worker directors and its preference for bargaining in the private sector.

The Liberal Party published its proposals on 23 March 1976 (just a year to the day before Liberal MPs were to gain some significance in the industrial democracy debate with the introduction of their pact with the Labour Government). They opposed the union power orientation of the TUC 50–50 ideas and called for three types of participation, which were spelt out a year later in a book by one of their more prominent MPs (Cyril Smith, 1977). The first, called 'organic participation', involved the creation of workplace councils in all companies with more than twenty employees. This would be coupled with widespread disclosure of information plus rights to prior consultation on decisions that would sometimes have to be jointly approved. This would introduce an element of joint decision-taking in factories and would be matched by the second part of the programme, which the Liberals called 'systematic participation'. Two-tier board structures would be set up in companies with more than two hundred employees and the top-level board would comprise an equal number of shareholders and employee representatives. But they would emerge through a joint ballot, so that they would not directly represent sectional interests. The shareholders would vote for the workers' representatives as well as their own, and vice versa. The third part of the programme involved job enrichment programmes to give individual workers a say over their jobs.

The Conservative Party did not submit any formal evidence, but various ideas emerged from leading Conservative MPs and generally indicated a swing towards worker directors provided they were introduced slowly and involved all employees. The first such proposal was sent as evidence to the Committee in April 1976 from the Bow Group. It called for legislation that would eventually provide for board representation of all workers after a three-year transitional phase. Next, the One Nation Group of Conservative MPs published their proposals in a pamphlet called *One Nation at Work* which was blessed with a foreword by the Party leader, Margaret Thatcher. She said the document reflected 'the concern that we all feel about the damage which is being done to our country by continuing conflict between different sections of the community' and that it also illustrated 'very clearly our Conservative belief that all employees have a right to be involved in the way that their enterprises are run, that they have a positive contribution to make, and that their full participation will not only bring greater satisfaction to their work, but will also make for more efficient management and a healthier economy'. The pamphlet itself wanted participation to grow from the shop floor upwards with workers ultimately, perhaps after a five-year period, being able to have one-third of the seats on a supervisory board in a two-tier structure, with shareholders and outside interests having the other two-thirds. It thought this would be logical if boards were to have to take equal account of the interests of employees and shareholders. The pamphlet also backed voluntary share-ownership schemes, especially in smaller companies.

From about the same time as these two policy suggestions emerged, Jim Prior, the Conservative's employment spokesman, outlined his various thoughts in a series of speeches. Basically they amounted to his support of legislation to lay down minimum standards on matters such as the equal treatment for shareholders and employees, plus wider disclosure of company information to employees. Then a code of practice could go further, and could include worker directors on supervisory boards.

By this time, therefore, all three main political parties were confirming their gradual conversion to the idea of worker directors being introduced in some form or other.

Evidence from Europe

One major factor pushing all Britain's political parties and other UK institutions towards worker directors up to this stage was the development of policy within the EEC. In November 1975, a month before the Bullock Committee started work, the EEC published its latest proposal for worker directors in the form of a Green Paper entitled *Employee Participation and Company Structure*. This revised an earlier 1972 Green Paper for a Fifth Directive harmonising company law across the Common Market (see last chapter) and its main change was a new emphasis on flexibility with special provision for transitional arrangements so that EEC member countries would not have to make sudden changes. It stuck however to an ultimate target of worker directors on the top level of a two-tier board structure (while recognising there could be a transitional single-tier period and even a different transitional structure). It suggested that all employees, not just union members, should participate in elections (an idea the Bullock Report acknowledged as a possibility but did not recommend). Employees should also be able to choose whether to accept or reject the whole idea in a ballot (unlike the German system, which is mandatory, but in line with the later Bullock recommendations). And it said extended collective bargaining did not form a suitable general base for EEC legislation (reflecting the fact that the UK is far ahead of most other countries with its bargaining arrangements unfettered by the law).

The EEC commissioner in charge of preparing this diplomatically balanced document was Finn Gundelach, who gave verbal evidence to the Committee in March 1976 and said that, when the Fifth Directive eventually came into force, it would undoubtedly include a mandatory requirement for all member states to provide for employee representatives on boards of companies.

So this harmonisation proposal was continuing to move – albeit very slowly – down a similar path to that of the more advanced European Company Statute which had been produced as a draft in 1975 for use by companies that traded in more that one EEC country and wanted to adopt a new form of incorporation. This draft statute provided for worker directors elected by all employees to have one-third of the seats on the supervisory top level of a two-tier Euro-company structure. The other two-thirds would comprise representatives of shareholder and outside interests.

Gundelach's remarks to the Committee confirmed the general drift of EEC policy towards worker directors and the Green Paper put a broad interpretation on the ideas:

It is clear from developments which have been and still are taking place in many Member States, that the time is ripe for the reform of certain social institutions, companies included, to take account of some important evolutions which have been gathering momentum for some time. The first evolution is the increasing recognition being given to the democratic imperative that those who will be substantially affected by decisions made by social and political institutions must be involved in the making of those decisions. . . . The second is a growing awareness of the need for institutions which can respond effectively to the need for change.

The Bullock Report seized on this notion of the 'democratic imperative' and suggested that it constituted a pressure for change which could provide an agreed basis for the UK debate on participation.

The Bullock Report also noted that by the end of 1976 some eight West European countries had schemes of one kind or another in operation which secured, or at least made possible, the representation of employees on company boards: Austria, Denmark, France, West Germany, Luxembourg, the Netherlands, Norway and Sweden. Of these the French provision, dating from 1966, is perhaps the least effective while the German models, of up to a 50–50 two-tier split, are the most highly developed and date from 1951-2. The Dutch system, introduced in 1971 is something of a curiosity because, while a workers' council has a major say in who sits on a Dutch supervisory board, no employee of the company and no official of a union with negotiating rights may be nominated. Originally the German system had the main impact on UK thinking, but then Sweden (which has union-based minority workers' representation on a unitary board) and later Denmark (which also has minority representation but has a sort of '1½-tier board' solution to the one- or two-tier problem) have also influenced the debate.

Members of the Committee visited Sweden and Germany and a research project was set up to supplement evidence on foreign experience. The project was carried out by two academics–Eric Batstone of Warwick University (who had been one of the authors of a controversially critical study of the early years of the British Steel Corporation worker director experiment) and Paul Davies, a labour lawyer from Balliol College, Oxford. Their brief was to review and evaluate published evidence on the workings of industrial democracy (so they did no original research), and their findings (Batstone and Davies, 1976) were published in July. They were critical of the limited impact that worker directors, (usually not union-based), had on decision-making in European companies, a conclusion that could lead either to the interpretation that worker directors are fairly useless or to the Bullock Report solution that one must therefore strengthen them by giving them parity of representation and by firmly anchoring them to a company's trade union and bargaining structures in a single-channel approach.

The Committee at work

Often a government sets up a royal commission or a committee of inquiry in the hope that it will dispose for an indefinite period of a problem about which there is great public or political outcry but no simple solution. The Bullock Committee was not entirely such a creature. While it emerged partly out of a government wish to slow down moves towards worker director legislation, its terms of reference and its make-up ensured that it would not be lost and forgotten in the mists of time–even if it were not immediately turned into law. This was guaranteed by the appointment of

Jack Jones, who, as primary creator and guardian both of Labour's social contract and of the TUC's worker director policy, exerted an overall and detailed authority alongside the chairman, Lord Bullock. Jones himself did little if any detailed drafting, but his presence was alway felt and hardly anything went through without his approval. (As one industrialist half-jokingly said later, 'even we behaved ourselves when Jack was present'.)

So to a large degree the primary outcome of the Committee was guaranteed from the start, although the latter half of the terms of reference did provide scope for it to be critical of the impact that worker directors might have. It was thus inconceivable that it would not produce a scheme for trade union-based worker directors to be introduced where employees, not employers, wanted them with a boardroom representation of between a third and a half. Indeed, Jack Jones seemed to the industrialists to be suggesting at the start–in line with the TUC's earlier views–that the Committee was superfluous and need not bother to meet. But under the patient chairmanship of Lord Bullock the Committee rapidly settled down to participate in some very detailed analysis and debates.

It is the primary job of a chairman of such a committee or commission to steer his colleagues through their work so that at the end they produce as united a front as possible. At best this means one unanimous report; at worst two reports without a clear majority for either. In between are a host of shades of addenda, supplementary notes, self-contained notes of dissent or even simply reservations written into the main report itself. The previous major industrial relations report in Britain–that of the Donovan Commission in 1968–is a prime example of this because all its twelve members signed the main report but virtually everyone also found ways of recording individual views and disagreements within or alongside the main report. The story of the Bullock Committee at work is therefore a story about Lord Bullock's unceasing efforts to achieve the same sort of result, efforts that were eventually to fail primarily because the TUC team budged on only one or two points and the industrialists insisted on producing a full minority report.

Months of debate
The Committee's year fell into two main phases with October 1976 being the breaking point between them. It was at this point, when the Committee went to the Civil Service Staff College in Sunningdale for a working weekend, that the final majority and minority split came and both groups went their own ways. The first ten months of the Committee's life, up to that weekend, can then be divided into three subsections. There was a long initial period stretching from December to May–June when the debate was open, constructive and without major splits. Then, in May and June, a key paper was drafted and redrafted by Lord Bullock and George Bain which sketched out a possible report and so helped to clarify thoughts, though the Committee still did not split. That mood continued through to the end of July when, with the August–September holidays and TUC and Labour annual conferences, there were fewer and less well attended committee meetings and the members were spending their time reading the evidence in detail, holding informal dis-

cussions among themselves, and preparing their positions for the decisive Sunningdale weekend.

During the months until the summer holidays, the Committee met for a complete day on most weeks and attendance was high. The Committee decided early on that it would not investigate specific forms of below-board-level participation or special styles of employee–management relationships or other co-operative theories, although it would obviously need to look at union organisation from the shop floor upwards and the issue of employee representation in general to see how what is called 'sub-structures' could underpin a joint board. It then swung into detailed considerations of a wide range of issues on which considerable agreement was apparent across the Committee on subjects such as the functions and operating methods of directors, where major company decisions were made, the role of middle managers, the confidentiality of company information, how a worker director system might be 'introduced (or 'triggered', as it became known), and the spread of trade unionism.

Already however one key figure was emerging as the main opponent of worker directors: he was Sir Jack Callard who, the TUC people rapidly decided, would never sign the sort of report they would put their names to and who really did not seem to approve of any participation that went further than ICI's consultative methods which he constantly advocated and praised. On the other hand, Heath (whose company, GKN–a fairly progressive company in some participation fields–had interests in German companies where he seemed quite to like his worker directors) and Biggs (who personally could envisage banks having worker directors) seemed far more potentially accommodating. This is not to say that these two men wanted the TUC's ideas: the point rather is that they *could envisage* worker directors in their companies whereas Callard could not. Later he was to become the anchor man of principle for the minority.

The Bullock–Bain 'core report'

Throughout these early months however the Committee avoided openly interpreting its terms of reference during meetings and Lord Bullock managed to keep a broad debate going. Then, late in the spring, Lord Bullock and Professor Bain produced their paper. Although broadly similar to the final majority report of seven months later, they stressed that it was only intended to be a possible basis for consensus. The idea was that it might become what was described as a 'core report' around which virtually everyone could group before going off Donovan-style to do their own thing–a strategy that would have enabled Lord Bullock to fulfil his chairman's primary role of achieving a virtually united basic report. The Bullock–Bain paper began by saying that its starting point was an assumption that there would be legislation on worker directors; that what it was proposing was not a panacea or a once-for-all solution but a beginning of a long process of industrial change. The authors then listed twelve points as a first step 'in the hope they may provide common ground for at least some members of the committee'.

The twelve points were: the basic duties of directors should be to take equal account of shareholder and worker interest; it would be best not to legislate on below-board representation but to allow it to develop flexibly; legislation should apply initially at least to companies with two thousand or more employees; the worker directors scheme should be optional to the extent that it should be up to workers to decide whether they wanted it–unlike the mandatory German system; the worker directors should be union-based in a single-channel system; the worker directors should be employees of the company concerned, not full-time outside union officials; all directors should have the same basic duties and responsibilites but the worker directors should be free to report back to their members even though neither the members nor the union could mandate them on strict policy lines; the representation should be on a unitary, not two-tier board (a '1½'-tier board midway between the two emerged later); the proportions on the board should be split into three parts because it was already clear that the Committee could not reach consensus on 50–50 with no third party (the precise '$2x + y$' formula emerged later and phrases like '$3x$' and then '$2x + 3$' were being used at this time in the Committee's debate); groups of companies and multi-nationals should be included; training of worker directors was essential; there should be an introductory period for such a scheme. These ideas were refined and detailed during the following weeks and months with several other discussion papers being introduced by people such as Nicholas Wilson and Professor Wedderburn (together and separately) on company law and by David Lea on union structures.

Encouragement abroad

In May and at the end of June members of the Committee made their two foreign trips–first to Sweden and then to West Germany. These trips not only consolidated ideas that were forming in the minds of some of the majority group but also provided some of the lighter moments of the year. One event in particular is recounted with relish by those involved. This was when, during the trip to Sweden in May, a number of committee members were to be found together one night, stripped and drinking schnapps, in the sauna at the home of the chairman of the Swedish state holding company.

The visit to West Germany, which lasted for three days at the end of June, coincided with a formal visit by Britain's relatively new prime minister, Jim Callaghan, to see Chancellor Schmidt. The idea was born in advance that a joint meeting should be arranged by Schmidt with both the Callaghan party and the Bullock group. So on the evening of 30 June the Bullock group was ushered into the Cabinet room in Bonn where Schmidt, flanked by German ministers, industrialists, union leaders and academics, was waiting along with Callaghan, Tony Crosland (the foreign secretary) and a party of aides and diplomats. Here, said Callaghan, are my people over from Britain to learn from you all about your worker director system, which has helped your country so much, so that we can design our own system well. And here, said Schmidt, are all my experts to tell you how well it works here. In roughly these words the two 'teams' were introduced to each other, and through an evening party and dinner they discussed industrial democracy.

The enthusiasm with which Callaghan later in 1976 started to talk about German economic miracles and the contribution of the country's worker directors undoubtedly owed a lot to the enthusiasm of Schmidt that evening and his apparent interest in seeing Britain go down a similar road. Schmidt suggested that such a move would show a new era was starting in Britain and (according to the Bullock Report) predicted that foreign investment would be attracted, not driven away. 'Such a view was implicit in the remarks made to us during our visit to Germany by the Federal Chancellor, Dr Helmut Schmidt, amongst others, who expressed the belief that the implementation of employee representation on company boards would have a positive influence on the whole British economy and would not be inimical to foreign investment in the UK', said the Report later.

Callaghan's growing enthusiasm for the subject (which was however to be tempered by the scepticism and opposition of many of his Cabinet colleagues in 1977 and by concern over the row the Bullock Report caused) emerged strongly in a speech he made at the Labour Party annual conference two months after the German trip when he said:

Until there is agreement on the place of the human being in our industrial society we shall push and pull at the economic levers in vain. We have expected too much from economic mechanisms and have paid insufficient attention to the most important element of all–the human element. The working environment is the most unresolved problem in our complex industrial society. We have people who are better educated, better informed, who have escaped from the deference of my youth and who now look to Government, employers and trade unions to provide a framework and an environment that befits their high status.

The Bullock Committee's two foreign trips also produced some sharpening up of views among the committee members. In Sweden, some members were impressed by the way there was only a minority of worker directors on the Board and that the unions basically were relying on laws providing for extended collective bargaining to broaden industrial democracy. The Swedish unions' philosophy is that they do not want to blur the union adversary role till financial participation puts them in a position of near-control of industry. (Wedderburn fairly rapidly tried to alter this interpretation of the Swedish position among his fellow committee members by pointing out that the unions in Sweden needed the new laws to wipe out earlier un-British semi-statutory restrictions on bargaining– British unions had free bargaining already and so did not need to bother with this hurdle.) Nevertheless, even some TUC supporters were impressed by the Swedish mixture of extended bargaining, the minority board representation, and extensive disclosure of company information. The feasibility of worker directors on a unitary board (albeit in Sweden in a minority) was also noted.

But perhaps the major contribution to the debate came in the area of company secrecy and confidentiality. There had been (and still is) a lot of concern in UK companies that their commercial secrets will leak with a worker director system. In Sweden the committee heard even from a leading banker that there need be little problem in practice: confidentiality is often fixed flexibly and sometimes information is graded so that some can be released to the worker directors only, some to their advisory 'economic committee', some to the equivalent of shop stewards, and some to all workers.

The trip to Germany produced more mixed reactions which stemmed from the basic polarisation of the whole UK issue of industrial democracy between the interests of employers in industrial efficiency without power-sharing, and the motivation of union leaders for hastening industrial and political change. In Germany the industrialist members of the Committee saw a system that worked well, with worker directors officially hived off from their unions and located in a supervisory board. On the other hand, the TUC leaders saw a system that was not, in their eyes, effective because the worker directors were remote both from their union roots and from the power centre of the management board. On a less political level the committee members had some worries allayed by German bankers about investors avoiding worker director companies (or countries), and some of the TUC people also felt that German worker directors tended to be paid too much. (The Bullock Report proposed later that they should only receive their normal pay as employees plus expenses.) The TUC members were also a little embarrassed by a left-wing German professor who suggested that co-determination was bad because it took the workers' eyes off the primary need to change the social system!

Methven resigns

By the time these visits were over early in July, what was to emerge as the majority group on the Committee was well established. It contained Lord Bullock, who saw the political inevitability of worker director laws in a historical sense and wanted to help design them satisfactorily, and Professor Bain, who did not see the TUC ideas as any great ideological breakthrough but thought, and still thinks, that worker directors could be a useful supplement to collective bargaining. Then there were the four main ideological supporters – Jack Jones, David Lea, Bill Wedderburn, and Clive Jenkins – who saw what they were after as a major move forward in the exercise of worker power through the unions' structures although they were not all agreed as to how far such a system should be presented as replacing conflict with co-operation. By this time it was also becoming clear that they had bagged their biggest catch since the Committee started – Nicholas Wilson, the City solicitor who carried special weight because he was a Department of Trade advisor on company law. Basically he did not believe, for legal reasons, in two-tier boards, but he did believe in worker directors. So he joined the majority group and then wrote a powerful dissenting note saying the power-oriented '$2x + y$' formula was wrong.

The other initial unknown quantity, John Methven, left the Committee on 15 July and the quality of the Committee's debates undoubtedly suffered as a result. His problem was that he had become director-general of the CBI and was being lent on by his extrovert 'boss', Lord Watkinson, the CBI's new president. Watkinson wanted him to come off the fence and join in an 'implacable opposition' to the statutory enforcement of union-based worker directors. Jack Jones however said there were no objections to Methven staying even though he had moved from being an 'independent' to an 'employer'; but Methven succumbed to other pressures and left. This could be seen as a miscalculation by the CBI because, from its point of view, Methven would have been far more useful during the following months working inside the Committee, especially since, as a former lawyer, he could have joined the Wedderburn – Wilson debates as an expert. Methven had started off sympathetic to the notion of worker directors and decided that ultimately he would make up his mind on the basis of how they would affect the efficiency of industry. By the time he left he was swinging against the idea and was becoming increasingly concerned about the growth of union power–an issue that would have almost certainly made him dissent at least from single-channel ideas even if he had not joined the CBI. But with his CBI position he might well have become the leader of the minority group. As it was, when he left, the group lacked cohesion and drifted aimlessly for some time.

Conflict at Sunningdale
So on the weekend of 16 October at the Civil Service College at Sunningdale, the Committee assembled–without Biggs, who was on a long trip abroad–for their decisive meeting. Everyone arrived with their own personal views established, and they all realised that the weekend was the final chance for consensus to be built up. A first majority draft report had been prepared by the secretariat–although Lord Bullock was prepared to see it torn up and re-done if a new basis for consensus could be found. Bullock opened the meeting and then did a *'tour de table'*, asking each person individually to state his position on the draft report. He did not go straight round the table because, the factions having grouped themselves together, that would simply have polarised the position. Instead he chose people in his own order: gradually it emerged that, to quote one of the TUC supporters later, 'the industrialists had been nobbled' by the CBI. The bombshell that was dropped by Heath and Callard was that, not only did they want a two-tier board, but also they would not go along with a single channel–in other words, they wanted the system based on all employees, not just trade unionists, and they wanted the worker directors pushed 'upstairs'. Such a stance was contrary to all the TUC people's thinking about making the board representation part of the normal union machinery and company operations. Bullock himself had toyed with two-tier ideas earlier but had also come down on the side of political reality, as he saw it, and favoured one tier. That was the end of consensus.

Although they did not tell the rest of the Committee at the time, Heath and Callard apparently arrived at Sunningdale with the bones of their minority report in draft in their suitcases. But since they did not reveal this, the other members of the Committee believed that there was no minority report in draft until several weeks later. The industrialists insisted that they could release nothing more than the chapter headings of what might be in their draft until they had seen what the majority group were preparing–a tactic that was to lead to some acrimony.

The industrialists' rationale for producing a minority report was that they had accepted terms of reference on being appointed which required them to show *how* a worker director scheme might be introduced. However this led to some bitter exchanges between Heath and John Methven at the CBI, where a new CBI general policy document, *Road to Recovery,* was being produced which went no further than the CBI's participation agreements. Methven and Watkinson would have liked the industrialists to fall into line with this and break loose from the Committee's terms of reference; but they were not prepared to do so and at one stage Heath said that even though he may have been a CBI nominee on the Committee, he was not a delegate to be told what to do.

The best thing, the industrialists concluded, was to follow the instincts of some major companies (including Heath's GKN) and put the worker directors on a fairly weak supervisory board where they could do least harm, leaving a company to be managed by the lower-tier professional executives.

But the argument on the Committee about tiers was nothing to the bitterness about the single-union-channel issue and the two industrialists gained little support during the Sunningdale meeting from Bullock who, having seen the Bain research–showing there was 70 to 80 per cent unionisation in large companies–thought it would be impractical to pretend one could or should run an employee representation system based on anything but the already established representative system, the trade unions.

So Bullock had failed in his primary objective of achieving a large measure of consensus. Heath went off to confirm to the CBI that he and Callard were not going to follow all the implications of the CBI's 'implacable opposition' but were going to do a minority report. He then asked his personnel director at GKN, Jim Parsons, to finalise a minority report on the basis of GKN's evidence to the Committee. This was done in liaison with a senior personnel advisor, Trevor Owen, at ICI (Callard's old company). Eventually the minority report emerged as a document opposing statutory worker directors in principle but containing a reluctant method of putting them into practice. Later Heath was to say at a press conference launching the document: 'I don't want to put the minority report into operation in GKN.' But this was somewhat milder than his thoughts on the majority report which were 'turgid dogma which would cause bloody chaos'.

The majority group also then swung into action with the help of the Committee's small secretariat, headed by Robin Hope, a civil servant seconded by the Department of Trade. The main drafting group comprised Bain, Wedderburn and Lea with a lot of input from Lord Bullock, while Jack Jones vetted much of what was produced and Clive Jenkins concentrated on a growing interest of his, trade union education. Nicholas Wilson also helped to produce drafts on company law issues, sometimes jointly with Wedderburn, which kept him involved in the majority camp.

This left Norman Biggs as the odd man out. Without him the split was 7–2, with Wilson included in the seven but providing a dissenting note. So when Biggs returned from his foreign trip at the end of October, he was immediately grabbed by the two industrialists and was pressured by the CBI and his City colleagues. He was also tempted to join Wilson in his majority-plus-dissenting-note position, and the two men talked about this possibility. Ultimately however the combined unrelenting forces of the industrialists plus the CBI and City lobby made this elderly mild-mannered man join the minority group and also provide, from his City base, an appendix to their minority report pleading financial institutions as a special case for exemption (Chapter 7). So the split was 7–3. (The industrialists however put a different–intriguing but rather dubious–gloss on these figures: this is that Wilson was really with them in spirit and was tied to the majority group only by the company law preference for a one-tier board. If one therefore moved him on to the minority vote and also included Methven, then there would have been only a 6–5 split, with Bullock giving the so-called majority its lead–if he stood to one side it would be a 5–5 dead heat. Where, the industrialist surmising continues, would that have left Bullock with his wish to produce a practical solution?)

Eventually the majority group finished its drafting on Saturday 4 December–it held ten formal meetings on its own after the Sunningdale weekend in addition to a series of informal sessions. Its report was presented to the minority group at a meeting of the Committee the following Tuesday, 7 December. This was a period of somewhat tetchy disagreements between the two sides about whether they had adequately kept each other informed about what they were each saying, and Jack Jones successfully pushed through some changes in the minority report– for example objecting to the industrialists saying the TUC group was 'doctrinaire' and that they did not represent the 'authentic voice' of the trade union movement in the private sector, which was against worker directors. Nevertheless, with Lord Bullock absent (he was taken ill on 8 December and was convalescing in Oxford), the reports were signed at a full meeting of the Committee on 14 December, Lord Bullock having put his signature the day before in the Radcliffe Infirmary, Oxford.

The Report

The Bullock Report, having been signed and sent to Edmund Dell, secretary for trade, on 14 December, was read by some Cabinet ministers over the Christmas recess and was then published on 26 January 1977. With a striking blue cover, it ran to a total of 205 pages embracing the majority report, a dissenting note and the industrialists' minority report with its appendices.

The majority report

The majority report began by outlining social, economic and industrial changes that made industrial democracy reforms justifiable. It discussed all the issues involved with a clear preference throughout for both the principle and the detail of TUC policy and then made two main recommendations. The first was that employees should have a statutory right to be represented by trade union-based worker directors in a single-tier board structure on a '$2x + y$' basis; but this should not be mandatory on all companies over a certain size as it is in Germany; instead, it should only operate where the employees and unions wanted it. Second, the law should be changed so that all company directors (whether or not a company had worker directors) should have to take equal account of the interests of employees and shareholders.

The Report's analysis of the social and economic changes was widely accepted as fair and accurate by both critics and supporters of its later proposals. It talked in terms of increasingly large industrial enterprises concentrating economic power in the board rooms of fewer and fewer companies which were becoming increasingly remote from the communities they served and the people they employed. It pointed out that the one hundred largest manufacturing enterprises in the UK had accounted for

40 per cent of the country's net output in 1971, compared with only 25 per cent in 1953, and said: 'The power and complexity of the industrial enterprise and the remoteness of decision making led to demands for large companies to be more responsive to the needs of society in general and of their employees in particular.'

This led its concluding chapter, influenced by Lord Bullock, to adopt a broad historical perspective and say that Britain's problem was basically a failure to draw out the energies and skills of its working population:

It is our belief that the way to release those energies, to provide greater satisfaction in the workplace, and to assist in raising the level of productivity and efficiency in British industry—and with it the living standards of the nation—is not by recrimination or exhortation but by putting the relationship between capital and labour on to a new basis which will involve not just management but the whole of the workforce in sharing responsibility for the success and profitability of the enterprise. Such a change in the industrial outlook and atmosphere will only come about, however, as a result of giving the representatives of the employees a real, and not a sham or token, share in making the strategic decisions about the future of an enterprise which in the past have been reserved to management and the representatives of shareholders.

Inspired by Lord Bullock, the Committee then went further down the road of the new responsibilities for trade unions than either the critics of union power or union leaders determined not to reduce their bargaining strengths would find entirely credible: 'We believe that the change in attitude of the TUC and their willingness to accept a share of responsibility for the increased efficiency and prosperity of British companies offer an opportunity to create a new basis for relations in industry which should not be allowed to pass.'

And Lord Bullock then added a final touch of historical realism in the last paragraph of the Report:

The fears expressed in the 19th century in face of proposals to give more people the right to vote did not stop short of subversion of the constitution and the dissolution of society. Once the franchise was extended, however, the fears were forgotten and the Reform Acts were seen as essential to the country's stability and prosperity. We believe that over 100 years later an extension of industrial democracy can produce comparable benefits and that our descendants will look back with as much surprise to the controversy which surrounded it as we do to that which surrounded the extension of the political suffrage in the 19th century.

How '$2x + y$' would work
The Report proposed that its worker director system would apply to groups of companies and subsidiaries (including multinationals) with two thousand or more employees. It was estimated that this embraced some seven million employees in 750 enterprises (a total of 1800 companies including subsidiaries). It would reduce the existing sole power of shareholders over a company's affairs by retaining for the new joint board—the report dubbed it a 'reconstituted' or 'policy' board—a board's normal powers of initiation of policies. But, because of the property ownership aspect of such a charge, shareholders were left with a right to veto matters such as acquisitions and sales of company assets. (This amounted to a watering down of the original TUC position, which had wanted the board to be supreme.) At the same time, the power of shareholders in takeover

situations would be reduced because one company could not take over another without the approval of the latter's policy board (and therefore the employees as well as the shareholders). The shareholder representatives on the board (normally top management) and the employee representatives (normally shop stewards) would have equal statutory duties and responsibilities and would not be mandated delegates of their constituents. But this neat specification was blurred by the Report saying that the worker directors would however be accountable to their constituents whom they represented and to whom they would have to report back on their work.

The system, watched over by an Industrial Democracy Commission, would operate only when one or more trade unions, recognised by the company for at least 20 per cent of all the employees, demanded a ballot of *all* the employees to see whether they wanted worker directors to be operated through the recognised unions. Thus not all the unions recognised in the company need be involved in the 'triggering', as the Report dubbed it. There would then be a union-run ballot of *all* employees, including non-unionists, and the scheme would go ahead only if there was a clear majority in favour *and* if the pro-vote amounted to more than one-third of the full-time work force. (This was written in to stop a scheme going ahead by a small majority of a minority of the work force.) All the unions recognised in the company would then have the right to participate in a joint representation committee (JRC) of lay (normally shop steward) representatives which would form the basis for the scheme. Ideally all the unions would agree to join the JRC; but the Report did not make the introduction of a scheme conditional on their doing so because it did not want to enable one small minority union opposed in principle to worker directors (like the Electricians, which have a handful of members in many companies) to be able to hold up developments. On the other hand, it did say that nothing should happen till all the unions that had opted in and joined the JRC had reached full agreement on how the scheme was to operate. The JRC, which could develop as the hub of the whole system, would itself decide how to elect its board representatives. It would also negotiate with the company on matters such as the size of the board and, therefore, on how many representatives there would be.

The '$2x + y$' formula would mean shareholders and employee representatives each having an equal number of representatives–meeting the TUC's 50–50 parity claim in a modified form. The two 'x' groups would then jointly choose (with an appeal to the Commission in cases of deadlock) the third 'y' group which would be an odd number greater than one but smaller than 'x'. The Report laid down some sample statutory fallback sizes for boards which would be enforced where a company could not jointly agree with the JRC. For companies with 2000 to 9999 employees '$2x + y$' would be $4 + 4 + 3$; for 10,000 to 24,999 employees it would be $5 + 5 + 3$; while for over 25,000 it would be $7 + 7 + 5$.

The shareholders' representatives would be chosen in the normal way through annual shareholders' meetings while the employees' representatives (normally shop stewards) would emerge through a method chosen by the JRC. This could involve a vote on the JRC itself, a ballot of union members, or even (though Bullock did not *recommend* this) a ballot of all employees. To begin with the '*y*' seats could be filled by any surplus exist-ing shareholder directors not given seats in the shareholders' '*x*'. This would apply till the next annual general meeting providing shareholders with a chance to decide which of their old representatives they wished to stay. (The *Investors' Chronicle* conducted a survey and estimated on 25 February 1977 that a total of between 1000 and 1600 directors would have to leave the board rooms of the companies involved, or the boards would have to grow in size on average from eleven directors to an un-wieldy nineteen to accommodate the employee representatives.) The Report suggested that the '*y*' could be representatives of senior manage-ment from inside the company or existing non-executive directors, experts such as solicitors or bankers, or a full-time trade union official (who would almost always be excluded from the employees' '*x*').

The system could be 'triggered' by unions either in a subsidiary company with more than two thousand employees or in a holding company with subsidiaries totalling more than two thousand–even though the holding company itself might only have a small headquarters staff. The holding company would have the right to nominate the '*y*' group in its subsidiaries where the subsidiaries' two '*x*' groups could not agree. (One point the Report's recommendations did not cover is that not all large companies would be treated equally under this provision–for example ICI has only one main board, with most of its 'subsidiaries' organised as large divisions and not incorporated under company law. So the divisional boards would not be covered unless the top board voted for them to have worker directors, although a company like GEC and GKN, with a lot of proper large subsidiary companies, could be caught at the lower levels. Any legislation would therefore have to consider whether to try to find a way to include ICI-style divisions. Alternatively it could try to stop companies with structures like GKN or GEC avoiding worker directors by changing the status of their subsidiary companies into non-statutory divisions–although some companies were considering doing this anyway early in 1977 to beat any legislation.)

The Report rejected appeals for exemption that it had received from organisations representing companies in banking and insurance and from broadcasting and the press on grounds of confidentiality and press freedom (see Chapter 7), as well as shipping, construction, and hotels and catering on other grounds such as high labour turnover and employment of part-time labour, and the geographical spread and fragmentation of a company's activities. (Abroad there have been exemptions or special pro-visions for certain publishing and financial institutions, and sometimes worker director laws have initially been introduced only for certain types of manufacturing and other industries.)

It also went further than many foreign schemes by doing its best to make sure that multinational companies, both those foreign- and British-owned, did not escape the proposals. It accepted that British law could not force British-based boards to have employee representatives of foreign subsidiaries any more than it could impose British worker directors on the top boards, located abroad, of foreign-based multi-nationals. But it was determined to catch what it could and said that representatives of British employees should be able to take up the full quota of employee seats on the boards of British-based multinationals. In foreign-based multinationals British employee representatives should have a full quota on the British subsidiaries. As with subsidiaries in general, however, the Report recognised that special arrangements needed to be made to solve the problem of the two '*x*' groups not being able to agree on the '*y*'.

In the general case of ordinary British groups, as has been said, it decided logically that a holding company needed to have commercial control of its subsidiary and so should have the right to choose the '*y*' when there was a failure to agree on the subsidiary board itself. The Report felt able to come to this decision because the employees and unions would have the opportunity to sit on the holding board and so could affect its decision on who the subsidiary's '*y*' should be. But, since they clearly could not sit as of right on the top board of a foreign-based multinational, the Report did not feel able to allow such a multinational to choose the '*y*'. It therefore reverted back to a deadlock-breaking system proposed for ordinary British companies and said that there should be an appeal to the Industrial Democracy Commission: it then went further and added that, in making its decision, the Commission should consult both the British Government and the foreign multinational itself. This proposal however whipped up a lot of opposition from multinational companies, which warned the Government about the potentially serious consequences of denying them an absolute right to choose a clear majority of the subsidiaries' directors.

There was no recommendation in the Report about whether the worker director system should lead to similar 'parity' representation on executive committees and other management structures below board level. But the assumption was first that sub-structures would have to be built or adapted from existing arrangements to support the board and second that it would be up to the workers' '*x*' to persuade the new top board to build in as much management power-sharing as they wanted into these structures.

Mr Wilson's dissent

The note of dissent to the majority report written by Nicholas Wilson added a significant dimension to the Bullock exercise. The point that firmly anchored Mr Wilson to the majority group was that, as a company lawyer, he could see no justification for changing Britain's statutory company structures. He therefore favoured a single-tier board and opposed switching over to the two-tier type of board structure that the minority industrialists advocated as a way of removing the employee representatives on to a weak top-tier supervisory board, away from day-to-day management. But he also firmly backed the justification of worker directors and accepted both that they should be union-based and that they should operate throughout groups of companies. On these points he was considerably more radical than the industrialists, although he was worried about using the law to force the pace of change too quickly.

But on other points he was clearly on the industrialists' side in not wanting to give the worker directors enough seats to be able to wield, through voting strength, a significant say over management decisions. He arrived at his conclusion not by arguing about the rights or wrongs of union power but by suggesting that both the alternatives of a 50–50 split or the production of '*y*' element would not work in practice. There should be no rigid formulae; he said the number of worker directors–in a minority position–should be calculated against the size of the work force.

Worried about the potential divisiveness and complexity in the '$2x + y$' formula, he said:

Equality of representation is said to be justified by the requirement that employee representatives should have equality of responsibility with other directors. But this is to confuse two quite distinct issues: representation is concerned with numbers and proportions, whereas responsibility is not capable of qualification. What is meant by 'equality of responsibility' is that *each* member of the Board has identical duties and, since all directors would, if the majority's proposals are adopted, be obliged to have regard to all the interests of employees, there is neither inconsistency nor contradiction in proposing minority representation whilst expecting all directors to have identical responsibilities. If equality of responsibility is used in any other sense, it must of necessity assume a degree of coherence within groups of directors and a polarisation of their attitudes which is at variance with the consensual method by which, as the majority acknowledge, Board decisions are generally reached.

In this passage however Mr Wilson is arguing from a company lawyer's, not the trade unions', view of boardroom responsibility (although his lack of interest in parity bears some resemblance to the steelworker directors' views–see Chapter 12). He is thus ignoring (or, rather, implicitly rejecting) the central point of the TUC's 50–50 and '$2x + y$' parity argument: that the unions' willingness to share fully in the responsibilities of boardroom decisions depends on their being able to share fully and equally in the power of decision-making.

The industrialists' minority report

The basic aim of the industrialists' minority report was to design a system of worker directors that would give the least possible power over management decision-making to employees in general and trade union representatives in particular, while encouraging participation below board level. It therefore started off by complaining that the Committee should have been asked 'whether', not 'how', there should be a worker director system and then went on, with some CBI-encouraged reluctance, to propose how a system could be introduced by law if the Government persisted with its line.

It proposed that the law should be changed to make all board directors take the interests of shareholders and employees equally into account. Then there should be a statutory requirement for companies, within four years, to set up company participation councils below board level. After such a council had been operating for three years in a company, the employees should have the legal right to vote for a worker director system–seven years from the start of the process. This would involve not just union members but all employees, who could have one-third of the seats on the top supervisory level of a two-tier board structure of holding but not subsidiary companies. Financial institutions and subsidiaries of foreign companies should be exempted.

In a separate summary of their proposals the three industrialists explained that one justification for worker directors was changing the legal status of employees:

There is evidence of widespread feeling in the country that the time has now come when those who work in industry should have their interests recognised in company law in the same way as shareholders' interests are recognised. If this premise is accepted, it seems to follow logically that both shareholders and employees should be represented within the Board structure.

They also said that one could not 'stand wholly outside the trends that are taking place in other countries of the EEC'. In addition, board representation might help improve Britain's economic and industrial performance by harnessing the understanding and co-operation of unions and employees and it also might help eliminate what the industrialists described as 'chronic economic illiteracy'.

The industrialists began their minority report by saying that, while they had agreed with the majority group on some things, they differed on fundamental issues. They considered that the majority's proposals were oriented towards the TUC's union power ambitions and were 'not likely to be in the interests either of people who work in industry or of the nation'. It was 'unwise to impose "democracy" on those who are unwilling or unready to receive it', so participation should be developed from the shop floor upwards and be based on all employees. Any legislation therefore should have three aims: to improve the effectiveness of companies in generating wealth for the whole community; to ensure that board directors were equally legally accountable to employees as well as shareholders; to satisfy the aspirations of employees for involvement in decisions closely affecting their work.

The majority's proposal for worker directors on a unitary one-tier board was rejected as incompatible with the role of such a board, which was 'the apex of a company's management team consisting primarily of persons with appropriate specialist and/or professional experience and training to fit them to plan and control the company's operations as executive directors'. The introduction of 'powerful sectional interests' would also upset the comparative objectivity of board decision-making and might 'provoke confrontation or extend the scope of collective bargaining into top-level management decision-making'. The employee representatives might also find themselves in the 'wholly invidious position of being obliged to sit in on discussions to which they might have nothing to contribute because they were not properly equipped to contribute to this particular type of deliberation'. The membership of boards would also be disrupted and managers would become increasingly disillusioned and frustrated said the industrialists and added:

The proposals on proportions of representation [$'2x + y'$] on unitary Boards could also be regarded as the thin end of the wedge, a method of infiltration, which could eventually lead to trade union/worker control of what are in effect the management Boards of the private sector of industry. There is no evidence in any part of the world to suggest that this form of control would be likely to be beneficial to British industry.

Worker directors should therefore be located on supervisory boards which would not involve themselves in the detailed decision-making of present boards or even with initiating or determining policy, but should be primarily concerned with the 'quality of management'. They should exercise general supervision over the conduct of a company's affairs with powers to approve appointments to the lower-tier board of management, to dismiss on a unanimous supervisory board vote one or more members of the management board, to fix management board members' salaries and to receive regular reports from the management board on the progress of the company with a right to any information affecting profitability or liquidity. The supervisory board would also have the responsibility of submitting to shareholders all major proposals for items such as winding up the company, changing its articles of association or capital structures, large expansion or contraction plans and therefore employment prospects, and dividend payments.

The supervisory board (in a modification of the '$2x + y$' idea) would consist of three equally-sized groups, one representing employees, another representing shareholders and a third of independent members elected by, but not directly associated with, either of the two other groups. The employees' representatives would include at least one member from shop floor, salaried staff and management groups. These representatives should also have been employed by the company for at least ten years, have been members of a participation forum for at least three years, and been adequately trained.

These then were the proposals put forward by the three industrialists, with quite a different objective from those of the majority report. But, in proposing their minority ideas – which they described as 'the best way of fulfilling what we regard as a far from satisfactory remit' – they were going far further than the country's industrial and financial establishment would have wished.

Chapter 16

Reactions to Bullock and Issues for Debate

There can have been few reports prepared for a government by men eminent in their own fields that received such a hostile response as the Bullock Report. It was attacked with one of the most vitriolic and damning campaigns ever mounted by Britain's industrialists; it was received with some embarrassment by government ministers, who found it difficult to say very much in its favour but were tied to its principles by Labour's 1974 general election manifesto; and it was absorbed by much of the trade union movement to begin with as an aberration of Jack Jones and one or two others which would involve them in changes of role and behaviour that they had not begun, and did not much want, to think through.

One initial problem was that, for a variety of reasons, there was little supporting fanfare on publication day. Lord Bullock was still away so could not take the press conference and carry out the radio and television appearances that are usual on such occasions. And the Committee itself was so sharply split that there was no one else who could credibly take the chair and stop a press conference decaying into a squabble between the two groups. So some semi-formal briefing was done by the two sides. The minority group used GKN's London headquarters where the three industrialists explained their views. But the majority group did not appear at all (apart from on television programmes) and left it to a civil servant from the Department of Trade (Robin Hope, the Committee's secretary, was away with a bout of flu) informally to guide journalists through the Report at a session ironically held in the United Services Club in Pall Mall which the Government was using for sundry purposes till its new occupants, the Institute of Directors, moved in later!

In place of a public press conference, Lord Bullock issued a personal statement to coincide with publication in which he explained his view of the Report in the context of boosting the survival of Britain's mixed economy:

The Report starts from the assumption of a mixed economy and it is my firm belief that nothing will do as much to guarantee the continuation and increased efficiency of such a mixed economy as change along the lines we have proposed.

He said that opposition and apprehension in advance of worker director schemes abroad had always proved ill-founded and added that he hoped the younger generation in management and the unions would read the report carefully because it was their world–the world of the twentieth century–that the Report was talking about, and it was they who would

241

have responsibility for making a success of it:

I do not know what action the Government will take on our report but of one thing I am certain: that the question of employees' representation has been placed on the agenda of British politics and will not easily be removed.

Rough deal for Bullock

The main problem facing the Report was the great strength of scepticism and opposition to its proposals which even led Edmund Dell to depart from his Cabinet brief when answering questions about the Report in the Commons on the publication day. His lack of conviction about its union-based contents was to grow more obvious in later months during Cabinet battles as he insisted that a basis for consensus had to be found. On the day of publication however his job in the Commons was to deliver a statement, which had been fought through a somewhat divided Cabinet. It stuck to the Labour general election manifesto and social contract line. This meant in TUC terms that the Government was pledged to prepare legislation providing a statutory right for union-based worker directors to hold an equal number of seats with shareholder representatives.

Mr Dell's statement said that the Government was about to start consultations with the TUC, CBI and others and made it clear that this would be on the 'general basis of the recommendations contained in the majority report' (so indicating, in line with TUC wishes, that the minority report should be seen as a non-starter – although some of its ideas were adopted by ministers later). He then stated that 'we shall bring forward legislative proposals this session' (legislative proposals in this context meant a White Paper) and said he wanted a 'lasting settlement', a phrase that often cropped up during the following months as a reason for the Government not rushing into contentious Bullock-style proposals. Having given this formal qualified welcome to the Report – which only dealt with the private sector – he then went on to provide a sop for the TUC by showing that the Government was prepared for more radical developments in the nationalised industries where, he announced, the Government had 'decided that employees in these industries should be given the right to representation at Board level'. He then went on implicitly to warn that only lesser developments could be expected in central and local government because of issues of community interest and parliamentary principle and he finished by echoing Lord Bullock's personal views:

The Government's aim is to see democracy extended from our political to our industrial life. That is an essential ingredient of the social contract. Just as political democracy has been accepted by all our people, so we believe industrial democracy – at all levels from the shop floor to the Board itself – will come to be regarded as part of the accepted fabric of our national life and open a new chapter in industrial relations and in our industrial performance.

Within minutes however, as he faced questions on his statement in the Commons, Dell was showing that his personal lukewarm interest contrasted sharply with the statement his Cabinet post required him to make to placate the TUC, and he became increasingly flexible and conciliatory in the face of Tory and other criticisms. For example, he indicated an immediate interest in adopting a two-tier rather than a unitary board system – which was a considerable concession to make to the Bullock critics within an hour or two of the report being published. From that point onwards, the TUC leaders were never sure how much help–or opposition–they could expect from Mr Dell, whom few if any of them knew, let alone understood.

The wide publicity that had been given to the proposals of the Bullock Report in the weeks before it was published meant that its opponents had had plenty of time and opportunity to marshal their forces. Senior civil servants had also been seeing drafts of the Report through 1976 and had various lines of opposition ready at their fingertips, and the CBI (briefed by the Bullock industrialists) launched its campaign of opposition three weeks before publication.

On the publication day and in the days following, a mass of condemning statements was issued by individual companies, employers' federations, banks and other City interests. Their general line was that the report's proposals were undemocratic (because it gave statutory rights to union members only), that its real purpose was to extend union power, and that it would do harm to business performance by demotivating management, slowing down managerial decision-making and driving foreign investment out of the country. In short, it would do nothing for industrial efficiency and everything for the march of union-based socialism.

Practical issues ignored

The real practical issue that was hardly touched on in this political battle was what the unions wanted to do when they got to the board room. Did they intend to shed their adversary role and move into a coalition with management in a full partnership, which, taken to its logical conclusion, would mean them giving up their opposition weapons such as strikes? Or did they simply regard the board room as an extension of their collective bargaining without any change in their role? Or, in between these two, did they think that they would be able to bridge the gap between these two extremes and boost both their own bargaining strengths and the industrial efficiency of British business by participating where possible and falling back on bargaining where they needed to?

These points have been raised earlier in this book but need to be restated now for several reasons. First, the Bullock majority report glossed over them. Second, the minority report and the industrialists who launched attacks on the Bullock Report failed fully to articulate them–they talked in terms of the simple awfulness of union power, not of whether or how that power could or should be harnessed. Third, the relative silence from the trade unions that followed the publication of the Report showed that union leaders were well aware of the dichotomy that they posed.

As a result TUC leaders wisely decided that, since the unions were still split on the basic issue, it would be best if the industrialists were left to make the running. The problem with this however was that the unions' dichotomy over bargaining versus participation and the general public dislike of connotations of union power meant that, by the summer of 1977, the Bullock Report had only a handful of sincere committed advocates left. The Prime Minister, Jim Callaghan, was known still to be interested but was worried about the general opposition to the Report and the possibility of rows and splits both in Labour ranks and with industrialists. The idea was still being pushed hard in the Cabinet by Michael Foot, Albert Booth and some other left-wingers, and there was a lot of TUC activity behind the scenes. But even Jack Jones, sensing the change in the political climate and seeing the wages side of the social contract vanishing in the acrimony of the unions' annual conferences, realised the time might not be ripe to push such a contentious issue too far in the private sector. Union power was back in the headlines as a major issue (thanks to disputes like that at the Grunwick film laboratory) and it was less easy to argue that the unions were maintaining their willingness to shoulder responsibilities for economic and industrial success when their conferences (including Jack Jones's own union in July 1977) were throwing out all ideas of partnership with the Government on wage restraint. So it was extremely difficult by the middle of 1977 to find a platform on which to push Bullock forward beyond the fact that it had been in the 1974 Labour manifesto, that there were ministerial (and prime ministerial) pledges to prepare legislation, and that it was (however lukewarm many unions might be about it) part of the social contract. But such pledges counted for little when the Government could not even gain a majority on the floor of the Commons without Liberal support.

Overall, therefore, the Bullock Report got a rough deal–attacked by its critics, and not pushed openly by its union proponents.

The CBI's campaign
During the early months of 1977 the industrialists' lobby and the CBI made a major impact on public and governmental thinking. Following the initial onslaught during the week the Report was published, the pressure was kept up from all sorts of directions and the president of the American Chamber of Commerce (UK) in London even publicly warned that American companies viewed the Bullock proposals with 'disbelief and dismay' and hinted that US investment could suffer.

The CBI's overall policy was then published in May 1977 in a booklet with a name that was a play on Barbara Castle's 1969 policy document (*In Place of Bullock:* CBI, 1977). But from the start in February the CBI refused formally to discuss with the Government three issues: 'The imposition by law of trade union nominated directors on to company Boards; parity of representation between shareholder elected and employer or trade union nominated directors; the monopoly given to the trade unions to choose worker directors.' All it wanted was legislation on participation agreements. It was thus setting its face firmly against the points of principle wanted by the TUC (and some of the industrialists' minority report ideas). It even threatened that its members might not be willing to co-operate actively with the Government's industrial strategy if there were unfavourable legislation.

This enabled the CBI to bring considerable detailed pressure to bear in Whitehall, and within two months of the Report being published, it had informally reached one possible fall-back package with the Government which it might tolerate even though it would not welcome it. This involved changing the law on employees' interests being taken into account in the board room; designing company law so that there was a two-tier structure and a voluntary system of worker directors that

companies could adopt; and providing for a two- or three-year programme of CBI-style participation agreements (although the legal enforceability point had still not been solved). Finally it was thought that
the Government would then have to go one step further for the TUC and
provide for worker directors, usually union-based, to take up one-third of
a board room's seats in a two-tier structure after a period of time – maybe
two or three years or more – had elapsed. This would be objected to
loudly, but not too angrily, by the CBI and could, it was thought, be
presented as a major watering down of the Bullock Report because it
would mean ditching the parity aspect of the '$2x + y$' formula, moving the
worker directors to a more remote supervisory tier, and delaying any
such innovations till below-board-level participation had been built up.

These ideas were being discussed when it still seemed likely that there
would be a Bullock-based White Paper *and a Bill* by the end of 1977. In
fact, as events turned out, it provided the groundwork on which Liberal
MPs and others in more powerful Whitehall positions could build as the
Government's parliamentary situation disintegrated during the later
spring and summer.

The TUC stands back

Meanwhile, at the TUC views were not so united. Broadly, there were
few private sector union leaders enthusiastically backing the Bullock
concept and even fewer who had enough interest to be prepared to adopt
a negotiating posture with the Government in order to find a politically
feasible solution. The problem was that, in the private sector at least,
most union leaders fell into one of three camps – they were either, like the
Communists, ideologically opposed to the notion on political grounds; or,
like the Electricians, opposed in principle on industrial blurring-the-lines-
of-conflict grounds; or, like most of the rest, were unwilling to face up to the
challenges involved and instinctively preferred to stick to old-style clear-
cut bargaining relationships, especially at a time when economic problems made many boardroom decisions unpalatable to workers. Only one
or two private sector unions, during a TUC survey of union views in the
early summer, showed any positive interest – they included the clerical
workers union (APEX), which opted for a two-tier solution, and the bank
employees (NUBE), which seemed broadly in favour of the Bullock
ideas. But among the others, most unions either opposed the idea or
(like the National Graphical Association) insisted on terms such as a
clear-cut 50–50 split that were quite clearly unattainable. Even Clive
Jenkins found the report that he had signed rejected in a far-left coup by
his own union's (ASTMS) annual conference. But David Basnett at the
General and Municipal Workers shifted his ground and tacitly moved in
behind the Report by saying it was not radical enough – extended bargaining would be more effective and so eventually helped build a
compromise.

Behind this mixture of lethargy, conscious over-bidding on terms and
outright opposition lay the fact that neither the Bullock Report nor the
TUC had satisfactorily explained how much of a change board representation was supposed to make to normal union conflict-based traditions.
On the one hand Len Murray had been stressing the responsibilities involved in collective bargaining and had tried to show that boardroom

245

representation was only an extension of this, provided the worker directors had parity of representation with the shareholders. But there was also a general suspicion that the impression being given by both Murray and the Bullock Report was that the unions were supposed to be moving into a new era of co-operation, in which, union leaders felt, they would risk losing many of their bargaining freedoms and strengths. Indeed, in a foreword to the TUC's guide to the Bullock Report, Murray talked of 'a new relationship of equality and co-operation between capital and labour, which provides for joint determination of company strategy'. As 1977 wore on and the social contract with the Government on wages began to founder, such an industrial partnership began to look more hollow.

Then, from the left wing of the argument, Professor Wedderburn, a member of the Bullock majority group, wrote an article in the May Day edition of *Tribune*, the left-wing Labour newspaper, which opposed any notion of integration of union activists into company affairs in any sort of permanent coalition: 'Effective workers' representation on Boards through trade union machinery would reflect a basic reality including conflict of interest. That is why it is right to speak of the plan as a "new dimension" of collective bargaining.' His main objective was to warn the Government off legislating what he called a 'cosmetic plan for an "unreal partnership"'; but in so doing he also cleared some of the air about whether or not the British unions had any interest at all in going down the path of German-style co-determination.

The TUC was also trying to bridge the credibility gap at this time and wrote in one of its internal discussion documents in April 1977:

Trade unions would still be free to oppose management policies, both at Board level and through collective bargaining, but they would also, through Board representation, have the opportunity for a more continuous involvement in the actual formulation of policy and consideration of alternative strategies.

Put like that however it still appealed to few union leaders and, indeed, strengthened the Bullock opponents among politicians and industrialists.

With these problems and unresolved differences of opinion, the TUC headquarters did three things in the first half of 1977. First they kept the public debate as low-keyed as possible because of their own internal divisions—a tactic that dampened down the divisions but also meant no one was speaking up publicly for the Bullock concept. Second they maintained pressure on ministers to introduce a White Paper and Bill for the private and public sectors based on the Bullock ideas. Third, as a fallback and a way of uniting their unions, they put special—but unsuccessful—pressure on the Government to introduce at least a general statutory right to union-based worker directors in nationalised industries.

Throughout their discussions with government ministers during these months, the TUC pressed for their basic concepts of a union-based 'single-channel' scheme, with 'parity' between worker and shareholder representatives, on a single-tier board. Gradually they shifted on some of these points—for example they saw an advantage in a Danish-style of '1½'-tier board where management had a clearly defined structure with responsibilities laid down by the main policy board which included the worker directors. But they stuck to the parity issue for some time (although some unions wanted this hardened, with the '*y*' element being dropped to leave a straight '$2x$' or 50–50 split). But the final point on which they stuck resolutely was the single-channel issue of the scheme being union-based.

Lack of government enthusiasm

Squeezed between these conflicting positions–and with the CBI considering itself increasingly powerful as the Labour Government's parliamentary position declined–senior ministers set out to try to find a compromise that might lead to lasting legislation. Within a day or two of the publication of the Bullock Report the Prime Minister gave a public commitment to the preparation of legislative proposals by the end of the summer. This left two ministers in the forefront. One was Albert Booth, secretary for employment, who had been promoted from minister of state when Michael Foot moved to become leader of the House of Commons in 1976. Although a member of the white-collar (TASS) section of the AUEW, which was firmly against worker directors, Booth stoutly set himself up as the guardian of the TUC's and of Jack Jones's policies and argued for the legislation of the Bullock Report. He did however see the advantage of trying to build in as much flexibility as possible, stressing that a Bullock system need be a fallback only when voluntary negotiations failed.

(The significance and usefulness of such a fall-back idea depends on how it is presented. On the one hand the Bullock system would not be mandatory in that it would be up to unions and employees to opt for it. And there would be nothing (apart from some superable legal intricacies) to stop the law being designed to allow worker directors to be elected through voluntary agreement between a company and its work force or unions, without 'triggering' a statutory procedure like Bullock's. Then one would only need to 'trigger' as a fall-back when all else failed. It is at this point that the problem arises, however, because a statutory fall-back could then become regarded as a penalty for those who could not voluntarily agree among themselves–which is hardly the best basis on which to introduce such a system.)

The Cabinet minister in charge was Edmund Dell, who came under different pressures from Booth and who had no significant union-based links or any special lines of communication with the TUC. He said he recognised the manifesto commitment and agreed with Lord Bullock that industrial democracy could well help the mixed economy to survive. But he was equally, if not more, concerned about the rights of all individuals, not just trade unionists, about the impact of worker directors on managerial efficiency, and about the prospect for international investment in the UK. He thus cast about for ways of watering down the Bullock proposals and (after a flying visit to Germany) wondered whether one could do a trade-off in which the TUC either accepted parity on a two-tier supervisory board or a minority of worker directors on a single tier. He was also concerned to build in a continuing role for non-unionists, which the Bullock Report had said was feasible to a limited extent without recommending a specific continuing role for non-unionists.

Dell noted in a speech to the Society for Long-Range Planning on 24 February 1977 that there was common ground between the two factions on issues such as the need to ensure that management efficiency was not impaired, that there must be commitment by all sides to the purposes of the company, that there was a need for improved participation of some sort or other, that there should be flexibility wherever possible in the arrangements, and (with some dissenters) that worker directors could sometimes be applicable. But this common ground glossed over the basic principled differences and left the Government with a situation that Dell summed up aptly in the same speech:

Clearly we have here an issue which can bitterly divide industry at a time when the economic future of this country crucially depends on a united effort for industrial expansion. Yet the issue is here, and ways forward must be sought. But they must be sought, and this is the intention of the Government, on the basis of a determination to find consensus if that is possible, to establish a lasting settlement which will not in its passage through Parliament bring only bitterness and dissension.

Then in May came three events that undermined the TUC's position. First on 24 May, the Manifesto Group of right-wing Labour MPs (of which Giles Radice, author of the 1975 Industrial Democracy private members' Bill, is a leading member–see Chapter 14) issued its policy. This carried a lot of weight with Labour and Liberal MPs and suggested, among other things, that after a three-year interval there should be a 'parity' worker director system but that it should be crudely based on all employees, not just the unions. With this proposal the Labour MPs thus went against the sacrosanct 'single-channel' policy of the unions in a crude all-employees approach which ignored industrial reality.

Next, on 26 May, a policy document appeared from the 1972 Industry Group (made up of about a hundred Labour-supporting industrialists, bankers and businessmen). Its chairman is Lord Houghton, the former Labour MP and trade union colleague of Jim Callaghan when both were in the Inland Revenue Staff Federation. The 1972 Group produces its reports either on its own initiative or because some Labour minister has privately indicated that a paper on a certain subject would be useful. In this case the initiative is thought to have come directly from the Prime Minister, who wanted to find out if there could be any consensus for worker directors among industrialists. This report also watered down the Bullock idea but in a novel way which tried to replace compulsion with a voluntary approach and regarded statutory enforcement only as a fall-back provision. Its idea was that legislation should only give unions a statutory right to 'trigger' negotiations on how a board system could be introduced, not trigger a set Bullock-style system (although of course there was nothing in the Bullock Report to stop voluntary negotiations). This was intended to give management and shareholders a say, through the negotiations, on what should be introduced. The Report envisaged that workers should have one-third of the seats on a 'participatory board' with a separate management structure and that all employees should be entitled to vote in any ballot.

The third event, which happened at the same time as these reports appeared, was that the Prime Minister appointed an informal Cabinet sub-committee of ministers to try to sort out the TUC–industrialists, Booth–Dell, deadlock. The minister he chose to chair this committee was a leading 'moderate', Shirley Williams, secretary for education, who also held the post of paymaster-general, which gave her a ministerial committee chairman's role. Her own views on the subject of industrial democracy were largely unknown, although she had shown her concern that responsibility should go along with any new power when she appeared with Jack Jones and others on Professor Galbraith's BBC 2 'Age of Uncertainty' programme a couple of months earlier. She said then that she agreed with Jones about the need for individuals to participate in society but added: 'The much more difficult half of the battle is in involving the individuals in the sharing of responsibility. So I go along with Jack on participation but I think the much more difficult stage is the stage of shared responsibility' (*The Listener* 7 April, 1977).

'Single channel' of union power

Out of these developments, one point emerged above all the other objections to worker directors that had developed over the previous couple of years. It was that the basic fear of union power, coupled sometimes with a lack of understanding about the unions' established dominant role in British shopfloor relations, can easily lead politicians of all colours (not excluding Labour) to join up with industrialists and many other interests to thwart union ambitions. In this case, a gradual swing in public opinion over shopfloor picketing and other union powers, plus the inability of the unions any more to deliver a firm wages policy, plus the Labour Government's increasing dependence on other interest groups to keep itself in power, made a wide-ranging union-based worker director scheme stretching across all industries a non-runner.

The final sticking point was central to this issue of union power – it was the single-channel approach in which the unions insist that any statutory rights and any worker director organisation should be based on the unions and the unions alone. This emerged at a meeting on 14 June between ministers and the TUC, where Dell reaffirmed the Government's commitment to preparing legislation on industrial democracy which would include an *essential* trade union role (which is not the same thing as an *exclusive* role).

Dell then outlined his views, which were far different from the Bullock starting point of five months earlier. He said he favoured a two-tier board, although he stressed that the top level where the worker directors would sit would have powers over major issues such as financial and strategic planning, the approval of management decisions, shareholders' dividends, the appointment and pay of managers, and personnel policies. But there could only be a gradual move towards 'parity', which would be described only as an 'agreed objective' and the starting point would be a minority of worker directors. In addition, he added, moving away from the 'single-channel' approach, there could well have to be provision for all employees to vote and maybe even to stand to be worker directors. Parliament would have to lay down ground rules for how any joint representation committee operated. (The Bullock Committee had envisaged this committee as consisting of union shop stewards drawing up their own ground rules and negotiating their methods of operation with management.) Mr Booth tried with little success to plead the case for a union-based system, even if all employees were allowed to vote in elections.

So the 'single-channel' issue became the most important principled break-ing point, and, after a subsequent meeting of the TUC Economic Commit-tee, Len Murray set out the TUC's position in a somewhat curt letter to Mrs Williams in which he bluntly stated: 'The single channel of trade union representation is a central principle of the trade union movement . . . any statutory expression of collective rights must be related to the trade union movement if it is to lead to stable industrial relationships and is to be compatible with collective bargaining arrangements.' He added that there could be no question of 'entrenched rights' for senior management to have a seat on the employees' side of the Board (as had been suggested by some Ministers and as happens in Germany). He said that industrial democracy not based on the unions would be a 'step backward, not a step forward', and urged the Government at least to introduce the parity union-based concept in the nationalised industries (where trade unionism is so wide-spread that the all-employee issue is less strong).

This letter made it clear to Ministers that there was little point in producing a White Paper giving some non-unionists certain rights because it would be savaged by the TUC's annual Congress. So a Ministerial Committee, chaired by Mr Callaghan, decided at the end of July to keep a draft White Paper, prepared by Mrs Williams's committee, under wraps till the autumn. This White Paper draft indicated that early legislation in 1977-8 would probably be limited to fringe issues such as making company directors take equal account of employees' and shareholders' interests and allowing them *voluntarily* to set up two-tier boards with worker directors. But any legislation giving employees statutory rights to board seats might well have to be left till later, although a possible scheme was being considered by some Ministers. This envisaged a union-based system, with identifiable occupational groups (such as middle managers) having some rights of separate appeal and representation. The worker directors could sit on a fairly powerful two-tier board structure along Danish rather than German lines but would only have one-third of the seats to begin with. Parity would only follow after five years or so but first there would be a three-year run-in period before any worker directors were allowed.

Eventually these ideas formed the basis of a White Paper which was published, and launched personally by the Prime Minister, on May 23, 1978. The document, called *Industrial Democracy*, had many 'green edges' nationalised industries but said nothing about the Civil Service or local government. Overall it was, politically, a success, and was received favourably even by some staunch opponents of the Bullock Report. But industrialists still objected to statutory enforcement of union rights, while trade unions wanted parity in the boardroom and a faster programme of implementation.

It also, significantly, bridged the trade union gap between Bullock supporters and advocates of extended collective bargaining whose views had been set out by the GMWU in June 1977 in a pamphlet called *Industrial Democracy in the Light of Bullock*. A compromise had been reached between the two groups at the TUC's annual Congress in September 1977 when legislation on both extended bargaining and worker directors was called for, and the White Paper adopted this in a modified form.

Points for debate

Throughout the Bullock debate various key points constantly emerge that will continue to arise whenever a worker director system is considered. They therefore need to be remembered beyond the Bullock battle. They include employees' rights in law; how many worker directors there should be (the parity issue); whether they should be union based; how many tiers of boards there should be; and the relative power of shareholders and employees.

Employees' rights and interests

Behind all the debates lies the issue of the rights of an employee (with or without worker directors) to be treated equally with shareholders. This means boards taking equal account of the interests of both groups and is an idea which few industrialists reject. It is however much more far reaching than it sounds because it means, for example, that in a takeover or a factory closure the financial interests of the shareholders have to be weighed against the job interests of all the employees–both those who may continue working in a more profitable company and those who may be made redundant in the process. It also leads on logically to wide-ranging sharing of power between the representatives of capital and labour and raises questions about the property rights of companies and managements' 'right' to manage.

In the boardroom context, if introduced without worker directors, it involves an extension of the already somewhat complex and delicate balancing act that directors have to carry out under existing company law. They have to balance the interests of both present shareholders (who will have varying interests for a number of reasons, including the type of shares they hold) and future shareholders (whom no one can fully identify). It can be argued that adding the interests of employees to this list will simply compound an existing type of problem but will not make it insurmountable. (The Conservatives' 1973 Companies Bill which fell with the 1974 general election would have changed the law to enable, but not to compel, directors lawfully to take this extra interest on board.)

However it is equally logical to query how directors, elected only by shareholders, can be accountable to employees as well. This raises the question of what sort of machinery one could create (unless one was simply to leave the responsibility un-monitored) to enforce the accountability. From here it is but a short step to argue that, if employees are to have their interests equally considered, then they should have an equal right to elect who they choose to sit on the board.

This then is a legalistic approach to why one should have worker directors if one considers there is a need to change the status of employees, although it does not necessarily mean that the workers have to elect their own directors: the Liberal Party has proposed that shareholders and workers should together elect all the directors. It also does not necessarily mean that one has to have a full statutory voting system. A first step to a system of worker directors could be just to change the law to *allow* some directors to be elected by workers–at present they all *have* to be elected by shareholders.

The majority Bullock Report recommended that 'all directors should continue to be required to act in the best interests of the company but that in doing so they should take into account the interests of the company's employees as well as its shareholders.' But it did not argue that because of this there should be worker directors: it started instead from the other end, assuming there would be worker directors and, along the way, recommended that in any case the change in the employees' status should be made.

The minority group of industrialists on the Bullock Committee, while not being too keen on the whole concept of worker directors, did accept that giving employees' interests recognition in company law would logically mean that there should be both employee and shareholder representatives on boards.

The parity issue

The argument about whether there should be parity between the shareholder and employee representatives is the most crucial aspect of the worker director debate apart from the union role because, irrespective of the precise powers or number of board tiers involved in a system, the percentage of the boardroom seats will be the visible sign of the worker directors' potential power.

At one end of the scale there is a small minority representation, where the worker directors wield no significant power but do have some powers of persuasion and an ability to pick up company information (as in Sweden, for example). At the other end there is full joint control.

Throughout the argument in the UK there is the TUC's case that parity of responsibility derives only from parity of representation – that is, one cannot expect shop stewards and unions to change their habits and shoulder joint responsibility for boardroom decisions when they have less than an equal say with shareholder representatives because there is then no genuine power-sharing. The Bullock Committee's '$2x + y$' formula attempted to straddle this problem by providing the 'y', jointly chosen by the two shareholder and employee 'x' groups, to act as a moderator between the two vested 'x' interests, as a vehicle to import non-executive directors, and as a way of providing a deadlock-breaking mechanism when the two 'x' groups could not agree.

In fact, the '$2y + y$' formula was a modification accepted for reasons of political expediency by the TUC which had started off wanting a straight 50–50 parity split, and several of its unions (and left-wing groups like the Institute of Workers' Control) objected to this watering down of potential union power. This came out clearly in a book by two leading members of the Institute of Workers' Control, Ken Coates and Tony Topham, called *The Shop Stewards' Guide to the Bullock Report* (Coates and Topham, 1977), which said that the shift away from a straight 50–50 split showed a 'new emphasis on collaboration with management' compared with the TUC's initial 50–50 position, which it said had been 'veto powers for workers' representatives'.

However there is another aspect to the '$2y + y$' idea which has been put forward by the TUC to placate these worker control critics. This is that a '$2x + y$' board room could be seen as a bargaining forum in which, when facing trouble, the employee representatives allow themselves to be outvoted by the combined force of the shareholders' 'x' and the 'y'. Then, having decisively lost, the worker directors would be free to opt out and go back to the shop floor to open the battle against the board's decision anew. Such a board room could then indeed be regarded as a supreme extension of collective bargaining with no watering down of traditional conflicts between capital and labour and no blurring of union functions, because when labour loses it could fight again on the shop floor. Such an approach would hardly be conducive to boardroom harmony and would almost certainly drive managements into making their decisions elsewhere. In fact, it illustrates how far back into the collective bargainers' camp the TUC had to go to sell its ideas to some of its activists. (Such bargaining freedom would not exist, for obvious reasons, with a straight 50–50 split where there would be equal responsibility, or indeed with 50–50 plus an independent chairman, because the unions could not constantly be forcing a chairman who was to retain his credibility to use his casting vote.)

Some unions, conversely, might settle for a minority representation as an easy way out of the issue because it would not upset their established habits too much and would give an insight into management operations, although most manual workers' unions in manufacturing industry would see it as the starting point of pointless collaboration with management. It could involve, say, just two worker directors on a board of eight or ten – or even a third or more up to a half. There would however be no major change in the power balance of the company's decision-making and the employee representatives could therefore opt into or out of decisions without their own or the board's credibility being endangered too much. And they would usually not have to bear responsibility for swinging the decisions with their votes (unless they were canvassed when the other directors were split on an issue). It is also sometimes argued that a minority worker presence might have more influence than their proportional representation would suggest because the other directors would not want it to become known that they had ignored the workers' views. And of course, if the law were changed to make the board equally responsible for the interests of shareholders and employees, the influence of even minority employee representatives would be considerably enhanced.

It should also be noted that the relative strength of the two sides of a board will not always be immediately evident from the official split-up into, say, '$2x + y$' or three-thirds. This is because, except where there is a straight 50–50 split, the actual balance of power will depend on how the third group (or the independent chairman, if he is the only balancing factor) is chosen. The Bullock solution, of both sides jointly agreeing the 'y' and appealing as a last resort to an Industrial Democracy Commission to resolve a deadlock on the choice, maintains a form of parity. But the Bullock minority report put up a proposition that would turn its three-thirds idea into shareholders' control because it said that its proposed third third

should be elected by an affirmative vote of at least two thirds of the employee elected representatives and of the shareholder elected representatives voting together. . . .In the event of a continuing failure of the requisite number of candidates to achieve a two-thirds vote, the matter should be referred to a general meeting of shareholders who should appoint the independent members.

This means in effect that the shareholders control the third third because their board representatives could block any employee candidate they did not like and then have their own choices endorsed by the shareholders' meeting. In this way, the formula proposed by the minority group ensured that the supervisory board could be shareholder-dominated.

There can be no doubt that, despite the TUC's emphasis on bargaining, the greater the proportion of seats in the board room occupied by union-based employee representatives, the harder it would be for the unions throughout the company to maintain their old habits. There is nothing to stop them trying to maintain these habits, of course; the point rather is that a board would not function effectively, and in one way or another would not remain the centre of corporate decision-making, if habits did not change. It would be easy enough under almost any worker director system — certainly one with less than a parity split — for a company to switch the places where it makes its decisions from one company board or committee to another, especially if the company were a part of a conglomerate or international group. Indeed, it would very often be up to the union representatives to persuade a company that they did have something to contribute through the containment of conflict, and the acceptance of decisions, to make it worthwhile to the company not to move its decision centres elsewhere.

Role of the unions – a 'single channel'?

The issue of how formally a worker director system should be fixed on the trade unions or whether it should be left open for all employees to be involved is a highly contentious one which raises issues about individual rights and even universal suffrage as well as about union power and industrial logic. And it is made more complex because it involves first a question of principle about who should be the recipients of any legal rights – that is, unions alone or all employees – and second a practical question of whether a worker director system would be most beneficial for all concerned if it were operated through the 'single-channel' sort of union organisations and structures or through a separate representative system.

On the issue of principle, there is the question about whether workers who of their own free choice decide not to belong to a union should consequently be denied the right to board representation, and whether indeed the principle of 'one-worker-one-vote' should obtain. The difficulty with this individual rights argument in practice (though in principle it is widely regarded as having a sound basis) is that the unions *are* the existing representative system in Britain for workers, and that a worker director system would need some sort of collective representative basis (unless a company's management were to be left to nominate the worker directors). In practice, even if the rights were given to all employees, the union activists would take over the system where unions existed. When there were no unions, as is argued later, there would be no effective independent worker director system, irrespective of who has the statutory rights. So the statutory rights issue has only a limited *practical* importance.

The second question is which system would be most beneficial – one based on the unions or one run in the way that old-style consultative systems have functioned, separate from union structures. The answer to this question depends on whether one sees a worker director system as a catalyst to harness new responsibilities from union activists and shop stewards and so reform labour relations, or as an exercise in paternalism which hopefully might even displace the unions or at least form a German-style non-union co-operative system. If one follows the catalytic reformist route then the system must obviously be based formally on the unions—even if, to meet the individual rights argument, the statutory rights were based on all employees and then shop stewards took the system over where they exist. To achieve this, one could give the statutory rights to all employees but say that any system had to be based on the unions where they represented more than a certain proportion of the work force. However, basing the system on the unions does, as has already been discussed, raise problems about the union role and loyalties of worker directors to their fellow shop stewards. To take the alternative route and say that the system must be run separately from the unions would avoid these problems of conflicts over the role and loyalties of the unions but would equally throw away the reformist potential of a worker director system and would fail to stand any chance of gaining the confidence of shop stewards.

Linked with these questions, as was evident from the outcry after the Bullock Report was published, is a political fear among industrialists and others that the unions are out (as indeed they are) to add another statutory right to the growing industrial democracy type of powers they wield over Britain's industrial and economic affairs.

Because of all these issues it has been suggested that, since the unions are so well established, as Professor Bain's research showed, they could afford to waive their demand for the statutory rights to be vested in them alone because they would in any case dominate the system—as the Labour Manifesto Group of MPs argued. It would be against their nature however for unions ever to accept permanently that basic rights they have fought for should be given to non-union employees. This is partly a gut reaction to non-unionists and partly a fear that employers would try to maintain rival non-union employee representation systems instead of adopting the single-channel approach.

The Bullock majority report rationalised the unions' position by rightly arguing that, since unions are established in the big companies, usually with shop steward-based structures, they provide the logical ready-made apparatus for worker directors. The conclusion of the report therefore was that there was no reason to give statutory rights for worker directors to anyone else. To hanker after the German system of non-union works councils and worker directors (though in practice union activists usually gain the council and board seats) would be to ignore the existence of the 300,000-strong British shop steward system. These sorts of shop stewards do not exist in countries like Germany, and in Britain they are unlikely to subside into oblivion just because a potentially rival statutory system is created alongside. A non-union worker director system might therefore appeal to some industrialists, frustrated by unions' often all-too-apparent inability to keep agreements; but it would hardly help the harmony of the company's employee relationships and would not, as has been said, be the catalyst for increased co-operation among the union activists that

could emerge from a worker director system. Nor would it encourage reforms in union structures and methods of the sort that could spring from
the JRC idea and many shop stewards would work to undermine it–or
would just ignore it. So it is logical to base any system on independent
(but not necessarily always TUC) unions, with some statutory encouragement for the protection for non-unionists.

In practice this raises the problem of what to do with non-unionists in
three categories. The first is a non-unionised company, the second involves the few non-unionists that may exist in basically unionised groups
of workers; and the third covers groups of people in unionised companies
whose own area of that company–say middle and senior management–is
traditionally not unionised.

The first two groups do not pose serious problems for the vast mass of
industry. In the non-unionised company the gift of a worker director
system will in practice rest with the management irrespective of
who has the statutory rights. This is because either there will be no
employee organisation, in which case the only way to the board would
be through management selection, or there will be an employer-dominated employee organisation (if it were not employer-dominated it would
qualify for the title 'trade union' under present employment law), which
would usually only do what the management told it. So, in practice, the
non-unionised company is not an issue on either a principled or a
practical basis. Indeed, the nature of the company would mean that the
employees would gain nothing from a right to worker directors being
vested in all employees.

The second example concerns the few non-unionists to be found in
areas where unions, recognised by management, have virtually all the
workers in their membership. These non-unionists have therefore chosen
to opt out of the established, management-recognised representative
system of the company, so it could be argued that by exercising that
individual right, they forfeit their right to be involved in any of the
company's collective employee affairs. On the other hand, it should be
remembered that some people may opt out of unions for anti-TUC or anti-
Labour Party reasons and therefore might opt into a non-union collective
worker director system; but few industrialists or personnel experts would
be prepared to endanger their established industrial relations by catering
specially for this usually very small minority beyond giving them some
voting rights. The Bullock Report suggested letting all employees vote
initially on whether there should be a system and recognised, though it
did not recommend, that they could be allowed to vote (but not stand for
office themselves) in subsequent ballots, the latter being a widely
canvassed compromise.

The third group is the most important in any statutory system because
it can involve large numbers of employees–say salesmen, middle
managers or various white-collar groups–for whom there may be no
trade union tradition in a particular company. Most industrialists and
personnel experts *do* want to cater for these people, although union
leaders say they should only be involved, apart from voting in some
ballots, if they form themselves into representative organisations that
qualify as independent trade unions. Other ways of including them would
be to give them ways of collectively raising their case and maybe en-

couraging them to form managers' associations which could have a limited, boardroom presence separate from the overall union system.

Behind all these considerations, is the issue of union power, with its political overtones. This is not however as clear-cut as the unions' critics make out. As has been pointed out earlier, a union-based worker director system using company employees and not outside union officials on the board does not necessarily strengthen – and indeed could weaken – central union power. And even without weakening that power, there is still an important potential for employers to harness the co-operation of their employees.

This leads on to the question about whether the worker directors would sit as individuals, as employee representatives, or as mandated union delegates. Clearly in any representative system (whether union-only or all-employees) the worker directors would be representatives, just as ordinary directors represent shareholders now. But only one or two people on the far Left of Labour Party politics have suggested that the employee representatives should be *mandated* on what policies to adopt by their union members, let alone by outside union interests, and the Bullock Report was explicit in saying that a worker director would be 'in breach of his duty' as a board member if he 'voted in a particular way solely because of the instructions of his trade union'. Of course the mere fact that as representatives they would have to report back to their constituents and stand for election and re-election means that they would have to reflect their members' views. They would also inevitably be influenced sometimes by their unions' policies; but, since the objective of industrial democracy should be to increase the rights of individual workers, not central union power, it is generally accepted that the unions should advise and not seek to control.

Tiers of power

The point about whether there should be a supervisory board two-tier system or a unitary board, and the point about whether worker directors should be on both subsidiary and group boards, hinges around two interlinked issues of primary importance. The central issue is the more political and concerns how much power worker directors should wield over company fortunes in general. Linked with this is the more practical issue of how free top managers should be to get on with their regular business without interference.

There is a whole spectrum of possibilities here. For example the worker directors will have the least power if (as the minority Bullock Report suggested) they sit only on supervisory boards of holding companies, because the main management work will be done by the management boards and other less formal day-to-day managerial decision-making, while the key policy decisions will be pushed down to the subsidiary company's boards. The worker directors could therefore find themselves in a powerless position unless they had a statutory right to a sufficiently large proportion of the board's seats (which in practice they would not have) to be able to call the management board and any informal management committees to account and impede the subsidiary companies' board decisions.

In practice, as has been seen since the Bullock Report was published, union leaders interested in worker directors are prepared to recognise the logic of allowing management to get on with its day-to-day work but are not prepared to be shunted off into a fairly meaningless supervisory forum like that designed in the minority Bullock Report. On the other hand, while ultimately the unions may want to have worker director seats on the top boards of conglomerates and major holding companies, it is unlikely that they would be able rapidly to organise themselves sufficiently, especially in multi-industry groups. So to begin with, unions might therefore be willing for practical reasons to start with subsidiary boards, although they would want the statutory right to cover any level.

The primary lesson the unions have learned from both the British Steel experiment in the UK and from experience abroad is that there is no point (apart from communications) first in being on a board with few powers (like the German supervisory board, which cannot initiate corporate policies) and second in being on a board in a system that allows all the key decisions to be taken by management individuals and committees meeting outside the boardroom. Equally, there is a fair measure of agreement between industrialists and unions that the employee representatives do not generally want the statutory right to a function in the execution of board decisions, so there is unanimity about the need for managers to feel and be free to go about their business—although the employee representatives would want the power to agree on the board what that devolved managerial autonomy amounted to and would presumably also want lower-level participation in the carrying out of board decisions.

It was for reasons such as these that the TUC and the Bullock majority group swung away from the two-tier supervisory board concept, which they felt isolated the employee representatives too far away from main management decision-making. They also found that in practice a sort of semi-two-tier system operates in Britain at present with the main boards being separate from management operations even though top managers sit on the board as shareholders' representatives. In any case, as has already been said, the TUC wanted worker directors to operate where the power lay if they were to bother with the idea at all.

So the primary issue is the amount of power given to whatever board tier contains the worker directors, rather than how many tiers there are. But this is not to suggest that the number of tiers itself is unimportant because, in principle, a two-tier structure has a different nature from a single-tier system. Broadly, but not always, a two-tier structure involves the worker directors less with management and more with non-executive-style shareholder representatives. Both groups will probably be part-timers, although there may be some full-time top management in the shareholders' group or as a third element. Normally the members of this board are intended to appoint the members of the management board and then only to supervise and oversee from a discreet distance rather than become involved in the job of management. So their ability to initiate policies will have to be limited so as to leave management free to manage. However, while such a situation may appeal to some people who want to limit the worker directors' power, the corollary is that there may well be a correspondingly limited trade union commitment to co-operation with management, and the system may well therefore have less of a catalytic impact on the reform of union and management attitudes, practices and relationships.

On the other hand a unitary board–like the Bullock Report's policy board–is intended to be operational and, although the worker directors would normally still be part-timers, there will be a preponderance of full-time top managers among the other board members. Normally these managers will take up the seats of the shareholders' representatives 'x' in a '$2x + y$' type of structure so that any non-executive directors go into the third or 'y' slice. This dual role of the top managers in the board room appeals to some advocates of worker directors because it brings the worker directors directly into contact with people who both represent the company's owners (the shareholders) and have the direct responsibility for executing the decisions the board makes. On the other hand, industrialists fear that such a close relationship may harm managerial freedom.

But there is a flexible sort of halfway system operated in Denmark, which was praised in the Bullock Report. This emerged in the Government's July 1977 draft White Paper and is sometimes called a '1½-tier board' because management sits on the board proper and then goes off into its own structures to carry out the decisions reached. Under the Danish Companies Act of 1973, there is a board of directors including worker directors (in a minority, though this is not significant here) and top management representing shareholders. This board runs the company's policies and appoints a management board of one or more members to carry the policies out. It is up to the main policy board to decide how much power it is prepared to delegate to the management structure because, statutorily, it is in charge of corporate policy and decision-making, unlike the situation in Germany.

The attraction of this for the UK is that it allows for any sort of management structure–from the most informal, where a managing director operates informally with colleagues, to the most bureaucratic, where there are formal committees. One point of argument in the UK about this idea has been whether the management level's job and responsibilities should be laid down by law, or should be decided by the policy board so that the worker directors can have a say in how much is delegated. People who wish to curtail the worker directors' impact to a more supervisory function will, in this argument, opt for the law to lay down specific management responsibilities to ensure that the management tier has freedom. Worker director advocates on the other hand will opt for the division of duties to be left to the policy board to decide.

Indeed, the logic of the term 'policy board' can be seen as being that the body should decide the policies of the company itself, and therefore how it is run, and so be more than a supervisory level but not so potentially interfering as a straight management board. It is the logical answer if one is designing a power-sharing as opposed to a cosmetic system, and it also should leave enough freedom for management to do its own job (although there will still be employee demands for lower-level participation on how the management tier's decisions are executed).

Shareholders' rights

There is one more factor, in addition to the spread of policy-making decisions between different boards and management structures, that determines the ultimate power and influence of worker directors. It is the way that control over a company's affairs is divided between the board and the shareholders' annual or special meeting. The Bullock Report linked the issues by proposing that on five key subjects the policy board should have the power to initiate policies and that, while there should be no provision for this power to be delegated to management, shareholders should have the reserve right to approve or veto the policies initiated by the board. The five subjects were: winding up the company, changing memoranda and articles of association, payment of dividends, changing the company's capital structures, and selling off a substantial part of the undertaking. For example, the board–with its worker directors– would have the power to decide whether or not to initiate a policy that could cause mass redundancies, but the shareholders would have the final say where the fate of their investments were at stake. This recognition that shareholders, as owners of the company, should have some say over the disposal of its assets was a modification of the original, more radical TUC stance, which proposed that the new board should be the supreme authority with the shareholders' meeting wielding only similar statutory powers to those of the employees' representative body (the JRC, for example, as proposed in the Bullock Report). However the TUC came to realise that such a diminution of shareholders' rights would not be politically acceptable to any government in the foreseeable future.

The alternative view (although the minority Bullock Report did not go into this in any detail) is that shareholders, as the owners of a company, should not have their rights to control their property reduced at all and that they should therefore reign supreme. This however is not a logical stance to take up if one accepts (as most industrialists say they do) that the board should take equal account of the interests of shareholders and employees. It would be illogical to initiate such a change aimed at recognising the workers' investment of their livelihoods without accepting at the same time that some of the final rights of the shareholders should be correspondingly reduced–just as it has been argued that such a change should be accompanied by the introduction of worker directors to ensure that employees' interests are taken equally into account.

The formulation chosen by the Bullock Report–reserving some primary ownership decisions for shareholders–strikes a balance between the interests of the two parties because it would hardly help worker directors to operate effectively if the management (through the shareholder directors) could constantly try to undermine the position of the worker directors by referring back to the shareholders to overrule board decisions that had been pushed through the board by the worker directors. Equally, if shareholders lost all primary powers, there would be few people or institutions interested in investing in UK companies.

Finally of course, a Bullock-style worker director system depends on one basic shareholders' right being removed: their ability to choose how their company is run, or, to put it another way, their power to stop the introduction, or reduce the effectiveness, of a worker director system. The reason for this is that the Bullock majority group believed that, given a right of veto, shareholders and management would almost always stop any effective worker director scheme and would introduce either sham alternatives or none at all. Nevertheless, a case could be made out (although the Bullock Report did not accept this) for management, through shareholders, to appeal to some central authority if they could show that the worker directors or their trade unions were perpetually trying to run the company against the joint interests of the shareholders and employees. If such a protection were devised, it would have to be phrased carefully to ensure it was used only for major cases–say, a union's external politically oriented policies being forced through into the board room–and not simply as a way of frustrating the worker directors. And it could in any case be argued that the Bullock Report's sort of '*y*' element would build in this protection and make an outside appeal unnecessary.

Shareholders and takeovers

A further significant reduction in the power of shareholders emerged in the Bullock Report's suggestion that the right of one company to acquire control of another simply by obtaining more than 50 per cent of its shares should be abolished. The logic for this is that in a worker director system the employees working in the company that might be taken over should have a say in addition to those owning its capital–who make their views known by selling their shares. The Bullock Report however approached this fundamental change through a discussion of the relationship between holding companies and subsidiaries. (An allied problem, not discussed by the Report, is that, in takeovers, the employees rarely know the employment plans of the incoming company, which will affect their livelihoods. On the other hand, shareholders are told financial plans.)

The Report suggested, on the main takeover point, that its '$2x + y$' ideas should apply to both holding companies and to subsidiaries but added that, while the '*y*' co-opted members on an ordinary or holding board should be jointly chosen by the two '*x*' groups, they should be chosen for subsidiary companies by the full board of the holding company. This was done to ensure that the holding company could in fact control its subsidiaries (and further protections were suggested for multinationals). But this idea, which raises a number of practical problems about the management of large groups, runs into special problems with takeovers. This is because it would mean that a company acquiring over 50 per cent of a company it wanted to own–and thereby becoming the holding company–could change both the shareholders' '*x*' and the co-opted '*y*' elements on its victim's board and so gain control despite the views of the workers' '*x*'.

As the Bullock Report explained:

We take as an illustration of the problem an independent company of which the Board has been reconstituted, with equal numbers of shareholder and employee representatives and an agreed third group of co-opted directors, and in which industrial relations and productivity have improved consequent upon the increased participation in its affairs. A second company, contrary to the wishes and recommendations of the independent company's Board, acquires a majority holding in the latter's shares. If the independent company automatically becomes a 'subsidiary' of the second company (as it would if the definition in Section 154(1) of the Companies Act 1948 remained unchanged) the second company would be able not only to replace the shareholder representatives on its Board but also, by virtue of the proposal above for a residual power for holding companies, control the appointment of its co-opted directors. A transaction on the stock market would thereby destroy what employees in the hitherto independent company had come to regard as effective employee representation on their company's Board.

So the Bullock Report–in a proposal that indicates the wide and as yet little understood legislative ramifications for companies of introducing industrial democracy–proposed that no takeover should become effective until the old board of the company being bid for had approved the idea. Some people would argue that this would remove the entrepreneurial share-trading basis of a successful capitalist-based free market system; but from the industrial democracy point of view it is essential (and was recognised as so by Nicholas Wilson) if worker directors are to have credibility. However, with reforming zeal inspired by Professor Wedderburn, the Report went on to propose that this restriction on the ability of the mere buying of shares to determine a company's ownership should apply to all companies, whether or not they had statutory worker directors.

Summary and the European significance

These reviews of the major points arising from a worker director scheme in general and the Bullock Report in particular have intentionally dwelt more on the theoretical than the practical aspects of the issues involved. This is mainly because some of the broad practical issues have been looked at progressively throughout this book. But there is another reason: it is that so little is known in detail about how major company decisions are made and executed that it would be foolish to try to interpret in detail how the proposals would for example affect the running of GEC (with its many subsidiaries but only a small head office dominated by one man, Sir Arnold Weinstock) or ICI (which has a divisional structure and is far more bureaucratic with complex committee structures). It is only too easy, because so little is known, for industrialists to argue convincingly that a 50–50 or a '$2x + y$' split board, while it *might* boost employee confidence, would make a nonsense of efficient management and harm the quality of directors' decision-making.

Such arguments however do little to help a constructive debate along, and a much better informed debate and evolution of worker power in the board room or elsewhere could develop if more were discovered and understood about the workings of companies, their management practices, the motivations of top industrialists, and the groups to whom the industrialists feel the most accountable, as well as the views of the workers.

The theory is also important because one is dealing with the law– present and future–and some of the Bullock majority group, realising this, were aware of the possibility of affecting Brussels policy. Whatever happens on industrial democracy in the UK during the next year or so, the operations of companies will increasingly be governed by a mixture of British and EEC laws. The way that the theoretical arguments turn themselves into law in Brussels and London will govern the way that some companies choose to operate. It is quite possible, for example, that the EEC's Fifth Directive on the harmonisation of company law, under which all companies in EEC countries would in the interests of fair trans-

European trading have to bring their company law practices, including worker directors, into line, may not come into being for many years. This is partly because of inertia within the EEC bureaucracy and partly because at least one EEC country–France–may permanently block the proposal.

The Euro-Company Statute–designed for those companies trading across European frontiers which for some reason or another decide to opt for a Euro-wide legal entity rather than their home-based laws–is however more likely to come into force somewhat earlier. It would then be open for British companies to opt out of British company law and choose the Euro-Statute if it provided a softer worker director option. For example, if the Euro-Statute provided for a three-thirds split in a two-tier structure with the worker directors based on all employees and located in a weak supervisory board, plus all-employee plant level works councils, it might prove more attractive to a British company if more power-sharing union-based laws were to emerge in the UK.

The 1978 White Paper

The White Paper *Industrial Democracy* which the Government eventually produced in May 1978 was a compromise between the sharply conflicting views of industrialists and union leaders. It stood by the basic Bullock Report principle of employees, through their unions, having statutory rights to boardroom representation, but watered down the impact.

The proposals started with a muted version of the trade union extended bargaining claim. This was adopted in the White Paper as a statutory obligation for companies with more than 500 employees to consult a committee of union representatives about major company plans before decisions were made. Then this committee, which would be a Joint Representation Committee as proposed in the Bullock Report, would have the right after three or four years to claim (in companies of 2000 or more employees) one-third of the seats in a Danish-style one-and-a-half-tier boardroom structure. As a result of Dell's influence, the White Paper also said that 'homogeneous' groups of more than 100 non-union employees might be allowed to claim a boardroom seat.

The White Paper also said that the Government intended to legislate to allow companies to introduce a two-tier board structure quite apart from any industrial democracy developments, so as to separate policy-making from management. (A further White Paper *Changes in Company Law* published on July 20, 1978, indicated that any industrial democracy legislation might also deal with the statutory obligations of directors towards employees.)

The industrial democracy White Paper was conciliatory in tone and stressed that its ideas were only statutory fallbacks and that voluntary arrangements were to be encouraged. It backed developments in the nationalised industries but said nothing about the civil service or local government. Overall it was, politically, a success, and was received favourably even by some staunch opponents of the Bullock Report. But industrialists still objected to statutory enforcement of union rights, while trade unions wanted parity in the boardroom and a faster programme of implementation.

Chapter 17

Other Campaigns:
The Public Sector and
Control of Pension Funds

While the main battles on industrial democracy were being fought in 1976 and 1977 on the way that the Bullock Report might affect the ownership and management of the private sector of industry, two other related events were taking place. One, on which the unions were having some success, was the spreading of worker power in management through the unions in the public sector, especially the nationalised industries. The other, which foundered early in the summer of 1977, was for union members to have a statutory right to a 50–50 joint control of the management of pension funds; had it been implemented, this would have given unions a wide-ranging measure of control over the country's industrial investment.

Plans for the public sector

When the Government set up the Bullock Inquiry late in 1975 to look into industrial democracy in the private sector, it also set up parallel inquiries into the public sector. But because of its own special interest in state-owned and -run industries and services, the inquiries had no publicly announced precise terms of reference and all their work took place as far away from the public gaze as senior civil servants could manage. The inquiries in fact were organised within Whitehall by civil servants themselves and basically amounted to the Government, through its relevant departments and with some co-ordination from the Treasury and the Civil Service Department, inviting the employers and unions in the individual industries and services concerned to consider what sort of industrial democracy advances they wanted. Alan Lord, a second permanent secretary at the Treasury who left for a senior post in Dunlop before the work was completed, was the only civil servant publicly known to be in some sort of charge, so the work, especially in the nationalised industries, was therefore sometimes known as the 'Lord Report'. In fact, Mr Lord only submitted a memorandum to ministers just before the Bullock Report was published setting out the various and widely differing stages of participation reached in the nationalised industries and pointing to the problems of enforcing a single solution for the future.

Eventually the public sector inquiries settled down into three main sections. First, the Treasury co-ordinated inquiries in the nationalised industries, which involved these industries' own sponsoring government departments (Energy for example for coal, electricity and gas, and

Industry for the post office, shipbuilding and steel) consulting with the managements and unions involved on where they wanted to go.

Then the Department of the Environment (which also had some nationalised industry interests, such as British Railways in the above exercise) co-ordinated an inquiry in local government to the extent that it encouraged those involved through the local authorities' own bodies such as the Association of Metropolitan Authorities, and through the individual unions and the TUC's Local Government Committee, to try to come to some understanding among themselves about what should happen.

In addition the Civil Service Department (CSD) looked at what should happen in central government – that is the Civil Service – and in what are known as 'fringe bodies' such as the Manpower Services Commission, the Civil Aviation Authority and other semi-autonomous government organisations. The CSD also had a co-ordinating role over this exercise and the local authorities to ensure that what civil servants call the 'read across' between government departments made sense – which means ensuring that one department does not do something that might form an embarrassing precedent for another. The target was to feed all this work into the White Paper which the Government was preparing in 1977 in the wake of the Bullock Report on industrial democracy in the private sector, but it was clear by mid-1977 that there would be no radical developments.

Linking all the public sector work was the basic consideration of how to marry industrial democracy, where workers elect representatives to help run their places of employment, with a parliamentary democracy and the elective principle, where people in general elect representatives to run their country and localities. Consequent on this is what is known as the ministerial responsibility to Parliament for nationalised industries – the minister involved having been charged by Parliament to look after his nationalised industries in the interests of the nation, as represented by MPs, and not in the interests of any sectional group, such as an industry's employees. This links with the question of how far unions and employees ought to be given the right to go beyond employment issues in determining the purpose as well as the operations on their employer's businesses (see Chapter 7).

But, as ministers began to realise during 1977, it also illustrates the practical problems as well as issues of principle involved in employee participation. Civil servants and ministers could increasingly be heard during 1977 deploying the same sort of practical arguments in identical terminology to that used against the Bullock Report in the private sector. Speaking as guardians of the taxpayers' and rate-payers' money, as opposed to shareholders' investments, they could be heard worrying about the impact of industrial democracy on managerial efficiency in the nationalised industries and public services, about the high cost of expensive delays in decision-making that extended consultation and participation could cause, and about whether the role of the unions should not in any case be limited merely to looking after their members' interests on relatively short-term employment issues.

To make it clear however to ambitious union leaders that the Government was not prepared to weaken on the principles involved, Charles Morris, minister of state at the Civil Service Department, made some all-embracing points when he dealt with the local and central government issues in Parliament. On 11 February 1976 he told the Commons:

Industrial democracy in the public sector presents special problems because of the role of Parliament and local authorities as representatives of the electorate and, so far as the nationalised industries are concerned, because of the ultimate responsibility of sponsoring Ministers in Parliament. It is fundamental to the working of democracy as we know it that elected representatives take decisions and act in the interests of the community as a whole: that principle cannot be breached. But within the need to preserve the accountability of elected representatives and the requirements of the public interest, employees and their representatives in the public services should be given the maximum opportunity to contribute their views on matters of legitimate staff interest.

Although there has been plenty of room for disagreement between the Government and the unions over how far 'legitimate staff interest' might stretch, the civil service unions did accept the basic points that Mr Morris was making and told the Government in the autumn of 1976 that their ideas for extending industrial democracy 'respect the accountability of Ministers to Parliament and of Parliament to the electorate'. In the local government area however–where superficially it is less difficult to imagine employees sitting on councils or their committees than it is to imagine civil service clerks sitting in Parliament or in Cabinet committees –the unions did not accept the electoral principle so fully. And even in the nationalised Bank of England, the 3500 employees' internal staff association suggested that two staff members should be elected to the Bank's august Court of Directors.

Nationalised industries

The debate in the nationalised industries (there are more than twenty of them employing some 2.5 million workers) on industrial democracy was complicated in November 1976 by the publication of a report from the National Economic Development Office on relationships between the Government and the industries. The report was produced, at the request in June 1975 of Harold Wilson when he was prime minister, by a team headed by the NEDO's director general, Sir Ronald McIntosh.

The report (National Economic Development Office, 1976) was highly critical of the unstructured, un-trusting, and confusing relationships between governments and civil servants under both main political parties on the one hand and of the management of the nationalised industries on the other. It suggested that for each major nationalised industry there should be a two-tier structure with a policy 'council and a separate corporation board. The Policy Council would be chaired by a president appointed by the Government. Other members of the Council would include senior civil servants from the Treasury and the relevant sponsoring government department, the chairman of the corporation board and other board members, trade union representatives, and members representing consumer and other independent viewpoints. The chairman and members of the corporation board would be appointed by and accountable to the Policy Council, which would be accountable to Parliament through annual reports and appearances before parliamentary select committees. The Government could, in extreme circumstances, overrule the Council. The job of the corporation's board–presumably made up of full-time top management, although a trade union presence was not ruled out – would be to run the corporation within the framework of objectives, strategies and criteria set by the Policy Council. Although the NEDO report intentionally did not analyse the aspect of industrial democracy because of the parallel Bullock and Whitehall inquiries, the unions would share power with the Government and other interests on the Policy Council.

While few people quarrelled with its analysis of the problems, the report's recommendations found little favour in Whitehall or among many of the nationalised industries. This was partly because of the way it proposed formally to institutionalise arrangements in a highly structured way between the Government and the industries and because it set up two tiers of authority – the council and the board – each with its own president/chairman. In some ways however the NEDO ideas bear some relationship to the ideas of the National Coal Board in the coal industry where the Government (through ministers from various departments rather than civil servants) comes together with both sides of industry on a top tripartite committee. The industry then gets on with its own affairs with lower-level structures. Ideas of involving civil servants more directly in the policy-making of nationalised industries, instead of letting them operate the levers of power more remotely from within their own government departments, had also surfaced elsewhere by early 1977, with two civil servants appointed to the British National Oil Corporation and the steel industry considering a similar sort of idea.

Such a direct representation is quite different from the normal system in which, although the minister responsible appoints all the board members, he does not expect them to act as his representatives and rarely if ever tries to influence what they do. Instead he relies on his own power of appointing and re-appointing the people involved and on the power of civil servants within his ministry and the Treasury – together holding the purse strings – to exert the Government's wishes from Whitehall. The NEDO and other similar ideas would change this often unhappy and fractious relationship by forcing the Government more into the open. The NEDO report recognised however that the civil servants who were put on to a policy council would thus have the possibly conflicting 'dual roles of reflecting the policies of their Ministers and sharing collective responsibility for decisions of the Policy Council'. But it then pointed to the Oil Corporation precedent and added that, abroad, civil servants sat on the supervisory boards of public enterprises in France, West Germany, Sweden and Austria.

Ideas being developed by Sir Charles Villiers, the chairman of the British Steel Corporation, in 1977, tried to embrace the problems raised by the NEDO report without creating a two-tier council – board structure. At the same time he set out a new form of industrial democracy through what he called a 'steel contract'. The plan included a new top-level management – union consultative (as opposed to policy-making) steel council and a new single-tier policy board. Although the precise relationships of these bodies were not immediately clear, the significant innovation was the membership of the policy board, which would be developed from the existing corporation board. In May 1977 Sir Charles suggested, without filling in many details, that they should include not only representatives of management and unions but also part-time representatives of the Government (presumably civil servants rather than coal industry-style ministers), consumers (presumably from the Iron and Steel Consumers Council), and even competitors (possibly the private sector steel producers). The precise purpose and practicability of such a gathering of conflicting groups was not immediately obvious except as a starting point for a debate about how the conflicting owner, worker, consumer and other 'social' ambitions in a state-owned enterprise could be brought together for the good not only of the individual interests but of the country as a whole.

A White Paper on nationalised industries in April 1978 rejected the main NEDO ideas but the Steel Corporation took six trade unionists (and two civil servants) onto its 20-man main board in August 1978, so boosting the Bullock debate in nationalised industries.

Almost before the Bullock Report was published, some union leaders decided that, at the very least, they must ensure that the Government pushed industrial democracy forward in this area. Such a policy had two advantages for the TUC's Bullock supporters. First it meant that the TUC could use its influence on the Government directly, as the employer in the nationalised industries, to push forward legislation then being prepared for the Post Office and to try to ensure that its union-based and other demands were included in the general legislation. Second, there was less opposition among the TUC's own ranks to worker directors in the public sector. Certain unions, notably the AUEW, could therefore be harnessed as potential worker-director supporters in the TUC's debates and conference votes at a time when much of the union movement was showing scant interest. Overall, therefore, progress in the nationalised industries would it was hoped buttress and give added credence to the unions' claims for legislative rights in the private sector. So, having established in January 1977 that the nationalised industries would be included in any private sector Bullock-based legislation, the TUC's nationalised industries' committee approved a six point Bullock-based policy on 10 March 1977 with only Frank Chapple of the EPTU dissenting. This was something of a coup for the Bullock camp in the TUC, because union leaders who voted for the policy included some erstwhile opponents. They were: Ken Baker of the General and Municipal Workers, Ray Buckton of the Locomen (ASLEF), Geoffrey Drain of the Local Government Officers (NALGO), Len Edmondson of the Engineers (AUEW), Jack Jones (who had, significantly, just become the committee's chairman), Bill Sirs of the Steelworkers (ISTC), and Sidney Weighell of the Railwaymen (NUR). The legislation should, the TUC said, include six points:

Unions to have the right to initiate the process of Board representation; parity–if on the '$2x + y$' basis, the 'y' element to be jointly approved by the other two sections; representation to entail reconstitution of the existing Boards; this option to be available to all nationalised industries under the Industrial Democracy (Companies and Nationalised Industries) Bill; joint machinery of the recognised unions to select workers' representatives; the trade union machinery to report back through the above machinery.

Despite the overall TUC optimism, however, little happened.

There remains the problem of how far ministers should be prepared to go in reducing their own authority over the nationalised industries in the interests of giving worker directors a meaningful role. Should there, in other words, be a ministerial equivalent in the public sector to the Bullock Report's proposals for shareholders to have veto powers, despite the worker directors, over certain key issues to do with their rights as owners of a company? Clearly the answer to this is that the Government could no more abdicate all ownership interests than private sector shareholders would be prepared to sit back and leave all decisions to top managers and worker representatives. By early in 1977, there seemed to be general agreement in the Government that a minister should retain power over certain key issues – such as the way in which large sums of public money are spent – as well as guarding the national interest in general. This meant a minister would need powers to control, for example, investment decisions involving government finance and those affecting international obligations – say on the functioning of the British National Oil Corporation's North Sea international interests, or the power station construction programme of the nationalised electricity supply industry, or the aircraft development plans of the aircraft industry. Such a power could be exercised by ensuring that the Government had its own representatives occupying a sizeable proportion of an industry's top board seats – perhaps through some scheme based on the NEDO (or coal industry or steel) ideas, although this could dilute the impact of employee directors. Or it could simply establish that, worker directors or not, certain board decisions could never be taken without ministerial approval – just as the Bullock Report acknowledged the need for shareholders' reserve veto powers.

There is a parallel problem over a minister's existing right to make all appointments to a nationalised industry board. Unions would not want anyone interfering with their choice for their representatives and would also want to have a joint say in any independents. The idea however that the Government would not have a say over the people running state boards strikes horror – for national security reasons if for no other – deep into the corridors of Whitehall. The issue was side-stepped in the Post Office arrangements where it was agreed that the unions would only put up enough names to fill their 'x' seats available in the '$2x + y$' formula and that the minister would consult both sides of the industry before appointing the 'y' group. In a relatively co-operative industry such as the Post Office has been, this had a chance of working effectively despite inter-union squabbles; but the same spirit of co-operation would not always be present elsewhere. This therefore means there are three options: one is to operate the Post Office system and hope it works; the second is to insist that more names are put up than are needed, or at least that the unions accept the minister's right to reject candidates (which could occasionally create a crisis in industries like the railways if a minister for example tried to keep a Communist Party member off the board); third, and probably most practically, there could be a compromise whereby the minister does not veto appointments but has a method of removing a member on certain grounds.

The Civil Service

While the debate about the nationalised industries shows the extent to which parliamentary and industrial democracy can be married in industry, it is far more difficult to do so in the Civil Service and local government, and this is accepted by the TUC. Charles Morris's remarks earlier in this chapter were aimed at emphasising this and at showing that there was little if any sympathy for union representatives going outside their normal employment subjects.

Broadly the claims from the unions in the Civil Service can be split into two groups. There was the worker director approach taken by Jack Jones (mentioned in Chapter 7), from the point of view of government industrial workers, which envisaged the fairly widespread creation of management boards within a government department to accommodate worker representatives. This was also taken up as a possible experiment by the white-collar civil service unions collectively in a joint submission to the Government in the autumn of 1976 from what is called their National Staff Side. But the Staff Side saw this only as experiments and basically opted for most advances to be made by extending the Civil Service's Whitley traditions with wider arrangements for bargaining and consultation. In a way, they were adapting the private sector's extended collective bargaining alternative to worker directors for use in the Civil Service—and thereby inevitably raising the question of whether they were aiming at gaining power by extending conflict-based techniques instead of adopting a worker director system which could lead to new co-operative methods with increased shared responsibilities.

In an appendix to its evidence, the Staff Side listed those areas of the Civil Service that it thought suitable and unsuitable for experimentation with management boards. It realistically thought that statutory bodies such as the Defence Council and the Board of Inland Revenue would not be appropriate (although some union leaders have argued that, since the Board of Inland Revenue only executes but does not create government policies, it could be a candidate). It thought that boards running the Government's Property Services Agency, the dockyards, and Royal Ordnance factories were possibilities, but realised that something like the Civil Service Department's permanent secretary's management group (a weekly top staff meeting) would not be appropriate. Of all its ideas, probably the most easily acceptable in Whitehall were proposals that staff representatives should be involved in management review committees looking into special problems like the efficiency of an organisation or training arrangements. But even here there would still be a lot of resistance to such a representation being institutionalised by law instead of merely being left to the top civil servants and ministers to invite a trade union presence.

Basically, the Civil Service Staff Side's proposals were aimed at giving the unions more power through traditional means, and they met some resistance in Whitehall on the grounds that the unions should not extend their adversary powers into areas controlled by Parliament. The unions wanted extended prior consultation on government estimates, cash limits, new legislation and the location of work, in so far as these affected the interests of staff. They also wanted more information and increased industrial relations rights on arbitration and recognition subjects (which were already applicable to the private sector but denied to many state employees), plus new conciliation arrangements.

These are all employment issues, so on the surface appear to be subjects over which there would be little dispute. The problem however is that the ramifications of employment issues can be interpreted extremely widely – for example, tax changes in the Budget alter the staffing needed by the Inland Revenue; a government policy reached for environmental reasons on the location of offices affects where civil servants live and work; government estimates and cash limits affect every aspect of state employment from whether a man has a job to how much he is paid. So there is a lot of opposition within Whitehall to any developments that would institutionalise a union's right to advance consultation and so potentially put government policy-making and execution at risk. But there is far less resistance to *ad hoc* arrangements which do not bind governments and the Civil Service with precedents.

Local government

Paradoxically, worker participation in the affairs of local government is at one and the same time both a less sensitive and a more sensitive issue than that in the Civil Service. On the one hand local government decisions do not directly affect the national interest, and it is also easier for progressive Labour groups to initiate their own ideas. On the other hand individual people – the electorate – are likely sometimes to react more strongly against worker power weakening their own local council votes, and it is also easier for groups like Conservative councillors, opposed to the extension of union power, to resist or cancel advances. But perhaps most important of all, there is the shadow of Whitehall and the central government watching over developments, determined not to allow anything to happen in local councils that might set a precedent for central government. Ministers therefore would not want locally to dilute the elective parliamentary principle which they are determined to maintain in Westminster.

The unions in local government have had varying views on what they want and some even started out claiming seats with full voting rights on the councils. They have cited as precedents the fact that teachers in the education field and doctors in the National Health Service (which in 1977 was making its own moves towards worker participation, with a government proposal that trade union representation should be increased to one-third on regional and area health authorities) had had seats on various sorts of management boards for some years. The difference however is that the doctors and teachers have sat as expert employees rather than as trade union-based employee representatives.

But there has been strong employer opposition among local council bodies to any statutory introduction of employee involvement on councils or committees, and there has also been specially strong opposition to employee representatives having voting rights. One or two Labour-controlled councils in 1976 and 1977 however planned, or started, experiments by using their ordinary powers to co-opt people on to councils by issuing 'standing invitations' for them to attend. Basildon District Council in 1976 co-opted four employee representatives on to the Council itself and two representatives on to most committees. All had the right to speak, but not to vote. By early 1977 however they seemed to have had little impact on the decision-making or the management of the Council's affairs

–partly apparently because of lethargy on the part of those involved. The Labour-controlled Greater London Council proposed a similar scheme at the end of 1976 but this fell foul of the change of governing party when the Conservatives took over in May 1977.

The Association of Metropolitan Associations echoed the views of many councils when, speaking for itself and other local authority associations, it said in December 1976:

Full participation of representatives of employee unions as voting members on the council or committees of local authorities is not acceptable. Although one or two authorities have developed, or are developing, proposals for having employee representatives present at meetings of committees in a non-voting capacity, this is also felt to be unacceptable by the majority of the Associations.

The Associations, strengthened in their views by the Conservative victories in the May 1977 local elections, were therefore rejecting two major points, although they did also acknowledge the right of councils to initiate their own experiments. First, they opposed any Bullock-style statutory right being given to unions and their members to opt for committee or council representation. Like industrialists in the private sector and senior civil servants, they did not mind worker representation where the company (or in their case the council) decided to award it on an *ad hoc* or even permanent basis – which is quite different from giving employees statutory rights. (It should however be added that the absence of statutory rights could cause more chaos in local government, where – as the GLC situation showed – if there are no statutory rights one political party can cancel the employee representation plans created by its predecessor.) Second, they were also opposing full employee participation: there can be shades of participation involved here grading from sitting only on employment-oriented committees without voting rights to sitting on all committees and the council with voting power. There could also be arguments about the proportion of the seats employees should have – Basildon opted only for minority representation in its experiment.

Because it could see the firm opposition that was building up among the councils, and because it did not want to raise problems that could have a spin-off effect, damaging its progress towards industrial democracy in the private sector and nationalised industries, the TUC eventually soft-pedalled in this area and agreed in February 1977 to press only for one-fifth of the seats on council committees, without voting rights, plus the extension of the old education arrangements to include representatives of non-teaching as well as teaching staff. It also wanted lower-level participation arrangements and linked all this with a separate request that an existing ban on council employees standing for election as councillors in the normal local elections should be lifted. But even these proposals, which were considerably more limited than those on which some unions had started out, met with little enthusiasm from the local councils. The councils also pointed out, in talks with the TUC and the Government, that the Redcliffe Maud Report on local government in 1974 had recommended against the unions' demand that council employees should be able to become councillors in the normal way.

Summary

At the same time that it has been pushing for increased union-based employee rights to power sharing in the private sector, the TUC therefore has been calling with a varied degree of urgency for parallel arrangements in the public sector. But by early 1977 it realised that the parliamentary and electoral principle in national and local government would raise so much opposition that it could be counter-productive to push it too hard – especially when there was a strong anti-Bullock tide running. As some ministerial advisors mischievously murmured, a concentrated civil service campaign to persuade ministers of the worst managerial horrors that industrial democracy could bring to their own government departments might cause a massive Cabinet backlash against the whole worker director concept. This was because, even though they had not actually claimed boardroom-style seats in the Cabinet room in Downing Street, the unions were knocking on the doors of the Government's decision-making centres.

Control of pension funds

In the middle of 1976, when the Bullock Committee was carrying out its inquiries, a new form of potential 50–50 control of industrial finance was launched on to a rather bemused commercial world by Stan Orme, who had moved from his Northern Irish responsibilities to be Minister of State for Social Security. In his new post he soon found a report awaiting him which opened up new avenues for the spread of an extreme radical form of industrial democracy by giving him the opportunity to propose that union members should, Bullock-style, have the statutory right to share in the management of their pension funds.

A large number of companies already have negotiating arrangements with their trade unions to determine the amount of money that should be paid into pension funds: indeed, some companies consider such an exercise to be essential since the cash comes out of the total amount of money they have available for payment to their employees, past and present, and they want their unions to appreciate the sums involved. But the significance of the new development goes considerably wider than workers, through their unions, extending their collective bargaining on wages into the 'deferred pay' area of pensions. This is because what Mr Orme came to propose was a statutory right for union members to claim joint management – worker control of the management of the funds, not just of how much money was paid into them each year. The crucial underlying factor here is that such new, potentially widespread control of pensions would give the unions an ever-increasing joint control over the massive industrial investments that many businesses depend on for survival. This is trade union-based financial participation (or economic democracy, as it is sometimes called) taken to its logical conclusion. Its target is the same as the Meidner collective share ownership plan in Sweden and other ideas developed along the same lines elsewhere, including a share ownership scheme proposed for the UK by a Labour Party working party in 1973 (see Chapter 13). The key difference between these share ownership schemes (or capital funds as they are sometimes known) and pension funds is that the former would only

273

provide a relatively slow buildup of significant amounts of investment over periods of thirty years or more, whereas joint control of pensions would happen overnight, and so would give the unions, through their members, a much faster control of some key investment decisions, albeit a form of control that they would gain to some degree through any worker director system.

The major importance of this lies in the size of pension funds in the UK. They are increasing as more manual workers' and other schemes are introduced; the CBI has pointed out that pension funds in the UK early in 1977 had some £20,000 million invested and that this sum was growing at a rate of more than £3000 million a year. John Hughes, vice-principal of Ruskin College in Oxford (and a part-time deputy chairman of the Price Commission from June 1977), put this new form of participation in its full socialist context in the London Business School's Stockton lecture on 10 March 1977. He pointed out the implications of the trade unions becoming (in effect) joint shareholders in companies as well as, within the companies, gaining increasing measures of joint control over management decisions – so that in effect there would no longer be a capitalist system with which to be in conflict:

Certainly equipped with the Trojan Horse of the pension funds, organised labour cannot for long be kept outside the citadels of corporate power. But by the same token this must represent a turning point from the organisation of negative power to the deployment of positive power, initiative, and social responsibility in the industrial society of the future.

Direction of investment
It was this prospect of unions using the pension funds to exert power over company investment policies – for example backing job-saving rather than profit-making investments – that most horrified industrialists already worried enough about the growing statutory and institutional power of the unions. This horror was increased when the TUC drew up a proposal in 1977 for a new state agency to be created which would be responsible for channelling investment into areas of high unemployment in industry. This agency's money, the TUC told the Wilson Committee on the City, should be drawn from North Sea oil profits, insurance companies *and the pension funds,* and its work would be monitored by a joint committee of ministers, union leaders and employers. It would thus be added to the string of jointly run government agencies (see Chapter 4) that are taking the unions into the policy-making and executive area of government affairs, as well as expanding the government's state control of companies' investment policies. It would also be adding a new dimension to the concept of industrial democracy by giving the unions direct influence over pension funds themselves, then over the way these and other funds were invested, with maybe later further power through workers' share ownership capital funds.

The idea of workers being given some statutory rights over the investment plans of their pension schemes was mooted in a general Labour Party policy paper in 1972 called *Labour's Programme for Britain,* and it cropped up again in the TUC's Economic Review for 1975:

In the past the tendency has been for pension schemes to be administered by employers through trustees and management committees without any trade union participation. There have been instances of pension funds being used within the company at less than market interest rates or invested overseas. There have recently been suggestions that funds could be more generally used as a cheap source of finance for industry. The benefits from a pension scheme depend on the yield from funds and it is therefore vital that negotiators make major efforts to establish joint control of both schemes and their funds.

At that time the Occupational Pensions Board, at the request of the Government, was looking into what statutory provisions there should be on disclosure of pension funds business and the TUC said in its Economic Review that it had taken this opportunity to call for 'legislation to ensure full disclosure to members and their trade unions under the supervision of a statutory body and full participation of their members in the management of schemes'.

Trade union interest in the pensions field has stemmed from three main sources, apart from the more political interest of getting to grips for its own sake with the power centres of industry. First, partly because statutory pay policies of the 1960s and 1970s have restricted increases in take-home pay, and partly because of changing social attitudes, pension schemes have been extended from white-collar staff to manual workers and there has also been a rapid growth of nationalised industry schemes. Second, at a time of rising unemployment, trade union leaders have sought new ways of inducing governments to direct finance into depressed industries (although that would not necessarily produce the best financial returns demanded in the 1975 TUC Review). The union logic of harnessing the pensions industry funds in this way – an interest that has grown with the high unemployment of 1976-7 – is that these funds really belong to the workers anyway and are simply being held pending the workers' retirement, and so should be used for the benefit of other workers. Third, there was growing trade union anger that holders of investment funds were not investing sufficiently in British manufacturing industry and so were hindering the recovery of Britain's economy. And fourth, in any case the existing management of some pension funds were not always proving to be sufficiently expert and were producing mixed results, including for example getting caught in the mid-1970s secondary banking crisis.

Handing over a significant control of pension funds to employees however raises the problem that the interests of a trade union in trying to direct pension funds into high unemployment areas and other ailing industries may well not be compatible, as has just been suggested, with an employee's own long-term interest in making sure the cash appreciates sufficiently to provide him with an adequate pension on retirement. In pure socialist terms this may not matter too much, because the State would in any case provide a large basic pension in real terms and would step in to 'save' the pension fund, so effectively killing it off in its private sector form.

Up to now however, where there has been joint union-based control of pension funds – in the nationalised industries, for example – there is no evidence of the union representatives wanting other than the best financial returns for their funds (albeit themselves too often not having sufficient expertise to know whether the fund is doing the right thing or not). For example, the funds covering employees in the coal mines, Post Office, electricity supply and local authorities have invested in property in the UK and abroad, and the electricity and Post Office funds have gone into North America. Indeed, up to now there is little significant difference in the investment strategies of funds with or without union involvement, apart from the fact that they usually steer clear of South Africa.

It is logical to assume however that this would change if there were widespread trade union involvement and this is demonstrated by the views of David Basnett, general secretary of the General and Municipal Workers, whose union is one of the most expert in Britain in the pensions field. It trains union trustees and representatives for its own and other unions and people who have passed through its hands now influence the funds of companies like British Leyland, Pilkington, GKN and Turner and Newall. Basnett explained his policies in a newspaper interview (*Daily Mail*, 20 June 1977). He said that his union was represented on the pension trustee boards of fourteen out of the country's top one hundred companies and that the trustees were trained to be aware of the 'social and economic consequences of their investment decisions'. He explained for example that the Pilkington pension fund had recently decided, because of union views, not to make an investment abroad, and he rejected a suggestion that this decision might be against the pensioners' interest by saying:

There is a self-interest at work here. If we send investment funds abroad so that our ability to create wealth declines, taxes will have to rise and our pensions will be worth less. . . . Pension funds represent an important part of our surplus wealth and we are concerned that it should not go on purposes of no economic value such as works of art or the Brighton Marina.

Mr Orme's White Paper

It is clear from this that the fairly placid, low-key and not very expert sort of union pension trustee of the past is likely to change, and central unions will want to influence the decisions that their members' representatives urge on the various funds. This will increase whatever happens to Mr Orme's 1976 White Paper because there is a trend towards increased employee, often trade union, involvement. This is happening with the backing of employers who do not object in practice to such employee influence but do object to the trade union power overtones of union members, not all employees, being given a statutory right to 50–50 representation. This is precisely the same objection as employers raise to the worker director proposals – namely, that it is one thing for companies to agree voluntarily to employee-, even union-based, involvement in management, but it is quite another thing for it to be imposed as a statutory union-based right.

In May 1977 the CBI estimated in a booklet called *Who Should Manage Pensions* that 43 per cent of the members of pension schemes in the CBI's largest companies had full participation in the investment and other management of their schemes and, of these, a fifth were trade-union based. So it claimed that there was no need for participation to be forced by legislation. Meanwhile, on the political and financial level, the City would argue that, quite apart from being ideologically wrong, union

interest in the direction of pension and other industrial investment is unnecessary because Britain's industrial problem is not a lack of cash but
how the investment is used.

Mr Orme's White Paper stemmed from a report by the Government's
Occupational Pensions Board (which itself was to be reformed as a tripartite style agency) early in 1976 suggesting that ministers should introduce a Code of Practice setting out how employers could arrange for their
employees to participate in the running of pension schemes. Mr Orme
took this and plumped for full legislation giving trade unions the statutory
right to 50–50 control of their pension schemes. He was thus applying the
TUC worker director proposals of statutory rights for union members
only to pensions control. But, also like the TUC and the Bullock Report,
he did not plan to force the trade unionists to do anything they did not
want to. He also accepted, as did the TUC in the Bullock situation, that
generally only trade unionists employed in the company–and not outside
trade union officials–should sit on the governing boards.

From one point of view Mr Orme was therefore only taking the logical
step of proposing to extend the industrial democracy ideas of worker
directors into the pensions area of a company's operations, although the
way he did it embarrassed the unions because of the political row it
caused and because of their own lack of expertise. At the same time however, from another point of view he was planning to introduce potential
trade union control of a large slice of Britain's economy–its industrial
investment. This underlines why the CBI decided, as it did with Bullock,
to mount its opposition not on the detail but on the trade union power
principle of whether such statutory rights should be vested in the trade
unions. By the spring of 1977, Mr Orme proudly declared he had a parliamentary Bill ready to present to the House of Commons. But his plans
foundered, like the full Bullock Report, in the problems caused for the
Government by its parliamentary position and in the general swing of
public opinion against institutionalising single-channel trade union
power. What would have happened to such radical proposals as Mr Orme
put forward in a different political climate is hard to judge (and the idea
has far from been forgotten in Labour circles). But in terms of 1977, he
went too far too fast, and so played into the hands of the CBI which
seized on his proposals as an even more damaging socialist plan than
worker directors.

Chapter 18
Summary

The conclusions of a survey of the spread of industrial democracy through the political, economic and industrial institutions of Britain need to cover both a consideration of whether the parties involved can cope with the changes of role required and whether the potential gains are worthwhile. There is also the question of what developments these issues point to in the future.

It was not a primary purpose of this book to map out some instant panacea for the future, but rather to illustrate, by putting them into context, that the social contract and the Bullock Report were not an aberration of a few power-hungry union leaders but were in fact logical stepping stones in what has been a continuing development of union and worker power in a modern economy. But the drawing of some conclusions is inevitable and they are based on the premise that the unions are, and will continue to be, a permanent and potentially constructive force within British society, and that to try to legislate them into insignificance would be both wrong and counter-productive within the present political system.

This suggests first that 'social contracts' will remain, with sympathetic governments, but will vary in their effectiveness as wage policies. Second, the unions sometimes, but not always, have a role in such quasi-political institutions as the Manpower Services Commission. Third, industrial democracy needs to be given a boost through legislation so that the momentum developed on employee participation in the past year or so is not lost. Despite all the problems involved, for such a law to be effective and to act as a reforming catalyst it would have to provide statutory rights for worker directors. But there is no need for the subject to be rushed. The rights need not come into force for some years and could be preceded by statutorily encouraged voluntary back-up provisions covering any and every other form of participation that employers and unions might want to try. There would also need to be stepping stones, as safeguards, providing preconditions to employees arriving in the board room.

These conclusions are based on the political reality that unions do exist, and that it is counter-productive to regard them simply as negative forces responsible for the country's economic failures and as threats to individual freedom. There is also the economic and industrial reality that the present system of confrontation does not work very well. A positive and constructive initiative is needed that encourages managements and unions to rearrange their relationships but does not try to force alien attitudes rapidly on groups that either do not want to, or could not, absorb them and benefit from them. The aims should be to expand workers' rights and to improve shopfloor co-operation and participation, while not impeding managerial efficiency, and so to increase industrial efficiency.

Compacts with governments

For many years, and especially since the Second World War, governments have tried to come to terms with the trade unions about the level of wage rises. From a wage freeze introduced in October 1948 by Sir Stafford Cripps, then Labour's chancellor of the exchequer, and on through successive Conservative governments (with a Council of Prices, Productivity and Incomes in 1957 and a National Incomes Commission in 1962) until the Labour Government started afresh (see Chapter 2) in the 1964-70 period, various mixtures of voluntary persuasion and statutory enforcement have been tried. Few have lasted more than two or three years, and the firm wage limits of the social contract have proved no exception. Gradually, however, throughout this thirty-year period since the Cripps's freeze, the trade unions have begun to exercise more influence over the formulation of the policies, and the TUC in recent years has increased its central authority to speak on behalf of the unions and then to try to persuade them to abide by agreed limits, for a time at least.

The two most significant pay policy events are of course the Heath Government's attempt at tripartism in 1972 and the Labour Government's social contract of 1974. The first showed a Conservative government trying to come to terms with the realities of union power but failing fully to understand the nature of trade unions. It was also not willing to offer sufficient changes in its own policies to 'buy' co-operation from a union movement that had been at loggerheads with it for two years over its earlier pay strategies and its labour laws.

The ensuing Labour Government did reach a compact with the unions, by offering them socialist reforms in return, ultimately, for pay restraint within the social contract'. Here the unions faced fully up to their responsibilities and, for a time at least, showed the sort of authority and willingness to stick by agreements that their critics had always called for in the past. Many of these critics however were still not satisfied, because they disapproved of the 'corporate state' overtones of governments doing deals with leaders of unions (and maybe with employers) as representatives of vested interests. And they specially disapproved of the degree to which the Labour Government gave the unions the social and industrial reforms they wanted. Then the wage restraint problems that the social contract ran into in 1977 were seized on by these critics as proof that the unions could not act responsibly and that they should never have been 'bought off' by the Government in the first place.

This is specially relevant, because it shows the problems that the unions face in Britain today; there may be parallels here between their political experience with the social contract and how their possible industrial influence in board rooms might be regarded. On the one hand, if they continue with their old-style conflict methods and refuse to do deals with governments, they will be criticised for being irresponsible. If they do deals without being seen by their members to wring some return from the Government, their deals will be ignored on the shop floor. (Indeed, the failure of the social contract to bring unemployment and prices under control led to the shopfloor dissatisfaction with this aspect of collaboration and responsibility–an attitude that some union officials were reporting led to a spin-off shopfloor reaction against any Bullock-style co-operation with management.) On the other hand, if they do deals that do wring some special policies out of the Government, and if they do design wage restraint according to their own interests, they are criticized by their detractors for having too much power over the Government and therefore over the country's affairs.

Although similar in principle, these problems are not however so great in practice as the issue of boardroom representation. This is because, to use the worker director debate analogy, compacts with governments are really 'extended collective bargaining' with unions maintaining a freedom to do or not to do a deal, and with a consequential ability to walk away from too formalised or too rigid a deal when traditional shopfloor pressures build up. The TUC is not here fully locked into the board room –that is, the Cabinet room–with all the co-operation that that would involve. On the other hand, when it walks away a little from a Government with which it has a soundly based social contract, it need not lead to outright conflict, just as unions that fail to come to terms with employers on some issue in a well ordered industrial relations procedure do not at the same time foul up all their relationships. It would of course be ludicrous (and no one is suggesting this) to try to lock the TUC, boardroom-style, into a permanent relationship with a government where wages deals had to be struck. This is because, from a purely practical point of view, leaving any constitutional or democratic issues aside, the Government would not have the freedom to govern the country and react to all the home-grown and international pressures it has to cope with. Correspondingly, the unions, being organisations that are naturally governed from the shop floor upwards rather than the union leaders downwards, need to be free to react to such shopfloor pressures, which come from all sorts of different types of workers and situations and do not have anything like the cohesion and similarity of interest that one would find in most individual companies. Only occasionally can the Jack Jones style of social contract leadership succeed, as Jones himself had to realise in 1977, when, during his final year as general secretary of his union, the wages side of the social contract which he had fostered was rejected against his wishes by his own and other unions' members.

So the industrial democratic relationship between the unions and the Government cannot be regarded as permanent and unchanging in the way that boardroom worker directors ought to be. It will change with economic fortunes, with swings in public opinion about the power of the unions, and of course with changes in the political party in power, and it may involve the inclusion of wider interests than just both sides of industry. The importance of the social contract in the longer term has been that it has shown how a responsible relationship could be fostered between the unions and a politically sympathetic government. The 1974 contract however, while providing various gains in employment and trade union law, did not eventually do enough on matters of immediate concern to individual union members such as jobs and the relationship of prices to pay.

But it will always be much more difficult for a Conservative government even to start such a deal, let alone maintain it, because Conservatives could not embrace the socialist policies wanted by the unions. As Thomas Balogh said in his 1970 Fabian Pamphlet *Labour and Inflation* (see Chapter 3), when he advocated a *'contrat social'* between the unions and the Labour Party:

. . . the Tories have their turn and we shall see how a party, whose whole economic philosophy is based on competitive pressures which are no longer effective, will cope with the problem of inflation . . . . The process of trying to frighten the unions with legislative regulation and withdrawal of supplementary benefits to strikers' families has begun. It is most unlikely that this tactic will succeed. The Tories . . . are precluded from the sort of new "Contrat Social" which is advocated . . . .

Balogh was of course writing here in the context of 1970 and the Conservatives' Industrial Relations Bill; but the pressures from back-bench Conservative MPs do not change all that much and will always make it difficult for a Conservative government to get to first base with the unions. Even when such a meeting of minds does take place, Tory ideology would make anything but the most stand-offish relationship hard to achieve. This is not to say that the TUC would refuse to have dealings with a Conservative government, or that temporary understandings could not be reached. Prior to 1964 the union leaders usually got on well with Conservative administrations, and the tradition remains that it is the TUC's job to do business with whatever political party is in power. But it is one thing to 'do business', and quite another to strike wholehearted compacts.

Tripartism in government agencies

Union leaders' involvement in the running of quasi-political Whitehall agencies such as the Manpower Services Commission is perhaps the least challenging and problematical for the role of the unions. This is because the agencies work at one or more stages removed both from the political arena of government – union compacts and from the shopfloor friction of industrial democracy in the work place. Also, the agencies are usually run by pragmatic men well used to the problems of industry who will have been chosen for their jobs partly because of their ability to come to terms with the vagaries and weaknesses of both unions and employers.

This does not mean that the unions' involvement in such agencies is unimportant, because a TUC (and CBI) presence can, for example, ease the path for employment policies to be adopted by companies and unions or can give a special credibility to the efforts of conciliators in a labour dispute. Equally however, as some problems at the Advisory Conciliation and Arbitration Service have shown, especially over union recognition issues, the presence of the TUC can introduce a bias against non-TUC unions and can sometimes even slow up back-stage work on matters that might not be wholly favoured by the TUC.

But the constitutional implications of the agencies should not be overlooked, because they do take vested industrial interests (the CBI and TUC and others) into a partial policy-making and wide-ranging executive role in government business (see Chapter 4). Ultimately, if the trend continues, the question will arise about how far such vested interests should be allowed to go outside purely, or mainly, employment issues such as jobs and training, conciliation and arbitration, health and safety at work and equal rights for women. The TUC for example has ambitions to link up with the Government and City interests in an agency on the allocation of industrial investment (Chapter 17), which would raise a lot of opposition, and in any case there are other ways (including through board rooms if they get there) that the unions could influence such a subject.

There is an added risk that an agency might collapse because of a clash either between the interests on its governing council or between it and the Government. The most vulnerable here is the Advisory Conciliation and Arbitration Service, especially in times of pay policy, when a Government might try to impose its will on conciliators, but also over other contentious issues.

Provided on balance that the co-operative approach engendered by these agencies outweighs any problems that the system might create, however, they are likely to continue to be seen as valuable ways of involving both sides of industry in improving the efficiency and standards of industry.

Co-operation at work

It would be an easy solution against the background of all the conflicts and power struggles of British industry to conclude that it would not be in the national interest to have any new laws significantly extending the power of employees at work, and especially that it would be suicidal to give them and their unions access to board rooms. On the one hand, it could be argued, managements, demoralised by years of conflict with trade unions and employees and undervalued by Labour governments and society at large, are both unwilling and ill-equipped to respond to such an almost revolutionary change in their environment, which would be disastrous for industrial efficiency. And the industrialists above them, with their interests as owners or managers, are not willing to abandon or share their positions without a massive fight.

On the other hand, union leaders, hungry for power, are apparently unwilling and incapable of taking responsibility for the agreements they sign. Certainly they should not be allowed to extend their power-bargaining and their lack of reliability into new areas of company affairs, let alone into the board rooms that so successfully run British industry today. Indeed, the union leaders themselves do not know whether the workers' representatives would be co-operating or engaging in conflict were they to be in the board rooms. And in any case, it could be added, the union members have shown no interest in their union officials or shop stewards becoming managers or directors or in the affairs or the long-term well-being of their company: all they want is their pay packets every week so long as they choose to be employed.

There is however an alternative view, which is less glib and somewhat more rádical and it is the main conclusion of this book. It starts off by recognising that unions exist, that they represent a growing number of workers who want some sort of collective representation, that they are therefore an established part of British life, but that they could become more constructive in their operations.

As far as individual workers are concerned, many British companies often seem to take too little positive account of their employees' interests, whatever many industrialists and senior managers may claim. What companies do do of course is to take their employees into account in the interests of the shareholders, not for the employees' own sake. Thus employees' interests will be watched on a negative basis by managements wanting to ensure that their plans are not thwarted by industrial action or other employee opposition. So, for example, in the interests of the shareholders they will need to design redundancy payment schemes that allow them to shut factories as economically and with as little fuss as possible. Now this may well be good and efficient management and is often necessary for industrial success. But it should not be confused with employees' interests being taken into account for their own sake. It is a conclusion of this book that employees' interests *should* be taken equally into account, and that this logically means (as even the minority industrialists' group on the Bullock Committee recognised) that they need some boardroom representation to guard those interests.

Next, the pace of industrial and economic change has now reached a point where trade unions can no longer (if they ever could) effectively represent the aspirations of their members through shopfloor bargaining or company- or industry-level pay deals. This is because the major decisions that dictate the terms of one day's shopfloor bargaining or what a company or industry can afford to pay will have been considerably determined by board- or other senior management-level decisions weeks or even years earlier. So any employer who acknowledges (as most do) the right of his employees to be represented by unions on pay and allied employment matters should recognise their right to a say in the wider business decisions that affect their working lives.

That is the argument for the employees' *right* to be represented by unions on a wider scale. The industrial logic that supports this right stems from the fact that many companies and industries do not at present function effectively. Managers too often fail to manage efficiently; unions fail to honour their bargains or adopt constructive industrial policies; and the two together do not make either a very profitable partnership or a very constructive conflict. Because of increased education and affluence mixed with shopfloor and bureaucratic frustration and occasional economic hardships, employees are therefore losing whatever faith they may have had in the system. The result is alienation from work, and industrial and economic failure.

One solution is to find a catalyst that might change the attitudes that lie behind these failings rapidly enough to force the necessary changes but slowly enough not to do more harm than good in the process. This would require the involvement of the unions through their individual members in a wider and more responsible role in company affairs, which should be recognised by the community as their right, in the hope that the new involvement and management changes that it would create would remove some of Britain's industrial conflict.

Catalysts through the board room

For such a catalyst to have an effect, it needs to be contained in legislation so that it acts as a spur to managements and unions to continue the move towards increased employee participation that the debate of the past few years, and especially the Bullock Report, has helped to engender.

Despite all the problems involved, a statutory right to board representation of employees – that is a worker director system – is almost certainly the only possible single innovation that would be legally enforceable without upsetting the voluntary system of British labour relations, that could encourage co-operation rather than conflict, and that could correspondingly encourage managements and unions to reform their systems. It could give a new legitimacy to the job of management which would have a chance to manage by consent (as the Bullock Report said) and could give a new legitimacy of positive and constructive authority to trade union shop stewards who are the real power and responsibility centres of a work force and of a trade union. (It is no good harnessing the co-operation of the union leaders if the shop stewards remain in opposition.) Just as the trade-off for national governments in social contracts is union acceptance of pay policies, so the trade-off in shopfloor-based industrial democracy should be co-operation in increasing industrial efficiency – and this could become the benefit for the community.

The two main alternatives to worker directors – CBI-style participation agreements and the union-backed extended collective bargaining – would not have the same potential advantages. The participation agreements (which the CBI proposed as *gifts of management* rather than *rights of workers*) would be too slow in moving towards significant participation because in their early years many of them would almost certainly be involved only with communications and limited consultation. They could however be regarded as one of the stepping-stones to worker directors.

The unions' alternative of extended collective bargaining does not rate as a potential statutory solution on its own. First, it would be extremely difficult to enforce (as would participation agreements) without the risk of moving down the American-style road of legally binding agreements and arbitrations with definitions of when an employer is or is not bargaining in good faith. Such a legalistic approach is not the purpose of the exercise. Second, and more important, extended collective bargaining would not produce rapid results and could extend conflict-based bargaining without the potential of a boardroom participative approach. Third, if extended to its logical conclusion with union-negotiated agreements on all major company affairs, it could impede efficient flexible management far more than having employee representatives in the board room. On the other hand, like participation agreements, it might be the best path for some managements and unions to agree voluntarily to follow, especially since it would not force changes of role where they might be counter-productive.

Giving a statutory right to worker directors would of course (as has been seen since the Bullock Committee was set up) create a major stir among industrialists. They would complain (not surprisingly) of the risk of trade union bargaining being transferred from the shop floor and the negotiating table into the board rooms, so that rational policy decisions could no longer be taken. They would quite understandably say that unions have not shown themselves able or willing to shoulder permanent boardroom-style responsibility, that company management would be disrupted, and that managers at all levels would be de-motivated.

Many of these risks have been quite genuinely advanced by industrialists and managers who have been aroused to near fury by the singlemindedness of the Bullock Report's allegiance to the TUC cause. One of the main problems of the report, as has already been said, stemmed from the terms of reference that the TUC won in Whitehall battles during 1975 (see Chapter 14), which directed it down the TUC's path and alienated all its opponents. Whether the primary opposition to the whole notion of changing the status and power relationships of industry through a worker director system would have been just as strong however the report may have been presented, is open to argument.

Flexibility and safeguards
The lesson to be learned from the exercise may be that if Britain were to travel further down this path a government would need to work for the greatest consent possible. This consent need not be won in the way that several Labour Cabinet ministers wanted during the post-Bullock Report debate, by watering down the union content – and therefore the potential impact of a union-based worker director system. The alternative could be to approach the issue gradually and flexibly – much in the style of the Government's mid-1977 draft White Paper – while recognising and accepting the reality of the presence of unions. A date could be set – maybe five years from the day legislation comes into force – for the unions to have a statutory right to instigate a worker director system by the broad methods suggested in the Bullock Report.

To stop companies being irrationally impeded by a rush of badly based union claims, one could find a number of safeguards and other options. First, there could be the three- to five-year gap. Second, there could be stages to be reached during this period such as – most importantly – all the unions' shop stewards coming together on a joint body (like the Bullock Report's joint representation committee) in dealings with management, say, two years before the final date to show that they could work together. If the inter-union friction that might develop in many companies made such a co-operation between all the unions impractical, then there need be no statutory right to board representation because it would be against everyone's interests to burden a board with employee representatives of unions that had not even started to be able to work together. But such a situation need not stop other forms of voluntary participation.

Other stepping-stones – including CBI-style participation agreements – could also be built in, and even when the initial five years had elapsed there could still be a run-in period of perhaps three years for any new scheme, with minority worker representation *en route*. Consideration might also be given to providing an appeal system for managements that felt they could mount a case that board representation was prejudicial to the *joint interests* of their employees and shareholders, as well as a special employees' seat being given, at least to begin with, on a joint board to a senior management representative.

Perhaps the most important safeguard would be for the subject not to be approached in the singleminded way of the Bullock Report. One answer therefore would be to set up an agency (the Bullock Report called it an Industrial Democracy Commission) that would be charged with encouraging and assisting any and all forms of employee participation and industrial democracy that employers and unions–together or separately– might ask for. This work could be backed up by some form of code of practice setting out all these options, which could range from basic communication, job enrichment and profit-sharing to workers' co-operatives, extended collective bargaining and voluntary worker directors. The result could be that, while the statutory right would ultimately apply only to worker directors, there would be statutorily backed (but not enforced) encouragement for all forms of participation. Any legal enforceability of these other methods would create such problems that it is not worth considering, but they could be statutorily encouraged by managements and unions both being required to submit, jointly or separately, annual reports of the innovations they had introduced and of the progress of established practices, say, to the Departments of both Employment and Trade (or any new agency). The requirement to do it jointly or separately might well put an onus on unions to assess progress and might also sometimes prevent managements presenting bromide summaries.

The objective of all this would be to use the catalyst of a worker director law to induce reforms in companies so that, while some would eventually 'trigger' a worker director system, others would use the statutory encouragement of the code of practice to use other methods. Most important of all, the development of legislation should not be seen by either unions or managements as a Bullock-style crusade for a specific form of worker directors. Given that flexibility, it might avoid the pitfalls of appearing prejudiced.

A boardroom scheme and individual rights

To be effective as a catalyst both to management and unions, and to provide the employees with a proportional voice, there would probably ultimately have to be the possibility of parity on a board between the shareholders' and employees' representatives; a minority of employee representatives however is a logical stepping-stone to a full system and would allow new relationships to be tried out first. Some third voice beyond a single lonely chairman might well also be introduced when parity was reached as an answer to the problem of breaking dea dlock and introducing outside views (like but not necessarily identical to the Bullock '$2x + y$' formula). The arguments for and against parity and for how many tiers of board there ought to be have been discussed in the chapters on Bullock. One of the most effective solutions has seemed to be to introduce the parity representation on what has come to be known as the '1½-tier' solution, where the employee representatives sit with industrialists on the company's main policy board which has considerable powers. There is then a clearly defined separate day-to-day management level below, whose duties the Policy Board has a distinct role in fixing. Decisions would then have to be made about how to relate below-board-level participation to that management tier, so that the worker directors did not find themselves losing face with the shop floor because of a lack of employee involvement in executing policy decisions reached by the main board.

The operation of the board representation would generally have to be based on trade unions, because the unions are almost always the representative organisations for bringing management and employees collectively together (as recent employment legislation has recognised). To base the operation on all employees without any recognition of single-channel concepts would be illogical: not only would it disrupt existing union-based employer–employee relationships, but it would also cast away the potential catalytic effect that board representation, and the moves during the run-up years, could have on inter-union co-operation and the expertise and efficiency and responsibility of unions and shop stewards.

Of course, there is the compelling argument that the rights of individuals should not be obliterated by union power. Concern about this raises the question of whether the industrial logic of basing the operation of worker directors on the unions is strong enough to justify pushing aside the interests of non-union minorities and vesting the actual *statutory rights* on the unions. The easy answer (and the one that gained a lot of support in the post-Bullock debate) would be to reject the overtones of union power and plump for all-employee rights. The supporting industrial logic would be that, since about three-quarters of workers in large companies likely to be affected by any legislation are already unionised, the unions would dominate the operation of the system whoever had the rights. But to follow that argument might waste the chance of the catalyst for industrial reform, because it would cause endless arguments in individual companies about the precise rights and operating roles of the unions and so might dissipate the essential shop steward support that would be needed to make a worker director system operate constructively. For that reason, the alternative of vesting the statutory rights in unions recognised by a company, with strong recommendations about the need to recognise and accommodate identifiable non-union groups, and with provision for all employees to vote in some key ballots, could lead to a better system.

This does not mean that non-unionised workers need be denied board representation, because giving statutory rights to one group of people (in this case members of trade unions) does not deny the right to others voluntarily to apply for board seats, with the possible encouragement but not the enforcement of the law.

It is those people in basically unionised companies but whose own area of that company – say middle and senior management – is traditionally not unionised that would lose out when the mass of unionised groups in their company elected their representatives to the board room. This group, which first makes up a sizeable proportion of the company's employees and second partially holds those key positions in management, will feel the maximum pressure from any participation schemes. They therefore need not only their normal employee rights, but also special constructive motivation. The orthodox, ideological union view is that they should, in pure 'single-channel' style, be excluded till they join the union. The liberal individual-rights approach is to give them equal rights to board-room representation. This might well be an industrially disruptive solution, because more often than not a white-collar union with members closest in status to the special group would object to their inclusion, owing to an instinctive objection to non-unionists and a practical hope that exclusion might force the people concerned into its membership.

So the best industrial answer might lie between these two extremes and could involve those concerned gaining representation in the board room either by joining an established union (which could be encouraged by any industrial democracy code of practice) or by forming their own independent staff association, which would have to gain certification as being independent of the company to gain recognition and therefore the rights. This second alternative would be strenuously opposed by the TUC because it would mean giving some recognition to non-TUC organisations, but it might be the best answer, especially for senior management. Despite such opposition, there could also be a case for a senior management representative to have a seat on a board, if not in the employees' group then at least among any third grouping.

Could it work – could people cope?

This leaves the question posed at the beginning of the chapter about whether the people and organisations involved can cope with such a change in their methods of operating and whether the potential gains are worthwhile. It is at this point that any advocate of a worker director system (unless he is ideologically committed to the idea as a means of changing society) will have to admit that such a move is something of a leap in the dark, especially since the result will, if it is successful, mean a radical change in industrial society.

The issue of the power-oriented aspects of the TUC's policies have been discussed earlier in this book in relation to the more conservative employee participation notions of industrialists, and the question must be left open as to whether ultimately the unions, with all their adversary traditions, will be willing and able to put enough of their conflict on one side to co-operate constructively with management in the creation of the wealth of industry, even if the conflict still breaks out over how that wealth is to be shared out.

The reservations of industrialists loath to chance the future of their board rooms in such a gamble (precisely illustrated in the Ford Motor quotation used in the introduction to this book about whether the unions wanted 'coalition' or 'constructive conflict') is fully understandable. But since industrialists have been working for years to turn the present, often destructive, conflict in industry into a more positive and constructive relationship and have too often been unsuccessful, a more radical approach can hold attractions. Reservations will quite understandably remain, however, so a slow introduction period for any scheme, plus government-sponsored encouragement for virtually any other sort of participation, would lessen the problem while not necessarily diluting the overall catalytic impact on management and unions. A final fall-back of an appeal from a management when it feels the livelihood of its business could be endangered would be another protection.

Overall, there is no reason why managements should not be able to accommodate the introduction of a direct employee voice into their topmost deliberations; and, from the point of view of sheer organisation and time required, board representation holds few problems that would not apply to any other participation or extended bargaining system reaching up into the higher levels of a company. So industrialists who argue about the time-consuming and organic problems are really complaining about participation in general, not about worker directors in particular. And, in the context of wider union and worker involvement in management affairs, participation of some sort or other will come.

It is true of course that employees so far have shown little interest in doing much about the wider ambitions of some of their union leaders, even though they might realise the potential advantages. But the union leaders themselves, apart from one or two at the TUC and elsewhere, have done little to start a debate on the issue of widening the role of employee influence. It is in fact much easier for the average run-of-the-mill union leader to opt for the extended bargaining option (which need involve him in little extra expertise or effort) – or to opt for nothing at all – than it is to grapple with the wider ramifications of board representation for his shop stewards. Equally, it is easier for a union official to concentrate on his present pay and employment conditions questions than to raise enthusiasm about an involvement for him or his shop stewards in wider issues – especially since shop stewards in board rooms could reduce the powers of the outside union official. This lethargy is not only the union official's fault: rather it is the fault of the shoestring approach to the business of trade unions adopted by most union leaders. It is also the result of a fear among general secretaries and others that building efficient and ambitious research and other bureaucracies within union headquarters and branches might provide power-bases for far-left theorists who will try to change the unions.

However, union officials might gain a different response if they went out and explained to their members that they had within their grasp the potential to take part in key decision-making that would affect livelihoods in the future.

There is of course also a conflict between the natural short-term interests of the shop floor and the longer-term interests of board members who should be making decisions based not on the size of next week's pay packet but on technological, commercial, political or other considerations of the next five years or so. This time-scale conflict of interest, which could also apply to any wide-ranging participation once the workers' horizon is lifted above the shop floor, is sometimes put forward as a reason why workers and directors cannot be compatible. But this need not be true. Just because union members up to now have naturally fixed their sights on the time-scale dictated by their own area of influence, the pay packet, does not mean that they would not gradually see the sense of longer-term horizons (and so quite possibly ease the top managers' jobs) if they were given an opportunity to participate in the wider decisions involved.

This is a different argument (although they are often blurred together) from the more often accurate suggestion that union members do not want their stewards or officials to become involved in the job of taking management decisions. But even this bland assertion might prove to be somewhat erroneous if the opportunity to take part in the making of management decisions were advertised as being an effort to make the shop stewards' job a more positive, rather than merely reactionary, occupation.

All this still leaves the primary problem of how to fit the participative style of boardroom representation with the unions' traditional collective bargaining on wages and other issues and with regular management systems. This is not a question of union expertise (which could and should be improved): nor of management or union resistance to change; nor of shop stewards being unsure of their role when they find themselves party to unpleasant decisions; nor a question of whether stewards are participating or bargaining in the board room (because for many years the relationship will be that of bargainers). Rather it is a question of whether union members would be prepared to allow their representatives to be locked into a relationship in the board room which agreed redundancies, or the overall size of the company's annual financial budget that is to be allocated to wages—and then to use their normal bargaining only to sort out how the redundancies would be effected or to divide the wages proceeds up between them. This is perhaps the most difficult question of all and it is the risk of disputes arising from this—and the tensions of the 'balance of power confidentiality' problem discussed in Chapter 7—that could break a worker director system. It would have to be worked out company by company and some worker director schemes could fail as a result.

Such problems are not a reason for blindly turning away from the potential catalyst for reform. It is more constructive to accept that British trade unions are based on bargaining traditions, that they will not immediately change their nature by going into the board rooms, but that the opportunity for them to do so might help to speed the reform of the operation of British industry, with managements harnessing co-operation of their shop stewards who in turn, as part of the union movement, gain new rights and responsibilities whether they eventually decide to finish up in the board room or not.

It was forward thinking such as this which lay behind the Labour Government's May 1978 White Paper on industrial democracy, with its proposals for extended consultation and worker directors, and behind other developments in 1978 such as worker directors being introduced to both the Post Office and British Steel main boards. These and other moves showed a positive way forward.

The other alternative is for companies to continue the conflict with the unions, slowly reducing it on the fringe by means of communications and other exercises. Some companies might move towards power-sharing of a participative nature at their own speed, that is very slowly, with little real constructive participation but some 'sham democracy'. Union leaders could of course continue to do their occasional deals in Downing Street but in the main would be forced by industrial and political realities to leave their shop stewards (where the union power really lies) to carry on with traditional conflict tactics. The unions and managements would remain as they have been for years, and there would be no constructive pressures on them to change the way they run their own affairs, the way they relate to each other, or the way unions often fail to shoulder responsibilities and the managements fail to respond effectively.

That is the easy answer, the one that has done Britain little good over the past few decades.

Part IV
Addendum 1983

Chapter 19

The Start of the Thatcherite '80s

The two alternatives posed at the end of the last chapter were for Britain to embrace systems of industrial democracy such as worker directors or to continue with the industrial conflict which had done the country little good in the past. In May 1979 a Conservative Government came to power with Mrs Margaret Thatcher as Prime Minister, and showed during a devastating recession that there is another possible route to the reduction of conflict in industry and to the management of a stable economy.

Mrs Thatcher's Government harnessed the impact of the recession, which started in 1979-80, and sharpened its effects – with a consequent escalation of unemployment to well above 3 million – before she was re-elected in 1983. There was political support for those who wanted to curb trade union power and shun collectivism and consensus policies, because the Government adhered to harsh economic disciplines. The new legitimacy for the role of management, sought by some of the supporters of the Bullock Report in the late 1970s, was therefore achieved (at least temporarily) by putting trade unions and workers out of work instead of putting them into the boardroom.

In the private sector a tough Government stand on issues like the level of interest rates, sterling and State industrial aid enabled managers to respond positively and toughly to market forces. Responding also to rapidly changing markets and production technologies, companies sliced with initial enthusiasm through unnecessary waste. They then cut even more deeply, but often more reluctantly, into the base of British manufacturing industry. Labour forces of some companies such as GKN, Unilver, Dunlop and ICI were cut by up to 30 to 50 per cent. In the public sector, while the surgery was less harsh, Mrs Thatcher's determination not to succumb to most of the pressures for leniency accepted by her predecessors led to similar changes and to confrontations which the Government usually won.

There was also legislation aimed at limiting trade union operations on subjects such as closed shops and picketing and on cutting legal immunities for some forms of industrial action.

The debate about the legitimacy of trade union influence and worker power on which the premises of the 1970s ideas were based was therefore turned upside down. Industrial democracy was neither well enough developed nor widely enough accepted to grow during an industrial and economic crisis. Trade union leaders were on the retreat, and workers were not likely to be interested in trying to share responsibility for industrial decline.

'You don't have democracy in a lifeboat – not if you have any sense – and for many companies today and in the future lifeboats may be the order of the day,' said Sir Alex Jarratt, chairman of Reed International (*Financial Times* 25 September, 1980) in a comment that summed up the prevailing mood but perhaps over-estimated the length of time that dictatorial rule can last.

But as Lord Bullock observed on the day his report was published, the subject of employee representation will not go away. There is always the possibility of British legislation on industrial democracy emerging from membership of the Common Market. There is also the chance of home-bred legislation: both the Labour Party and the new Social Democratic-Liberal Alliance had policies derived from the Bullock debate in their 1983 general election manifestoes.

The threat of such legislation, however distant, means that both the Thatcher Government and organisations such as the Confederation of British Industry constantly warn that companies might one day be forced statutorily to develop policies if they do not do so voluntarily. However employers were motivated more during the 1979-83 period by a need merely to communicate with their employees in order to prepare the way for the cutbacks of the recession. At the same time, employers' interest in increasing the economic involvement of employees led to a slow steady increase in profit-sharing and share ownership scheme. The rising levels of unemployment also helped to stimulate worker interest in another form of industrial democracy: worker co-operatives.

Tripartism out of fashion

There was little room in the early 1980s for the tripartite notions of the earlier decade. The crumbling of the social contract (see page 61), which failed eventually to serve the interests of either the Labour Government or trade union members, cast serious doubt on the viability of pacts between Governments and trade unions. Although Mr Jack Jones during his heyday looked like one of Britain's great national leaders of the twentieth century, he failed to provide the leadership needed for the labour movement to emerge from the failing social contract. And he also lost the support of grass root trade union members who, in turn, undermined the image of trade unionism in the 1978-79 'winter of discontent'. Moreover, Mr Jones failed to groom a powerful successor to follow him when he retired, and the trade union movement had no leader of importance or significance during the period of the first Thatcher Government.

But at an economic and industrial level tripartism continued, albeit in a lower gear, through institutions such as the NEDC, MSC and ACAS, which kept trade union representation on their governing councils. The NEDC's economic development committees (Little Neddies) covering individual sectors of industry remained in being, though with less sense of purpose than in the late 1970s. Sir Geoffrey Howe, the Conservative Chancellor of the Exchequer from 1979 to 1983, constantly stressed his own interest and support for Neddy activities. But the top council — the NEDC — had little impact.

From democracy to involvement

The Bullock debate of the late 1970s had a seminal effect on management thinking that far exceeded the impact of the Bullock Report itself. Hurried along by the possible threat of legislation, many companies in manufacturing industry — especially large concerns — introduced new systems of employee consultation and tried to involve their employees in some decision-making on issues close to their daily working lives. Some of the initiatives were mere tokens and many companies did nothing at all. But, starting from a low base, what was done was significant.

The election of the Thatcher administration removed the immediate threat of Bullock-style legislation although Mr Jim Prior, Employment Secretary from 1979 to 1981 and a 'wet' from the Left-wing of the Conservative Party, said he would like to enfranchise legally the views of long service employees. Speaking personally he said in 1980 'I have a very strong view that it is wrong that an employee with 40 years' service, who is not a shareholder, does not have a say in the future of his company and whether it is taken over'. However such ideas came to nought and the prospect of early legislation receded. As a result some managers felt more free to experiment with shopfloor involvement now that they did not have to explain their actions in the context of Bullockry. But the more usual reaction was to slow down progress because the issue was no longer on the agenda for action by top management.

Then the Thatcher ethos of lauding individualism at the expense of collectivism caught on. Many managers in the private sector discovered that they could often take decisions without having to negotiate, let alone consult, with their union representatives. Personnel and line managers in both the public and private sectors by 1982-3 could be heard condeming the way that the trends of the 1970s had made their employee relationships too 'meetings-orientated'. This was specially prevalent in businesses such as BL and the Post Office which had been the subject of major industrial democracy experiments (see next chapter). But throughout British industry those companies which were genuinely concerned about 'employee involvement', as the subject came to be called, continued to develop direct means of contact with employees. They used Japanese-style quality circles, briefing groups and other means, including new forms of electronic communication, to try to harness the support of employees for the dramatic changes being forced by the recession, by rapid technological advance and by increased competition, especially from the Far East.

Those companies which had little genuine interest in involving their employees, also saw the need for greater communication in advance of bad news. They increased their information-flow to employees but not their consultation. As a result there was a lot of exaggeration during the period 1979-83 about how much companies were really doing to improve employee involvement (the words 'participation' and 'industrial democracy' almost disappeared from common usage). Organisations like the CBI produced surveys and other evidence to prove that improvements were being made and over-estimated the improvements. The surveys were not always accurate, often reflecting what companies thought the survey organisers wanted to hear.

Some industrialists were concerned about how little was really being done in many companies. Between 1980 and 1983, two successive CBI presidents — Sir Ray (later Lord) Pennock and Sir Cambell Fraser — made a theme of the need for more to be done and the CBI issued employee involvement guidelines in September 1979.

A more radical stance was taken by Sir David Orr, then chairman of

Unilever, who called for a 'bargain' between individual companies and their unions in which 'more information and full consultation' would be offered by a company in return for 'the certainty that no one will go on strike except as a last resort and after all procedures have been exhausted' (*Financial Times* 10 November, 1981).

The swing away from collectivism was underlined by Dr James McFarlane, director general of the EEF and a former GKN senior executive, at the CBI's annual conference on 2 November, 1982: 'There are two quite different ways of looking at employee involvement and participation. One is mechanistic and related to structures. The other is organic and related to people'. He then incorrectly added: 'The two views are not mutually supportive. They are opposed'.

This remark was aimed at underlining the tough anti-legislation line being taken by the EEF, but it also revealed how opposed the EEF is to any significant advance on participation because it is quite possible for a willing employer to merge the two 'mechanistic' and 'people-related' approaches.

But the main interest among most companies by this time was to use communication to persuade workers to accept bad news rather than to build new and co-operative methods of involving workers in the running of companies. The challenge as the economic climate changed would be for companies to adopt more positive involvement policies, if only to avoid the risk of an employee backlash.

Chapter 20

Systems

Backwards and forwards – some practical examples

The following sketches illustrate the trends of the 1979-83 period by looking at some of the examples dealt with originally in Chapters 11, 12 and 13. They show the collapse of the forced experiments of the late 1970s at British Leyland, the Post Office and the British Steel Corporation. As will be seen, too little attention was paid in advance to what these schemes were supposed to achieve and to how they would relate both to executive management and traditional labour relations. And they all fell foul of the Thatcherite management style. (The Harland and Wolff plans never got off the ground. Consultation in the public utilities and the coal industry – which are not dealt with in this chapter – dropped back to old-style public sector arrangements, shedding the more adventurous participation ideas of the 1970s.)

In the private sector there are two main examples to illustrate the best that happened. The experience at ICI shows how a well-based system can weather storms, while Unilever shows how a series of consultative company councils have been expanded voluntarily and slowly, despite the political and economic climate. One or two other examples are briefly mentioned. Finally, there are accounts of the expansion of worker co-operatives, which became more significant, and of the development of profit-sharing and pension fund management.

A short life at BL

The elaborate system of participation committees introduced in BL at the beginning of 1976 lasted little more than two years. It was hit progressively by management and trade union frustration, by the arrival of a new tough management style when Mr (later Sir) Michael Edwardes became chairman, and eventually by the sudden closure of the Triumph factory at Speke in Liverpool early in 1978 following a bitter 17-week strike.

Mr Pat Lowry (who retired from BL early in 1981 to become chairman of the Advisory, Concilliation and Arbitration Service) remarked in 1975, that employee participation was a 'delicate flower' which could 'wither in the frost of managerial suspicion and mistrust' (see page 158). This happened so quickly that Mr Lowry's greater fear that it would 'perish through over-exposure to the hot house of our political system' did not have time to be realised. It was not Thatcher nor even Edwardes, but the system's own deficiencies, which were really to blame, although it is extremely doubtful whether it could have survived for long in the tough and explicit approach to problem solving favoured by Edwardes.

Three tiers of committees were set up in 1976, and the system was in full swing later that year in the cars section of BL, with truck and bus division following more slowly. But the aims, as opposed to the structure, of the system were not set down specifically enough by the 1975 Ryder Report. In keeping with the mood of the time, the system was over-formalised and meetings-oriented rather than topics-oriented. Trade unions refused to discuss anything that was part of their traditional collective bargaining, and management shield away from contentious issues because they were scared the shop steward union representatives would walk out. Issues such as closures, redundancies and manning were not dealt with, and fundamental problems such as quality and productivity were touched on only superficially and in general terms. Productivity issues in particular were avoided by employee representatives lest they undermined their separate collective bargaining positions.

'Participation developed a life of its own that had little to do with the real business' said one senior manager. 'For example it was debating whether we ought to be producing 1 million or 2 million cars a year when in fact we were so uncompetitive we were only managing 600,000 and falling. It was all based on the belief that the Labour Government would turn BL into an engine of change by funding a high-wage and job-secure business. But nothing was being done on basic problems of design, or over-capacity, or manning. Managements were diverted by all the industrial democracy from doing the things they ought to have done'.

Union officials were firmly excluded from the system, partly because the architects (BL management plus the Ryder Committee's resident expert, Mr Harry Urwin of the TGWU) were trying to harness the loyalty, energy and commitment of shop stewards for a new era of labour relations. But, as sceptics had forecast from the start, the shop stewards who were members of participation committees tended to become detached from the shopfloor. Quite often, those on the top committee were also unable to communicate properly with their members because of the confidential or complex nature of the information they received.

The shop stewards became disillusioned when they discovered that they could not have a major impact on management decisions in any one meeting. Like many proponents of industrial democracy in the 1970s, they had mistakenly imagined that management decisions were suddenly taken at a given point in time and that, by obtaining a voice at the appropriate level in the company, they could influence those decision. They did not understand that management decisions gradually evolved at many levels in a company and could not be so easily hijacked.

By the time Edwardes arrived as chairman in November 1977, managers were becoming disillusioned and cynical. The shop stewards were also far from happy but were unwilling to give up what had been gained. It quickly became clear that participation through lengthy discussion was not the Edwardes style and this was proved when the Speke closure was anounced with no debate. The unions then tried to get the system changed and lodged demands which included seats on the board and a right to veto management decisions. When these ideas were rejected they withdrew in September 1979 and the experiment was over. 'The participation procedure is not working as it should. Decisions are being brought to the table, put before the committee, and that is the end of the story' Mr Grenville Hawley, national secretary of the TGWU had said a little earlier (*Financial Times* 17 March, 1979).

But it was not all total failure. Some managers say that an understanding obtained in 1976 and 1977 on productivity targets for the new Mini — later named the Metro — enabled that car to be launched in 1980 with far less trouble than was usual for important new models. Some pension and health and safety arrangements also evolved from the participation system and some of the shop floor committees still exist under different names. It could well be argued that this list of achievements should be regarded as sufficient achievement for the first two years of a new system.

Researchers from the Tavistock Institute sat in on the participation exercise throughout and their early findings showed that the scheme had worked well at the top level. Senior shop stewards, such as the controversial Derek Robinson from Longbridge (who was sacked during the Edwardes era in a controversial demonstration of managerial prerogative), became highly co-operative and involved. But the role and performance of lower level committees were not so good. Overall the system might have performed better if it had survived for longer, but it is arguable that it had no chance of exerting influence on management decisions in a company that was tackling a major high-speed turn-round programme such as that adopted under Edwardes.

Such a radical change in industrial relations systems, accompanied by the rough management style of many of BL's plant managers introduced during the Edwardes era, carries the risk of a backlash. A long strike at BL's Cowley plant in the spring of 1983 showed how a workforce can eventually react. The union official who took control of the strike, Mr David Buckle of the TGWU, indicated the build-up of frustration almost a year earlier: 'This has been a dam-building period for management which has clawed back 40 years of trade union advance. There's practically no shop steward involvement in shopfloor targets and conditions. At present it is a waste of time to put a view to management that they don't want to hear' (*Financial Times* 23 August, 1982).

By 1983 BL had developed a less far-ranging and formal system of communication and consultation. This was basically aimed at reducing contact with full-time trade union officials to a minimum and expanding management communications with individuals and small groups of employees so that employees and trade union representatives were kept informed without reducing managerial prerogatives. A new general procedure agreement signed in April 1982 for BL cars had a section called 'provision of information'. It included a BL Cars Review to meet twice a year, attended by management with shop stewards negotiators and full-time union officers, to discuss 'business matters of significance which are relevant to the company as a whole'. Plant Reviews were also provided for following the Cars Review meeting, and a middle tier was developed in some subsidiary product companies like Jaguar.

This is basically a communication system with little consultation, let alone participation, although some relevant consultation has developed in a few plant committees. The emphasis is on passing information to small groups and individual employees and on harnessing support for management decisions through quality circles, briefing groups video films, and other similar methods.

In another exercise more akin to involvement in job design than ordinary participation, workers from various levels and skills in parts of Austin-Rover were being involved during 1982-83 in value engineering studies on problems like the design and production of particular parts of a car to make them easier or cheaper to produce and to improve shopfloor methods and layout.

Disagreement in the Post Office

The Post Office worker director system, introduced at the beginning of 1978, was not a success. It was terminated at the end of 1979, when its two-year experimental period expired, by an antipathetic Government acting at the behest of an unsympathetic top management.

Like other developments in the 1970s, too little attention had been paid during the gestation period to the practical managerial purposes, as opposed to the procedures and structures, of the new board. 'No one ever decided precisely what it was supposed to do and there was no common agreement or understanding about the objectives,' says one expert closely involved. The board, with a total of 19 members, was too large to be an effective decision-taking body and the real power lay elsewhere, notably in a monthly executive management board meeting.

The union people involved were all full-time professional or lay union officials, as their designation of union nominated members (UNMs) indicated. They received no special boardroom pay. Some had worked in the Post Office for as long as 30 years, a statistic which the TUC later contrasted critically with the fact that most of the management on the board were new to the industry.

There were four national executive members who were Post Office employees on full-time secondment to their unions as well as three trade union employees — the POEU's research officer and a national organising secretary and treasurer from the UPW (later renamed the Union of Communication Workers). The main function of these union nominees was to attend the monthly Post Office board meeting. But they were not fully occupied at other times because they were barred from any trade union negotiating work. So they tended to pester management and pursue less controversial industrial relations issues. In the board meetings they often only contributed on issues in an industrial relations context, which they felt was right during the experimental period because it was here that their expertise lay. However they also usually shied away from contributing to boardroom debates on major labour issues and disputes because of potential conflicts of interest — although one or two sometimes gave hints of their own or their unions' views. The UPW representatives were criticised at their union's conference in 1978 for having taken a boardroom stand against UPW policy on Sunday postal collections. Overall, their behaviour often irritated management. Sir William Barlow, who became chairman of the Post Office in 1977 from an engineering industry background, found the lengthy union-inspired debates in the boardroom hard to tolerate.

There is however room for doubt about how much top management tried to involve the union members. 'We are not expected to formulate policies but to give advice on their policy initiatives — and that's something of a limitation', commented Mr Peter Shaw, one of the POEU's two members, (*Financial Times* 22 May, 1979). 'We don't vote. It's not a faction fight and we sit all mixed up together. But it's a chairman's consensus and the chairman is a strong man who likes to have his own way.'

There have been suggestions that the management in the telecommunications part of the business were less in favour of the whole experiment than those in the postal part. Certainly Mr Shaw felt that the degree of management commitment needed to make the experiment a success was lacking. The unions did however benefit from having a considerably increased amount of management information. A code of confidentiality and disclosure was agreed and most information obtained could be taken back to meetings of union executive committees.

Eventually, after labour problems in the Post Office worsened over issues such as the shorter working week, it was clear that the experiment had not improved industrial relations. Nor had it met other jointly agreed criteria concerned with improving the effectiveness and speed of the making and implementation of management decisions. The management then decided not to join with the unions in asking for the experiment to be continued after the first two years. Led by Sir William Barlow, the management felt that the business was being damaged by the slowing down of boardroom decisions and by the union members' problems with conflict of interest. The trade unions disagreed and complained that there had not been enough time for such a dramatic experiment to settle down and prove its worth. But Sir Keith Joseph, the Industry Secretary, had little love for such boardroom expressions of trade union power and was quite happy to follow the line requested by Sir William (who resigned in 1980 because he had had enough of life in the politically fraught goldfish bowl of the nationalised industries). In an announcement from the Department of Industry on 12 December, 1979, Sir Keith noted that 'broadly the unions are in favour of a continuation whilst management and a majority of the independent members of the board are not'. In the 'absence of agreement that the two year experiment should continue the board appointments made for the purpose of that experiment will terminate at the end of the year'.

At board level Morrisonian-style representation returned on its own. Mr Derek Gladwin, southern regional secretary of the GMWU, who had sat on the old board, was given a seat on the Post Office board. And Mr John Lyons, general secretary of the EPEA, sat on the British Telecom Board till he announced his resignation in July 1983 in protest at the second Thatcher Government's plan to sell a majority control of the business to the private sector.

During 1978 union nominees had also taken seats on advisory regional boards and local committees in the Post Office and these were later terminated, with little opposition.

They had operated alongside existing consultative arrangements and seemed to have made little mark. Both levels of participation were studied by teams of academics, the boardroom membership by a Warwick University group led by Eric Batstone who had been involved in the 1976 critical study of the early BSC worker directors' scheme, and the regional and local levels by Dorothy Wedderburn of London University.

More conventional forms of consultation at national and regional levels replaced the board representation and separate structures were set up when British Telecom was hived off from the Post Office in 1981. Union officials then claimed that they were not consulted enough — and the management could not really disagree with allegations that the union representatives were only consulted just before final decisions were reached.

So by 1983 the postal and telecommunications businesses were more or less back to where they were before Tony Benn started the worker director initiative in 1974-5. Some critics may argue that the failure of the experiment in a business with such a long history of well-developed consultation proved the futility of worker director systems. That would be a wrong conclusion, as would other suggestions that the Bullock formula of '2x + y' failed in its one and only major test.

The boardroom experiment was clamped on top of established bargaining and consultative procedures without sufficient attention being paid to how it was supposed to work and influence management decisions and workers' views. The postal unions have weak and non-existent official organisation and representation outside their London headquarters and this, coupled with the fact that non-bargainers were nominated direct by the unions' headquarters, meant that the direct lines of contact proposed by the Bullock Report to operate through shop steward committess to a '2x + y' board were largely absent. There were also serious conflicts of interest between the union members' roles as union representatives and as board members, which their specially designed non-bargaining role did little to help. But the experiment was not a disaster; it was just not a success.

Changes at BSC

The worker director system at the British Steel Corporation took a potentially big step forward in August 1978 when six trade unionists (and two civil servants) went on to the main corporation board (see pages 169 and 268). But the arrangement did not survive the industrial upheavals of the next few years, during which the corporation's workforce was cut from about 210,000 in 1977 to 79,000 in 1983. Eventually, after many problems, the national board representation was terminated by Mr Patrick Jenkin, Tory Secretary of State for Industry, just before the June 1983 general election.

The six appointed in 1978 were trade union representatives from the main unions (apart from the EPTU which refused to be involved). They were paid (in 1983) £4,750 a year on top of their basic steelworks wage. Unlike their counterparts in the Post Office, they were BSC employees, not full-time trade union officials. There were two from the ISTC and one each from the AUEW, GMWU, TGWU and the National Union of Blastfurnacemen (NUB). By 1983 they had dwindled to two, partly because of a failure to agree on whether the trade unions or the board chairman should choose the candidates.

The arrival of Mr Ian MacGregor as BSC chairman in the summer of 1980, and the spin-off from the national steel strike earlier the same year, were the final turning points. The major union, the ISTC, was ambivalent throughout and many of the board members never had a clear and effective relationship with top management, their own plants, the unions or the TUC Steel Committee — although some individuals did have good and useful relationships in individual steelworks.

They had little influence on the board although Mr Ian MacGregor was known sometimes to listen patiently to their views. He took notice of one or two he came to trust and was not prepared to let the unions decide when a board member should be changed. Early in 1981 the TUC Steel Committee agreed after some debate to continue with the system, even though the role of the board had been dramatically reduced. At the time it was feared that Sir Keith Joseph, then Industry Secretary, might want to kill it off.

The TUC annual report of 1982 reflected the frustration but showed more optimism than was justified. It said that the board members 'ability to exercise an influence on events is non-existent in present circumstances, but they continue to provide a channel through which a trade union view can be put on current issues, which it will be possible to develop when circumstances change'. In October 1982 the TUC Steel Committee backed a one-day BSC strike by calling on all the employee representatives to resign. Although this call was not fully obeyed, the fact that it was issued underlined the basic problems of the system.

Eventually in March 1983 Mr Patrick Jenkin gave official notice of the scheme's termination. He projected this as being part of a new general Government policy on the size and shape of nationalised industry boards which had been introduced following a report made in 1981 to the Prime Minister by the Central Policy Review Staff (the Downing Street 'think tank' which was abolished in 1983). This report had recommended smaller boards with more influential non executive directors having business experience. Mr Jenkin's decision meant that an experiment in government-nationalised industry relations, which since 1978 had involved two civil servants from the Treasury and Industry Department sitting on the corporation board, also ended. (After 30 June, the only person from a trade union background on the board was Sir John Boyd, retired AUEW general secretary who, in old Morrisonian tradition, was appointed as a TUC worthy.)

Lower in the corporation there were still five trade union representatives acting as worker directors and sitting on business committees (divisional or group boards having been abolished) of certain product groups such as sections and commercial steels, strip mill products and steel tubes. These appointments were the gift of the corporation itself and so were not abolished as a result of the Jenkin statement. Seen in low key participation terms they were regarded as successful and valuable, and plans were drawn up for them to be kept and maybe expanded.

In tune with the times, the gradual disappearance of the highly structured employee director system gave way during the lifetime of the first 1979-83 Thatcher Government to more shopfloor oriented consultation arrangements to deal with the impact of closures and demanning in individual plants. After the ISTC announced a formal withdrawal from all joint consultation in 1980, these arrangements were developed on an *ad hoc* basis. 'Slimline Committees' evolved in some plants to discuss changes in working practices, to negotiate lump sum bonus schemes, and to monitor results. The consultation on slimline committees, and in other plants on works councils which survived the 1980 ISTC blast, range over important business issues such as productivity and output, quality and delivery, and energy usage. Local shop stewards are usually involved, although some full-time officials also attend. The corporation has also used 'quality circles'.

Survival at ICI

Perhaps the most durable of the consultation systems developed in the 1970s is that at ICI where there has been little change or upheaval, despite heavy cutbacks in the company's UK workforce from about 95,000 in 1977 to just over 60,000 in 1983. Often management has taken action without putting their ideas through the consultation system. For example in 1981 the management was accused of deciding to merge its plastics and petrochemicals divisions and of deciding to shed 4,000 jobs in its fibres division without consulting the shopfloor (*Financial Times* 6 March, 1981).

But the system has survived these and many other stresses. While trade union leaders have often been far from happy about their influence, their sense of realism has stopped any suggestion that the scheme should be boycotted or scrapped.

The central business and investment committee meets at national level four to six times a year instead of the twice originally envisaged. The total scheme was reviewed in November 1978 by a delegate conference when full-time trade union officials met the employee delegates. The existing arrangement was endorsed, subject to the role of a central agenda forming committee being strengthened on both agenda formation and progressing items under consideration.

The consultations have rarely had a direct and measurable impact on company decision-making. But, on the other hand, senior managements acknowledge that the existence of the committees, and the need for managers to account for themselves to the employees, must of itself change the style and, maybe, sometimes the course of decision-making.

Steady growth in Unilever

Unilever's arrangements for communication and consultation expanded rapidly in the late 1970s and early 1980s to the extent that company councils existed in 32 of the Anglo-Dutch group's 38 companies in the UK by 1983. These councils involved 55,000 of the total 66,000 UK workforce in 1983 (down from a total of 90,000 in 1977). They are echoed by various lower level consultative arrangements in factories and work groups. The companies involved vary in size from over 14,000 (Birds Eye Walls) down to 100-200 employees. But two important companies in the group, Batchelors and SPD, by 1983 had not formed councils at company-level.

Much of the impetus for the developments came from Unilever's head office in London in the form of discreet encouragement, but each company's management has been left to make progress at its own speed and in its own way.

The company councils consist of directors of the company plus elected representatives drawn for all sections of the workforce including management, whether unionised or not.

In one instance — at Thames Case — a council called a company communications group has been set up jointly involving full-time trade union officials as well as employee representatives, elected in individual factories, and management. This structure emerged from a working group set up in 1976 by Thames Case with SOGAT (Society of Graphical and Allied Trades) to devise a way of improving employee relations.

The style of each company's council meeting tends to vary according to the style and enthusiasm of the management and employee representatives involved, ranging from occasional management lectures and discussion about the need for economies and labour efficiency, to genuine consultation on production, marketing and sales. Agendas often tend to be dominated by subjects of concern to management. Generally, they range over the state of a company's business, sales and marketing, budgets and production plans, manpower forecasts and recruitment, organisational changes, and safety, health and new technology.

There is no suggestion of any attempt at joint decision-making, although on a few occasions management plans, for example, to rationalise production and cut a labour force, have been delayed or changed as a result of employee representation. A sharp distinction is made between consultation within the council framework and collective bargaining in union-based machinery. For example, a council may be told of future plans, including possible new investments or closures, up to two or three years ahead of an event. Later, the details of a closure such as the redundancy arrangements are negotiated with trade unions within the collective bargaining machinery.

The trade unions generally seem to have accepted, or at least decided to tolerate, that the councils are based on all employees. In any case, union people tend to dominate the whole consultation system throughout the unionised parts of Unilever because they, rather than non-unionists, come to the top in shopfloor elections.

While union officials and shop stewards are prepared to complain about the separation of powers, many of them see the benefit of being able to obtain and discuss management information without any union commitment in the consultation arena, leaving the unions free to negotiate later in the collective bargaining machinery. Sometimes shop stewards stay away, or even formally boycott, consultation meetings when they are in dispute. Companies do not escalate these upsets into formal crises, and after a time the shop stewards return.

The Birds Eye company council (before it was merged with Walls in 1983) had 42 representatives from nine locations consisting of one-third nominated by the workforce, one-third agreed between the workforce and management, and one-third management. The company council met quarterly with factories' site councils being given one month's advance notice to allow time for issues to be tabled. A liaison group prepared the agenda two weeks before the meeting, which generally lasted a full day, followed by reports being telexed immediately to all factories where site consultative councils prepared reports for the employees.

The site level councils vary but can, for example, consist of one-third representatives elected from work groups, one-third delegates appointed by trade unions, and one-third members of management. They meet not less than every three months. Major factories also have monthly departmental or production line consultative meetings where managers and supervisors pass on and discuss information directly affecting the work group involved, such as output, sales, quality and safety.

Any elected representative can put an item on a site council agenda but in practice they are usually management-run communications exercises and the agendas often include routine health and welfare issues. For example, the location of a cycle rack dominated a meeting in 1982 of the Lowestoft factory's council, even though 170 redundancies were on the agenda, (*Financial Times* 23 August, 1982). But local management would stress that it is giving the employees information it would not have given even operational managers in the mid 1970s which is an advance, even if the shop stewards can still complain that they have little real impact on company policy.

Worker co-operatives flourish

While formal boardroom and trade union-based methods of industrial democracy declined after the end of the 1970s, worker co-operatives mushroomed. Whereas in the early 1970s there were thought to be not more than 40 co-operatives in the UK, the total grew to 300 with 5,300 workers in 1980 and then to 500 with 6,400 workers in 1982. These statistics were prepared by the Co-operative Development Agency (CDA) which was set up in 1978 by the then Labour Government to provide a general boost to co-operatives. The CDA was then kept in being, after some heartsearching, by the 1979-1983 Thatcher Government as part of its general policy of encouraging small businesses.

So co-operatives have established themselves as a significant, though still tiny, part of Britain's small business community. This is mainly the result of changing social attitudes, with some people wanting to have the freedom to run their own businesses, coinciding with the dramatic increase in unemployment.

A 1982 report by the European Commission estimated that as many as 1,500 jobs a year had been created by co-operatives in the UK, and in France where there are more than 35,000 people working in 900 co-operatives. The report also estimated that more than 350,000 people were employed in co-operatives across Europe and reported rapid growth in Italy as well as France.

Co-operatives appeal for different reasons to politicians of all colours. While committed Socialists see them as ways of replacing capitalism with collective ownership, Liberals favour them because they can remove much of the conflict in industry and spread industrial common ownership. High Tories also like them because they involve would-be entrepreneurs banding together to pool their individual skills, usually without any trade union involvement.

But, whatever the political inspiration, co-operatives do not find it easy to survive because they often have an excess of ideological dreams and fervour. They are often short of management and marketing skills and cash for product development and expansion. While the CDA found that 290 were created in the period 1980-2, 95 closed of which 80 were less than six years old (*Co-ops: A directory of industrial and service co-operatives.* CDA London, 1982).

The rapid growth of unemployment led official bodies such as the MSC to help fund co-operatives for redundant workers, although many did not stay in business for long. A large number of regional and local co-operative agencies also sprang up around the country and left-wing local councils such as the Labour controlled Greater London Council tried to set up co-operatives as part of their programmes for job creation. Churches also became involved, both in local job initiatives and in a debate that followed the publication in September 1981 of 'Laborem Exercens', the encyclical letter of Pope John Paul II on human work which specifically encouraged the formation of worker co-operatives (Catholic Truth Society, London, 1981). A conference held in the Catholic Plater College in Oxford in July 1982 was told by Mr John Kay of the Christian Association of Business Executives: 'Previous

Popes have smiled benignly on co-operatives, co-partnership common ownership and co-management schemes in very general terms; John Paul II comes remarkably near to proclaiming it as the much sought after "third way" which can borrow what is best in free enterprise and socialist doctrines while rejecting the errors of both'.

Such ideas gain quick support from middle class liberals. This was illustrated by the foundation in November 1978 of Job Ownership, a small organisation nominally headed by Mr Joe Grimond, the former Liberal Party leader, and run by Mr Robert Oakeshott who was one of the 1977 Anglo-German Foundation study team on the Spanish co-operative at Mondragon (see page 196). Job Ownership helped to organise the Plater College conference and earlier advised journalists on *The Times* newspaper who formed 'Journalists of *The Times*'(JoTT) and drew up abortive plans to acquire their newspaper between 1978 and 1980. Job Ownership also helped organise a significant example of a workforce partnership being formed (in 1983) from an old family company — Richard Baxendale and Sons, manufacturers of Baxi fires and other heating equipment.

According to the CDA, the average number of workers in all co-operatives was about 17 or 18 in 1982. They ranged from computer software writing businesses to wholefood shops, and about half the businesses were in retail distribution, catering and food. Over one-fifth were in various forms of design and building and the same number again in printing and publishing. The numbers included community and neighbourhood co-operatives, where local interests shared ownership with the workers.

A few trade union leaders also became interested in co-operatives, notably in Wales where the regional TUC investigated one or two rescue possibilities and prepared plans to set up a co-operative development centre modelled on the Spanish Mondragon example.

Trade unions have in general remained disinterested although the Labour Party produced a discussion document in its *Socialism in the 80s* series ('Worker Co-operatives', The Labour Party, 1980) which included a £100 million a year plan for employees to have a legal right unilaterally to take over a company from its shareholders and turn it into a co-operative. But this policy mainly grew only from disenchantment in the Labour movement with large-scale nationalisation and with the failure of the limited co-operative initiatives launched by the 1974-79 Labour Government at KME (which eventually expired in 1980) and at Meriden (which passed to liquidators in 1983).

The final development which gave a boost to the growth of co-operatives was the vast increase in management buy-outs where the managers of a company bought a business from its previous owners. In some cases shopfloor employees provided some of the purchase funds and when the former State-owned National Freight Corporation was the subject of a buyout, employees bought a sizeable proportion of the shares.

Taken together, all these developments mean that, while there is no prospect of worker co-operatives becoming a significant part of the British economy, they have emerged from the doldrums of the first three-quarters of this century. In the mid-1980s they partly meet the mood of the times, providing people from many backgrounds and political ideals with a different form of ownership, management and industrial democracy, while at the same time playing a small part in the creation of jobs.

Financial participation

Financial participation also developed between 1979 and 1983, encouraged by employers who wanted to make their employees more aware of economic and financial affairs so that they are encouraged to moderate their pay claims and boost productivity. The main system is profit-based share ownership schemes, boosted by tax concessions introduced first by the Labour Government at the behest of the Liberal Party in the 1978 Budget, and then by the Conservative Government's Budgets of 1980 and 1983.

But these tax concessions did not lead to profit-sharing schemes being introduced by companies as quickly as had been expected, possibly because the corporate losses of the recession made such profit-based notions seem less relevant. By the end of March 1983, Inland Revenue records showed that there were 344 profit-based share-ownership schemes approved under the concessions first introduced in 1978, and a further 215 schemes under save-as-you-earn share-ownership tax concessions introduced in the 1980 Budget.

Employee share ownership also expanded during the 1979-83 Conservative Government's privatisation exercises in the public sector. In a new initiative for nationalised industries, employees of businesses such as British Aerospace and Cable and Wireless bought shares at preferential terms when these State assets were partially sold to the public. A more radical move occurred in National Freight where, as has just been mentioned, employees joined with management in a £53.3 million management buyout.

Employee involvement in the running of pension funds also increased, developing more dramatically than participation through profit-sharing and share ownership. Plans for 50-50 control of schemes (see page 273) proposed in a 1976 Labour Government White Paper were not turned into legislation. But participation expanded voluntarily, involving both non-unionised representatives and trade union nominees (who sometimes received investment advice from their own unions or the TUC).

Other examples

One notable example of a company developing a consultation system which kept the ideas of the 1970s alive occurred at Toshiba, the Japanese electronics company. After it parted from its previous UK partner, Rank, and re-started television set production in Rank's former premises in Plymouth, the company agreed in 1980-81 to a significant sole bargaining rights deal with the EPTU. This gained considerable publicity for its 'flip flop' or 'pendulum' system of arbitration, where an arbitrator has to decide in favour of a case from management or labour and cannot split the difference. Equally significant was the formation of an 'advisory board' elected by all the workforce which has access to a considerable amount of company information, reviews the company's performance and plans, and can recommend policies to the company. The workforce is split into ten constituencies for electing the representatives, which include one constituency for the six senior managers.

But there were few other such examples and the existing worker director schemes in the private sector (see page 158) did not develop. One academic study showed the limitations of eight such schemes: 'All of them were originated and most were implemented by management...In their design and rationale they showed the dominance of managerial forms of thinking. Commonly the schemes were designed to establish a mechanism of participation that would stress consensus values in the organisation, framed by the actions of management. The schemes were designed to legitimate existing managerial control, not to supply a counterweight to it'. (*Do Worker directors work?* Department of Employment Gazette, September 1981)

One potentially significant but little-noticed development came at the start of 1982 when the CBI agreed to promote consultation jointly with the TUC in the NEDC's annual steering brief for Little Neddies. Together they encouraged companies to set up consultative arrangements which would discuss proposals from Little Neddies. The steering brief said: 'Where such (consultative) machinery does not exist, council parties would wish companies to set it up and unions to provide the necessary level of specialist support so that discussions could develop and lead to effective joint action'. This action often included companies accepting advice offered by 'ambassadors' from the Little Neddies, and it made some impact in a few industries (*Financial Times* 28 January, 11 and 12 May, 1982). This led to improvements in job involvement in some companies, although progress was patchy.

Chapter 21

Statutory Policies

Statutory developments

There were no new major laws in the years following the main Bullock debate affecting industrial democracy, although both the Labour Party and the Social Democrat-Liberal Alliance included policies steming from that debate in their 1983 general election manifestoes. The main development in the period was the apparently growing possibility of legislation emanating from the European Commission. The proposed Fifth Directive (see page 224) continued to move slowly through the Common Market's policy machinery, but was overtaken by a new initiative on employee consultation and communication. Known as the Vredeling Directive, this was named after the Dutch Common Market commissioner who launched it in 1980. However the implacable opposition of some groups of employers and company directors — particularly in the UK — and of the British Conservative Government meant that progress remained slow.

In the UK, the 1979-83 Thatcher Government legislated in two fringe areas. First the Companies Act 1980 obliged employers to take employees interests into account when making decisions. This meant that a long debated issue (see pages 214 and 251) came onto the Statute Book. But the innovation had little impact, contrary to some expectations that such a move might have a considerable influence on management decisions as case law developed. Company boards found they could easily show that they had taken the impact of decisions on employees into account.

The second development emanated from the Employment Act 1982 as a result of a House of Lords amendment to the Employment Bill which was adopted by the Government. This required companies with more than 250 employees to describe in their annual company reports the action they took during the year to introduce, maintain, or develop arrangements aimed at: providing employees with systematic information of concern to them as employees; consulting employees or their representatives on a regular basis so their views could be taken into account; encouraging employee involvement through profit-sharing and other means; and increasing economic understanding among employees. This requirement did not have much impact on companies' employee involvement policies: but it did remind companies that there was still a risk, even under a Thatcher regime, of some legislation in this area.

Vredeling and the Fifth

The Vredeling initiative was launched in 1980. It was an attempt by a few left-wing European politicians and trade unions to curb the power of multinational companies by forcing them to disclose information to employees about their general plans and about specific decisions. Certain other groups of companies operating in the EEC — dubbed 'national companies of complex structure' — were included after multinationals complained they were being victimised. The European TUC took a lead in promoting the proposals which were vigorously resisted by companies, particularly by American multinationals and by the Institute of Directors in the UK, which made opposition to any European legislation in this area a cause célèbre.

Closure of European factories by multinationals fuelled the European TUC's determination to encourage a radical policy. But multinationals warned that they might invest outside Europe if they felt their right to manage was being put at risk. (*Financial Times* 17 September, 1982). The companies feared they would have to inform employee representatives about detailed plans of future products and projects. They were specially worried that a proposed 'bypass' provision that had been suggested would enable workers from a European subsidiary to invade foreign corporate headquarters to seek secret information and demand the right to negotiate on company decisions, which could then be delayed.

After lengthy haggling in the European Commission and the European Parliament, the Commission adopted a draft directive in the middle of 1983. This covered groups of companies with 1,000 or more workers in the EEC. It proposed that once a year they should provide information giving a clear picture of trends and prospects of a company's structure, finances, sales, employment and investment. Where information was not provided employees could appeal to a company's headquarters and after 30 days the company could be taken before a tribunal. Employees should also be consulted in good time on management plans likely to be of serious consequence to them and attempts should be made to reach agreement. The plans should not be implemented till the employees' opinion had been received or until 30 days had elapsed after the information was passed on. There was also provision for employees to set up multi-plant committees, but companies were given the right to withhold sensitive information.

This was a considerably watered down version of earlier drafts. It protected companies from having to hand over secret information, from having to disclose information frequently, and from having to cope with direct appeals to the hierarchical management structure when workers felt their rights had been ignored. But the main European employers' body, the Union des Industries de la Communauté Européenne (UNICE), continued to oppose it. In the UK, the CBI and the Institute of Directors pushed the campaign, believing they could rely on Mr Norman Tebbit, Employment Secretary, to kill it off, or at least to block it indefinitely in the European Council of Ministers.

Meanwhile, the Fifth Directive had also been watered down. By 1982 it proposed a choice broadly based on German, Danish and Dutch experience. Workers could have between one-third and one-half of the seats on either the top supervisory board in a two-tier structure, or as non-executives on the management board of a single-tier structure. Another option would be an employees' representative body adjacent to board level. Alternatively, the employees could have a say in the co-option of representatives to a supervisory board, or could negotiate with a company on how to use one of the above choices.

In an attempt to ensure that all the options could have an 'equivalent' impact on company decision-making, the European Commission was proposing in a statement dated September 1982 that there should be certain common principles, and that there should be special arrangements to underpin any negotiated option.

Although there was little prospect of either the Vredeling or the Fifth Directive affecting companies before the end of the 1980s, the threat of such legislation upsetting ownership and managerial rights and practices kept lobby groups active. The potential threat also led even the most right-wing UK Government ministers to warn companies of the risk of legislation if they did not introduce employee involvement voluntarily.

Policies in the UK develop from Bullock

The Conservative Government's policy in the mid-1980s was that there should be no legislation forcing companies to communicate with or involve their work forces. But there was a very faint possibility that a statutorily-backed Code of Practice might one day be introduced as a first step.

The Social Democrat-Liberal Alliance produced a policy for its 1983 general election manifesto which looked like a direct descendant of the Bullock Report. It contained earlier Liberal Party policies together with a watered-down version of the previous Labour Government's May 1978 post-Bullock White Paper (see page 263). This was hardly surprising since both Mrs Shirley Williams and Mr Edmund Dell, who had both played key roles in the Bullock debate as Labour Government ministers, were by then leading figures in the Social Democratic Party (SDP). The policy included an Industrial Democracy Act which would set up an Industrial Democracy Agency and encourage participation at all levels. Profit-sharing and worker co-operatives would also be helped. Employee councils would be set up in all places of work with more than 1,000 employees. At a top level board directors would be elected jointly by employees and shareholders, or there would be a representative council with some co-determination rights.

The issue which dogged the Labour movement's Bullock debates in the late 1970s of giving unions' sole rights in a single channel system was dealt with by the SDP in a policy document published in 1983 (SDP Council for Social Democracy, Policy Document No 4. *Industrial Relations II: Industrial Democracy*). Saying that 'where trade unions are involved in organisations they should have a crucial role in participation', this attempted to give established trade unions a secure role without alienating those who did not want non-unionists to be disenfranchised.

The Labour Party produced a much more radical policy which had been agreed with the TUC. It bore the indelible stamp of Mr David Lea, the senior TUC official (now an assistant general secretary) who had helped formulate Jack Jones' worker director ideas in the 1970s. The policy aimed to harness general trade union support for the previously contentious Bullock proposals. It put Labour's planning agreement policy of the 1970s on a sounder base by giving union officials a specific role, and it recognised the importance of local rather than national initiatives and of devolved as well as centralised company management.

The Joint Representation Committees (JRCs) of the Bullock era were significantly renamed Joint Union Committees (JUCs), and were expanded to involve full-time officials as well as lay representatives. Trade union leaders' arguments in the late 1970s over board representation versus extended collective bargaining were partially bridged by a JUC being given powers to set up minority or parity representation on a company policy board. A JUC would also have rights to information and consultation. This would all be linked to other industrial and economic planning through a new concept of a company's agreed development plan, and through sectoral planning committees and other arrangements which would be encouraged by financial and other powers operated by the Government.

These Labour and SDP-Liberal Alliance policies were broadly in line with the ideas being developed in Brussels. But they were out of tune with the prevailing mood in the UK (and elsewhere in Europe) where trade union activists were more concerned with protecting both jobs and their traditional bargaining role than with branching out into uncharted territory. Managers had little interest in such ideas. The policies looked top heavy and over-structured, especially for the new electronics and other industries that were replacing the heavy traditional manufacturing industries for which the Fifth Directive and Bullock ideas had been primarily designed.

Chapter 22
Conclusions

A lack of progress

Looking back to the 1970s it cannot be claimed that much was achieved by the great industrial democracy debate and the experiments, apart from the establishment of the debate itself as a continuing issue. The TUC and Labour Party produced somewhat arid policies, full of structural and procedural rules that eventually had little appeal to any but the most committed activists. Experiments foundered, partly because they were introduced without sufficient preparation, partly because management were either totally opposed or were just not committed enough, and partly because the trade union and workforce foundations were not sound enough.

Mr David Lea at the TUC kept the basic precepts of Bullock alive in Labour policy documents but failed to inspire many supporters. By the early 1980s there was no figure such as Jack Jones among the unions' top leaders to push ideas forward which gradually seemed more arid and less relevant. Indeed the SDP's modified version of the 1978 White Paper in 1983 looked dated. The same is broadly true of the Common Market's highly structured ideas, even though they often only included what many managements should accept as good practice.

But, while it might be argued that the advocates of industrial democracy did not pursue their cause very effectively, management was successful in doing all it could to slow down the development of new policies. Industrialists avoided entering debates wholeheartedly, offered few constructive ideas, and, in the public sector, suffered the experiments with less than full commitment.

There are deep party political divisions in Britain, firmly rooted in the polarisation of a class and status conscious society which is echoed in the hierarchical and adversarial traditions of industry. Consequently industrialists and trade unions rarely, if ever, offer to work together and share power constructively. Often both see it as being in their own best interest to perpetuate the prevailing adversarial system, while still complaining when they are hurt. There are few examples of industrialists trying significantly to increase employee and trade union influence in their company on a constructive basis, because they fear that eventually such an initiative could lead to a change in the balance of the power of ownership and management.

Events in the US have shown how much more can be achieved with less class-based shopfloor confrontation, less politically-oriented trade union attitudes, and a more confident and less self-defensive management. US companies have offered 'survival bargains' in which trade unions or employers have gained more management influence; workers have more job security, and companies have co-operation for changes. A United Auto Workers deal with Ford was a pacemaker — and it was led by management. A participation programme was included in the 1983 three-year deal struck by the United Steelworkers of America with the major US steel companies, which also included temporary cuts in pay and holidays to fund new investment and increased job security and lay-off benefits.

These examples illustrate why it will often be argued in the UK during the mid-1980s that the old prescriptions have had their day. The new interest in individual relationships, plus the impact of technological change on both employment and communication, will seem to many people to make subjects like Bullock, the Fifth Directive and Vredeling (which were designed for old, large-scale labour-intensive manufacturing industries) look outdated. Are such ideas relevant to new electronic businesses and service industries which operate in small and relatively classless factories? And on a more political level, will the experiences of the recession and two Thatcher Governments produce new attitudes and relationships that will require different policies?

The people who argue that a new approach is needed most convincingly are employers who want to bury the debates of the 1970s about the rights and power of employees as deeply as possible so as to resist any future employee or trade union onslaught on industrial ownership and management. They argue that small groups of people working in new style industries do not have the adversarial hang-ups of the past and that, left to themselves, companies will have better informed and motivated employees.

There is some truth in this. There appears to be less labour unrest in newer industries, and attitudes in high technology businesses are certainly less adversarial and union-oriented than in older manufacturing factories. Employees are more naturally and easily motivated and involved in smaller high technology businesses than in car factories or steel mills. But there are also some similarities. The frustrations and militancy of working far from a remote top-level management, especially in a foreign owned company, can occur in an electronics company as easily as in a car manufacturer. The lines of authority, frustration, and conflict may be drawn differently, but they will not be banished by changes in political attitudes or technological advance.

The management and trade union challenge

So, in the mid 1980s, when there is no prospect in Britain of any far-reaching legislation on participation, the challenge to change from the conflicts of the past rests with management, unions, and employees. The changes of the 1979-83 period give management a chance to break out from traditional attitudes, in the way that US companies have done, and offer partnerships to both unions and employees for collective and individual issues.

Trade unions need to realise that nationally-organised statutory bureaucratic solutions are not on offer in the 1980s. They therefore need to change their focus, aiming for constructive representation of their members in individual companies and plants. Companies need to make sure that employees feel fully consulted about the issues that surround them each day and that they have full access to information and consultation in detail about what is happening at the topmost managerial levels in the particular company or group.

There is still a role for the law to persuade and encourage employers to do more. The Thatcher regime and the recession have not removed the need for a dramatic change in the industrial democracy of Britain. They have merely passed the challenge to management and trade unions to find a more practical alternative to the debilitating conflicts and inertia of the past.

Bibliography

1: Books

The following books have either been quoted in the preceeding chapters or have been extensively consulted:

Alexander, K. J. W. and Jenkins, C. L. (1970) *Fairfields: A Study of Industrial Change.* The Penguin Press, Allen Lane, London.

Bain, G. S. (1970) *The Growth of White-Collar Unionism.* The Clarendon Press, Oxford.

Barnes, D. and Reid, E. (1980) *Governments and Trade Unions — The British Experience 1964-79.* Heinemann Educational Books and Policy Studies Institute. London.

Beynon, H. (1973) *Working for Ford.* Penguin Books, Harmondsworth.

Brannen, P., Batstone, E., Fatchett, D. and White, P. (1976) *The Worker Directors: A Sociology of Participation.* Hutchinson, London.

British Steel Corporation Employee Directors with Bank, J. and Jones, K. (1977) *Worker Directors Speak.* Gower Press, Teakfield, Farnborough.

Clegg, H. A. (1976) *Trade Unionism under Collective Bargaining: A Theory based on Comparisons of Six Countries.* Basil Blackwell, Oxford.

Clegg, H. A. (1972) *The System of Industrial Relations in Great Britain.* Basil Blackwell, Oxford.

Coates, K (1981) *Work-ins, Sit-ins and Industrial Democracy.* Spokesman, Nottingham.

Copeman, G. (1975) *Employee Share Ownership and Industrial Stability.* Institute of Personnel Management, London.

Cullingford, E. C. M. (1976) *Trade Unions in West Germany.* Wilton House Publications, London.

Dickson, P. (1977) *Work Revolution.* George Allen & Unwin, London.

Eccles, T (1981) *Under New Management — The Story of Britain's Largest Worker Co-operative.* Pan, London.

Edwards, Sir Ronald and Roberts, R. D. V. (1971) *Status, Productivity and Pay: A Major Experiment. A Study of the Electricity Supply Industry's Agreement and Their Outcome, 1961-1971.* The Macmillan Press, London.

Flanders, A. (1970) *Management and Unions, The Theory and Reform of Industrial Relations.* Faber and Faber, London.

Goodman, J. F. B. and Whittingham, T. G. (1973) *Shop Stewards.* Pan Books, London.

Grant, W. and Marsh, D. (1977) *The CBI: The First Major Study of the Role of the Confederation of British Industry in the British Political System.* Hodder and Stoughton, London.

Gyllenhammar, P. G. (President of Volvo) (1977) *People at Work.* Addison-Wesley Publishing Company, London.

Hoe, S. (1978) *The Man Who Gave His Company Away. Biography of Ernest Bader.* Heinemann, London.

Jenkins, C. and Mortimer, J. E. (1968) *The Kind of Laws the Unions Ought to Want.* Pergamon Press, Oxford.

Jenkins, D. (1974) *Job Power: Blue and White Collar Democracy.* William Heineman, London.

Jenkins, P. (1970) *The Battle of Downing Street.* Charles Knight & Co, London.

Kolvenbach, Dr. W. (1978) *Employee Councils in European Companies.* Kluwer, Deventer, The Netherlands.

Marsh, A. I. and Evans, E. O. (1973) *The Dictionary of Industrial Relations.* Hutchinson, London.

McCarthy, W. E. J. (1964) *The Closed Shop in Britain.* Basil Blackwell, Oxford.

McCarthy, W. E. J. and Ellis, N. D. (1973) *Management by Agreement. An Alternative to the Industrial Relations Act.* Hutchinson, London.

Meidner, R. (1978) *Employee Investment Funds.* George Allen and Unwin, London.

Nichols, T. and Beynon, H. (1977) *Living with Capitalism: Class Relations and the Modern Factory.* Routledge & Kegan Paul, London.

Oakeshott, R. (1978) *The Case for Worker Co-ops.* Routledge & Kegan Paul, London.

Purcell, J. and Smith R. (1979) *The Control of Work.* Macmillan Press, London.

Roeber, J. (1975) *Social Change at Work: The ICI Weekly Staff Agreement.* Gerald Duckworth & Co, London.

Simpson, B. (1973) *Labour: The Unions and the Party.* George Allen & Unwin, London.

Smith, C. (M.P.) (1977) *Industrial Participation.* McGraw-Hill (UK), London.

Storey, J. (1980) *The Challenge to Management Control.* Kogan Page, London.

Taylor, R. (1978) *The Fifth Estate — Britain's Unions in the Seventies.* Routledge & Kegan Paul, London.

Thomas, H. and Logan, C. (1982) *Mondragon — An Economic Analysis.* George Allen & Unwin, London.

Thornley, J. (1981) *Workers' Co-operatives — Jobs and Dreams.* Heinemann Educational Books, London.

Webb, S. and Webb, B. (1901) *Industrial Democracy.* Printed by the authors, London.

Wedderburn, K. W. (1965) *The Worker and the Law.* Penguin Books, Harmondsworth.

Weekes, B., Mellish, M., Dickens, L. and Lloyd, J. (1975) *Industrial Relations and the Limits of Law: The Industrial Effects of the Industrial Relations Act, 1971.* Basil Blackwell, Oxford.

Wigham, E. (1973) *The Power to Manage. A History of the Engineering Employers' Federation.* Macmillan Press, London.

Young, M. and Rigge, M. (1983) *Revolution from Within — Co-operatives and Co-operation in British Industry.* Weidenfeld & Nicholson, London.

2: Pamphlets and other publications

The following pamphlets, booklets, official reports and other similar publications have either been quoted in the preceeding chapters or have been extensively consulted:

Advisory Conciliation and Arbitration Service (1977) *Code of Practice 2: Disclosure of Information to Trade Unions for Collective Bargaining Purposes.* HMSO, London.

Advisory Conciliation and Arbitration Service (1982) *Advisory Booklet No. 8: Workplace Communications.* ACAS, London.

Anglo-German Foundation for the Study of Industrial Society (1977) *Worker Owners: The Mondragon Achievement* by Campbell, Keen, Norman and Oakeshott. Anglo German Foundation, London.

Anglo German Foundation (1979) *What do the British want from Participation and Industrial Democracy?* by Heller, Wilders, Abell and Warner. Anglo German Foundation, London.

Balogh, T. (1970) *Fabian Tract 403: Labour and Inflation.* The Fabian Society, London.

Batstone, E. and Davies, P. L. (1976) *Industrial Democracy European Experience: Two Reports prepared for the Industrial Democracy Committee.* HMSO, London.

Biendenkopf Report (1970) *Co-determination in the Company.* Translated from the original German by Duncan O'Neill. Legal Research Committee of the Faculty of Law, Queens University, Belfast.

British Institute of Management (1975) *Employee Participation: A Management View. Report of a Working Party under the Chairmanship of Bernard Cotton.* BIM, London.

British Institute of Management (1977) *Employee Participation: The Way Ahead, incorporating a Guide to Participative Practice.* BIM, London.

Bruce-Gardyne, J. (1978) *Meriden — Odyssey of a Lame Duck.* Centre for Policy Studies, London.

Bullock, Lord (1977) *Report of the Committee of Inquiry on Industrial Democracy.* HMSO, London.

Cassidy, Bryan (1973) *Workers on the Board: A Study in Employee Participation.* Conservative Political Centre, London.

Coates, K. and Topham, T. (1977) *The Shop Steward's Guide to the Bullock Report.* Spokesman Books, Bertrand Russell Peace Foundation Ltd, Nottingham.

Commission of the European Communities (1975) *Employee Participation and Company Structure.* Office for Official Publications of the European Communities, Luxembourg.

Commission of the European Communities (1975) *Statute for European Companies: Amended Proposal for a Regulation.* Office for Official Publications of the European Communities, Luxembourg.

Commission on Industrial Regulations (1972) *Report No 31: Disclosure of Information.* HMSO, London.

Commission on Industrial Relations (1974) *Study 4: Worker Participation and Collective Bargaining in Europe.* HMSO, London.

Confederation of British Industry (1973) *The Responsibilities of the British Public Company.* CBI, London.

Confederation of British Industry (1976) *Involving People: CBI Proposals for Employee Participation.* CBI, London.

Confederation of British Industry (1977) *Communication with People at Work.* CBI, London.

Confederation of British Industry (1979) *Guidelines for Action on Employee Involvement.* CBI, London.

Confederation of British Industry (1981) *Current Employee Involvement Practice in British Business.* CBI, London.

Conservative Political Centre (1968) *Fair Deal at Work.* CPC, London.

Conservative Political Centre (1976) *One Nation at Work,* CPC, London.

Co-operative Development Agency (annually from 1979) *Annual Report and Accounts.* HMSO, London.

Co-operative Development Agency (1980, 1982) *Co-ops: A Directory of Industrial and Service Co-operatives.* CDA, London.

Department of Employment and Wilson, N. A. B. (1973) *Manpower Papers No 7: On the Quality of Working Life.* HMSO, London.

Department of Employment Tripartite Steering Group on Job Satisfaction (1975) *Making Work More Satisfying.* HMSO, London.

Department of Employment Work Research Unit (1975) *Work Restructuring Projects and Experiments in the United Kingdom.* DE, London.

Department of Industry (1975) *The Contents of a Planning Agreement: A Discussion Document.* DI, London.

Department of Manpower Services (1975) *Industrial Democracy: A Discussion Paper on Worker Participation in Harland and Wolff.* HMSO, Belfast.

Donovan, Lord (1968) *Report of the Royal Commission on Trade Unions and Employers' Associations 1965-1968.* HMSO, London.

European Trade Union Confederation (1982) *Survey and Documentation on Disputes in European Subsidiaries of Multinational Groups of Companies.* ETUC, Brussels.

Fabian Trade Union Special (1979) *Industrial Relations Law and the Conservative Government* Lewis, Davies and Wedderburn. NCLC Publishing Society, London.

Her Majesty's Stationery Office (1969) *In Place of Strife — A Policy for Industrial Relations.* HMSO, London.

Her Majesty's Stationery Office (1975) *The Attack on Inflation.* HMSO, London.

Her Majesty's Stationery Office (1976) *Occupational Pension Schemes — The Role of Members in the Running of Schemes.* HMSO, London.

Hilgendorf, E., Linden and Irving, B. L. (1976) *Workers' Experience of Participation The Case of British Rail.* Tavistock Institute of Human Relations, London.

House of Lords Select Committee on the European Communities (1981) *Employee Consultation.* HMSO, London.

Industrial Participation Association (1977) *Industrial Democracy: An Acceptable Solution.* IPA, London.

Industrial Participation Association (1979) *Guidelines for Voluntary Company Codes of Practice on Participation.* IPA, London.

Industrial Participation Association (1982) *Industrial Participation: A National Framework.* IPA, London.

Industrial Society (1976) *Democracy in Industry.* The Industrial Society, London.

Industrial Society (1977) *Participation and Industrial Democracy: Survey of Company Practice, Attitudes and Plans.* The Industrial Society, London.

Inns of Court Conservative and Unionist Society (1958) *A Giant's Strength: Some Thoughts on the Constitutional and Legal Position of Trade Unions in England.* The Inns of Court Conservative and Unionist Society and Christopher Johnson Publishers, London.

Institute of Directors (1980) *The EEC Vth Directive — A Trojan Bullock?* IoD, London.

Institute of Directors (1982) *Company Law in Europe: The Vth Directive and the Harmonisation Programme.* IoD, London.

Institute of Personnel Management (1976) *Workers' Participation in Western Europe 1976* IPM, London.

Job Ownership (1978) Job Ownership, London.

Kolvenbach, Walter (1982) *Co-operation between Management and Labour.* Kluwer Law and Taxation Publishers, Deventer, The Netherlands.

Labour Party (1967) *Report of the Labour Party Working Party on Industrial Democracy.* Labour Party, London.

Labour Party (1972) *Labour's Programme for Britain: Annual Conference 1972,* Labour Party, London.

Labour Party (1973) *Capital and Equality: Report of a Labour Party Study Group.* Labour Party, London.

Metra Oxford and Hemingway, J. and Keyser W. (1975) *Who's in Charge? Worker Sit-ins in Britain Today.* Metra Oxford Consulting Ltd., Oxford.

National and Local Government Officers Association (1977) *Industrial Democracy.* NALGO, London.

National Economic Development Office (1976) *A Study of UK Nationalised Industries: Their Role in the Economy and Control in the Future.* HMSO, London.

National Swedish Industries Board (1976) *Board Representation of Employees in Sweden: A Summary from a Survey.* Liber Fölag, Stockholm.

1972 Industry Group (1977) *Industrial Participation. Proposals for an Acceptable Solution.* 1972 Industry Group, London.

Paul II, John (1981) *Laborems Exercens: Encyclical Letter of the Supreme Pontiff John Paul II on Human Work.* Catholic Truth Society, London.

Price, R. and Bain, G. S. (1976) *Union Growth Revisited: 1948-1974 in Perspective.* Industrial Relations Research Unit of the Social Science Research Council, University of Warwick.

Radice, G. (1974) *Fabian Tract 431: Working Power: Policies for Industrial Democracy.* Fabian Society, London.

Royal Arsenal Co-operative Society (1979) *Mondragon: The Basque Co-operatives.* Royal Arsenal Co-op, London.

Ryder, Sir Don (1975) *British Leyland; The Next Decade.* Abridged Version of a Report by a Team of Inquiry. HMSO, London.

Social Democratic Party (1982) *Democracy at Work: A Policy of Partnership in Industry.* Green Paper No 6. SDP, London.

Social Democratic Party (1983) *Industrial Relations: Industrial Democracy.* Policy Document No 4. SDP, London.

Trades Union Congress (1966) *Trade Unionism: Evidence of the TUC to the Royal Commission on Trade Unions and Employers' Associations.* TUC, London.

Trades Union Congress (1972) *The Chequers and Downing Street Talks, July to November 1972.* TUC, London.

Trades Union Congress (1974) *Industrial Democracy: Report by the TUC General Council to the 1974 Trades Union Congress.* TUC, London.

Trades Union Congress (1976) *The Social Contract 1976-77.* TUC, London.

Trades Union Congress (1977) *Industrial Democracy — Including Supplementary Evidence to the Bullock Committee.* TUC, London.

Trades Union Congress (1977) *TUC Guide to the Bullock Report on Industrial Democracy.* TUC, London.

Trades Union Congress (1979) *Employment and Technology: Report to the 1979 Congress.* TUC, London.

Trades Union Congress (1982) *Economic Planning and Industrial Democracy: The Framework for Full Employment. Report to the 1982 TUC Congress and Labour Party Conference.* The Labour Party, London.

Trades Union Congress (1982) *Regional Development and Planning: A TUC Policy Statement.* TUC, London.

Trades Union Congress (1983) *The Battle for Jobs: TUC Economic Review 1983.* TUC, London.

Walker Kenneth (1977) *Worker Participation in Management: Problems, Practice and Prospects.* Bulletin of International Institute for Labour Studies, Geneva.

Wider Share Ownership Council (1977) *Employee Share Scheme.* WSOC, London.

Index

Adam, Kenneth
  survey of Esso Petroleum managers, 106
Adamson, Sir Campbell, 59, 60
Added value schemes
  at Ionic Plating (GKN) 152–153; ICI, 185
Advisory Conciliation and Arbitration Service
  (ACAS), 5, 30, 37, 40, 45–48, 281, 282, 294,
  297
  and disclosure of information, 140
Alexander, Professor K.
  on trade union directors in *Fairfields* (1970), 169
Allen, Alfred (later, Lord) of USDAW, 28
Allen, W. P.
  first trade union director on nationalised rail, 210
Amalgamated Union of Engineering Workers
  (AUEW), 302, 303
  makes distinction between private and public
  sectors, 75; participation problems due to union
  organisation, 91; power of district committees,
  92; employee director at Bonser, 159; TASS
  section against worker directors, 247; union
  support for worker directors, 268
America, 139, 191, 193, 199
  American unions, 7; individual-based industrial
  democracy, 182, 183, 184, 187; worker shares
  schemes, 185; car workers prefer Detroit
  assembly tracks, 200; president American
  Chamber of Commerce (UK) opposes Bullock,
  244
Anglo-German Foundation for the Study of
  Industry
  report on Mondragon (Spain) worker
  co-operatives, 196
Armaments manufacture
  and Lucas Aerospace, 80–81; workers' attitude in
  these industries, 83; Jack Jones on defence
  strategy, 79–80
Armstrong, Sir William (now, Lord), 19, 20
Association of Members of State Industry Boards,
  107
Association of Metropolitan Authorities, 265, 272
Association of Professional, Executive, Clerical and
  Computer Staff (APEX) and use of information
  at Lucas, 87; support for Bullock and two-tier
  system, 245
Association of Scientific, Technical and Managerial
  Staffs (ASTMS)
  use of Industrial Relations Act for recognition,
  16; study of Rolls Royce redundancies, 87;
  Bullock Report rejected at 1977 Annual
  Conference, 22, 245 see also Jenkins, Clive
Attack on Inflation, The, (White Paper, 1975), 36
Attlee, Clem, 210
Austria, 225, 267

Bader, Ernest (of Scott-Bader)
  company shares given to its employees, 193
Bain, Professor George (of Warwick University)
  report on white collar trade unionists (Price &
  Bain, 1977), 108; independent member of Bullock
  Committee, 220, 226, 227, 232; sees worker
  directors as supplement to collective bargaining,
  230; research showing 70–80 per cent unionisation
  in large companies, 232, 255
Baker, Ken (GMWU)
  votes for Bullock-based policy on nationalised
  industries, 268
Balogh, Thomas (now, Lord)
  uses term *contrat social*, in Fabian pamphlet
  Labour and Inflation (1970), 33, 281
Banking
  and worker directors, 83; managers as union
  representatives, 107; reaction to Bullock, 232, 243
Bank of England, 42
  staff association suggests two staff members on
  Court of Directors, 266
Barber, Tony (later, Lord), 46
Barclays Bank
  and employee share ownership, 186
Barlow, Sir William, 301
Basildon District Council
  co-opted employee representatives, 271
Basnett, David (GMWU), 33, 51; 'economic
  contract', 61; support for social contract, 28;
  opposition to worker directors, 28, 76; in 1977
  accepts Bullock as *one* route to industrial
  democracy, 77; moves in behind Bullock report
  with extended bargaining, 245; on pension funds,
  276
Batstone, Eric
  Bullock research paper, *Industrial Democracy:
  European Experience* (1976), 136, 225
Benn, Anthony Wedgwood, 31, 87, 114, 302
  and planning agreements, 38, 216; on
  participation in media, 82; several initiatives on
  participation, 175; industrial democracy in the
  Post Office, 178; backed three co-operative
  projects, 192
Berry Wiggins (Bitumen and Refining)
  experience of form of worker directors, 159
Bevin, Ernest, 26, 220
Bewley Cafes, Dublin
  worker co-operative, 193
Beynon, Huw
  author of *Working for Ford*, 73
Biendenkopf Commission (1970)
  German report on worker director scheme, 137
Biggs, Norman (later, Sir), 227
  appointed to Bullock Committee, 219; puts City

of London case against worker directors in Appendix, 83, 232

BL, *see* British Leyland

Board of Inland Revenue, 270, 271

Boilermakers
élitist craft attitude at Harland and Wolff, 177

Bonser Engineering
selected employee director, 159

Booth, Albert (Secretary of State for Employment)
address to Industrial Society on managers and participation, 121; on job satisfaction, 202; support for Bullock, 244, 247, 249

Bow Group
evidence to Bullock Committee, 223

Brannen, P.
critical study on worker directors in British Steel Corporation, 170, 171

BRD Company, 152

Bristol Channel Ship Repairers
worker directors and share ownership scheme, 158, 159

British Aerospace, 308

British Aircraft Corporation
sit-in in 1975, 191

British Airways
union rivalries on planned joint committee, 177

British Employers' Federation
agreement with TUC (1963) on training shop stewards, 85

British Gas Corporation
new consultative arrangements exclude discussion on corporate plan, 166

British Home Stores, 186

British Institute of Management (BIM)
desire to represent employed managers, 108; *Employee Participation – A Management View* (1974), 117

British Leyland (BL), 58, 76, 87, 113, 151, 154–158, 276, 295, 297
and participation of shop stewards, 69; combine set up in 1975, 92; and legitimacy of management, 99; piecework to measured daywork problems, 120; compromise on 'single channel', 131, 154; three tiers of participation committees (1974), 154, 298; company-wide conference, 155; industrial action over siting of paint shop, 155; evidence to Bullock, 157; cost of consultation schemes, 158; small experiment with group working, 200; a short life at, 297–300; Speke closure, 297, 298; the Mini, 299; Cowley plant, 299; Cars Review, 299

British National Oil Corporation, 267, 269

British Rail, 76, 265
Tavistock Inquiry, 163

British Steel Corporation (BSC), 169–175, 267, 297, 301
worker director experiments, 84, 139, 258, 263; worker director scheme, 1977, 169; board member from UPW, 1967–1977, 210; changes at, 302–303; workforce cut, 302; 'slimline committees', 303

British Telecom, 301
hiving off from Post Office, 301

Brown, George (now, Lord George-Brown)
experiment in participation at Fairfields, 168

Buckton, Ray (ASLEF)
votes for Bullock-based policy for nationalised industries, 268

Budget, the
bargaining on, 36

Bulletin of the International Institute for Labour Studies (Jan. 1977)

article on 'ascending' and 'descending participation', 198

Bullock Committee of Inquiry on Industrial Democracy (Bullock Report), 4,8, 23, 30, 65, 66, 71,104, 111, 121, 124, 137, 142, 145, 177, 179, 195, 215, 221–240, 284, 293, 294–295, 302, 315
evidence from Ford Motor, 7, 102, 117, 119; and planning agreements, 38; suggested Industrial Democracy Commission, 42, 84, 235, 237, 253, 286; and CBI, 59, 222, 243–245; John Lyons against, 70; TUC view, 74; evidence from Communist Party, 75; Joint Representation Committees (JRCs), 82, 91, 94, 127, 285, 313; Norman Biggs' appendix to minority report, on banks and insurance companies, 83, 232; and inter-union disputes, 94; on confidentiality, 96; on new legitimacy of consent, 99, 105, 121; evidence re 'them and us' mentality of workers, 100; reserves certain rights for shareholders, 101; evidence from ICI, 112; evidence from GCE, 119; on blurring of distinction between consultation and negotiation, 130; evidence from Unilever, 147–148; evidence from British Leyland, 156; on British Steel, 173; '$2x + y$' could be adapted for nationalised industry, 180; how '$2x + y$' would work, 234–238, 252, 261; road to Bullock, 205–220; first official meeting 12 Dec. 1975, 221; Liberal Party proposals, 222–223; Majority Report, 233–238; Minority (industrialists) Report, 238–240; no proper launching of Report, 241; reactions, 241–263, 285; policies developing from, 312–313

Bullock, Lord (formerly Sir Alan), 99, 221, 226, 227, 233, 294
Chairman of Committee of Inquiry on Industrial Democracy (1975), 219; 'core report' on first steps, 227; 'political inevitability' of worker director laws, 230; failure to obtain consensus, 232; influences concluding chapter on Britain's industrial problem, 234; issues personal statement in place of press conference, 241

Cable and Wireless, 308

Cadbury Schweppes, 151
Cadbury set up consultative works councils in 1920s, 163

Caja Laboral Popular (Spain)
savings bank connected with Mondragon scheme, 196

Callaghan, James, 14, 33, 39, 248
opposes Barbara Castle's *In Place of Strife*, 14; on deal with unions, 31; meeting with Chancellor Schmidt, Bullock group and others in Bonn, 228–229; and reactions to Bullock, 243

Callard, Sir Jack, 232
member of Bollock Committee and President of Industrial Participation Association, 219
main opponent of worker directors, 227; brings draft minority report to Sunningdale, 231

Cannon, Sir Leslie of EPTU
on worker directors, 76

Carr, Robert (now. Lord), 46
and Industrial Relations Act, 15, 214; idea of a national training agency, 43; on Conservative Cabinet sub-committee on consultation, 214

Carron, Lord
then President of AEUW joins board of Fairfields, 169

Carter Committee (Government Inquiry on the Post Office) opposed to worker director system, 181

Castle, Barbara, 11, 46, 140, 189
In Place of Strife (White Paper), 13, 14, 15, 16;

not allowed to speak on industrial relations at
1971 LP Conference, 30; issues consultative
document (1970) on worker directors, 208–209
Central Policy Review Staff, 303
Changes in Company Law (White Paper, 1978), 263
Chapple, Frank (EPTU), 117
against worker director schemes, 76; against TUC
policy for nationalised industries, 268
Chrysler, 76, 151, 175
planning agreement, 38, 153; participative
schemes developed during 1976, 153; and
dropping of worker directors' scheme, 153, 158
Churchill, Sir Winston
quoted in *A Giant's Strength*, 10
Citrine, Lord, first chairman of nationalised
electricity (1947), 164
Civil Aviation Authority, 265
Civil Service
Whitley councils set up in 1919, 163; approach to
industrial democracy, 79, 270–271
Civil Service Department (CSD)
industrial democracy schemes for Civil Service
and 'fringe bodies', 265
Civil Service Unions
and staff represeanatives on some management
boards, 80; on industrial democracy in public
sector accept accountability to Parliament, 266
Clegg, Professor Hugh
and Donovan Report, 12; and conflict tradition
of labour relations, 132; and importance of
Whitley Committee 162–163
Closed Shops, 24, 55–56, 217, 293
Coal Industry
and miners' crisis, 21
Tripartite Group set up by Labour Government
and general participation, 167–168
Coates, Ken
joint author of *Shop Stewards' Guide to the
Bullock Report*, 252
Cole, G. D. H., 209
Collective Bargaining, 33, 66, 77, 124, 125, 127–128
extension from shop floor to corporate decisions,
6, 131–132, 137, 215, 284; and Employment
Protection Act, 22; and shop stewards, 68, 70;
and Bullock (John Lyons' letter in *The Times*),
70; TUC view given to Bullock, 74; extension in
public sector, 75; Compen's report on Harland
and Wolff, 89; and 'bargaining creep', 130; and
Ford Motor 149; at 1977 TUC Congress, 250
Combines
and union officials, 92; Leyland combine, 92
Commercial Secrecy, 96–97
Commission on Industrial Relations, 41
1972 report on company information, 140
Committee of Inquiry
in place of Bill on industrial democracy,
217–220; becomes Bullock Committee, 221; terms
of reference, 218
Communist Party, 73, 76, 131, 269
against worker directors in private sector, 75,
245; evidence to Bullock, 222
Compacts with Government (1948–1977), 279
Companies Bill (1973), 214, 251
Companies Act 1980, 310
Company Accountability
and ICI evidence to Bullock Committee, 112; *see*
Shareholders' rights
Company Law Reform (1965)
Fabian Society pamphlet by Professor
Wedderburn, 219
Compen (NI), Belfast
and resource centre for workers at Harland and

Wolff, 88–89
Computer Machinery Co., 159
Confederation of British Industry (CBI), 11, 40,
41, 57–60, 108, 109, 242, 244, 294, 295, 309,
311
lack of negotiating experience, 19, 20; employee
participation policies, 44, 244; support of
school-leavers' work scheme, 45; and ACAS, 46;
weakness in relation to TUC on MSC, 56; report
(1973) on need for change in company
responsibilities, 112; on participation agreements
(1976), 117, 215; statutory backing, 133; attempt
to review current consultative systems, 142; on
profit sharing, 186; attacks whole basis of
Bullock Inquiry, 222; Methven withdraws from
Bullock Committee, 230; campaign against
Bullock, 243–245; on pension funds, 274; on
legislation re participation in pension investments,
276; participation as gifts of management, 284;
1982 annual conference, 296
Confidentiality
and 'balance of power', 94, 95, 96; solution to
problem in Sweden, 96, 231
Conservative Government, 5, 11, 30, 34, 43, 46, 67,
281, 293, 308, 310
emphasis on union support, 5; repeal of
Industrial Relations Act, 9; *Fair Deal at Work*
(April 1968), 15; lack of understanding of unions,
17; initiative with TUC and CBI on pay, 17;
opposition by Jones and Scanlon, 28; and
NEDC, 39, 40, 48; and Robens Report on *Safety
and Health at Work*, 43; and CBI, 60;
participation based on individual, 183; and
'quality of working life', 201; memorandum from
TUC, 212; and EEC policy on worker directors,
213; Cabinet sub-committee on consultation,
214; and recession, 293; budgets of 1980 and
1983, 308
Conservative Party, 57, 188, 202
policy (1970) includes manpower board, 43; and
expanded NEDC, 55; and CBI, 59, 60; suggests
Conservatives should join unions (1976), 107;
'green paper' on profit sharing, 186; no formal
evidence to Bullock Committee, 223
Consultation
definition, 123; employee development by
industrialists, 140; *see also* Employee
Participation and Participation
Consultative Committees, 129
and consultative developments, 142; at ICI,
145–147; Unilever, 147–149; Ford Motor, 149,
150
Contrat social, 33, 283
Cooley, Mike (past President of TASS), 81
Cooling Off Periods (conciliation pauses), 14
Co-operative Development Agency (CDA), 306, 307
Cooper, Lord, (GMWU), 28
Cotton, R. E. (Chairman of Samuel Osborn & Co.
Ltd.)
and report: *Employee Participation – A
Management View*, 117
Council of Engineering Institutions recommends
members to join unions, 108
Council of Prices, Productivity and Incomes (1957),
279
Cripps, Sir Stafford
wage freeze October 1948, 279
Crosland, Anthony, 228
Cryer, Bob, 194
Courtaulds
factory occupation, 192
Cousins, Frank, 26, 205

resigns from Government on pay freeze, 11

Daubler, Professor
German labour lawyer quoted in *Industrial Democracy: European Experience*, 137
Daly, Lawrence (NUM), 28
Davies, Paul
joint author *Industrial Democracy: European Experience* (1976), 137, 225
Defence Council, 270
Dell, Edmund
Secretary for Trade and ex-ICI, 220; Bullock Report received, 221, 233; statement in Commons on Bullock Report, 242; wishes to water down Bullock, 247; speech to Society for Long-Range Planning, 248; against 'single channel', 249; *Industrial Democracy* (White Paper, 1978), 263
Democracy in Industry
Industrial Society booklet, 159
Denmark, 189, 225
system of worker directors, 259
Department for Economic Affairs, 168
Department of Employment, 42, 46, 47, 213
impetus for job satisfaction schemes, 199; and worker directors, 212;
and nominations for Committee of Inquiry, 218
Department of Industry
funds for co-operatives, 194; small firms division conference (April 1977), 194
Department of Manpower Services, Belfast discussion paper (1975), 176
Department of the Environment and industrial democracy in local government, 265
Department of Trade, 218
Diamond Commission, 53
Diamond, Lord, 188
Directors,
two-tier boards, 231, 244, 245, 250; Investors' Chronicle survey, 236; Bank of England, 266; *see also* Shareholders' Rights and Worker Directors
Disclosure of Information, 140, 141
Dockyards and national security, 80
Donaldson, Sir John, (President of NIRC), 10, 16
Donovan Report, The (Royal Commission on Trade Unions and Employers' Associations (1968)), 11, 205, 206–207, 220, 226
voluntary reform, 12; legal retraints, 12; influence of Professor Hugh Clegg, 12; criticism by Lord McCarthy, 13; recommends company-wide bargaining, 127; concentrates on problems of strikes, 207
Drain, Geoffrey (NALGO)
on participation of public service unions, 164, votes for Bullock-based policy on nationalised industries, 268

Economic Policy and the Cost of Living, 32, 33
Edmondson, Len (AUEW)
votes for Bullock-based policy in nationalised industries, 268
Education and Training of Shop Stewards, 10, 69, 84–86, 119
Edwards, Sir Michael 297-299
EEC (Common Market), 51, 52, 201, 212, 213
employee participation policy, 98; proposals re participation (1976), 190; Green Paper on employee participation, and Gundelach evidence, 224; harmonisation of company laws, 205, 262–263
Electrical and Plumbing Trade Union (EPTU), 308
opposition to worker directors, 76, 131, 166, 177, 245; leaders welcome co-ordinating council in

electricity supply, 165; interest in job enrichment exercises, 198
Electrical Power Engineers Association, 301
Electricity Act (1947)
unions not to enter boardroom, 164
Electricity Supply, 164-166
Electricity Council, 165; National Joint Co-ordinating Council (1977), 165
Ellis, N. D.
joint author, *Management by Agreement: An Alternative to the Industrial Relations Act* (1973), 131, 132
Employee Participation, 78, 79, 83
definition of, 123–125;
Leyland scheme includes 'combine', 92; and Arnold Weinstock, 114–116; and Ford Motor, 116–122; insufficient preparation at Leyland, 120; various methods of, 123–138; trends in private sector, 139–160; ascending and descending participation, 198
Employee Participation and Company Structure
EEC Green Paper (Nov. 1975), 224
Employee Share Ownership, 184–197
seen as way to raise cheap capital, 184, 185
Employment Act 1982, 310
Employment Protection Act 1975, 30, 32, 34, 47, 86, 96, 128, 189, 207, 216
comprehensive framework of employment law, 22; legal problems could arise for unions, 22; and disclosure of company information, 87, 140; and influence on managers to join a trade union, 107
Energy Commission, 42
Engineering Employers' Federation (EEF), 296
and employers' rights to manage, 101; against worker directors, 215
Equal Opportunities Commission, 40, 42
Employment Service Agency, 43
plan to abolish, 1977, 45
Esso Petroleum
results of management survey by Kenneth Adams, 106, 107; communication methods with employees, 141
European Commission, 306, 310
Fifth directive 1983, 310, 311–312, 313, 315
European Company Statute, 224
European Economic Community (EEC), 311
European Trades Union Council, 311
European Parliament, 311
Evans, Moss, 51

Fabian Society
tea party, 27
pamphlet by Thomas Balogh, 33, 281; and by Prof. Wedderburn, 219; evidence to Bullock, 222
Fair Deal at Work, 15
Fairfields
experiment in participation, 168, 212; *Fairfields:* book by K. Alexander and C. L. Jenkins, 169
Fakenham Enterprises
creation of workers' co-operative, 192; help from Ernest Bader, 193
Feather, Victor (later, Lord), 15, 16, 18, 28, 30, 31
opposes *In Place of Strife*, 14; talks with Heath, 20; launches *Economic Policy and the Cost of Living*, 32
Felixstowe Dock and Railway Company appoints TGWU shop steward to board (1975), 158
Ferranti, 58, 87, 175
Fiat
and extended collective bargaining, 132; mixture

of assembly techniques, 200

Figgures, Sir Frank (Director-General of the National Economic Development Office), 19, 20, 40

Financial participation, 308

Fisher, Alan (NUPE)
appointed to board of Harland and Wolff (1975), 177

Flanders, Professor Allan, 132, 141

Foot, Michael, 23, 31, 202
urges Government Bill on industrial democracy, 217; loses first round, 218; support for Bullock Report, 244

Ford Motor
evidence to Bullock Committee, 7, 102, 117, 119; unsuccessful court action re non-strike bonus, 14; Halewood labour troubles, 73; Bob Ramsey's views on employee involvement, 100, 116; firmly based on adversary system, 145; emphasis on collective bargaining machinery, 149; sit-in in 1975, 191; failure of group working experiment at Halewood, 200

France, 190, 193, 225, 267
worker shares schemes introduced by De Gaulle, 186; workers' takeover in 1973, 192; 'humanisation of work', 199

Friends of the Earth, 194

Garnett, John
and letter from Sir Geoffrey Howe on employees' legal status, 214

Garringtons, 152

General Electric Company (GEC), 114, 115, 116, 145, 236
evidence to Bullock Committee on problems re managers, 119; participation document (1976), 150-151

General and Municipal Workers' Union (GMWU), 301, 302
David Basnett succeeds Lord Cooper, 28; alternative to worker directors, 131; Bullock debate at TUC Congress, 1977, 250; trustees and representatives trained on pensions, 276

Germany, 7, 43, 66, 85, 205, 213, 214, 224, 255, 258, 267
employee representation not confined to union members, 136; proposals for profit-sharing, 190; 'humanisation of work', 199; employee representation on boards, 225; Bonn meeting between British and German politicians and Bullock members etc., 228, 229

Giant's Strength, A (1958)
pamphlet by Conservative lawyers on union power, 10, 13, 16, 105

Golding, John, 194

Gormley, Joe, 28
and miners' strike, 21

Grant and Marsh
book on CBI (1977), 58, 59

Greene, Sir Sidney (later, Lord), 28
working party chairman (1970) on workers directors, 211

Griffiths, Ward (Ebbw Vale worker director), 172

Grundy of Teddington, 160

Grunwick Dispute, 46, 244

Guest, Keen and Nettlefold (GKN), 142, 151, 236, 276, 293
'charters for workpeople' schemes in some small subsidiaries including Shotton, 151, 152; information to employees' policy in all GKN companies, 153; Heath, Barrie on Bullock Committee, 219; evidence to Bullock Committee

used for minority report, 232

Guild Socialism, 169, 209

Gundelach, Finn
evidence to Bullock Committee, 224

Harland and Wolff, 97, 162, 176-178, 181, 297
worker director plan, 88, 175; report by Compen (NI) on need for training, 88, 177; problems of joint shop stewards committees, 91

Harper, Keith, 27

Hawley, Grenville, 299

Health and Safety Commission, 29, 30, 37, 40, 43, 201

Health and Safety at Work Act (1974), 128, 199

Heath, Barrie (member of Bullock Committee), 219, 227
brings draft minority report to Sunningdale, 231; disagreement with Methven, 231; would not follow CBI's 'implacable opposition', 232

Heath, Edward, 18, 19, 20, 21, 60
and enlargement of NEDC, 55

Heath Government, 5, 55
and tripartism, 5, 19, 20, 25, 34, 38, 40, 43, 213, 279; confrontation policies, 9; defeated, 21, 35; reasons for defeat, 22; use of NEDC, 40; and Manpower Services Commission, 43

Herbert, Alfred, 58, 87, 175

Holland
'humanisation of work', 199; supervisory board system, 226

Hope, Robin, (Bullock Committee Secretary), 232, 241

Houghton, Lord (Chairman of 1972 Industry Group), 248

Howe, Sir Geoffrey (Solicitor-General in Conservative Government) and Industrial Relations Act, 15, 214; Cabinet sub-committee on consultation, 214; letter to Industrial Society, 214; interest and support for NEDC, 294

Hughes, John (Ruskin College)
on use of pension funds, 274

Imperial Chemical Industries (ICI), 142, 145, 262, 293, 297
and company accountability, 112; four-tier structure of consultation, 145-147; consultative works councils in 1920s, 163; profit sharing scheme, 185-186; Callard and Methven views on Bullock Committee, 220; problem of subsidiaries and worker directors, 236; survival at, 303-304

Incomes Policies, 10
and ACAS, 47; and shop stewards, 69

Industrial Common Ownership Act (1976), 192, 193
initiative for movement (ICOM) by Ernest Bader, 193; financial help for co-operatives, 194; ICOM co-operatives, 195; unions play no significant role in ICOM enterprises, 197

Industrial Democracy, 3-8, 30, 35, 36, 65, 110, 124, 168, 201, 210, 216, 293, 294, 295
concept of changing balance of power, 4, 6, 111; Conservative view as 'employee participation', 6; Webbs' view, 6; as wider responsibility for shop stewards, 68; and conflict tradition of labour relations, 73; requires maximum disclosure, 97; and new breed of highly competent managers, 122; definition of, 123-125; in Sweden, 136; starting point for legislation, 143; Sir Charles Villiers' view at BSC, 174; working party (1966), 205, 212; Committee of Inquiry suggested, 217; Liberal Party proposals, 223; Dell's attitude in speech to Commons on Bullock, 242; and the

public sector, 264–272; and the civil service 270–271; and local government, 271–272

Industrial Democracy Commission
suggested in Bullock majority report, 42, 84, 235, 237, 253, 286

The Industrial Democracy Experiment and UPW Participation, 181

Industrial Democracy in the Light of Bullock GMWU document (June 1977), 250

Industrial Democracy: Labour Party report (1967), 22, 130
basis of Bill Simpson's speech at 1971 Conference, 30; also TUC policy document in 1974, 65, 130, 178, 183, 184, 215, 216

Industrial Democracy: European Experience (Eric Batstone and Paul Davies) Bullock research paper (1976), 137, 225

Industrial Democracy (White Paper, 1978), 250, 263, 290

Industrial Relations Act, 15–17, 21, 31, 32, 34, 55, 85
repealed (1974), 9, 216, 281; legally binding labour agreements, 12; 'union registration' chosen by TUC for main fight, 16; Jones allows TGWU to appear at NIRC, 29; subsequent increase of closed shops, 56

Industrial Relations and the Limits of the Law (Weekes et al 1975)
and closed shops, 56

Industrial Society, The
general programme re information to employees, 141; survey re participation in 41 companies, 143; booklet *Democracy in Industry*, 159; letter from Sir Geoffrey Howe, 214

Industrial Strategy
see National Economic Development Council

Industry act (1975)
and disclosure, 140

Industry Group 1972
policy document on 'participatory board', 248

In Place of Bullock (CBI policy document, 1977), 244

In Place of Strife (White Paper), 13, 14, 35

Institute for Workers' Control, 72, 101, 252

Institute of Directors, 311
wish to represent entrepreneurs and businessmen, 108

Institute of Personnel Management
speech at Conference (1975) by Bob Ramsey (Ford), 100, 116; survey of ten large companies, 144; Geoffrey Drain speaks on public service unions at 1976 Conference, 164

Into the Eighties: an agreement (Government/TUC joint policy document), 61

Investors' Chronicle
survey on number of directors in '2x + y' scheme, 236

Ionic Plating
participation scheme and added-value bonus, 153

Iran
Shah and workers' shares schemes, 185

Iron and Steel Trades Confederation (ISTC), 87, 302, 303

Israel
worker-co-operatives, 183–184

Italy
and extended collective bargaining, 132

Jenkin, Patrick, 302, 303

Jenkins, Clive (ASTMS), 230
appointed by Bullock Committee, 220; contribution on education to Bullock Report,
232; ASTMS Conference rejects Bullock, 245

Jenkins, Peter
The Battle of Downing Street, book on Barbara Castle's policy, 13

Jenkins, Roy
calls for talks with unions, 29

Job Ownership, 307

Job Satisfaction and Quality of Working Life, 198, 201, 202
Volvo's experiment in Sweden, 199, 200; tripartite group set up by Maurice Macmillan (1973), 201; work research unit set up by Michael Foot, 202; programmes proposed by Liberal Party, 223; Callaghan speech at LP Conference 1976, 229

Joint Representation Committee (JRC) (Bullock Report), 82, 91, 94, 127, 285

Jones, Jack, 4, 20, 28, 30, 31, 32, 36, 38, 51, 53, 101, 208, 210, 216, 220, 249, 270, 280, 294; and non-registration, 16; background of, 26; attends Fabian tea party, 27; quoted on incomes policy in *The Guardian*, 27; tells Labour Party Conference unions and party leadership are united, 29; article in *New Statesman* on industrial relations, 32, 211; key part in design of ACAS, 46; tactics to influence policy, 49; demands industrial democracy in Government establishments, 55, 79; for constructive union bargaining, 72; for 50–50 joint union-management in defence establishments, 79; and working party on industrial democracy (1966–1967), 205, 207, 208, 212, 213; and TUC working party on participation (1970) 211; and 50–50 basis for worker directors, 213; wanted Bill on industrial democracy, 217; loses first round 218; determined member of Bullock Committee, 218, 220, 221, 226, 230, 232, 233, 247; difficulty in mid-1977 to push towards Bullock legislation, 248; defeated on social contract wage restraint by own union conference, 61, 244; votes for Bullock-based policy on nationalised industries (March 1977), 268

Joseph, Sir Keith, 301, 303

'Journalists of *The Times*' (JoTT), 307

Kalamazoo
co-operative spirit, 188

Kaufman, Gerald (Minister of State for Industry)
on participation in Post Office, 179

Kirkby Manufacturing and Engineering (KME), 192, 194, 195, 196, 197

Labour and Inflation (Fabian pamphlet 1970)
Thomas Balogh advocates *contrat social*, 281

Labour Government, 4, 15, 28, 32, 33, 35, 49, 57, 175, 205, 249, 279, 298, 308
'social contract' with unions, 4, 5, 25, 45, 279; repeal of Industrial Relations Act, 9; declaration of intent on pay and productivity (1964), 11; voluntary pay norms (1965), 11; statutory pay freeze, 11; Trades Disputes Act (1965), 11; Donovan Commission, 12, 205; falls in 1970, 14, 209; returned to power, 21, 31; industrial strategy, 1976–1977, 36; 1976 White Paper, 308; 1978 White Paper, 312; and tripartism, 36, 40; and conciliation on pay, 46; and CBI, 59; supports TUC on shop stewards training, 85; and Whitleyism, 161; and nationalisation 1945 and 1964, 163; Tavistock Institute inquiry on British Railways, 163; agrees with NCB on need for incentive scheme, 168; and British Steel Corporation, 169; and boardroom seats on Post Office Corporation, 179; and profit sharing, 187;

refuses to legalise factory occupation, 191; and Industrial Common Ownership Act (1976), 194; on Board level representation in nationalised industries, 242; PM gives public commitment re legislative proposals, 247; commitment to include *essential* but not *exclusive* trade union role, 249

Labour Party, 4, 25, 28, 31, 35, 51, 109, 294 discussion document (1967) re industrial role of unions, 13; report (1967) *Industrial Democracy*, 22, 207; Liaison Committee with TUC formed, 26; closer relationship between unions and party leadership (1971), 29; and NUM, 26; study group report on profit-sharing (1973), 188–189, 273; influence of Jack Jones, 205; 1974 manifesto pledge on industrial democracy, 216; evidence to Bullock, 222; Callaghan on the working environment (Conference, 1976), 229; *Labour's Programme for Britain* (1972) and workers' rights re investment plans of pension funds, 274; *Socialism in the 80s* (1980), 307, 310; 1983 policy document, 312–313; lack of progress, 313

Labour's Programme for Britain (1972) on workers' statutory rights re pension funds, 274

Landsmens Co-ownership workers' co-operative based on shares given by owner (David Spreckly), 195

Lea, David (TUC's economic secretary), 206, 212, 220, 228, 230, 232, 314 and Bullock Committee, 39, 220, 230, 232; lecture to Civil Service College 1975, 41; and Diamond Commission on wealth and incomes, 53; with Prof. Wedderburn drafts Industrial Democracy Bill, 217

Lever, Harold rescue plan for Meriden, 196

John Lewis Partnership worker directors, 158; 'sham democracy', 188; paternalistic co-operative, 193

Liaison Committee (formed (1972) from TUC, Labour Party and Parliamentary Labour Party), 26, 27, 30–33, 35, 51, 52, 56, 211

Liberal Party, 212, 245, 251, 308, 312 and CBI, 60; and profit sharing, 187; call for statutory works councils, 215; proposals for industrial democracy, 223; MPs support for Manifesto Group policy on Bullock, 248

Local Government and worker participation, 271–272; Basildon District Council co-opts employee representatives (1976), 271; and GLC, 272

London Business School lecture (March 1977) by John Hughes, 274

London Passenger Transport Board, 209

Lord, Alan (Treasury Official, later Dunlop) 'Lord Report' on participation in public sector, 264

Lowry, Pat (British Leyland), 297 problems re participation, 158

Lucas Aerospace and shop stewards' proposals for socially useful products, 79, 80; article in the *Financial Times* (18 Feb. 1976), 80, 81; and APEX, 87

Lucas Joseph share ownership scheme, 186

Luxembourg, 225

Lyons, John (Electrical Power Engineers' Association) letter in *The Times* on Bullock, 70

MacGregor, Ian, 302

Macleod, Iain (Conservative Minister of Labour) cancellation of arbitration system, 10

Macmillan, Maurice, 47, 214

on employee participation, 20, 213; on MSC, 43–44; and 'quality of working life', 201, 213; founder chairman of Wider Share Ownership Council, 213

McCarthy, Lord (formerly Dr W. E. J. 'Bill') research director of Donovan Commission, 13, 208; on weakness of Donovan Report, 13; major work on closed shop (1964), 56; proponent of extended collective bargaining, 31, 132; appointed to joint board of Harland and Wolff, 177

McIntosh, Sir Ronald (Director General of NEDO), 266

Management initiatives re provision of information, 90; and confidential and commercial secrecy 97; employees' lack of faith in management ability, 98; 'legitimacy of the management function', 99–105; 'managerial rights', 100; re thinking of loyalties, 103, 105; styles, 118; need education and training for participation, 119; GEC objectives, 150; 50 per cent of BSC managers oppose worker directors, 171; disruption of middle managers, 198; *see also* Manager, The

Management by Agreement (McCarthy and Ellis, 1973) advocates a system of 'predictive bargaining', 131

Manager, The problems of trade unionism, 104–109; reluctance to strike, 109; effect of doctors' industrial action (1970), 109; resents participative changes, 118; new type can work with participation, 121; GEC guide to managers, 150; worker co-operatives need expert managers, 197

Manifesto Group (right wing Labour MPs) policy on Bullock, 248, 255

Manpower Services Commission (MSC), 5, 7, 37, 40, 42–45, 47, 51, 52, 56, 105, 113, 194, 201, 265, 278, 281, 294, 306

Marks and Spencer, 186

Marsh and Evans (1973) definition of 'industrial democracy', 123

Massey Ferguson sit-in 1975, 191

Meidner plan for profit sharing, 189

Melchett, Lord first Chairman of British Steel Corporation, 169

Meriden Motorcycle Co-operative, 158, 175, 192, 194, 195, 196, 197 help from Arnold Weinstock (GEC), 116, 194; Government financial help, 194

Methven, John, 59 member of Bullock Committee, 222; resigns from Bullock Committee when at CBI, 220, 230; dissension with Barrie Heath, 231

Metra Oxford Consulting Ltd study (1975) on sit-ins, 191

Milne-Watson, Sir Michael tells worker director to relinquish union links, 170

Miners' Participation Plans, 167

Miners' Strikes (1971–2 and 1973–4), 18, 21, 24, 167

Mondragon community of worker co-operatives in Spain, 196

Monopolies Commission, 42

Morris, Charles (Civil Service Department), 270 on industrial democracy in public sector (11 Feb. 1976), 265–266

Morrison, Herbert, 164 influence on worker director debate (1930s), 209

Multinational companies and Bullock proposals, 236–238

Murray, Len, 36, 38, 51, 132
on Bullock Report and responsibility of unions, 71, 72; on representation at board level, 75, 76, 245; and Donovan Commission, 206; foreword to *TUC Guide to the Bullock Report*, 246; single channel is central principle, 250
Mutuality
workers' rights on piecework rates in engineering, 128
National Association for Freedom (NAFF) and Post Office workers' industrial action, 23; and Grunswick dispute, 23
National Coal Board (NCB), 267
and methods to increase participation, 167; board member from mining unions, 210
National Consumer Council
evidence to Bullock Committee, 222
National Economic Development Council (and Office) (NEDC), 37, 39–40, 48, 55, 88, 294, 309
'little Neddies' and industrial strategy, 40, 52, 294, 309; report on nationalised industries and Government (1976), 168, 266
National Enterprise Board, 37, 40, 52, 75, 76, 175
National Freight Corporation, 307, 308
Union leaders on Board from TGWU and railwaymen, 210
National Graphical Association (NGA)
use of information at Odhams, 87; support for Bullock, 245
National Health Service
and worker participation, 271
National Incomes Commission (1962), 279
National Industrial Relations Court (NIRC)
successes and failures, 16, 17; Jones allows TGWU to appear, 29
Nationalised Industries
impact of Whitley tradition, 164; and Labour Government, 169; TUC's board representation plans, 211; 'Lord Report', 264; debate on industrial democracy in, 266–272
National Joint Co-ordinating Council for Electricity Supply (1976), 165
National Joint Industrial Councils, 163
National and Local Government Officers' Association (NALGO), 164
electricity supply members only want consultation, 166; favours worker directors in Gas supply industry, 166
National Staff Side (Civil Service), 80, 270
National Union of Bank Employees (NUBE)
broadly in favour of Bullock, 245
National Union of Blastfurnacemen, 302
National Union of Mineworkers
history of support of Labour Party, 26; and National Coal Board, 167, 168; reject NEDO report on Government and nationalised industries, 168
National Union of Public Employees (NUPE), 87
Nicholas, Sir Harry, 31
Norway, 225
idea of small factories, 199

O'Brien, Richard (Chairman of MSC 1976), 44, 113
Occupational Pensions Board, 275, 277
Office of Fair Trading, 42
Olslager, Lorelies, 80–81
One Nation Group
One Nation at Work pamphlet on industrial democracy, 223
Orme, Stan
and experiment in industrial democracy at Harland and Wolff, 176, 178; White Paper (1976)

on pension funds, 273, 276, 277
Orr, Sir David, 295–296
Owen, Robert, 190
Owen, Trevor (ICI), 232

Parliament, 3, 79, 162
and laws re unions' hold on industry, 3; and legal system re restrictive laws, 21; ministerial responisibility for Post Office, 179, 180; legislation (1977) on operation of the Post Office Corporation, 181; and ministerial responsibility for nationalised industries, 79, 265
Parsons, James (GKN)
and minority report to Bullock Committee, 232
Participation, 295, 298
definition, 124–125; trends in the private sector, 139–160; trends in the public sector, 161–181; US programme of, 1983, 215; *see also* Employee Participation
Pay Policies, 11, 17–21, 35, 36, 69, 279
Pension Funds, 5, 184, 273–277
unions demand rights, 5, 264; White Paper (1976), 37
Peugeot, 200
Philips Industries
evidence to Bullock Committee, 100; objective of NV Philips, 102
Picketing, 293
Pilkington
and pension fund, 276
Planning Agreements, 37–38, 216
and shop stewards, 71; in Industry Act (1975), 140; Chrysler presents first planning agreement to Government (Feb. 1977), 153
Plessey
occupation, 192
Plowden Report (1976) on energy policies, 166
Policy Council
suggested in NEDO report (1976), 266; dual roles of civil servants on, 267
Political Lobbying, 57
CBI appoints lobbyist, 60
Post Office, The, 95, 176, 209, 268, 269, 295, 297
nationalised in 1969, 162; Whitley council set up in 1919, 163; worker director system, 178–181; Post Office Corporation against power-sharing, 179; penision funds, 276; disagreement in the, 300–302; worsening of labour problems, 301; worker director initiative, 1974–5, 302
Post Office Engineering Union (POEU), 300
and worker director plan, 178, 180
Power Station Closure Programmes, 165
Power to Manage, The (1973)
EEF history by Eric Wigham, 101, 126
Press, The
freedom of and employee participation, 82
Prices and Incomes Board, 41
Prior, James
on consultation, 215; on steps towards worker directors, 223; on long service employees, 295
Prison Officers' Association, 86
Productivity Bargaining
and shared responsibility (Eddie Robertson), 126
Profit Sharing, *see* Employee Share Ownership
Public Sector
plans on industrial democracy, 79, 264–273

Quigley, Dr George (Ulster civil servant) scheme (with Stan Orme) to harness workers' co-operation, 177

Radice, Giles, MP, 248

private member's Bill on worker directors, 216–217, 220

Ramsey, Bob (of Ford Motor)
speech on 'them and us' attitude in British industry, 100, 116

Recession, 293

Redcliffe Maud Report, 272

Reed International
and advances towards employee involvement, 142

Research Facilities of Trade Unions, 86–90

Responsibilities of the British Public Company, The
CBI's 1973 report under chairmanship of Lord Watkinson, 112, 187

Retail Consortium, 55

The Right Approach to the Economy: Conservative policy document 1977, 55

Road to Recovery: CBI general policy document, 231

Robens Report on Safety and Health at Work (1972), 43

Robertson, Eddie
on productivity bargaining, 126

Robinson, Derek
member of study group on profit sharing (1973), 189

Roche, Bill
on problems in Leyland arising from 'divine right to manage' attitude, 120

'Role Conflict', 70

Rolls Royce
ASTMS study of redundancies, 87

Rookes v. Barnard, 22

Rothschild, Lord
refused chairmanship of Committee of Inquiry, 218

Rowntree
consultative works councils set up in 1920s, 163

Royal Commission on the Distribution of Income and Wealth, 53, 188

Royal Commission on Trade Unions and Employers' Associations
see The Donovan Report

Ruskin Research Unit, 86
on British Leyland's participation scheme, 69

Ryder Committee, on British Leyland, 154, 155

Ryder Report, 1975, 298

SAAB
experiment with assembly tracks, 199

Scandinavia
individual-based forms of industrial democracy, 182, 183, 184, 199

Scanlon, Hugh, 4, 20, 31, 101
negative opposition to efforts to deal with economic problems, 28; complete opposition to Industrial Relations Act, 29; preference for social 'compact' to social 'contract', 33

Schmidt, Dr Helmut (German Chancellor) on German worker directors, 228, 229

Scott-Bader, 193, 195

Scottish and Newcastle Breweries, 142

Scottish Daily News
shortlived co-operative project, 192

Scottish Stamping and Engineering, 152

Shareholders' Rights, 101, 102, 113, 134, 251, 260–262, 269
and reality of control of company, 103; TUC 50–50 scheme could displace, 212; in majority report, 234–235

Shipbuilding Industry, 178

Shonfield, Andrew
and Donovan Commission, 207

Shopfloor Democracy, 182–202

Shop Stewards, 10, 30, 36, 54, 65, 68–72, 99, 129
and training, 10, 69, 84, 119; co-operation made more difficult by Industrial Relations Act, 17; energies could be harnessed for management, 66; and proposals for Lucas Aerospace (1975), 79–82; and company-wide committees, 91–92; and benefits in co-operation, 92, 93; and conflict with union hierarchy, 94; and collective bargaining, 127; 300,000 stewards in UK, 139, 255; and role in consultation schemes, 145, 146, 147, 152; co-operation in Chrysler's planning agreement (Feb. 1977), 153; 400 attend company-wide conference at Leyland (1974), 155; reluctance at Fairfields for joint-control, 169; reluctance re boardroom seats at Harland and Wolff, 177; and participation in Post Office, 180; and ICI's profit sharing scheme, 185; job satisfaction schemes often opposed, 202; Bullock Report and new shop stewards committees, 221; responsibilities re takeovers, 234, 235

Shop Stewards' Guide to the Bullock Report, The (Coates and Topham)
book by Institute for Workers' Control, 72, 252

Shop Stewards Movement (First World War), 69

Shore, Peter, 218, 220
little interest in Labour pledge on industrial democracy, 216; wanted Committee of Inquiry rather than Bill, 217; formally sets up Bullock Committee, 221

Silkin, Samuel (Attorney-General)
on Post Office workers' industrial action, 23

Simpson, Bill, 29, 30

'Single Channel', 211, 246, 249, 250
union attempt to extend influence within companies, 130; compromise reached at British Leyland, 131, 156; wanted by unions at BSC, 170; as proposed in TUC's *Industrial Democracy*, 208; Bullock minority group against, 231; post-Bullock arguments, 246, 249–250, 254

Sirs, Bill (ISTC)
votes for Bullock-based policy on nationalised industries, 268

'Sit-Ins', 128, 190–192

Smith, Cyril, MP
book on industrial participation (1977), 223

Smith, Ron
and British Steel Corporation, 169

Social Contract, 4, 5, 7, 25, 28, 34–37, 53, 54, 57, 61, 85, 103, 279
unions' involvement on national planning and policy formulation, 9; unions accept short-term pay restraint, 22; event which opened the way, 26; original authorship of title, 33; used by TUC to move towards social change, 52; relied heavily on support of Jack Jones, 216

Social Democratic-Liberal Alliance, 294, 310
policy for 1983 gereral election manifesto, 312, 313, 314

Social Science Research Council (SSRC), 86
report: *Trade Union Support for Research*, 87

Society for Long-Range Planning
speech on Bullock by Edmund Dell (Feb. 1977), 248

Society of Graphical and Allied Trades (SOGAT), 304

South East Electricity Board
job enrichment method for clerks, 201

Spain
Mondragon worker co-operatives, 196

Spreckly, David

Index

business sold to work force, 195
Stagg, Norman, 181
Start of the Thatcherite '80s, 293–296
Status Quo
  arrangements, 128
Statutory Pay Freeze
  under Wilson Government, 11; under Heath
  Government, 18
Steel, David
  private member's Works Council Bill, 215
Steel Engineering Installations
  experience of form of worker directors, 159
Stock Exchange
  and rules about information on companies, 97;
  Weinstock's financial reconstruction covered by
  secrecy rule, 115
Stokes, Lord
  gives sales assistance in America to Meriden, 196
Strikes, *see* Unofficial and Unconstitutional Strikes
*A Study of the Electricity Supply Industry's
  Agreements and Their Outcome (1961–1971),*
  (Edwards and Roberts) on negotiation and
  consultation in electricity supply, 164
Sunderlandia
  worker co-operative, 193
Sunningdale Conference (October 1976), 226
  Bullock Committee meets and splits, 7 to 3,
  231–233
Sweden, 43, 85, 133 139, 199, 225, 252, 267
  part-time economic advisors to shop stewards,
  90; worker directors leave boardroom when
  wages discussed, 95, 136; and solution to
  problems of confidentiality, 96; and *status quo*
  arrangements, 128; worker director system,
  135–137; Meidner plan on profit-sharing, 189,
  273; Volvo's job satisfaction scheme, 198, 199;
  Bullock Committee visit, 228, 229
Swinden, Alan (of CBI), 212
System of Industrial Relations in Great Britain, The
  (Professor Hugh Clegg)
  on principles of Whitley Committee, 162–163

Taff Vale (1901), 22
TASS against worker directors, 268
Tavistock Institute, 299
  inquiry on participation in British Railways, 163
Tebbit, Norman, 311
Thatcher ethos lauding individualism at the expense
  of Collectivism, 295
Thatcher Government, 294, 303, 310, 315
Thatcherite management, 297
Thatcher, Margaret, 24, 219
  on unions as 'very important minority', 55;
  foreword to *One Nation at Work* on
  participation, 223
The Times, 307
Topham, Tony
  joint author of *Shop Stewards' Guide to the
  Bullock Report*, 252
Toshiba, 308
Trade Union and Labour Relations Act (1974), 30,
  32, 189, 215
  and closed shop, 217
Trade Union Research Unit, 86, 90
  survey on TU research departments, 86
Trade Unions, 65–77, 183
  political ambitions to change society, 4, 7; move
  into new policy-making roles, 5; joint
  responsibility role, 6; refusal to accept legal
  restraint on pay (1975), 11; Council of
  Engineering Institutions' view, 108; traditional
  role, 154; board directors sent to nationalised

industries other than their own, 210; dichotomy
  of intentions re board representation, 243
Trade Union Studies Project
  TUC, BBC and WEA television programmes for
  trade unionists, 86
Trades Disputes Act (1965), 11; (1906), 22
Training Services Agency, 43
  plan to abolish 1977, 45
Transport and General Workers' Union (TGWU),
  86, 298, 299, 302
  role of, 26; and Leyland, 87; and shop steward
  on board of Felixstowe Dock & Railway Co.,
  159; *see also* Jones, Jack
Tripartism in Government Agencies, 40–48,
  281–282, 294
TUC (Trades Union Congress), 7, 28, 31, 32, 34,
  35, 36, 41, 51, 52–53, 106, 109, 118, 139, 160,
  209, 230, 246, 300, 308, 309
  co-operation with politicians and industrialists,
  9; and shop stewards, 68, 71; declaration of
  intent on pay and productivity (1964), 11;
  acceptance of statutory pay freeze, 11; defeat 'In
  Place of Strife' policy, responsibility for stopping
  inter-union strikes, 15; choose registration as
  central plank against Industrial Relations Act,
  16; breakdown of talks with Mr Heath, 18, 19,
  20; backs miners' strike (1971–1972), 21; insists
  that Labour Government repeal Industrial
  Relations Act, 29; introduces 'Collective
  Bargaining and the Social Contract', 33;
  economic review for 1975, 37; and pension funds,
  32; and planning agreements, 38; and Bullock
  Report, 38, 71, 74, 101, 221, 222, 245, 268; and
  NEDC, 40; and Manpower Services Commission,
  42–43; support for school-leavers' work scheme,
  45; and ACAS, 46; how it works, 48–57; *Into
  the Eighties: an agreement* (Government/TUC
  joint policy document), 61; on reduction of
  conflict through industrial democracy, 72;
  Congress (1977) for both worker directors and
  collective bargaining, 72, 252; and training of
  shop stewards, 10, 84–86, 120; and research
  facilities, 86; and television programmes for trade
  unionists, 86; and research departments, 88; and
  extension of collective bargaining, 127; and *status
  quo* arrangement, 128; firm preference for 'single
  channel', 130, 208; steel committee at BSC, 170,
  171; for shop stewards rather than officials on
  Boards, 180, 210, 211; attitude to factory
  occupations, 183; against worker shares schemes,
  184; asks for legalising of factory occupations,
  191; evidence to Donovan Commission, 206;
  influence over nominations to public
  appointments, 210; working party (1970) on
  worker directors, 211; and 50–50 basis for
  worker directors, 212, 222, 252–253; and terms
  of reference for Committee of Inquiry, 218;
  three nominees on Bullock Committee, 220;
  Government to consult on Bullock, 242; leaders'
  doubts about Mr Dell, 243; lack of unity on
  worker directors after Bullock, 245; *Guide to the
  Bullock Report on Industrial Democracy* (1977),
  246; Local Government Committee views on
  industrial democracy, 265; Nationalised Industries
  Committee approves 6 point policy (March 1977),
  268; and employee rights in local government,
  273; proposals for channelling investments,
  274, 282; and joint control of pension funds,
  274–275; central authority increased, 279; *can
  work with Conservative governments, 281; annual
  report 1982, 303; Steel Committee, 303; lack of
  progress, 314

TUC Steel Committee, 170, 171, 173, 174
Turner and Newall, 276

Unemployment, 293
Unilever, 293, 295–296, 297
  plan for consultative and company councils, 145,
  147–148; steady growth at, 304–306; company
  communications group, 304–305
Union des Industries de la Commaunauté
  Europeéne (UNICE), 311
Union of Construction, Allied Trades and
  Technicians (UCATT)
  work done on efficiency by Warwick University
  academics, 87
Union of Post Office Workers (UPW)
  and industrial action over South African
  apartheid, 23; and worker director plan, 178,
  180, 181
Union of Shop, Distributive and Allied Workers
  (USDAW)
  PA used to look into sugar confectionery
  industry, 87
Union Mergers
  reasons for co-operation, 93
United Biscuits
  long established consultative procedures, 142;
  participation working techniques, 200
Unofficial and unconstitutional Strikes Donovan
  Commission (1968) favours voluntary reforms,
  12; TUC shoulders responsibility to try to stop,
  14
Upper Clyde Shipbuilders
  work-in 1971–1972, 168, 192; support of
  Wedgwood Benn, 175
Urwin, Harry, 46, 298

Vandervell Products
  'charter for workpeople', 152
Varley, Eric, 179
Villiers, Sir Charles
  speech to ISTC conference on a 'steel contract',
  (1977), 174, 267–268
Volvo
  car factory (Kalmar) job satisfaction scheme,
  198, 199, 200; new experiment at Skovde engine
  plant, 200
Vredeling Directive, 310, 315

Walker, Kenneth
  'ascending' and 'descending' participation, 198
Wandsworth Borough Council
  and worker co-operatives, 194
Warwick University study group, 301
Watkinson, Lord (President of CBI), 59, 186, 230,
  231
  report: *The Responsibility of the British Public
  Company*, 112
Wealth Policy of TUC, 52–53
Webb, Sidney and Beatrice, 6, 164, 197, 205
  on industrial democracy, 6; influence on trade
  unionism rather than co-operatives in industry,
  193
Wedderburn, Lord (Professor K. W. 'Bill'), 22, 208,
  229, 230, 232, 262
  with Lea drafts Industrial Democracy Bill, 217;
  member of Bullock Committee, 219, 228, 229,
  230, 232; article in *Tribune* on Board
  representatives as 'new dimension' of collective
  bargaining, 246
Weekes, B. (et al)
  Industrial Relations and the Limits of the Law:

*The Industrial Effects of the Industrial Relations
  Act, 1971*, 56
Weighell, Sidney (NUR)
  votes for Bullock-based policy on nationalised
  industries, 268
Weinstock, Sir Arnold, 122, 262
  article in company's newspaper (*Topic*) on worker
  participation, 114; memorandum to his managing
  directors on worker directors, 114–115, 145; help
  to Meriden, 116
White-Collar Trade Unionism, 108, 163
Whitehall
  and battle against worker directors, 216–218; and
  inquiries on industrial democracy, 264; resistance
  to Civil Service staff side's proposals, 270, 271
Whitley, J. H. (MP)
  and Committee on relations between employers
  and employed (1917–1918), 162
Whitley Traditions, 162–164, 270
Who Should Manage Pensions (CBI, 1977), 276
Wider Share Ownership Council, 185, 186, 213
  lobbying of industrialists re worker shareholders,
  187
Wigham, Eric
  on management rights in *The Power to Manage*,
  101, 126; and Donovan Commission, 207
Wilberforce Report, 18
Wilson Committee on the City
  TUC suggests new state agency for channelling
  investment, 274
Wilson, Harold (now, Sir), 32, 210
  speaks at LP Conference (1971) on industrial
  relations, 29; launches *Economic Policy and the
  Cost of Living*, 32, 33; requests report on
  Government and nationalised industries, 266
Williams, Shirley, 31
  chairman of Cabinet sub-committee on Bullock,
  249; watered down White Paper prepared, 250
Wilson, Nicholas
  on Bullock Committee (expert on company law),
  219, 228, 232, 262; joined majority group but
  wrote dissenting note, 230, 237–238
'Winter of Discontent' 1978–9, 294
Woodcock, George, 210
  and Donovan Commission, 12, 207; and *In
  Place of Strife* policy, 14; and Commission on
  Industrial Relations (CIR), 14
Worker Directors, 8, 9, 23, 32, 34, 36, 38, 42, 43,
  65, 67, 71, 75, 76, 107, 112, 121, 124, 125,
  134–138
  and British company law, 5, 133; and rights of
  shareholders, 5; and union ambitions, 5; and
  accountability, 17; opposition from David
  Basnett, 28, 76; in relation to planning
  agreements, 38; and responsibility of shop
  stewards, 68, 70, 71; opposition from Electrical
  Power Engineers' Association, 70; Communist
  Party view, 75, 222; and GMWU, 77; and
  Harland and Wolff, 88; and confidentiality,
  94–96; Watkinson Report firmly against, 113; and
  Arnold Weinstock, 114; opposition from CBI,
  118; in Sweden and Germany, 135–137; no major
  schemes in British private sector, 151, 158;
  Chrysler proposal replaced by participation, 153;
  at Bristol Channel Ship Repairers, 159;
  opposition from EPTU, 76, 166; and BSC,
  169–175; and share ownership schemes, 187;
  gradual support of all three main political
  parties, 224; Bullock majority and minority
  reports, 233–240; employees' rights, 251; methods
  of implementing 252–253
Worker Directors Speak (J. Bank and K. Jones

with BSC Employee Directors (1977)), 170, 172, 173

Workers' Co-operatives, 182, 184, 190–197
flourishing, 306–307; Co-operatives for redundant workers, 306; increase in management buy-outs, 307

Workers' Educational Association, 85

Working For Ford (1973) by Huw Beynon, 73

Work Research Unit (Department of Employment) report on work-restructuring, 201; unit set up on job enrichment (1974), 202

Yugoslavia
worker-co-operative based systems, 183–184